The Developing Individual in a Changing World

Klaus F. Riegel
John A. Meacham

The
Developing
Individual
in a
Changing
World

Volume I

Historical and Cultural Issues

AldineTransaction
A Division of Transaction Publishers
New Brunswick (U.S.A.) and London (U.K.)

Second printing 2009

Copyright © 2008 by Transaction Publishers, New Brunswick, New Jersey.

This book is printed on acid-free paper that meets the American National Standard for Permanence of Paper for Printed Library Materials.

Library of Congress Catalog Number: 2007024301
ISBN: 978-0-202-36129-1 (vol. 1) ; 978-0-202-36130-7 (vol. 2)
Printed in the United States of America

Library of Congress Cataloging-in-Publication Data

The developing individual in a changing world / [edited by] Klaus F. Riegel
  and John A Meacham.
      p. cm.
Originally published: Chicago : Aldine, c1976.
Includes bibliographical references and index.
ISBN 978-0-202-36129-1 (alk. paper) -- ISBN 978-0-202-36129-1 (alk. paper)
      1. Developmental psychology--Congresses. 2. Social psychology--Congresses. I. Riegel, Klaus F. II. Meacham, J. A.

BF712.I57 2007
155--dc22

                                                                    2007024301

Introductory remarks at the opening of the Conference

by Hans Thomae, *University of Bonn President, International Society for the Study of Behavioral Development* (ISSBD)

On behalf of the International Society for the Study of Behavioral Development, I would like to welcome you and thank you for your interest in the activities of this rather young society. I would also like to thank the Center for Human Growth and Development and the Department of Psychology for inviting us to the University of Michigan, and especially Professor Harold Stevenson, Chairman of the Conference Coordinating Committee, Professor Klaus Riegel, Chairman of the Program Committee, Professor John Hagen, Chairman of the Local Arrangements Committee, and all their co-workers who took part in the preparation of this meeting.

History of the society. The history of our society spans at least ten years if we include the preliminary meetings which took place in Amsterdam, Austin, Copenhagen, Chicago, Bonn, and Gardone (Italy). By mentioning these places I want to emphasize that this society, from the beginning, was the result of American-European cooperation. Through the initiative of our colleagues Robert Havighurst, Bernice Neugarten, Robert Hess, Robert Peck, Torsten Husén, Ingvar Johannesson, J. Kostaskova, Franz Mönks, A. Kossakowski, Marcello Cesa-Bianchi, and many others, the basis for this society was formulated and developed.

In 1969 we agreed upon a set of principles, rules, and an organizational structure which, due to the efforts of Professor J. de Wit, were approved by the Dutch government as the official by-laws of the society. The particular location for the legal incorporation of the society was chosen because many of the preliminary meetings took place in the Netherlands, and the first Biennial Meeting was organized by the Department of Psychology at the University of Nijmegen. However, this is not the only reason why the Netherlands provide a good headquarters for the society. Most of us will agree that creativity, tolerance, and open-mindness rank very highly in the Dutch culture, and these values and behavior patterns also fit very well the conception of our society.

Last year, this society tried to form closer cooperation with the Far East. Professor Takase from Kyoto University invited those of us who participated at the International Congress of Psychology in Tokyo to attend a special meeting. I hope very much that future meetings will take place in the Near East, South America, Africa, or in one of the socialist countries.

Goals of the society. The promotion of exchange of information among different nations and cultures is one of the major goals of this society. In addition, the society aims at integrating research at different age levels, with different methods and approaches. If we consider the barriers between child psychologists and gerontologists, or between the experimental and the clinical-observational approaches, these aims are quite ambitious. However, they seem moderate or conservative if we compare them with those of the International Organization for Research on Human Development, founded by Professor Kretchmer from Stanford University. His organization tries to integrate research in different cultures, different life stages, and different disciplines ranging from cell physiology, biochemistry, and embryology to pediatrics, child psychology, cultural anthropology, sociology, and many other fields.

One of the reasons for mentioning the International Organization for Research on Human Development is my hope that some day it may become a coordinating organization for biological as well as for behavioral developmental research. Our society would then form one of the branches of a larger scientific body centered around problems of development.

If for the present time we decide to concentrate our efforts on behavioral development, we expect to find at least a reasonable amount of common language among the different specialists. On the other hand, even the behavioral aspects of development include so many problems that for some time ahead our integrative aims will remain distant goals rather than close realities. Nevertheless, the theme for the second Biennial Meeting – The Developing Individual in a Changing World – defines some very concrete integrative issues in the study of behavioral development. Therefore I hope that the outcome of this meeting will prove that my predictions have been wrong.

Editors' preface

The theme of the second biennial meeting of the International Society for the Study of Behavioral Development – The Developing Individual in a Changing World – was chosen to be both a criticism of and a challenge to traditional developmental psychology. For all too long, developmental psychologists have been studying the individual as if he were developing in a socio-historical vacuum. For all too long, we have disregarded changes in the socio-historical conditions within which individual development takes place – changes in the conception of development, in the relationship between the individual and society, in the roles of the child, the adolescent, the adult, and the aged, and changes in the impact of education, communications, economics, and socio-political conditions.

Recently our orientation has begun to change and, in part due to practical demands, we have begun to investigate the impact upon development of early education, socio-cultural deprivation, mass communications, immigration, alternative living arrangements, medical care, and nutrition. At the center of attention have been both the young and the old, the child and the aged. In part this change in orientation has been made possible by our increased recognition of the theoretical relationships between individual and social changes and the need to analyze such changes with advanced developmental research designs.

The conference. With this orientation in mind, the theme was chosen and announced, along with recommendations for a number of subtopics which would be related to the overall theme. In contrast to the preparation for meetings such as those of the American Psychological Association or the Gerontological Society, the role of the program committee was not to merely select the best of the papers which were submitted. The task of the program committee was more challenging in scope and execution and included a major effort to solicit recommendations from a number of people, to encourage the organization of symposia around specific topics related to the theme, to rearrange the speakers and symposia into the most suitable framework, and to encourage the participation of speakers from a number of countries and a wide range of disciplines relating to human development.

After the list of symposia topics was completed, the organizers of the various symposia were given a free hand to select speakers, discussants, and a chairperson, as well as to decide upon the form of the presentations. Since these symposia were the foundation and structure of the whole conference, we should be deeply appreciative of those colleagues who made this effort of organizing the various symposia. In its final form the conference attained more the character of an invitational conference, rather than that of more traditional meetings. The enthusiastic response to this conference indicates that such conferences, organized around a broad and timely theme, may become an important mode for interpersonal scientific exchange.

In addition to the major symposia, the conference, held at the University of Michigan in Ann Arbor in August 1973, included a number of workshops, films, conversation hours, social events, and several 'mini-symposia', at which submitted papers could be briefly presented and discussion among the participants and the audience could take place. Altogether, more than 500 people from at least 24 countries attended. Although serious efforts were made to encourage as many non-Americans as possible to participate, the proportion of non-Americans participating was only 36 per cent. Although perhaps we should not be disappointed with these results, especially considering that the United States is relatively expensive to reach and to travel within, this percentage is relatively small considering that of the earth's 3 billion inhabitants only a few more than 200 million live in the United States. The inbalance is, of course, the main reason why the meetings of the International Society for the Study of Behavioral Development are being alternated between American and non-American locations. Preparations are already being made for the third biennial meeting, to be held in 1975 at the University of Surrey in England.

The present volume. The symposia in the present volume include a pproximately half of the papers presented at the conference. The problem of selection was a difficult one, both because there were many excellent papers and because the timeliness of many of the papers made it imperative to have these published as quickly as possible. Consideration was also given to the balance or representativeness of topics within the volumes. Unfortunately, many excellent papers presented at the conference ultimately could not be included.

Part I, *Historical and cultural issues*, contains symposia which address the problems of behavioral development from various points of view— historical, political, theoretical, and cultural. From these various perspectives, a number of content areas already familiar to developmental psychologists are discussed – Piaget's theory, perceptual development, socialization, language acquisition, etc. In addition, topics relatively unfamiliar to American psychologists are included: the contribution of early European developmentalists, such as William and Clara Stern, Alfred Binet, and Eduard Spranger; and an introduction to recent Soviet developmental theory.

Part II, *Social and environmental issues*, examines the effects upon individual development of changes in social and environmental conditions. Among the changes considered are the expanding effects of technology, such as the communications media, the importance of nutrition, and the design of playgrounds and other spaces for growing children. The impact of social organizations and interactions within small groups is examined, focusing upon preschool education, interaction within the family (infant education, caretaker-infant interactions, sibling effects), and personality development throughout the life-span.

We want to express our appreciation to many who contributed to the success of the second biennial meeting in Ann Arbor and who gave encouragement and advice for the present volume: the additional members of the program committee, Walter Emmerich, Hans Thomae, and Leon Yarrow; the Grant Foundation of New York City for providing funds to support travel, especially for young investigators from abroad; the Educational Testing Service in Princeton, New Jersey; the Department of Psychology, the Center for Human Growth and Development, and the Extension Service of the University of Michigan, Ann Arbor.

Klaus F. Riegel
John A. Meacham

List of contributors

Anagnostopoulou, Rena	*Vassar College, Poughkeepsie*
Anderson, Gene	*University of Wisconsin, Madison*
Andersson, Bengt-Erik	*Göteborg University, Sweden*
Angelini, Arrigo L.	*University of Sao Paulo, Brazil*
Beller, E. Kuno	*Temple University, Philadelphia*
Borich, Gary	*University of Texas, Austin*
Brainerd, Charles J.	*University of Alberta, Edmonton, Canada*
Carlson, Jerry S.	*University of California, Riverside*
Ciaccio, N.V.	*American University in Cairo, Egypt*
Cicirelli, Victor G.	*Purdue University, Lafayette*
Clarke-Stewart, Alison	*Yale University, New Haven*
Cole, Michael	*Rockefeller University, New York*
Coren, Stanley	*University of British Columbia, Vancouver, Canada*
Datan, Nancy	*University of West Virginia, Morgantown*
Diaz-Guerrero, Rogelio	*National University of Mexico, Mexico*
Doberenz, Alexander R.	*University of Wisconsin, Green Bay*
Dopyera, John E.	*Pennsylvania State University, University Park*
Eisner, Howard C.	*Duke University, Durham*
Elias, Marjorie F.	*Harvard University, Cambridge*
Eyferth, Klaus	*Darmstadt Institute of Technology, Germany*
Falk, Jacqueline M.	*University of Wisconsin, Green Bay*
Fein, Greta G.	*Yale University, New Haven*
Freedle, Roy O.	*Educational Testing Service, Princeton*

Garbers, Johan G.	*Rand Afrikaans University, Johannesburg, Republic of South Africa*
Gardner, Eric F.	*Syracuse University, Syracuse*
Girgus, Johan S.	*City University of New York*
Glick, Joseph	*City University of New York*
Greenfield, Patricia M.	*University of California, Santa Cruz*
Gutmann, David	*University of Michigan, Ann Arbor*
Hall, William S.	*Vassar College, Poughkeepsie*
Hardesty, Francis P.	*City University of New York*
Hargrove, Joy L.	*University of Michigan, Ann Arbor*
Harris, Adrienne E.	*Glendon College, York University, Toronto, Canada*
Helson, Ravenna	*University of California, Berkeley*
Heusinkveld, Henk G.	*University of Nijmegen, The Netherlands*
Higgins-Trenk, Ann	*Pennsylvania State University, University Park*
Hooper, Frank H.	*University of Wisconsin, Madison*
Jones, Pauline A.	*Memorial University of Newfoundland, St John's, Canada*
Kelly, Penelope	*Syracuse University, Syracuse*
Kessen, William	*Yale University, New Haven*
Klein, Jenny W.	*Department of Health, Education and Welfare, Washington, D.C.*
Klein, Robert P.	*National Institute of Health, Bethesda*
Kubo, Shunichi	*National Institute for Educational Research, Tokyo, Japan*
Kussmann, Thomas	*University of Bonn, Germany*
Lay, Margaret Z.	*Syracuse University, Syracuse*
Leckie, Gerard	*University of Nijmegen, The Netherlands*
Lehr, Ursula	*University of Cologne, Germany*
Leibowitz, Herschel W.	*Pennsylvania State University, University Park*
Leifer, Aimee Dorr	*Harvard University, Cambridge*
McIntosh, Elaine N.	*University of Wisconsin, Green Bay*
Manaster, Guy J.	*University of Texas, Austin*
Marjoribanks, Kevin	*University of Oxford, England*
Mecacci, Luciano	*National Research Council, Rome, Italy*
Miller, Louise B.	*University of Louisville, Kentucky*
Mönks, Franz J.	*University of Nijmegen, The Netherlands*

Monge, Rolf H.	*Syracuse University, Syracuse*
Neisworth, John T.	*Pennsylvania State University, University Park*
Neugarten, Bernice L.	*University of Chicago*
O'Leary, Sandra E.	*University of Wisconsin, Madison*
Olson, David R.	*Ontario Institute of Education, Toronto, Canada*
Overton, Willis	*Temple University, Philadelphia*
Papalia, Diane E.	*University of Wisconsin, Madison*
Parke, Ross D.	*Fels Research Institute, Yellow Springs*
Pascual-Leone, Juan	*York University, Toronto, Canada*
Peck, Robert F.	*University of Texas, Austin*
Pollack, Robert H.	*University of Georgia, Athens*
Porges, Stephen W.	*University of Illinois, Champaign-Urbana*
Przetacznikowa, Maria	*University of Krakow, Poland*
Rahmani, Levy	*Harvard University, Cambridge*
Riegel, Klaus F.	*University of Michigan, Ann Arbor*
Rosow, Irving	*University of California, San Francisco*
Rothbart, Mary K.	*University of Oregon, Eugene*
Runyon, David K.	*University of Wisconsin, Whitewater*
Salomon, Gavriel	*Hebrew University, Jerusalem, Israel*
Sameroff, Arnold J.	*University of Rochester*
Schludermann, Eduard H.	*University of Manitoba, Winnipeg, Canada*
Schludermann, S.	*University of Manitoba, Winnipeg, Canada*
Schmitz-Scherzer, Reinhard	*University of Bonn, Germany*
Scribner, Sylvia	*Rockefeller University, New York*
Shanan, Joel	*Hebrew University, Jerusalem, Israel*
Sheehan, Nancy	*University of Wisconsin, Madison*
Smith, Marshall S.	*Harvard University, Cambridge*
Smits-Van Sonsbeek, Betty	*University of Nijmegen, The Netherlands*
Starr, Susan	*Yale University, New Haven*
Strobel, David A.	*University of Montana, Missoula*
Thomae, Hans	*University of Bonn, Germany*
Toman, Walter	*University Erlangen-Nürnberg, Germany*
Torney, J.V.	*University of Illinois, Chicago Circle, Chicago*
Van den Daele, Leland D.	*Columbia University, New York*
Van Lieshout, Cornelis, F.M.	*State University Utrecht, The Netherlands*
Voyat, Gilbert	*City University of New York*

Walberg, Herbert J.	*University of Illinois, Chicago Circle, Chicago*
Whiting, Beatrice	*Harvard University, Cambridge*
Wilder, Larry	*University of Wisconsin, Madison*
Witz, Klaus	*University of Illinois, Urbana*
Wozniak, Robert H.	*University of Minnesota, Minneapolis*
Zimmermann, Robert R.	*Central Michigan University, Mount Pleasant*
Zivin, Gail	*University of Pennsylvania, Philadelphia*

Contents

SECTION I

Historical and theoretical issues
in the development
of the individual and society

Early European contributions to developmental psychology

A. OVERVIEW, CONTEXTS, AND SELECTIONS

by Francis P. Hardesty, *The City College, City University of New York*

Within the design of today's symposium, several features are salient. Disappointment may arise that these forego an unraveling of relationships between contemporary developmental psychology and conceptions of the nature of growth and development as generated by scholarly thought in classical antiquity, the Renaissance, or the Age of Reason. Similar sin might also be registered concerning the absence of reference to other systems of speculation, especially to the great educationists of earlier times – to Comenius, Rousseau, Pestalozzi, Froebel, Herbart or even to Dewey, Nohl and others more recent. Disappointment and sin cast aside, the soldering of 'early European contributions' to the title of today's symposium is not without a degree of substantial rationale. The prefixing becomes solid once it is held firmly in mind that it was only within the context of events attending the end of the nineteenth century that developmental and child psychology began to acquire the empirical and experimental footing associated with it today.

Despite diverse emphases historians customarily give to them, the works of our symposium subjects have a number of features in common. By way of introduction, I would like to stress only three.

Methods for studying the child. From the perspective of today's attention to cognition, cognitive processing and the new structuralism, the works of

Binet, the Sterns, and Spranger are early nodes directly contributive to the tradition. The subjects of our symposium exercised vigilant regard for third-party observation, the collection of empirical data, and for the transformation of these into a socially relevant and subsequently more precise grasp of how the developing individual construes, negotiates, and makes a physical, exogenous world over into one which is endogenously and personally his own. The significance of specific functions underlying sensory-motor processes with concomitant consequences for inner-structuring of cognition and affect were all vigorously pursued. The pursuit involved crisp recognition of the vital roles to be played by systematic experimentation into the functions of language and thought, and of the relating of these to behavior and clarification of the puzzle of differential individual reality.

It is of value to remember that the developmental and child psychologies fostered by our symposium subjects did not methodologically operate upon a field made ready by educationists or psychologists by training. Rather, they took their methodological heel from developments aligned with medical science and the advancements in physiology. While it can be shown that the works of Tiedemann (1787), Sigismund (1856), Kussmaul (1859) and others occupy significant positions in the sequence, the dramatic turn was taken in 1882 when Wilhelm Preyer published his *The Mind of the Child*. Here, made available for the first time, was an account of the developmental course of a single child based upon the application of a successive set of systematic, day by day observations extending from the very onset of life to the end of the third year. As might have been expected from his background in physiology, Preyer provided detailed description of physical patterns, giving prominent place to the progressive unfolding of musculature and motor functioning. But it was also Preyer who was to record the first systematic observations of the emergence and early phases of speech, spatial appreciation, memory, and other psychological functions. From the standpoint of the chronicle, it makes small difference that Preyer's interpretations of matters underlying his observations were destined to gain little subsequent acceptance. The precedent had been established.

A full generation of events was to transpire before the professional toddlers in the newly founded field of psychology were to acquire a degree of surety regarding the meaningfulness of Preyer's amorphous designations and the study of the child was to take on the empirical footing characteristic of it today. As the nineteenth turned into the early part of this century, the recognition of the child as an individual and the newly won methodology were to generate a range of insights coalescing with the excitement which accompanied the establishment of general psychology as an independent discipline a generation earlier. Cogent expression is given to the meaning of these events by one of our symposium subjects in the opening lines of one of his ground-breaking texts:

'In science and culture, progress has two paths. One starts from the ordinary, self-evident and matter-of-fact, and leads into the distance. It looks for the strange and mysterious, for the pathological and the exceptionally gifted, for marvelous forms of life, unknown regions, and strange mental phenomena.

'The other has no such distant goal yet leads to no less great discoveries. It deals with that which is quite near, seemingly known to all, and suddenly shows it to us in an entirely new light. It is the more tedious path ...

While it is true child care, education and instruction have always existed in human culture, it has been reserved for our times to look upon the child as an issue and suddenly to discover what deep mysteries and riddles man has passed by, blind and deaf, for thousands of years' (Stern 1914 a, p.1).[1]

The conceptual framework. It has been said that the trails blazed by yesterday's pioneers often fail to bear the burden of today's traffic. It likewise seems to be true that, in the area of human development, the original trail-markings have become obscure or looked upon as irrelevant. In weighing a jndudging the contributions of Binet, the Sterns, and Spranger, it is important to remember that their works were produced within a contextual framework different from yet similar to certain contemporary aspects of our field today. Their investigations were bounded by physical resources, development of apparatus, and other strictures imposed by the general level of technology available to them at their time and in their place. At quite another level, the contextual frame within which they operated was governed by a conceptual tradition which placed experience from the standpoint of the experiencing person at the very core of the definition and intent of a scientific psychology.

The conceptual tradition they pursued continues today, albeit a sub-configuration tempered by the larger, simultaneously more differentiated

---

1. The section underwent only slight editorial change in the fourth and subsequent editions of the volume. For a similar version in English see Anna Barwell's translation of *Psychology of Early Childhood* (1924) based on the third German edition.

and loosely integrated lid covering not only the science and discipline but the now established profession. The conceptual lineage of our symposium stands apart from the Hobbes-Darwin-Galton-Hull tradition or, put in a slightly different way, the Anglo-American derived associationist-behaviorist-habit formation view of human development and the nature of individual differences. Up to a point one could go along with Riegel (1972) and place the subjects of our symposium in that European conceptual posture extending from Rousseau and Pestalozzi through to Piaget. The point is, however, debatable. Suffice it to say that there is evidence for this position not only in the argument presented by Riegel but also in the portrayals of crises affecting psychology as recorded by Spranger in 1926, by Karl Buehler in 1927, and by Stern in 1931 dealing with the place of the discipline in the university.

Couched in humor, critique of a pure associationist-behaviorist scientism is to be found even earlier in the *Psychologists' Song* allegedly sung with great glee at the congress for education and child study held in Breslau in 1913. The fifth stanza reads:

> *Association – truly 'tis a word of magic!*
> *Twill, if you please, with greatest ease*
> *Break every problem's seals.*
> *And many seek with it alone to conjure*
> *A counterfeit so true that it*
> *The soul's real form reveals.*
>
> *Ideas check or aid each other*
> *They jostle, crowd and squeeze one another.*
> *And lo! A psychologic hash*
> *Comes from this clash.*
> (Stern, 1914b, p. 415)

The social and cultural frameworks. Our final commonality relates to broader movements underlying the social and cultural dynamics of change attending the turn of the century and perhaps continuing in the world today (Stern, F. 1965). Of the various ways trends in the sciences may be historically analyzed, the socio-transcendental approach has been the least explored and the most difficult systematically to articulate. Presentations of the history of psychology are no exception since they readily lend themselves to classification under the more prevalently exercised strategies associated with immanent history (e.g., Boring 1929, 1950), problem- or issue-centered history (e.g., Pongratz 1967 and Pastore 1972), the ideological approach (e.g., Riegel 1972) or other historiography.

Difficulties of the transcendental approach notwithstanding, it would be inappropriate to forego mention of the dramatic features of the social landscape shared by the developmentalists to be discussed, inasmuch as the socio-cultural climate at the end of the nineteenth century and extending into the first two decades of the twentieth century proffers striking parallels to changes in the world of today. It was an era of remarkable unrest and social upheaval, of widespread breakdowns and progressive reorderings affecting almost every facet of the social institutions constituting western societies of the time; an era the onset of which found the major powers of western society embroiled in skirmishes in Africa, Asia, in the Pacific and Caribbean; a time when England's poor worked long hours for minuscule wages and lived in desperate conditions; when a prominent judge, later to become president of the United States, asserted that many more workers would have to be killed before disturbances associated with the Pullman strike could be stayed; a time when Emile Zola was led to accuse French authorities of inflicting one of the greatest inequities of the century in the case of Alfred Dreyfus; and a time when no less than eight heads of state were murdered, and governments were territorized by assassins (*cf.* Tuchman 1966).

It was a period when the arts were to undergo revolution, universities were to be reformed, educational systems vastly revised and extended, and legal definitions of the mentally ill and handicapped were to be accommodated to fit the findings of medicine and psychiatry. The social and behavioral sciences were to be put on their feet and the older physical and natural sciences were to be confronted with paradigmatic changes, ushering in their own age of uncertainty (Sumler 1973). For psychology it was a period of rapid proliferation of its great theoretical systems and schools, the discovery of the individual, and of securing the establishment of the psychologies of the child, education, industry and other applications to the new array of vexing social problems.

For views regarding the nature and implications of developmental processes held by our symposium subjects. other features of the time were perhaps closer to home. For the Sterns, the Buehlers, and especially for Spranger, these relate to protests associated with European youth movements which coincided with the era's onset and which achieved a degree of socially institutionalized status in the ensuing decade.

Following almost a generation of rapid industrialization, urban concentration, increasing specialization in the technologies, unprecedented material prosperity and realignments affecting the full scope of its vital social institutions, Germany of the 1890s had obtained its place in the sun. Integrating a wide range of materials dealing with the effects on youth of the time (e.g., Lütkens 1925, Schelsky 1957, Schmid 1941). Rosen tells the story most poignantly:

'But large numbers of German youth saw nothing admirable in a society that was being overwhelmed by tides of commercialism and uniformity. For them there was no brave new world ... What they saw was a brassy, tarnished society, in which moral bankruptcy and social fraud were rampant. They were ... disillusioned by the world of their elders, whose values, traditions and institutions appeared treadbare and irrelevant ... they saw parental religion largely a sham, politics trivial ... economic activity deceitful ... education stereotyped, and the relations of the sexes ... shot through with hypocrisy ...

'By 1900 all over ... northern Germany one could find tanned, travel-stained young men, and later girls, in nondescript clothes ... on their backs a few simple belongings in knapsacks, and on the shoulders of at least a few, lutes and guitars that they played while wandering ... the Wandervögel developed a headquarters for each group ... embellished with their own hand made furniture, carvings paintings and leatherwork ... [Their] credo was goallessness' (Rosen 1970, pp. 7-9).[2]

These and other characteristics of the span of years intimately experienced by our symposium subjects warrant intensive psychological study. For it is to this period that today's much discussed concepts of cultural lag, generation gap, credibility gap, alienation, and like phenomena are immediately to be traced and have relevance for an adequate understanding of the developing individual in a changing world.

2. Treatises on the German youth movements often focus on their activities as forerunners contributive to the rise of National Socialism. These analyses generally fail to emphasize the changing constituency of the movements and the fact that the time frames of the 1890s, 1900s and the mid-1920s and later were different.

B. THE CONTRIBUTION OF WILLIAM AND CLARA STERN TO THE ONSET OF DEVELOPMENTAL PSYCHOLOGY[1]

by Klaus Eyferth, *Darmstadt Institute of Technology, Germany*

There are many parallels between today's theorizing in developmental psychology and thoughts on this topic at the onset of this century. The contemporary discourse fails to recognize its predecessors. This review does not intend to disclose the ancestry of these ideas; it has a focus relevant to the social and political conditions which provoke or inhibit psychologists in choosing the objects of their investigation today. Historical knowledge may support the understanding of these conditions. William Stern – in collaboration with his wife, Clara Stern – strongly influenced the course of psychology during the first three decades of this century in Germany, when the German scene had an impact on the international development of this science. The work of the Sterns exemplifies the intensity of international scientific communication and exchange at the turn of the century (cf. Allport 1938, 1968). The First World War was followed by a limitation of this exchange in psychology, and the growing discipline disintegrated into national subgroups. But this process alone does not explain why the contribution of the Sterns was consigned nearly to oblivion in Germany as well as abroad during the ensuing decades. It may be interesting to look at this process from the perspective of the development of scientific and political ideas.

The life of William Stern. Louis William Stern was born in 1871 in Berlin, the son of a not overly successful businessman. At Berlin University he was a student of Hermann Ebbinghaus, whom he followed to Breslau in 1897. Here he formulated the outlines that proved to be fundamental to all his future publications. Within an 18 year period, 12 books (most with several revised editions) appeared under his senior authorship, several co-authored by his wife. He published many articles and co-edited two newly founded journals. Most of his influential publications on developmental psychology stem from this period.

In 1916 William Stern accepted a position at Hamburg within an institution for adult education called the *Vorlesungswesen*. Immediately after the end of the First World War he was instrumental in founding the University of Hamburg in 1919. His departure from Breslau seems to have been motivated not only by a denial of an adequate academic position but also by the pull exerted by the liberal political climate in Hamburg and by the Sterns' growing involvement in progressive educational ideas. In Breslau he had already diverged from the paternalistic style of teaching by inviting his students to discussion groups and by organizing workshops or 'retreats' in the nearby mountains. He was in close contact with a group of students in revolt, the so-called *Jugendbewegung*. During his first years in Hamburg he lectured and wrote on such topics as coeducation, the participation of pupils in school government, and treatment of juvenile delinquency. Prior to Stern's venture into such areas, topics of this nature were not perceived as belonging to the province of academic psychology.

William Stern became one of the first full professors of the newly established University of Hamburg. He built up an extensive and influential psychology department on a basis that was founded by Ernst Meuman, who died in 1914. Immediately following the National Socialist seizure of power he was prohibited even to set foot in the rooms of his department. He left Germany, and after a short period in the Netherlands, he immigrated to the United States in 1934. Here he was established as a professor at Duke University in Durham, North Carolina, a position he held until his sudden death in 1938.

A comprehensive biography of Clara Stern has not yet been compiled. Apart from a note by their daughter that she met William Stern first during his studies in Berlin (Michaelis-Stern 1972), data pertaining to her life are hard to come by. Indications are that she received no formal professional training, but she collected and evaluated data for the studies she and her husband published together. Clara Stern died in 1945. It is difficult to imagine William Stern's developmental studies without her contributions.

The spread of Stern's influence. Before a review of these studies, the interruption of the impact of this research needs further consideration. There are several explanations. Though his main publication *General Psychology from the Personalistic Standpoint* received an early English publication (1938; in German 1935) Stern did not subsequently gain influence in the

United States. At the time of his emigration he had turned to a rather fundamental analysis of psychological methodology and theory. This philosophical orientation and its emphasis on the person as the unit of psychological concern were not in the mainstream of psychology in the United States at that time. Furthermore, Stern never became well acquainted with spoken English, although throughout his career he referred to and reported on American research in his publications. He had visited the United States at least twice prior to his immigration. He was a member of the prestigious conference held in 1909 during the twentieth anniversary of the founding of Clark University.

Following the ascent of National Socialism, Stern's contribution was lost to German psychology since his publications were consigned to the library stacks as prohibited reading, and most of his associates and students were obliged to resign from their academic positions after 1933. But all these facts do not sufficiently explain the discontinuation of his influence. The works of other German emigrants were accepted and extended in English speaking countries, and these psychologists were re-accepted by German psychology in the aftermath of World War II.

Psychology and social changes. William and Clara Stern promoted a branch of psychological endeavor that never contributed directly to the mainstream of thinking in psychological science. They did not pay the proper tribute for the acceptance of psychology into the fraternity of sciences. Their intentions cannot be defined in terms of the system of knowledge but only in terms of applicability of insights. Stern was active in editing two journals, the *Zeitschrift für angewandte Psychologie* (Journal for Appied Psychology) and the *Zeitschrift für paedagogische Psychologie und experimentelle Paedagogik* (Journal for Educational Psychology and Experimental Education). The aims of these periodicals characterize his involvement. For him psychology was a tool for meeting social demands. Although William Stern never became a practitioner and remained throughout his career an academician, he did not perceive of psychology as an institution that could exist autonomous from its obligations to society.

This perception of psychology as an instrument of social change was the fundamental cause of the inhibition of Stern's lasting impact on the development of psychology. During the revolutionary period of republican and socialistic movements following the collapse of the *Kaiserreich* in 1918, Stern's psychological intentions superficially seemed to be accepted. But this was an illusion. Psychology remained an academic institution. It continued to persecute any deviation from academic tradition. Neither in America nor in Germany did a programmatic change of the direction of psychology seem admissible. William Sterns' innovations were to be forgotten, since he did not strive to comply with the expectations of the academic profession.

William Stern was not at all a revolutionary. In some respects, he even maintained positions that seem to us now an uncritical reflection of the moral norms of his social background. Examples of this are suggested by his outspoken denial of infantile sexuality (1909), and his discussion of parental punishment practices (1914, pp. 345–350). However, he regarded psychology as a tool of social change, and this was a distinct departure from scientific tradition of his time.

The personalistic perspective. Beginning with his book *Person und Sache* (Person and Thing) (1906), Stern gradually built a philosophical system that culminated in his *General Psychology from the Personalistic Standpoint* (1938). He rejects the idea that psychology might adequately take the human being merely as an object of cognizance. Men are not sums of functions but persons. A person is not a thing, i.e., man is not understandable as an object, but only if his action and intention are taken into account. It is not possible here to discuss his philosophy in detail, but Stern's educational engagement, his pioneering work in applied psychology, and his programmatic turn toward differential psychology, all belong to an elaborated scientific system. For most psychologists, this approach has not been acceptable until recently with the advent of a more vigorously oriented humanistic psychology.

In order to evaluate the developmental work of the Sterns, within their historical context, we have to have a notion of the concept of differential psychology. *Differentielle Psychologie* (1911) was the title of one of William Stern's most successful books. It was intended to be programatic. At the turn of the century, psychology was engaged in determining general laws of the mind. It was Stern's position that this is only one side of the legitimate interest in human behavior and experience. The other side is represented by the investigation of individual differences. As early as 1900, Stern presented an outline of the methodological problems of differential psychology, in which the relation between experimentation and testing are discussed. The objective of experimental work in psychology is the relation between generalized variables and the search for invariants.

The aim of the test is to characterize an individual. As developmental research tracks the process of individual change it belongs to differential psychology. Stern was not much interested in growth as a function of age. He wanted to know what makes the world of the child qualitatively different from the world of the adult.

Stern's most well known but perhaps not his most significant contribution in this area was his introduction of the idea of the intelligence quotient (IQ). To him, intelligence is the ability to adjust thinking to new tasks. He denied the notion that intelligence is a unitary capacity. He saw intelligence rather as an intention that is not to be separated from what we would today term achievement motivation. Each age has its characteristic way of applying intelligence to performance but within achievement there is a continuity which can be related to chronological age by calculating the IQ. Stern never applied the IQ for the measurement of adult intelligence. In the third edition of his book on the measurement of intelligence (1920), Stern criticizes the overestimation of intelligence and 'the delusion that it might be possible to classify, to guide, or to treat someone correctly by just knowing his intelligence' (1920, p. VII). Stern's book *Psychological Methods of Testing Intelligence* was published in the United States in 1914. In the revised German edition (1920, pp. 275–279), Stern discusses thoroughly the problems of educational selection and calls for the reform of the public school system with the aim of providing equal opportunity to all children.

In 1914 the *Psychologie der Frühen Kindheit* (Psychology of Early Childhood) appeared. Here Stern analyses the question of the relative impacts of heredity and environment on individual development. He concludes that this is a fictitious issue and question. He maintains that separation of genetic invariants and of environmental components will never be possible. All learning is based on genetic disposition, but no disposition can be completely realized. Overt and observable traits cannot be reduced to their elements. Stern calls this the '*principle of convergence*'. Nativistic research which tries to isolate genetic roots of human performance necessarily resorts to categories of behavior which are ultimately irrelevant for the understanding of human interaction. This derivation of the convergence principle is one example of the confrontation of thing and person. An analytical decomposition of behavior cannot but lose the perspective of developmental continuity.

Studies of language acquisition. Another example of convergence is

Stern's treatment of language acquisition. Stern deliberately neglects the quantitative interpretation though he collected data directly relevant. Rather, he was concerned with the qualitatively varying function of language during the course of development. In 1907 Clara and William Stern published *Die Kindersprache* (The Language of Children). In their research they use longitudinal case studies as well as cross-sectional data. The empirical data are treated with a strong linguistic orientation. Special attention is paid to the change of linguistic categories used as instruments of communication. One point that seems characteristic of the Sterns' approach is the anticipation of important contemporary research topics.

'The main condition of language acquisition, the social stratification, has gained the least investigation. All children that were investigated belong to a well educated middle class; they are privileged to develop without inhibition. In terms of controlled observation, we do not know anything about language acquisition of children in proletarian or rural families' (1907, p. 254).

This remark from 1907 could quite well have provided an interpretative review of the state of empirical research in 1960.

In *Die Kindersprache* and in *Psychologie der frühen Kindheit* most of the conclusions are derived from description of individual development. Clara Stern recorded systematically the activities and utterances of her own three children. These observations are used to exemplify the problems and pecularities of each age. This method may be unacceptable for today's developmental psychology. However, it led the Sterns to describe many developmental phenomena that had not been reported previously.

A last example are the studies on trustworthiness or credibility of children testifying in judicial proceedings. In his book on early childhood, Stern discusses memory and the process of concept formation in terms of discrepancies between children and adults. The child's recollection or his statement of prior experience may reflect a reality which need not be identical with that of a adult person in the same situation. Clara and William Stern gathered instances of spontaneous recollection and forgetting in the age groups from one to seven years. They also experimented by showing children of different ages pictures of situations and posed questions to the children regarding pictorial contents after several days. This topic was the subject of several articles in two volumes (1920, 1926), wherein there are meticulous descriptions of factors which may influence or distort testimony of the child as a witness in legal proceedings.

Clara and William Stern did pioneering work in many fields of developmental psychology. However, their labors were brought to a sudden and dramatic end in 1933. The impact of this research does not lie mainly in the data which were collected. What was lost in the interruption of continuity of this psychological tradition was the theoretical work of William Stern and the orientation of research toward the aims of education. At least in the theory, his conception of intelligence was much more advanced than concepts that later enjoyed popularity for many decades. Stern's principle of convergence might have assisted in the avoidance of subsequent blind alleys in psychological research.

The Sterns set goals for their developmental studies that contrasted markedly with the intentions of academic psychology of their times. The critique of positivism is nearly a trademark of Stern's work. It implies a strong regard for the value system of the developing person, and it resulted in great social relevance of their findings and in direct application of research. In this respect alone developmental psychology still needs the teaching of Clara and William Stern.

C. THE REAL WORLD OF ALFRED BINET

by Gilbert Voyat, *City University of New York*

The world of Alfred Binet can be approached from several directions. It is quite natural to associate Binet with the concept of IQ testing, for which he is recognized as a pioneer and whose reputation still stands. Yet his personality and his professional endeavors were diversified to a great extent. The word which probably encompasses his status best is 'eclecticism'.

Pollack and Brenner (1969) note in their book dedicated to the experimental psychology of Alfred Binet:

'Binet can be best epitomized as a man with a diversity of interests and a tremendous capacity for hard work. He was continually observing the behaviors of his two daughters .... He wrote a small book and several articles on microorganisms and insects. He co-authored with André Lorde, several plays whose themes centered around abnormal behavior. He was interested in the effects of emotional and other non-rational influences on thought processes, and published a number of studies on suggestibility, esthesiometry, hypnotism, mental fatigue, graphology and cephalometry' (pp. x-xi).

If on the one hand Binet is recognized as the father of experimental psychology, due to his deep conviction in observation rather than theory, on the other hand it is evident that his contributions reflect a breadth of interest and knowledge. It is interesting to note that his educational background is original in relationship to other psychologists of his generation. Born in 1857, he first studied law, and he received a doctorate in natural sciences (a distinction Piaget later shared with him!) in 1897. By 1880 he published a first paper in psychology, 'On the Fusion of Similar Sensations', the first sentence of which symbolizes his theoretical belief at the time: 'We know that the association of ideas by similarity is one of the two principles which assure the succession of our thoughts' (p. 284). Although he departed from the ideas of Taine, his studies on intelligence led him to practice systematic introspection, independently from the Würzburg School, and led him to use a method which he called 'questioning method'. Its use culminated in his book dealing with the experimental study of intelligence published in 1903 (1922) the conclusions of which attested to his fidelity to the concept of imageless thought which goes beyond introspection. Concluding his book he noted:

'The American authors, who like to deal big, often publish experiments which deal with hundreds and thousands of persons; they instinctively follow this prejudice according to which probing value of a work is proportional to the number of observations. This is but an illusion; when a certain number of concurring observations has been collected, those which can still be added do not increase significantly the demonstrative value of the first ones; and, on the other hand, there is some danger in multiplying the number of subjects, since one risks to lose in quality what is gained in quantity .... A mental test applied hastily on anonymous subjects has only a proportionate value to the time that one spends; if I was able to shed some light through the attentive study of two subjects it is because I have observed them live and I have scrutinized them for many years' (pp. 297–298).

It is interesting to note this reflection and compare it with the intuitive knowledge one has of Binet as the father of experimental psychology and mental tests, where the purpose is to differentiate mental abilities among large numbers of children. What it means is that Binet was fundamentally unwilling to be bound by any particular method of investigation. More precisely, it is the nature of the problem studied which largely determined his method. One can define a continuum of experimentation ranging from precise quantified data to pure introspective considerations. The point is also that Binet, following his interests, adapted the experimental paradigm to them rather than have them defined by the experimental paradigm itself.

When one compares the actual state of developmental and experimental psychology today with the situation at the beginning of the century, one observes a reversal. I am here referring to the main trend: the specialization that one observes today, in the different realms of psychology, that deals not only with a specificity of topics such as memory, perception, intelligence, etc., but also with a specificity of method. This specialization has been accompanied by the massive impact of statistical methods in psychology. As Stevens (1964) notes: 'When description gives way to measurement, calculation replaces debate' (p. 1). One also observes that the language of the observations has changed during the century. Whereas Binet was involved in carefully describing behaviors in qualitative terms, the actual trend is to take large numbers of subjects and to substitute a mathematical language for a descriptive one.

The result is, I believe, a state of psychology characterized somehow by abstractions and models rather than a concern with real, individual subjects. The departure from individual observation has resulted in a change of focus in psychology. The fact that we are, most of the time, dealing with large populations implies a focus on problems rather than individuals. The subject is perceived as an abstraction within the paradigm of a well defined experimental problem. An exception has to be made for a part of clinical psychology, but undoubtedly the contemporary concern is to a large extent defined by the use of large samples, statistically treated. The actual tendency is to stress similarities or group differences according to statistical means, whereas Binet, for instance, emphasized individual differences carefully, noting their qualitative features.

For example, when Binet described the different times at which his two daughters learned to walk (1890), he came to understand the reason of the delay for the younger girl by stressing individual differences which went beyond a simple description of psychomotor features. He notes:

'The younger one, on the other hand, was a laughing turbulent child; when put on her legs, she remained immobile for some moments and then was suddenly pushed forwards by a desire to progress ... she cried out, she gestured, she was very amusing to watch; she advanced staggering like a drunken man, and could not take four or five steps without falling. Thus, the beginning of walking was delayed; she could walk alone securely only at the age of 15 months' (p. 297).

Binet intimately knew the life of his subjects, not only some partial, isolated experimental characteristitics or socio-economic data which are societal features as opposed to individual ones. Today, few developmental psychologists take their children as examples, and Piaget is at times perceived as an anachronism to have taken only three children as subjects at the beginning of his career. Yet it is significant to observe that Piaget's findings when repeated on a great number of subjects, in particular those dealing with the sensori-motor development, were essentially confirmed.

As far as observations are concerned, Binet displayed a quasi-mathematical level of description. The precision and the care of his language reflected both his deep commitment and his concern for objectivity. One cannot talk of his objectivity as based on statistical evidence since most of the time Binet reflected upon percentages only; one can certainly assess his need for factual evidence, and the precautions he took when dealing with comparative psychology. In his article dedicated to children's perception he noted (1890):

'In regard to numbers, we saw that children, who did not know how to count, could not perceive numbers of objects greater than five or six.

These experiments make us appreciate the value of those carried out on certain higher animals: monkeys and bears for example, have been made by various contrivances to perceive a certain number of objects. Because the more intelligent animals hardly exceed what small children can do, it is to them that they must be compared. Like children animals merely perceive the totality of a group of objects whereas adult humans, thanks to the use of language, actually count them, which is quite different. When we compare the animal to the adult human, we are therefore committing an error' (p. 582).

This comment is quite interesting since it sheds some light on Binet's differential view of children and adults as well as the implicit problem of generalization from animal data to adult psychological functioning. The isomorphism is neither immediate nor justified. The general problem of behaviorism and of ethology was already anticipated here.

The clarity of his observations as well as their systematic disclosure can be seen when reading the end of the same article:

'. . . if we glance at the path we have followed, we will retain the following facts relative to the two girls under our observation: (1) They show a great ability to compare lengths. (2) Among the colors, red is the first to be designated correctly. (3) A design representing the entirety of a known object is easily interpreted. Difficulties arise, however, in interpreting the fragments of an object or the signs of an emotional state. In all of this, the child does not seem to analyze her perceptions. (4) The child has difficulty in the use of personal pronouns which probably indicates a certain difficulty in perceiving her own personality. At four and a half a little girl can account for her dreams. (5) In recalling objects, the child is above all attentive to the use of the object' (p. 611).

Here we have a set of general but precise observations which cut across specific domains of psychology and tend to lead to the perception of the child as a total human being, not as a part or category of knowledge. The focus is the child. Binet not only referred to individual observations but, when the problem asked for it, he would experiment with large numbers of subjects. To take only one example, he begins his article dealing with the investigation of the development of visual memory in children (1894) by stating: 'Our investigations were carried out in the primary schools of Paris on more than 300 boys' (p. 348). After having described in detail the profile of his population, he states that his reason for using percentages is essentially to facilitate comparison. In this sense, statistics are used in order to help the comparison, not to define it. In any event, Binet made use of a variety of methods and was never determined by a specific experimental approach.

What was his production? How many articles did he write? How did his professional endeavor look?

Binet's creative energy. Binet's first article was published in 1880, and across the years he maintained an interesting output, until his death in 1911. In total, one finds 331 articles and books which were published either in collaboration or by himself; six publications appeared after his deat, and six were originally published in English. It is interesting to note that his average yearly production from 1880 until his death is 10.5 publications. Binet wrote 217 articles by himself which means that 67% of his production was written alone and 33% in collaboration. A further breakdown of his production allows the following considerations: from 1880 until 1899, Binet published 88 papers by himself, 83 were in French and five were in English. The latter are all concentrated within three years from 1895 to 1897.

It is noteworthy to observe the topics with which these particular papers dealt since they essentially addressed themselves to American psychologists and can give us some idea of the nature of this 'transatlantic' exchange. The first paper dealt with the mechanisms of thought (1895) and affirmed his theoretical position that thought goes beyond images. The following year Binet published a review of recent work in French psychology (1896) and in 1897 his output in English reflected his broad and eclectic concern: the first one dealt with Le Dantec's work (1897) on biological determinism and conscious personality, an intersecting paper between biology and psychology; the second one had to do with plural states of being where the influence of Charcot was clearly present (1897), and the last one consisted of notes on the experimental study of memory (1897). In the same year, one further paper was published in collaboration with Vashide and dealt with the influence of intellectual work upon the blood-pressure in man (1897).

Binet's total production of 331 articles and papers does not take into account the numerous translations which were done in various languages. During his first 19 years of publication 164 articles and books appeared; out of them, 88 were written by himself and 76 in collaboration. This is to say that almost half of his production is his (53.6%) and another half in collaboration (46.6%). Among the co-authors four names involved 61 publications: Féré with 10 publications, Henri with 10, Courtier with 21 and Vashide with 20. Altogether there were 13 co-authors which were part of Binet's first period of work. It is noteworthy that one publication was done with Charcot in 1893 and dealt with the psychological processes of mnemonic virtuosity (1893). A second period lasted from 1900 until 1904. During this time Binet published 51 articles. Among those only two were written in collaboration. Forty-nine were produced by him alone which represented 96.1% of his output. This meant that essentially Binet was working on his own.

It is interesting to note this departure from his previous period of work, which could be inferred to be a kind of withdrawal. Yet I think that the best characterization for this second phase of his life was renewal. Although he was certainly disappointed when the Collège de France chose Janet for a professorship and the Sorbonne chose Dumas (which meant that Binet never held a professorship), he nevertheless expanded himself in new directions.

He was, along with Ferdinand Buisson, instrumental in creating, in 1900, the Société Libre pour l'Etude Psychologique de l'Enfant. This group was not limited to psychologists and contained school teachers and principals concerned with educational, practical problems. After his death, this group became the Société Alfred Binet and still carries on today Binet's tradition of concern with educational problems.

The choices of the Collège de France and of the Sorbonne reflected the status of psychology in France at the beginning of the century: Janet never experimented, and Dumas dedicated only part of his activity to it. Binet had been strongly involved in experimentation of various types, but he was not chosen. Psychology was still part of philosophy.

This event principally affected Binet's career. He turned himself more and more towards educational problems. He became the natural choice of the Ministry of Public Instruction when it created a commission whose main purpose was to improve the teaching of backward children in 1904.

From this point of view it is important to note that the origin of measurement of intellectual abilities stems from a political decision bearing the mark of a socialist orientation: Binet was asked to find ways to improve the teaching of backward children, who as a result of a sort of 'open admission' had come to constitute a population of such a magnitude that teachers were faced with a difficult problem of heterogeneity within their classrooms. Psychological testing had thus an educational reason and was a late consequence of the extension of schooling to all segments of the population. It had been Jules Ferry, a leftist doctrinaire, who in 1880 had been instrumental in enacting the educational laws which made primary education compulsory across the French Republic. Until this time, education was essentially an elitist opportunity, but it was really the conflict with the Catholic Church which prompted Ferry to force a democratic system of education that was separated from the Church. In any event, the impact was clearly felt only 24 years later, which gives us some idea of the rate of development at this time in history: it took a quarter of a century to create a commission whose purpose was really to improve the educational system as a whole. The language used (improving the teaching of backward children) was in fact a euphemism for the paucity of school systems. The purpose of this commission was to improve the overall situation.

It should also be noted that in 1895 Binet became the director of the Laboratory of Physiological Psychology at the Sorbonne. This position did not entail a professorship. But the same year he founded with Beaunis the Review, l'Année Psychologique, which by 1908 was largely devoted to the enquiry of practical and social questions.

The year 1905 marks a change in Binet's productivity. From 1905 until his death, he published 110 articles; 80 are written by himself and 27 with Simon with whom he is traditionally associated. There are 30 papers in total which are published in collaboration during this third period of Binet's life. His main collaborator is undoubtedly Simon and Simon only. There is one publication with Lorde, one with Alice Binet and one with Vaney. In short Binet's collaboration with Simon is relatively late in his life and represents only 12.5% of his total individual production. Yet this collaboration remained a constant from 1905 until his death, with an average of 3.8 publications a year.

In summary, Binet's life contains three main periods: from 1880 until 1899, the accent is on a collaborative work with a number of people of different backgrounds; from 1900 until 1904 Binet publishes alone and from 1905 until 1911 essentially only with Simon. The overall trend is a slow pathway from theoretical and experimental focus towards a deep involvement in educational problems. In this respect Fraisse's reflections upon Binet (1963) are significant: 'A profound experimentalist, he (Binet) believed more in fact than theories. His docility towards facts led to several changes during his career' (p. 1–32).

Binet's points of view about teachers. It is interesting to further analyze Binet's concern about education in citing what he himself felt about teachers and principals. This again gives us some idea about the spirit of the time, the attitudes of people involved in education and of the relationship between psychologists and educators.

In one of Binet's studies (1895) which deals with the concept of fear in children he used several questionnaires which were distributed to a number of teachers. Although it is not my purpose to relate the findings themselves, the structure of Binet's presentation is worth mentioning. He began by first carefully describing the nature of the enquiry, the population it dealt with, proceeded in giving a definition of fear, the subjects of fear, the signs of fear, the state of health of fearful children as well as their intellectual characteristics, the moral character of fearful children, their relative number, the causes of fear as well as its treatment, and he ended this more than 30-page study with the following comment:

'... I think it is entirely useless to add that I do not feel that I have investigated the psychological mechanism of fear. To understand this mechanism one must conduct an experimental and physiological investigation of capillary circulation and respiration, the nature of which occupies me at the moment' (p. 254).

This paragraph is totally characteristic of Binet's relentless mind whose interest never remained limited to one domain of psychology.

To study this article from an educational point of view, Binet noted the kind of responses he obtained from the different teachers who had received the questionnaire. Approximately 250 copies had been distributed, and Binet complained about the indolence of the majority of educators but made the reflection that 50 teachers answered nevertheless. He further analyzed the types of replies and observed that some of them were, in a polite form, simple refusals to answer. Binet noted the way the teachers justified their attitude in citing one of the questionnaires which said that 'no circumstances have permitted me to verify feelings of fear in the children entrusted to my care' or 'the principal of the school and her assistants, after having deliberated on the question, agree on affirming that they have never noticed the slightest indication of fear in the students'. Binet expressed his feelings in a humorous yet precise way: 'Let us salute this happy school and pass on to others' (p. 224).

At the same time the comments of the teachers reflected how much the reality of the children's worlds was denied. Their denial was so obvious that Binet was prompted to express a value judgment on this kind of response. Binet's comment illustrated that he, too, was essentially a progressive man in education. One of the reasons for doing this study of fear in children was to show to teachers the reality of the problem. One wonders what type of person Binet was.

Binet as a person. Binet spent many years observing his two daughters. This clinical preoccupation 'undoubtedly affected his family life' (Pollack and Brenner 1969, p. X), and must have influenced his person in some ways. From this point of view it is interesting to refer to the drama that Binet wrote in collaboration with Lorde, a famous French dramatist of the first part of the century. Lorde was named the Prince of Terror and created the theatre of horror (Théâtre de l'épouvante). The name of the joint drama, which was first published one year before Binet's death, is *The Horrible Experience* (1910).

Binet's long-standing interest in art principally focused upon writing psychological studies of known dramatic authors and artists. He had published studies of this type as early as 1894, and this topic had remained a constant throughout his career. Yet *The Horrible Experience* was the only drama that he co-authored. In the introduction of the drama, Binet not only analyzed the author, Lorde, but also stated the conditions by which he came to be involved in writing the play itself. He slowly shifted from the position of an observer to the situation of an active participant under the influence of Lorde's powerful personality. Binet made the reflection that in each man there remain parts which are child like. He ended his introduction with the following comment:

'If André de Lorde would not have conserved deep inside him, impressions of childhood which were painful, he would not have given us this theatre whose feature is so original and powerful' (p. 16).

The point I want to stress is that Binet agreed to see his name associated with a drama. He departed from the position of an observer using his questioning method and became involved in the making of the play itself. Binet, in the same introduction, wrote, in regard to the mode of interaction that he and Lorde developed:

'... since his taste and mine are very similar, since I passionately love this theatre of anxiety where one expects, with heart-pang, that something terrible and chiefly mysterious will happen, I did not have the courage to continue the psychological analysis' (p. 10).

Binet was profoundly involved in the play itself, not as an observer but as an actor. The reason these facts are worth mentioning is that the content of the play can certainly be used to understand Binet as a person.

The drama itself contains seven players and the main actor happens to be a doctor (Dr. Charrier). The first part of the drama shows the doctor talking with the future groom (Jean) about his daughter Jeanne. Jeanne is going to leave for 53 days and upon her return will marry Jean. Part of Scene V is devoted to an interesting discussion about the idea of death that Charrier does not believe to be irreversible. After the departure of Jeanne, Charrier receives a visit from the official French executioner. They discuss the facts concerning executions since Charrier would like to carry on an experiment with the next executed person. They talk essentially about the technical details of how to recuperate the body as soon as possible. They agree on a procedure, and the executioner leaves. Immediate lyafterward, Charrier receives a phone call informing him that his daughter has just been wounded in a car accident. Charrier goes to see his daughter who dies, and he decides to attempt his experiment on her. The purpose of his endeavor consists in wanting to ressucitate the body, and during his attempt the hand of his daughter comes to squeeze his neck in such a way that nobody can free him from suffocation. The surrounding people are unable to prevent Charrier from being strangled literally by the hands of his own daughter. In the last scene, one of the actors, Maria, asks what has happened (she just came in) and Jean, the fiance, says: 'He wanted to try an experiment ... to ressucitate his daughter.' Maria then says: 'To touch death is a sacrilege.' To which Jean adds: 'One could believe that death has taken its revenge' (p. 82). At this point the drama ends.

Who would intuitively believe that Binet whom Fraisse and Pollack call the father of experimental psychology could have been part of such an intense dramatic play whose content carries obvious similarities with his life? These similarities have to do with what one can infer about his feelings for the naturalistic observations he was fond of. The deep meaning of the play reflects his covert feelings and certainly some sense of guilt.

I do not want to carry the clinical interpretation too far, and yet it seems to me that several facts emerge from this play. In some ways the drama is significant of Binet's strong feelings towards his daughters, whom he observed for many years. There is a sense of guilt but also of necessity in this drama. Binet's two daughters were the subjects of his observations; he must have had misgivings about it. He appears to have been conflicted over the necessity of psychological investigation and the fact that he took is own daughters as subjects.

One observes here also Binet's relationship with science, and this fact is equally meaningful. Experimenting and understanding the process of knowledge were in fact conceived by him as dangerous enterprises.

This drama, when inserted within the context of Binet's life, made him in many ways a profoundly human being who was concerned with the effects that psychological investigations could have upon other human beings. An experimentalist at heart, he certainly had ethical concerns. One might wonder if the reason does not lie in the fact that he intimately knew most of his subjects, their lives, and their personalities. One might also wonder if the fact that today one tends to experiment with large populations does not sometimes remove us from these difficult but real ethical concerns.

D. DEVELOPMENT AND VALUE ORIENTATION: THE CON-
TRIBUTION OF EDUARD SPRANGER TO A DIFFERENTIAL
DEVELOPMENTAL PSYCHOLOGY

by Hans Thomae, *University of Bonn, Germany*

At the International Congress of Psychology of Montreal (1954) G.W. Allport pointed to different traditions in American and Continental European theories of personality (Allport 1957). Although he was well aware of the dangers of oversimplification which threaten any comparison of scientific approaches coming from different continents he defined six basic differences between the American and English way of studying man and his behavior on the one hand and that of European, especially German, psychologists on the other. The first of these basic differences refers to the Lockean *tabula rasa* concept of human nature as preferred by the Anglo-Saxon tradition, and the Leibnitzian and Kantian idea of man as a self-actualizing entity as representative of the continental approach. The second difference is defined by the elementaristic preferences of English-American associationistic approaches compared with the different holistic or Gestalt ideas as they originated in Middle Europe between 1915 and 1930. A third difference, according to Allport, is defined by diver-gences in mood. American optimism and Sartre's as well as Heidegger's pessimism are mentioned in this connection. A fourth difference is related to the higher relevance of social interaction in all American compared to European studies. Furthermore Allport hypothesized that brain models are more favored by American psychologists and that these are more rigorous in methodology than European (especially German) psychologists.

As a participant of the Symposium in which Allport proposed his diagnosis I might say that his portrait was quite correct twenty years ago. However it is no longer correct for today. European, especially German, psychologists have learned to adapt to American standards and points of view, and in many instances the young German generation is more Lockean, elementaristic, optimistic, oversocialized, and methodologically rigorous than many colleagues from the US continent. On the other hand we can observe many symptoms of a remarkable change toward Leibnitzian thought in the States: Arthur Jensen's unfortunate evaluation of racial differences in intelligence is not the only example. The great emphasis on self-actualization, creativity, and self-consistency, as documented in the publications on clinical, developmental, and personality psychology during the last 15 years in America, is a more candid proof for this change which von Bracken (1954) called the 'humanistic shift in American psychology'. The same approximation of American psychologists to continental philosophies as defined by Allport (1957) can be observed regarding the 'elementaristic-holistic' issue and future-outlook problems, whereas continental psychologists took over the interactionist and the rigorous methodological approach. Therefore we may state that the differences as diagnosed by Allport (1957) twenty years ago disappeared to a great extent or were replaced by intranational differences defined by divergencies in theory, method, and cultural orientation. A history of the behavioral sciences will offer several explanations for this approximation. It certainly would be very narrow-minded if we would overlook the many social-political influences involved in this change. On the other hand, the history of science shows some changes which go back to the introduction of new techniques or to changing methodological orientations.

Rises and falls of Spranger's scientific influence. In any case, as far as our topic is concerned we can assume that Eduard Spranger as a representative of typically German *Verstehende Psychologie* is forgotten or unknown almost to the same degree for German and young American psychologists. If he is known at all, this is due to the efforts of Allport and his elaboration of a Value Scale (together with Vernon). However, whereas he was not better known in the United States twenty years ago than today he was one of the most influential men in German education and culture between 1945 and 1960. This was due to his reputation in Eastern Europe, in Greece, as well as in Japan. It was due, too, to his personal history which is characterized by a very steep career between 1915 and 1935 and many difficulties and even persecutions during the Nazi period. He even went into prison in 1944 (Bähr 1964). After the war the Russians appointed him as the first Rector of the Humboldt University at Eastern Berlin in 1945. He moved to Western Germany in 1946 where he was offered a chair at Tuebingen and guided the scientific and educational policies of postwar West-German politicians until the early sixties. His ideas of humanity and humanistic psychology shaped several reform plans in education; however when the big reformers started their work in out country his influence had waned already.

The reduction of his influence was especially large true regard to his psychological approaches and contributions. It is true, the book on psychology of adolescence, published for the first time in 1924, was used as a textbook in teachers' colleges and even some universities up to the sixties, although it had not been changed or revised since its first edition. And the same was true for the book on 'Lebensformen' (Types of men). However, at most universities since the late fifties and at all psychology departments of universities and teachers colleges in the late sixties his books were replaced by other ones, translated from American or at least oriented toward American psychology.

The 'Verstehen' approach. This complete exclusion of his approach is to be explained mainly by his anti-experimentalistic attitudes. An additional factor in diminishing Spranger's influence was the sociological criticism of the 'ideology of a separate stage of adolescence' (Schelsky 1957). Allport (1937, 1957) never denied the fact that Spranger was opposed to the approach to human nature which Wilhelm Wundt had opened. Spranger stressed *Verstehen* and understanding the stage under study by looking at some final or 'mature' state of the mind.

He defined development as that ordered series of changes which is experienced by the individual due to internal and external influences (1924, p. 18). However the internal forces were regarded as more influential (1921, p. 343). These internal forces are to be defined by tendencies toward the realization of a value in a final stage (1924, p. 17). Therefore the concept of 'value' is the most decisive one in Spranger's approach (Spranger 1921, p. 70; 1924, p. 166).

Value is defined by individual and cultural standards. Value in terms of individual standards is represented in the securing of survival, of social prestige or of political influence. However, these individual values are to be integrated into a structure which enables the individual to participate in the objective mind, that is, the culture or the cultural progress of mankind (Spranger 1909, p. 17; 1924, pp. 9–19).

From this point of view development is directed from adjustment to survival requirements toward self-realization, i.e., the realization of objective cultural values within a concrete individual existence. To understand development means to comprehend concrete actions, ideas, and even fantasies of the growing person with regard to the final aim of realizing the objective cultural values in the shaping of an individual personality.

It is quite evident that this approach to developmental psychology is influenced by philosophical and even ethical traditions. However Allport and Vernon (1931) demonstrated how the deductive way in which Spranger defined and described the main directions of value orientation can be translated into a method for empirical research. This Value Scale has been used for studies in personality and social psychology (Rodd 1959; Kelly 1955; Arsenian 1970; Simon 1970) and still is being translated and standardized in more and more countries (e.g., Roth 1972). Therefore there might be some chance that not only Spranger's philosophy of values but also his psychology of adolescence from a *Verstehen* point of view attracts some interest.

Adolescence as a process of testing and choosing values. Adolescence for Spranger is that stage of development in which experience becomes a challenge for the growing person to test the identifications with these different values or with different variations of the realization of these values (Spranger 1924, p. 31–49). Doing so the adolescent finds his self (1921, p. 345), i.e., that value-orientation which integrates his personal dispositions (or *Anlagen*) with the meaning, the possibilities and the challenges of a section or aspect of the objective culture (1921, p. 345; 1924, p. 49–51). Therefore adolescence according to Spranger is the decisive stage in the formation of personality (1924, p. 185). Although he does not overlook the relevance of development in early childhood he stresses the role of the adolescent years for the process of maturation. These years should not be regarded as transient stages to be defined by the formula, 'no longer child not yet adult' (1924, p. 18). The philosophy of 'youth culture' is defined here by internal standards. In order to become a person, i.e., one who has chosen himself a certain orientation toward society and culture, the adolescent must find his own identity.

This process of maturation of personality by finding his way through the challenges, temptations, and obstacles of different value identifications is described by Spranger in a somewhat dialectic way. A first step toward this maturation requires the individual to overcome childish identifications with the values of his environment, of identification with his parents and all other authorities. By experiencing himself in psychological distance from others the adolescent discovers himself, a loose pattern of desires, emotions, and ideas (1924, p. 52 ff.). The second step or aspect of the maturation process is defined by the gradual unfolding or discovering of a life-plan. This does not refer to real conscious planning; it refers to all aspects of the extension and differentiation of future-time perspective as being demonstrated in autobiographies and other personal documents.

The final step means restoration of the subject-society integration which had been disturbed with the beginning of the maturation process. Obviously it does not mean a restoration at the childhood level. Integration of the individual value-orientation and the objective culture at the late-adolescent level or early-adult level involves the knowledge of active participation, of an involvement or non-involvement which is completely dependent on the subject's own choice (1924, p. 49).

The dialectics of adolescent development as defined by dissociation or disengagement from familial and societal bondage, discovering present self and future perspective on oneself, and reassociation (reengagement) with society defines a very broad frame of reference which is described by Spranger by use of personal documents of different qualities. He himself states that this description is representative only for the time of the early twentieth century in Western Europe. After the war he gave characteristics of five youth generations beginning with that of the late nineteenth century up to the post-World War II generation in Western Germany (up to 1949) (Spranger 1950/1962, p. 25–57).

However limited as the empirical basis may be the pattern of development as postulated by Spranger could be demonstrated by several studies in the thirties as well as the fifties of this century at least for Western Germany. Furthermore this pattern anticipates several theories of adolescent development which were formulated especially in the United States. Finally the broadness (or you may say vagueness) of the statements combined with the pattern which allows consideration of any individual variation as the emergence of individuality is the main topic of the theory. But demonstrating this we do not want to prove that it is better to build philosophies of development rather than doing empirical work. We just want to test how much theoretical as well as phenomenological studies can help in guiding as well as manipulating research.

Empirical research related to Spranger's theory of adolescence. Whereas the increasing disengagement of the adolescent from his environment is documented only by casual observations there exists a great deal of empirical support for Spranger's thesis that this social disengagement is followed by (or caused by) a discovering of the self, 'of the subject as a world for himself' (Spranger 1924, p. 38).

Kroh (1929, 1940) and his disciples could demonstrate some symptoms of this discovery in the analysis of essays written by 10 to 16 year old students after the observation of a silent movie. Whereas the younger ones told the story (of a mountain-climber who is watched by his wife and his friends and who falls down after a wrong step) just in terms of the external events the older ones (beginning with 14 years) mentioned more and more the inside aspects of the story: the feelings of the climber and the people who watch him, the motivations, expectations, and ideas they might have in mind. This increasing relevance of the internal aspects of events was found in similar studies by Undeutsch (1965) in his students between 1950 and 1960. It could be shown, too, in a test by the author in which preferences between photos of different people had to be explained by younger and older adolescents: the younger ones mention the exterior (shape and face, hair, nose, ears, etc.); the older ones (after 15 years) refer more and more to the mental and personality qualities of the people shown in the pictures (Thomae 1954).

Bertlein (1961) found in studies conducted in the late fifties that German adolescents of that time showed even an increasing tendency to be engaged with themselves and to analyse their own emotions and reactions. In many reactions of the 15 to 17 year olds of his large sample he found indications of the feeling of an insular status as described by Spranger (1924, p. 38).

Similar correspondences between the findings of studies on adolescents conducted between 1925–1935 and 1950–1965 can be reported for the second aspect of maturation as defined by Spranger. The first symptom of the emergence of a kind of a life-plan or an extended future-time-perspective can be found in studies on adolescent ego ideals. Spranger (1929, p. 46) refers in this instance to a quotation from a German poet (Rückert) who stated that during this life stage everybody is faced with an image of that person he should become. In studies of Schmeing (1929) at Berlin (1932/33) and of Glöckel (1960) at Nuernberg, the decisive role of ego-ideals during adolescence was demonstrated in a very impressive way. Glöckel, who repeated Schmeing's study, stresses the great degree of similarity of the responses of these two generations of adolescents who actually grew up during and after two world wars. Persons of the immediate environment (like friends, relatives, teachers) were mentioned more often than glamour stars! In this instance the findings from Western Germany were very similar to those from Belgium, Spain, Italy, and Netherlands (Lutte 1970), from Paris (Zazzo 1965) and from Buenos Aires and different from findings from the United States (Havighurst *et al.* 1965, p. 18). Studies of Bertlein, Mönks (1967), and others demonstrate how much future time perspective extends and increases during the adolescent years. The orientation on values represented at first in persons one would like to be, later in abstract ideals, seems to be a fundamental process in the maturing person (Spranger 1924, p. 185; Thomae 1965, 1969, p. 213–237).

Studies which demonstrate the third aspect of maturation in adolescence as postulated by Spranger are related to the reintegration of the young person into society. We can refer here to different projects in which we compared attitudes of young people toward 'law and order', toward 'work', and toward 'marriage and family life' (Thomae 1969, p. 213–237). In 1929 Kelchner analysed essays of more than 1000 adolescents, mainly from the lower class, on the topic: 'Why guilty behavior must be punished'. Kelchner's publication documents very well the increasing intensity and independence by which the older compared to the younger adolescents discussed the problem. We repeated this study for the first time four years after World War II and found a new reaction among the different variations of the response (Thomae 1969, p. 227–229). Whereas in 1929 practically nobody doubted the absolute character of social norms, of law and the need of punishment in order to maintain order, approximately 20% of the postwar adolescents raised doubts. They referred to the change in norms due to which former German war heroes were treated as war criminals and to the situation of mothers who tried to steal coal or potatoes for their children in the years of economic deprivation (1944–1948). When this study was repeated in 1956 and 1966 this postwar effect could not be observed any longer. The discussion of the problem was quite similar to that observed by Kelchner, although we observed an increasing amount of psychological thinking regarding motives for crime, adverse developmental conditions in early childhood, etc. In any case the identification with social norms became more conscious and more based on arguments by the older than by the younger adolescents.

The same was true in studies referring to attitudes toward work, which could be carried out in 1929, 1951 and 1961 (Thomae 1969, p. 229). Here we observed changes in the 1961 sample who regarded work as a precondition for a meaningful life more often than the adolescents of the previous years. On the other hand the percentage of adolescents regarding work just as a necessary means for survival was highest in all cohorts and it increased, too, in 1961. The detailed analysis of the responses pointed to a very independent way of looking at work conditions, to a high degree of criticism, and of realism in the acceptance of the work conditions.

The attitude toward marriage and family life could be analysed by asking adolescents to write on their lives up to the year 2000 (see Gillespie and Allport 1955). Mönks (1967), who compared the responses of adolescents from the Netherlands and from Western Germany, stresses the great number of family-centered future time perspectives in girls, and of boys too. The very detailed description of their own desired family life demonstrated a very definite way of reintegration into the structure of society as it exists today. On the other hand there were responses to make the own family life better, to deal with their own children in a different way and to make things change. Therefore they reflected a thoughtful way of planning for the future. however a planning which remained as conservative as the reaction toward law and toward work.

Although this conservative tendency is not a major trend in Spranger's theory of adolescence it is implied in the sequence of psychological changes as defined by him starting with dissociation. At least for the generations covered by the studies reported here this sequence can be traced in many responses of adolescents of different cohorts and cultural background. Unfortunately we cannot report more recent studies using the same kind of methods. However, public opinion polls show that radical divergencies from this pattern are typical only for a minority.

Therefore Spranger's theory of adolescence in terms of value orientation and issociation-reassociation sequences can be regarded as valid at least as a frame of reference. On the other hand it would be misleading to conclude from this that holistic, Leibnitzian, and non-interactionistic approaches in developmental psychology are recommended as more promising than Lockean, elementaristic, and interactionistic ones. It is true that Spranger stresses the influences of internal forces, of internal regulating structures more than that of the environment. He very often refers to innate dispositions (*Anlagen*) as an explicative construct and refers to environment mainly as the manifestations of cultural values between which the young person has to make his decisions.

It is this orientation on 'innate' or hereditary factors for the regulation of development which raises the main problems in Spranger's work. Although he referred to different aspects of society in a more concrete way than many of his contemporary philosopher-psychologists, economy, state, and politics, as well as law and social order, are regarded as fields of possible action rather than as counterparts in an interaction process.

American theories of adolescent development and Spranger's theory. This is certainly the greatest difference between Spranger's approach and those of many English or American writers who use very similar categories or constructs to comprehend and/or explain processes of adolescent development. In Erikson's theory of adolescence as the time 'when a lasting ego identity' (1950, p. 137) emerges we can observe many similarities with Spranger's approach. It is true, Erikson like many other American writers is more influenced by the storm-and-stress model of adolescence of Stanley Hall. Therefore he stresses especially the role of 'a gradual accruing ego identity in safe-guarding against the anarchy of drives as well as the autocracy of conscience' (1950, p. 139). However he, too, stresses the responsibility of the individual to make the right choice between different value orientations: The individual must be able to convince himself that the next 'step is up to him and no matter where he is staying or going he always has the choice of leading or turning into the opposite direction if he chooses to do so' (Erikson 1950, p. 245).

However the necessity of making a choice, of deciding between different value orientations, is regarded here as the dependent variable of American society and cultural-political philosophy. Therefore the autonomy of the individual who searches for his self, who tests possible identifications with values and finally decides for or against some value areas is a very limited one. It is the individual in a certain social context and with a certain childhood experience who is faced with the alternatives of different value areas. Therefore, what may have been regarded by Spranger and some of his followers once upon a time as the emergence of a metaphysical 'entelechy' according to Erikson is a variable dependent on certain socializing conditions.

The same is true of Havighurst's theory of adolescence as a stage of 'becoming a person in one's own mind' (1963, p. 30). The aspects of the developmental processes regarded by Havighurst as typical for youth are very similar or almost identical with those of Spranger; however for Havighurst (1948/72) and even more for Garrison (1965) these aspects are identical with developmental tasks defined for an individual socialized by very definite environments and very definite social norms.

The greatest degree of similarity may be found between the Spranger and Ausubel theories of adolescence. The task of becoming 'internally' independent, of 'planning and discovering by own effort' as defined as one of the aims of adolescence has even more Kantian or Leibnitzian implications than some statements of Spranger. Ausubel furthermore defines as one aspect of the maturational process during adolescence the 'attainment' of new values on the basis of their internal validity or their relationship with important aims of the individual rather than due to loyalty towards parents or substitute parents! This is completely identical with Spranger's philosophy of adolescent growth. However, as an American, Ausubel sees the cultural-social-background and opportunities determining that process in a more detailed way than Spranger.

The striking coincidence between the Leibnitzian, less interactionist holistic approach of Spranger and the more socialized, interactionist partially psychoanalytically oriented approaches of Ausubel, Erikson, and Havighurst demonstrates that it is not necessary to conceive the pattern of adolescence as defined by Spranger mainly in terms of internal or even innate forces. This pattern is itself a product of socialitation and a socializing agent for each individual development. This is also demonstrated by the similarities of the responses of adolescents from different generations as demonstrated by the reported studies from Europe. As far as the conditions in society were similar, especially in the family, work, and community life, we got similar responses. When the situation had changed completely as in the immediate post-war conditions the responses changed at least in some important areas. And even if there are changes as, e.g., in the work conditions of the young apprentice or worker, it is the perception of these conditions which really is important (Baldwin 1969). Work is perceived to the same degree as a necessary tool for survival even in different socio-economic systems; and parents may be perceived as authoritarian even if they behave in a democratic manner.

Generally speaking we can regard Spranger's theory of adolescence as a broad frame of reference which is open for an 'Unfolding' theory of development as well as for a socialization or learning theory of development. The agreement of some core aspects of this theory with other theories points to a common set of experience which has a great degree of transcultural stability.

Spranger's contribution to a differential developmental psychology: The model and its variations. The broadness of the theory, too, is one of the main reasons why it allows for individual differentiations. The main aim of the whole process again and again is described as the decision for that value-orientation which coincides with the own self or gives opportunity for self-realization in the most effective way. Therefore the whole theory works only if it offers opportunities and aspects for the definition of individual variations of the general developmental course (1924, p. 20).

Spranger himself defined types of juvenile 'experiences' as variations of the general adolescence structure by using his typology of value orientations as a frame of reference (1924, pp. 332–264).

Therefore the dominance of religious, political, esthetic, social, or economic values is the main aspect for differentiation. Although this typology of value interpretations proved to be successful for many research aspects we doubt if it is the only and the best approach toward a differential developmental psychology. Some of his followers have defined different forms of development in terms of variations of the pattern of sequences as postulated in Spranger's theory. Wenke (1951) especially differentiated a more 'primitive' and 'pragmatic' type from the classical one. Jaide (1959, 1961) distinguished between a 'productive', an 'emancipatory', and a 'conservative' style during adolescent development. On the basis of clusters of rating data from a longitudinal study related to personality variables like activity, adjustment, responsiveness, ego control, etc., Uhr, Thomae and Becker (1969) found social class differences between certain developmental styles.

A review of these different approaches to a differential developmental psychology demonstrates that all of them are approximations toward an adequate understanding of individual sequences and patterns of change during the adolescent years. Compared to stage theories, especially oriented toward cognitive development, Spranger's approach offers many hypotheses and points of view for the design of a differential model which might be at least as specialized as Guilford's model of intellectual structure. However it certainly would be useless to introduce Spranger's theory completely unrevised. He himself knew this very well. Revisions seem to be necessary especially regarding the classification of values which should be replaced by psychological points of view. Furthermore we need new instruments and experiments to test the theory in terms of contemporary problems of adolescents. By the way, judging from the situation in our country his theory can cope with the new generation much better than sociological theories like that of Schelsky (1957) who diagnosed a continuous adjustment process from childhood into adulthood as reppresentative for modern youth.

In any case it seems worthwhile to use the suggestions implied in this approach and to realize that any learning theory of development assumes a great variety of developmental patterns, corresponding to the individual learning histories. The theory of intrinsic disengagement-reengagement as defined by Spranger offers assistance in solving this problem.

The development of women through history

A. ASTARTE MOSES AND MARY: PERSPECTIVES ON THE SEXUAL DIALECTIC IN CANAANITE, JUDAIC, AND CHRISTIAN TRADITIONS

by Nancy Datan, *West Virginia, University Morgantown*

The relevance of ancient myth to contemporary psychology is more than historical:[1] psychoanalysis teaches us that myths and traditions endure when they express components of individual consciousness. Thus, the contribution made by this study of women in religious tradition is twofold. First, and most obviously, it traces the evolution of sex role prescriptions and proscriptions which survive to the present day. Second, if ontogeny recapitulates phylogeny not only in the metamorphoses of embryonic development but also in the psychological development of the individual – that is, if the passage from infancy to adulthood recapitulates some elements of the intellectual and cultural history of mankind – then a study of the myths and religious traditions governing women and their relationships to men may yield insight into unconscious components of the sexual dialectic.

1. Moshe Kohn, literary editor of *The Jerusalem Post*, introduced me to *The White Goddness* in 1965, and so initiated the enquiry of which this paper is an expression. Professor Moshe Herr of the University of the Negev led me to the Midrash treating the rebellion of Korah, Datan, and Aviram (Numbers 16; Midrash Alef [Tehilim]). Their provocation is gratefully acknowledged.

Histories of religion have generally dealt with the relationship between man and his gods, or the emergence of monotheism, or the development of transcendent conceptions of morality and divinity. These considerations are peripheral to the present paper, which compares Canaanite, Judaic, and Christian traditions as they apply to the relationships between men and women and discusses transformations in these traditions within a psychoanalytic framework.

Canaanite worship, which might appear to have no more than historical interest, has been preserved as a part of the contemporary religious consciousness of Western civilization through the elaborate, repeated proscriptions of the priests and prophets of Judaism against whoring after false gods – the gods of the Canaanites. And the practices proscribed are the propitiatory rites intended to mirror and to ensure the cycle of seasons: of birth, death, and rebirth, festivals of mourning, sacrifice, and orgy, securing food for this season, and children for the generations to come.

The antagonism of the Jews to these nature rituals is first described at Sinai, when Moses descended from the Mount with the Tablets of the Law to discover his people dancing naked around a golden calf (Exodus, 32: 19–28) and caused three thousand men to be slain in expiation. But the backsliding of the Jews to the tempting practices of their Canaanite neighbours is recorded throughout the writings of the prophets, and as late as Ezekiel (8: 14) women are reported sitting at the north gate of the Temple, weeping for Tammuz.

It has been suggested by Eliade (1960) that the reversion to nature-worship among the Jews occurred during periods of economic peace and prosperity, while historical catastrophies, which transcended the annual healing of the seasons, caused them to return to the One God: 'And they cried unto the Lord and said, We have sinned, because we have forsaken the Lord and served Baalim and Ashtarot; but now deliver us out of the hand of our enemies and we will serve thee' (I Samuel, 12: 10). The rivalry between the God of the Jews and the Goddess of the Canaanites has else-where been described as a contest between the more 'primitive' female procreativity and the more sublimated male creativity by Graves (1966), who decries the contest, claiming that true male creativity is an act of homage to the primeval female goddess.

The antagonism between the patriarchal God of the Jews and the mother-goddess of the Canaanites is easily observed. Power resides in Astarte, who restores Tammuz and the earth to life; she is usurped by the God of the Jews, who has no female companion; and when something of the divinity of motherhood reappears in Christianity, it is through an asexual, virginal birth, in which female procreation is explicitly subordinated to divine, male creativity. From this perspective, it appears that Judaeo-Christian traditions originate in opposition to nature rites and become progressively distant from nature ritual until, finally celibacy is revered and sexuality implicitly repudiated. Moreover, this perspective implies that the unique creativity of women is progressively devalued and their status progressively lowered.

Baalim and Ashtarot. Pre-Mosaic nature worship was found from the Nile to the Euphrates, and although there were regional variations, apparently determined by the regional harvest periods, there was a common theme of birth, death, and rebirth which reflected the cycle of seasons: rainy and fertile in the autumn, winter, and spring, and dry and barren in the long Mediterrenean summer. The religious literature of Babylonia yields what is probably a representative indication of nature-worship, widespread in the Levant and borrowed from the Semites by the Greeks as early as the seventh century before Christ (Frazer 1955). The cycle of seasons is represented by the birth and death of Tammuz, who was annually mourned in the parched midsummer month which bears his name to this day in the Judaic lunar calendar. Tammuz was the young lover of Astarte, the divine mother goddess who represented the reproductive energies of nature; and at his death Astarte journeyed after him to the house of death, 'to the land from which there is no returning, to the house of darkness, where dust lies on door and bolt'. In her absence sexual passion ceased, and with its cessation all life was threatened with extinction. Finally, Astarte succeeded in freeing Tammuz from the queen of the dead and returned together with him to revive nature in the upper world, at about the time of the first rains at the end of the long, dry summer of the Middle East (Frazer 1955; Graves 1966).

Tammuz and Astarte were worshipped as Adonis and Aphrodite by the Greeks, and as Osiris and Isis by the Egyptians; common to all rituals was the battle fought by Astarte/Aphrodite/Isis to restore her dead lover to life, although the season of the festival of rebirth apparently varied. The rituals included mutilation – the prophets of Baal gashed themselves with knives to ensure, through their own flowing blood, abundant rainfall– sacrificial deaths, and orgies of sexual indulgence. All these were to be severely proscribed by Mosaic codes; yet it will be shown that Jewish

ritual did not eliminate nature worship but rather incorporated, chan-
neled, and refined many of the Canaanite practices.

In the image of God. 'So God made man in His own image, in the image of
God created He him', it was declared in Genesis (1 : 27), and proceativity
became a male domain. The powers of regeneration shared by Astarte and
Tammuz were transformed into the Power of Creation, wholly masculine.
Moreover, the Mosaic story of creation, it has been suggested (Graves and
Patai 1966), is itself a transformation of a Babylonian creation myth, in
which the Mother-goddess who bore the gods was a victim of their
rebellion and then surrendered her own body to serve as building material for the universe. The Babylonian Mother-goddess is represented in
the Mosaic story of creation as תהום [the deep]; similarly, other
ancient matriarchal deities are reduced to abstractions: chaos, darkness.

'And God said, let us make man in our own image, after our likeness:
and let him have dominion over the fish of the sea, and over the fowl of the
air, and over the cattle, and over all the earth, and over every creeping
thing that creepeth upon the earth.

'So God made man in his own image, in the image of God created he
him; male and female created he them ... and the rib, which the Lord God
had taken from man, made he a woman, and brought her unto the man ...
And the man said, The woman whom thou gavest to be with me, she gave
me of the tree, and I did eat ... Unto the woman the Lord said, I will
greatly multiply thy sorrow and thy conception; in sorrow thou shalt
bring forth children; and thy desire shall be to thy husband, and he shall
rule over thee' (Genesis 1 : 26–3 : 16).

As in the story of the Creation, so in the story of the Fall: earlier
matriarchal myths have been translated into a patriarchal framework:
Graves and Patai (1966) trace the familiar story of the Fall to an earlier
Sumerian legend in which the love-goddess Aruru creates a man of clay,
confers wisdom on him, and covers his nakedness. In the Mosaic retelling,
mortal woman tempts mortal man to knowledge, and both are punished
by God; it will subsequently be shown that Christian tradition judges Eve
even more harshly.

Divine prerogatives were clearly masculine. Moreover, Judaism instituted status differentials for mortal men and women which begin at
birth: if a woman bears a male child, she is ritually unclean for seven days,
but if she bears a female child, she is ritually unclean for two weeks
(Leviticus 12: 2–5). Male children are circumcised at eight days, marking

the establishment of the Covenant with Abraham and his descendants but also reminiscent of more dramatic forms of mutilation; furthermore, circumcision was not uncommon in the Near East but was typically carried out at adolescence and signified the transition to sexual maturity. Finally, if a son is a firstborn, there is a ceremonial payment of money to a Cohen (priest), recalling Abraham's willingness to sacrifice his son, for whom a ram was substituted, and human sacrifice thenceforth abolished – but retained in muted, symbolic form.

The birth of a girl is not marked by any ceremony, and the period of the mother's ritual uncleanness (in which sexual contact is proscribed) is doubled. Moreover, from menarche to menopause, women are ritually unclean for two weeks out of every four, for the week of menstruation and seven days thereafter (Leviticus 13; Mishnah, Taharot).

The constellation of rituals associated with sexuality, menstruation, and childbirth has been interpreted as a code of protective health measures; and there is little reason to doubt that the ritual bath after sexual relations and after menstruation, and abstinence after childbirth, did indeed have survival value. The cycle of sexual abstinence at menstruation and for a week thereafter, followed by a period in which the sexual pleasure of husband and wife is commended, is similarly interpreted as a means of encouraging fertility and population growth. This purpose, however, is served equally well by sexual licence. Moreover, other practices in Judaism favor population growth more directly: the abolition of infant sacrifice, and the preference given sons, making the birth of a daughter a signal to try again.

The system of menstrual taboos, of abstinence alternating with sanctioned indulgence, is more easily understood as a tempered, civilized vestige of the Canaanite cycle of orgy and mourning. Although to Western scholars, menstrual taboos have signified the subordination of women, and even disgust, a reading of Talmudic sources makes it clear that the sages viewed the menstruating woman as magically enticing and therefore very dangerous. In the Talmudic disputation over the color of menstrual blood, five, colors were finally determined to be unclean: 'like the blood of a wound', 'like the colour of sediment', 'the shade of the bright-coloured saffron', 'a colour like that of water which has had the earth of the Valley of Beit Kerem stirred into it', and 'the colour of two parts of water mixed with one part of the wine of Sharon' (Taharot). The Talmudic imagery suggests temptation rather than sanitation, as do derivative Moslem customs which require a woman to make herself unattractive during menstruation – implying that otherwise she would be especially desirable. This does not appear to be a denial of but rather an attempt at circumscribing the magic of woman.

The cycle of the seasons is retained in the Judaic calendar of festivals: the three pilgrim festivals, Passover (early spring), Shavouot (the first harvest), and Succot (harvest at the end of summer, when a prayer for rain is said), are the first holidays proclaimed as the Jews depart Egypt (Exodus 23: 14–16); indeed, some have suggested that Passover is a modified Canaanite spring festival (Graves 1966). Although some have claimed that Baalim and Ashtarot were the divinities of procreation, and the God of the Jews was a God of history (Eliade 1960), it is apparent that the God of the Jews is also a God of fruitfulness (Harrleson 1969); significantly, however, the Goddess and her lover have been replaced by a single male deity.

Mary, blessed among women. In Christianity, two of the major themes of Judaism are repeated in modified form: creation and the sacrifice of the firstborn son. The birth of Jesus from a human mother implies, on the one hand, a restoration of some measure of procreativity to women. On the other hand, while the sexuality of Astarte and Tammuz echoed human sexuality, there is no human echo to be found in the virginal conception of Jesus, and it might be argued that divine conception and birth usurp female procreativity even more decisively than did Judaic tradition. Campbell (1964) suggests that the motif of the virgin birth is derived from Greek mythology rather than from the traditions of the Levant, citing Leda and the swan, and Danae and the shower of gold, both instances in which the divine Zeus lusted after mortal women and not indicative of any divinity in the women.

Abraham's sacrifice of Isaac is repeated in the crucifixion of Jesus: but for Jesus there is no intercession, and he dies. And, finally, is resurrected: the theme of death and rebirth is older than Judaism; but Jesus died 'not as myth, not as symbol, but as flesh and blood, historically' (Campbell 1964). Frazer cites the testimony of an anonymous Christian of the fourth century who wrote that Christians and pagans alike remarked the 'coincidence between the death and resurrection of their respective deities' (1955), and he suggests that the coincidences of Christian and pagan festivals were too close and too numerous to be accidental, representing instead compromises which the Church was forced to make with rival systems of belief. It does not seem improbable, however, that the Church absorbed, rather than making forced compromises with, celebrations which were not out of harmony with its major themes of birth, death, and resurrection. In this way, for example, the Passover (the Last Supper) became the Easter celebration, and both retained the preMosaic theme of rebirth derived from the cycle of the seaons.

The Tree of the Cross recalled, and indeed rescinded, the Tree of the Garden and its message, in Christianity, of the Fall of Man (Campbell 1964). However, Christianity is based upon the spiritual Father and the virgin birth and a less indulgent attitude toward human sexuality: whereas Judaism commends sexual pleasure between husband and wife, Christianity commends celibacy (I Corinthians: 7: 1–2) and tolerates marriage. Furthermore, the judgment on Eve has become harsher:

'Let the woman learn in silence with all subjection. But I suffer not a woman to teach nor to usurp authority over the man, but to be in silence. And Adam was first formed, then Eve. And Adam was not deceived, but the woman being deceived was in the transgression' (I Timothy 2: 11–14). Thus, although Christianity abolishes certain constraints on woman (such as the menstrual taboos of Judaism) and restores to womanhood a role in creation, nevertheless, in the repudiation of sexuality which is implicit in the reverence for the virgin birth, Christianity has moved still further away from the nature-rituals out of which it sprang (Harrelson 1969) – and which can still be discerned in the cycle of Christian celebrations (Frazer 1955; Graves 1966).

Astarte, Moses, and Mary. This brief overview of Canaanite and Judaeo-Christian traditions does not reflect the roles of men and women in contemporary Judaism or Christianity nor does it include the extensive debates over women's rights in Talmudic Judaism and the Christian Scholastics. Quite the contrary: this overview was intended to recall the most familiar elements of Judaeo-Christian tradition and to trace pre-Mosaic contributions to these traditions. In the suggestion of common themes in Canaanite, Judaic, and Christian traditions, moreover, the purpose here is not to establish or to question the historical or theological validity of these traditions. It is rather supposed that these common themes arise out of needs which are common to all men and which find similar expressions. Thus, both the commonalities and the modifications seen in this succession of themes are relevant to an understanding of the evolution of religious thought and its implications for contemporary consciousness.

Freud has suggested that the God of the Jews can be compared to the the father of the Oedipal stage: powerful, terrifying, and punitive (1939, 1950). But we have seen that the Hebrews imposed their God upon an earlier tradition: The God of the Jews was preceded by the Goddess of the Canaanites – Astarte, the earth mother, the goddess of birth and death. And the Canaanite cycle of birth, death, and rebirth reappears, the earlier sexuality transformed to spiritual Fatherhood, in Christianity.

Psychoanalysis claims that ontogeny – the development of the individual – recapitulates phylogeny, the historical and cultural evolution of the race. Freud has proposed that Mosaic law represents one phase of this evolution, comparable to the stage in individual development in which the son desires his mother and the power of his father. Freud suggested further that this desire is part of the prehistory of the race, and that the event experienced symbolically by the child at the Oedipal stage occurred in fact in the formation of the Mosaic code, when the Jews murdered Moses, an Egyptian prince, and screened the memory of the murder with a network of law (1939, 1950).[2]

Neither the historical validity nor the unconscious dynamics of Freud's interpretation of Judaism are at issue here: rather, it is suggested that Freud's interpretation is incomplete. The Mosaic code served the God of Wrath – who is also the God of Justice and of Mercy: the Oedipal-stage father who is also the arbiter of conscience. Thus, partiarchy, the Oedipal deathwish, and its renunciation are only part of the significance of the innovation of Judaism: more significant is the muting of Canaanite natureritual, the abolition of human sacrifice and of orgy, and the elaboration of codes of law.

If Judaism can be seen as the historical analogue of the Oedipal stage in individual development, the nature-rites of pre-Mosaic worship reflect en earlier stage of psychodynamic development: Astarte, the earth mother, the goddess of birth and death, is the archetype of the benign/terrifying mother of the oral stage, and the cycle of orgy and mourning mirrors the infantile experience of alternating phases of gratification and deprivation. And in Christianity, the repudiation of sexuality implicit in the revernce

2. This interpretation has been challenged by Velikovsky (1960), who traces the Oedipus legend of the Greeks to Pharaoh Akhnaton, whom Freud identifies as Moses himself; Bakan (1958) has suggested that Freud felt a personal identification with Moses: the burden of leadership, enlightenment, and perhaps also the opposition to his leadership.

for virgin birth echoes the sexual renunciation of the latency stage, in the service of sublimated, 'higher' goals.

Astarte, Moses, and Mary, then, recall stages of psychosexual development and represent stages in the development of the relationship between man and nature, the relationship between man and his gods, and, finally, the relationship between man and his own nature. 'It is human to have a long childhood', writes Erikson (1950); 'it is civilized to have an ever longer childhood'. In the prolonged childhood of modern man, the longest and hardest learning is the delay of instinctual gratification in the service of a technological society, which eventually permits a more reliable gratification of these needs, if perhaps less sensational than the gratifications available in primitive societies. Judaism, at the time of its emergence and early codification, and Christianity, at the time of its emergence and early codification, may reflect stages in the progression of civilization from nature-worship to mastery over nature.[3]

Female and male: From procreation to creation. The progression symbolized by Astarte, Moses, and Mary is significant at two levels: first, the historical transformations represented by each form of worship resemble phases in the psychosexual development of the individual; and second, the progression from nature-worship to mastery over nature involves progressive subordination of the procreativity of women, as creativity and then procreativity become the domain of men.

It is sometimes contended that the evolution of Judaeo-Christian religious tradition has entailed the subordination of women. This claim ignores the historical origins of both religions, which at the time of their inception were comparatively progressive regarding status prescriptions for women. Nevertheless, the Judaeo-Christian God is male: this cannot be without consequence for the men and women of Western society, all of whom have some measure of religious consciousness, whether it is aetheism or orthodoxy.

It is suggested here that the contemporary consciousness of creative women, and men, is incomplete without an awareness of the Goddess who preceded God. But this consciousness is also incomplete if it does not incorporate the knowledge that the nature-rites disappeared as the need

3. The discussions of religious tradition would be incomplete without an acknowledgement of the continuing evolution, within Judaism and Christianity, of legislation adapted to changing historical circumstances.

to pray for procreation diminished, that is, as mastery over nature made propitiation of nature-gods unnecessary. Finally, as this paper has indicated, nature-rites have not, in fact, died out but have been incorporated, in muted and civilized form, into the very religions which proscribe them, suggesting that the mastery of nature has not eliminated the need for the celebration of birth.

B. TWO TYPES OF WOMEN WRITERS AND THREE PERIODS IN TIME: A PSYCHOHISTORICAL ANALYSIS

by Ravenna Helson, *University of California, Berkeley*

In ancient Greece artists were craftsmen. Their status was low because they worked with their hands, as slaves did. They were classified along with barbers or locksmiths, and it was technical aspects of their work that were valued – the ability to execute work according to norms and standards. In the medieval period, there were painters' guilds, and the guilds so closely regulated the training and daily routine of their members that there was little opportunity for individual expression.

But in the Hellenistic period, and again in the Renaissance, the roles of visual artists were redefined. In each age, artists became creators, and their personality traits became of sufficient interest to record. In the 14th century, artists were occasionally depicted as jolly pranksters, but in the 15th and 16th centuries they had separated from the guilds, and their image became clearer and more somber. Artists were now described as solitary, moody, melancholy, obsessed with their work, unconventional in sexual habits. Still later, as academies developed to regulate the education of artists and as the higher status of the artist was consolidated, the stereotype changed again, and in the 17th century the artist was regarded as an urbane gentleman. Good examples would be Bernini and Reubens.

This material, which I have taken from a book entitled *Born under Saturn* by Rudolf and Margot Wittkower, makes the point that the function and characteristics of artists vary with sociohistoric circumstances. This point is interesting to consider in the case of male artists, but it is of central importance for an analysis of creativity in women because it takes us away from naive questions about innate sex-linked characteristics as determining facts. As Linda Nochlin has said, outstanding artists never came from the aristocracy, and yet one does not assume that aristocrats lacked the little golden nugget of artistic talent but rather that a network of role obligations and customs precluded any substantial commitment on their part to the career of an artist. And so it has been with women through most of history.

But if roles and commitments are important, we need a differentiated conceptualization of how they are important, and how social factors and personality characteristics relate. The Wittkowers argue that the variability of artists from one historical period to another refutes the idea that there is such a thing as the 'creative personality'. Here is the familiar issue of 'situation vs. personality' writ large across the generations and centuries.

Scope and method. One sometimes studies the abnormal or unusual in order to see more clearly a process which is accentuated there. Let us adopt this strategy in exploring the relationship between historical situation, sex role, and the personality and product of the artist. If one looks to the past, a conspicuous fact is that there are only a few periods in history when women artists appear in sufficient numbers to be dealt with in even a semi-statistical way. When women artists are very rare, they are likely to be ignored, or to be treated as women rather than as artists, or vice versa. There is cognitive dissonance, and awareness of one role is suppressed. However, sex role, as I see it, is rather like a guild, which influences not only *whether* a person is admitted to the role of artist, or how grudgingly, but also contributes to the definition of the role of artist and its articulation with the role of patron, audience, power elite, etc. The imagery of the artist and the form and substance of the creative product will vary with the constellation and coloration of these roles. To illustrate this point of view, I shall describe two of the unusual periods when women writers were relatively abundant, trying to show how sociohistoric factors brought the feminine role and the role of the artist into relationship – very different relationships, as we shall see – and how the personality of artist and reader, and the characteristics of imagery and creative product, differed in each case.

After emphasizing the *differences* between the writers in these two historical periods, I shall suggest that the writers of each period of the past find a counterpart in a sample of women writers of the present. There thus appears to be a *recurrence* in personality type. Although historical situations vary, they too have recurrent features, and one of these is whether individuals in the role of artist are identified with the values of society or not. From this point of view, the personality typology of Otto Rank is useful, because he distinguished adjusted, conflicted, and creative types of personality on the basis of the individual's relationship to society. The adjusted person has learned to adapt his will to that of society; he wants what society rewards. The conflicted person is rebellious; he values his autonomy but suffers from guilt or inferiority feelings which lessen his impact or effectiveness. The creative person is one who has been able to work out a pattern of life which enables him to express his own individual will in a way which makes productive contact with the concerns of humanity. I shall not try to distinguish very clearly between the con-flicted and creative authors because whether an individual can work out a pattern of life which enables him to express his own will as an artist depends very much on the resources and opportunities the society makes available, and women artists have almost always been disadvantaged in the search for patterns of self-fulfillment. Finally, at the end of the paper I will make brief reference to Jungian type theory as a resource for bringing into relationship various characteristics of both male and female authors which are not readily understood on the basis of the Rankian typology alone.

For historical information, I have consulted several sources, but an article by Ann Douglas Wood (1972) is particularly helpful, one in which she contrasts the use and impact of the feminine role in two generations of women writers in 19th century America, presenting characteristics of a sample of ten writers in each period. In the interests of conserving time and space, I shall compare these periods in terms of a journalistic schema of what, who, why, and what then.

The pre-civil war period. This was a period of prosperity, manifest destiny, and widespread social mobility. Many men and women were eager to learn how to be middle-class in manners, attitudes and way of life. There was tension and uncertainty in the area of sex roles, because both sexes grew up with emphasis on achievement and equalitarianism, but there were very few opportunities outside the home for middle-class women. The Feminist Movement was protesting this fact, but the larger social compro-mise was an even more pronounced division of labor: men went into the world to make money; women remained at home, but with increased responsibility as arbiters of morality and culture. The 'new ideal woman' was much discussed.

Conditions were ripe for a lucrative new field, commercial authorship. It was new because the U.S. had relied heavily on British writers, who were prestigeful and to whom no royalties had to be paid. It was lucrative because several inventions had reduced printing costs, and because there was a great and increasing interest in reading, especially among women. Since this was a new field, it had not been definitely assigned to men. In fact, 'scribbling' was a recognized feminine activity.

A generation of women writers made the most of this situation. They were fabulously popular. In what were called the 'Feminine Fifties'

Hawthorne and Melville were neglected for Elizabeth and Susan Warner, Fanny Fern, Harriet Beecher Stowe, and many others.

Who were these women? They were middle class, upwardly mobile, unusually ambitious, energetic and lively. They lived in the cities. Most made 'successful' marriages but also taught or edited journals. Many supported the Feminist Movement. However, in their writings they were zealous to uphold the highest ideals of true womanhood. They were Rank's 'adjusted' type.

What they wrote was a new kind of fiction, the domestic novel with the sentimental heroine. The heroine was often an orphan or lonely child. The stories were emotional and the characters clearly sympathetic or villainous. Here is a paragraph from *Ruth Hall: A Tale of Domestic Life of the Present Time* (1855):

'It was so odd in Ruth to have no one but the family at the wedding . . . Where was the use of her white satin dress and orange wreath. What the use of her looking handsomer than she ever did before, when there was nobody there to see her?

'Nobody to see her?' Mark that manly form at her side; see his dark eye glisten, and his chiselled lip quiver, as he bends an earnest gaze on her who realizes all his boyhood dreams. Mistaken ones! it is not admiration which that young beating heart craves; it is love.'

This is the partly autobiographical story of a young woman with no mother, a heartless father and brother, stingy, critical and unscrupulous parents-in-law, and a devoted young husband who dies and leaves her without resources and with two babies to support. After much suffering, including a cruel rebuff from her well-established brother, an editor, she achieves success as an author of columns for newspapers. The tone of the book is sanctimonious and the herione's perfection unrelieved, but the author – her pen name was Fanny Fern – makes many acid criticisms of the way women were treated.

James D. Hart in *The Popular Book*, describes Fanny Fern as follows:

'She was in her mid-forties when she achieved success, a vivacious, coquettish woman hiding a blowzy face behind a stylish veil, but non-chalantly revealing the foot and ankle that dapper young men about town declared wonderfully well turned. Her head was a mass of curls and had been, in fact, ever since school days when she tore up a copy of Euclid to make curling papers . . . It was not her flighty yet florid style but a personality shining through her prose that impelled readers to tell the author, "I like your writings and I like you".'

Ann Wood, and also Helen Papashvily, in her book, *All the Happy Endings*, suggests that the women authors of this period used the sentimental heroine as a facade behind which to engage in a power struggle with the male sex. Fanny Fern provides particularly clear evidence for this, in her life and in her works. Wood also cites a humorous short story by Harriet Beecher Stowe about a parson who is completely dependent on his housekeeper to rescue him, as Wood puts it, 'from pitiful plights to which his ponderous brain has led him and in which his pathetic masculine pride threatens permanently to trap him' – plights such as trying to make the turkey hatch the hen's eggs. Women have a natural superiority, some of these stories seem to say, in the really important areas of life.

The post-Civil War period. The post-Civil War period was one of rapid and confusing social change. Cities grew wildly. Technological advances made the rich richter and more corrupt, and the contrast between rich and poor more marked. Fundamental beliefs about religion, social class, and democracy were undermined. However, the professions were developing, and they allowed some openings to women, so that a number of active, achievement-oriented women who might have been writers and editors in the 'Feminine Fifties' were now pioneers in the fields of medicine, social work, etc. Technological improvements in distribution methods had led to a sharp increase in the number and circulation of magazines, some of which were patronized by sensitive élites who were repelled by their contemporary world. Feelings of alienation were indeed widespread. In literature, they were manifested in utopianism, an interest in childhood, and, as we shall see, a return to regional roots, especially in New England and the South. These were the oldest areas and also those which had been most hurt by the Civil War and the loss of manpower in migrations to the city and to the West.

These were the conditions when a new generation of women writers appeared, the first in America to be taken seriously as artists. In contrast to the earlier group, these women were reclusive, shy and quirky, never wanting to leave the small towns or rural areas of New England or the South, attached to their parents, remaining single or marrying only late in life. The names we remember best today are those of Mary Wilkins Freeman and Sarah Orne Jewett.

What these women wrote was the Local Color story. Like their predecessors, the Sentimentalists, they wrote about women and their houses, but where the Sentimentalists had written expansive novels about the present, the Local Colorists avoided overstatement and cultivated lucidity in sketches or short stories about the past. Their women heroines were often old women, and the houses were often empty. There is a frequently quoted remark of Sarah Orne Jewett, that her head was full of old women and old houses, and when the two came together in her brain with a click, she knew a story was under way.

Some authors who worked in the Local Color genre portrayed a world of the past that had never existed and served only the purposes of nostalgia and escapism. Harriet Beecher Stowe in her later days was a writer of such works. But the better artists among the Local Colorists could not be called escapists. They had a much more complex attitude, part regressive, part tough-minded. They examined the old traditions lovingly, but with a sharp eye to their dark side in the past and their dark effects on the present. They used the despised, soured, or exhausted tradition to make criticisms of the present. The new generation of women authors was not interested in social roles except to show their effects on the inner life of individual who had played them out. Here is a paragraph from Mary Wilkins' 'A New England Nun', a story about how Puritan self-denial and adherence to routine can ultimately bind the personality and choke off its potential for growth and relationship.

'Louisa tied a green apron round her waist, and got out a flat straw hat with a green ribbon. Then she went into the garden with a little blue crockery bowl, to pick some currants for her tea. After the currants were picked she sat on the back doorstep and stemmed them, collecting the stems carefully in her apron and afterward throwing them into the hencoop. She looked sharply at the grass beside the step to see if any had fallen there.'

The sentimental heroine, as we have seen, served to give author and female reader a role-model who met their needs for achievement importance and expression without incurring the disapproval of violating role-boundaries or losing the benefits of femininity. In the later period, the symbol of the woman and the house would seem to have expressed the identity of the Local Colorist author as a woman in a declining region which had lost its manpower. But it is also a more general symbol of the psyche whose vital force is in abeyance. Thus it was also meaningful to any reader whose assertive impetus had deserted him in a contemporary world in which his traditional framework and emotional values – his house – seemed empty and dated.

The acute or prolonged sense of emptiness and deprivation converts, in images of woman, to witchery, and Ann Wood emphasizes the Local Colorists' treatment of this theme.

She says that 'the witch's only message is a curse against the society which has denied her a place'. We might add that the witch is the most universal symbol of the conflicted woman – one who has her own will but is thwarted by society, or by herself, from achieving it. Van Wyck Brooks said of Mary Wilkins: 'There was something fierce and primitive in her view of life, and the Furies existed for her'. This was a woman who fell in love, waited, married somebody else at 49, and knew what the scarce market in husbands did to the personalities of woman in the hamlets of depleted New England.

But I would emphasize, as Wood does not, that the urge to creative fulfillment on the part of the Local Colorists sometimes led them beyond conflict to truly creative expression. In fairy tales the hero or heroine is sometimes stopped by an old hag, but when she is kissed or befriended, the way is transformed. Both Wilkins and Jewett, in their separate ways, were befrienders of the old hag, and their originality, their place in American literature is closely related to this fact. But I will not prolong an attempt to differentiate the conflicted and creative. Sometimes the most creative thing one can do is to express the right conflict in the right way. Emily Dickinson, a creative genius of the Local Colorist temperament, the New England region, and nearly the same time period wrote sometimes of witch feelings,

> *I like a look of agony*
> *Because I know it's true ...*

and sometimes of transcendence,

> *The soul that hath a guest*
> *Doth seldom go abroad ...*

After earning the label of literary realists, meaning that they saw through social pretense, many of the Local Colorists developed in a direction that was called mystical. Certainly, they were interested in how the hold of an arbitrary present could be transcended. Although Mark Twain in his later works carried this interest the farthest, it seems to have been the women who first realized the deeper potentialities of the Local Color genre.

A contemporary study. What needs demonstration now is that Rank's adjusted and conflicted-creative syndromes, which I believe to be well represented by the Sentimentalists and Local Colorists, recur in other groups of women artists. For this purpose let us consider a sample of contemporary women authors of fantasy for children (Helson 1973). Two of the four subgroups of this sample are authors of 'heroic' fantasy, but it is the other two, somewhat older and more traditional, that seem to me to parallel the sentimentalists and the local colorists: they are the less creative and more creative authors of mildly comic or tender fantasy.

A comparison of these two groups of women shows large differences on the Dominance, Sociability, Communality, and Achievement via Conformance scales of the California Psychological Inventory (Gough 1969). The less creative group scores high; they can safely be labeled 'adjusted'. In work style, the 'adjusted' authors place high and the creative authors place low on a cluster of Q Sort items which contrasts extrinsic motivation – money, attention, reader-interest – with literary goals and absorption in an autonomous inner process. When their books are compared, the adjusted authors are found to place more emphasis on plot and analytical devices, to show more concern for the real world of everyday, and to be particularly prone to superficial and stereotyped attitudes. The creative authors emphasize setting (which is what Local Color is all about) and a concern with everyday life but with 'unusual phenomena of communication or perception' that convey the sense of a 'higher or deeper reality'.

Some of the less creative books are quite popular. A good example would be the *Mrs. Pigglewiggle* books by Betty MacDonald. The central character is a sensible and clever woman – a 'good witch' – who devises just the right and most hilarious remedy for the various behavior problems which beset the children of the neighborhood and are plaguing the lives of their parents.

The woman whose work received the highest rating on creativity was an English author, Lucy Boston. In the midst of a depression following a life crisis, Mrs. Boston came into possession of a remarkable house which was built during the crusades and which has figured prominently in most of her work. In her children's books it is called Green Knowe and is inhabited by a great-grandmother, Mrs. Oldknow. In one adventure it is almost overtaken by a witch. In an early book for adults the house is called Yew Hall. The elderly woman owner of Yew Hall explains that its walls are made of quarried stone with seams of air between. 'They breathe around me. Sitting alone here for the longest series of wordless winter nights, I feel neither shut in nor shut off, but rather like the heart inside living ribs'. And elsewhere she says: 'I believe that if my house were magnified as big as the sea it would show as much sparkle, as much rhythm and vitality, as much passion as the sea'. Like some of the Local Colorists, Mrs. Boston seems to live out an analogy between an ancient house and the full depths of her psyche.

An interpretation of the two patterns in women writers. I have tried to convey briefly the recurrence of images, characters and personality patterns from the two periods of the nineteenth century in these two groups from the recent present. Children's literature seems to be a field which attracts both types of writer, the one because it is a conventional field of activity for women and can be quite lucrative; the other because childhood and fantasy are congenial topics for individuals inclined to psychic withdrawal or inward-turning. I have described the first type as representing an adjusted pattern and the second, a creative-conflicted pattern.

It seems to me that Jungian theory, in addition to the Rankian concepts, helps to relate a number of the salient characteristics of these women artists, and further, that Jung's typology enables us to formulate the larger hypothesis (though I will not develop it here) that the patterns which have been described are associated particularly but not exclusively with women artists, that certain other patterns exist which are rare among women but common among male artists, and that still other patterns exist which show little relationship to sex. Jung, one recalls, spoke of two attitudes, extraversion and introversion, and four functions: sensation, intuition, thinking and feeling. He thought there were sex differences only in thinking and feeling.

The adjusted woman is the familiar 'lady-author' of best-sellers, motivated primarily by external rewards. In Jungian terms, she is identified with her persona, or social role. Since the feminine role is an important part of the persona, she expresses herself in terms of extraverted feeling. Her liveliness, her power struggles, her drama, her depiction of the world in good-bad terms, her moral platitudes, her pleasure in manipulation – all these characteristics fit descriptions of the person with extraverted feeling. She does not care to look within, so her work tends to be shallow, though it is often entertaining and sometimes provocative.

One would expect the introverted feeling type also to be common among women writers, and certainly the conflicted-creative author who emphasizes local color or setting does seem to fit here. In stories, setting is one of the main ways of expressing mood or feeling. Jung says that persons of this type are reserved, unadaptable, oriented to the past, and fundamentally concerned to realize for themselves the emotional or feeling aspects of an inner image. The witch is an image of what Jung called the shadow. The more positive image of the old woman and the house can perhaps be understood in terms of Jungian theory about the individuation process and the attempt to develop a relationship between the ego and unconscious. The author, in these terms, is relating her ego to an image of the feminine self.

C. PLANNED OBSOLESCENCE: HISTORICAL PERSPECTIVES ON AGING WOMEN

by Nancy Sheehan, *University of Wisconsin, Madison*

Although there is currently a good deal of discussion concerning the changing role of women in society, the double standard of aging seems to persist. Our contemporary notions regarding aging women still reiterate the historically persistent theme which associates aging in women with far more negative consequences than aging in men.

This paper will explore attitudes toward aging women (a) as they have been expressed historically from prehistory to the present, (b) as they have been expressed within the history of psychology, and (c) as they are expressed today. Historical conceptions of aging women were traced through two principle sources: the history of aging and the history of women. While one would expect a good deal of overlap between these two areas, there is, in fact, practically none. Historical discussions of aging rarely discuss women; historical discussions of women rarely discuss aging women. In reviewing these sources, as well as additional materials drawn from anthropology, archeology, mythology, and literature, it becomes evident that historical and philosophical discussions of aging women represent gross demonstrations of prejudice, superstition, omission, and neglect.

Until quite recently practically all discussions of women were written by men. These men seemed primarily interested in maintaining the *status quo* so that women outside of their conventional roles such as marriage and childbearing, that is aging women, received little attention. They selectively ignored or misrepresented facts concerning women in society, making women almost 'invisible' in historical writings (Rosen 1971). It has also been noted that while histories of men are written concerning their relationship to their environment, histories of women are written concerning their relationship to men (Holtby 1934). A classical example of this male-dominant perspective is John Langdon-Davies', *A Short History of Women* (1927) in which he discusses among other topics, 'the potentiality of every woman, given the right background, to become a witch' (Langdon-Davies 1927, p. 297).

In addition to these historical factors, issues regarding aging itself serve to confuse the search for information concerning the history of aging women. The two major questions regarding aging in women are: (1) at what age is a woman considered to be aging and (2) at what age does a woman identify herself as aging. Since aging, in many respects, is considered to be a culturally defined variable, these questions are answered differently in various times and cultures. Aging women do not necessarily constitute a similarly defined social group over different periods in history. Furthermore, as emphasized by a number of developmental psychologists (Birren 1959; Kessen 1960; Wohlwill 1970) age itself is a nonspecific term which can be used to refer to chronological age, social age, psychological age, biological age and/or physical age. Finally, as Simone de Beauvoir (1972) has pointed out, within earlier periods longevity was a privilege of the upper class. Consequently, no mention is made of the aged poor until the nineteenth century.

Given these limitations, we are left not with an accurate description of the history of aging women but with a preliminary attempt to disentangle 'the conflict between the actual position and the abstract position' of aging women (Bell 1973, p. 1). Consequently this paper does not represent, nor could it represent, a definitive statement regarding the history of aging women. Its major purpose is to sensitize the reader to the need to disentangle further the historical facts concerning aging women from the myths, prejudices, superstitions, and stereotypes which have, throughout history, obscured these facts.

By viewing our own attitudes toward aging women in light of this historical perspective, we may hopefully come to realize the degree to which our attitudes toward aging women are based upon prejudice which can be traced back to much earliers times. Perhaps through this process we may arrive at a first step in developing a viable survey of the history of aging women.

Ancient civilization. Information concerning prehistory is scant and often based upon far-ranging speculation. Archaeological and anthropological evidence has been cited which supports claims that within precivilization a highly developed matriarchate existed (Davis 1971). But other historians claim that these interpretations are ridiculous, labeling them as 'profeminine' views.

Neither point of view, however, mentions aging women. The only discussions concerning the role of aging women in ancient civilization is provided by Karl Pearson (1897, in Hall 1922) who theorized that the origins of witchcraft can be traced back to this matriarchy. Witchcraft was purported to have developed out of the struggle of old women to retain their power, with whatever means they could, from the younger generations. If this theory has any validity, it indicates that throughout the history of *man*, aging women have been associated with evil and super-natural powers.

Golden age of Athens. A review of the writings of the early Greek philos-ophers and playwrights reveals that their attitudes toward aging were similar to those of our youth-oriented culture. In contrast to the exalted glory of youth, the Greeks viewed old age as a time of unhappiness and despair. They also maintained a double standard of aging. Women were considered to reach their prime of life, and subsequent decline, significantly earlier than men. The loss of physical beauty was held as a constant threat to women.

These negative views are clearly expressed in the writings of Aristotle. A devout antifeminist, Aristotle believed that men reach the prime of life at age thirty-seven, women at eighteen. In addition to his views regarding the inferiority of women, Aristotle also had extremely negative views concerning aging. Aging, as he described it, is the process whereby the vital heat and moisture of the body are lost. This results in the decline of abilities – loss of memory, loss of physical prowess, etc. Old people are consequently by nature dry and cold with little pleasant about them.

Although Plato's views were not as vitriolic as those of Aristotle, he did share Aristotle's view that women experience an earlier decline than men, describing the prime of life as 20 to 40 for women and 25 to 55 for men. He also believed that women are weaker and not as wise or virtuous as men.

Lacey (1968), one of the few historians who has discussed aging women, cited evidence that these philosophical portrayals do not adequately represent the actual position of aging women in Classical Greece. Women in the Athenian democracy experienced increased freedom of movement with increasing age. Freed from restrictions, they were allowed to act as messengers, midwives, and funeral mourners. They were also freed from economic insecurity since by law children were obligated to support their parents.

The Roman Empire. Unfortunately, historical writings concerning the period of Ancient Rome (from 770 B.C. to 476 A.D.) provide us with few direct statements regarding aging women. However, there is evidence that the political changes of this era led to significant changes in the role of women and, subsequently, in family styles. These changes must have ultimately effected the role of aging women.

Simone de Beauvoir (1972) has suggested that before the establishment of the oligarchy, the early Romans, considering their old to be an excess burden, may have disposed of them by drowning. With the establishment of the oligarchic system, property rights were recognized – by placing power in the hands of wealthy male property owners. Thus unders this conservative political system, the rights of the old (men, that is) were upheld. The rights of women were denied. Women were placed under the strict control of their fathers and husbands. According to the historian Plutarch, Roman matrons of the eighth and seventh centuries B.C. were expected to be completely subservient: '. . . sobriety was insisted on, and silence made habitual, not to speak in their husband's company even on the most ordinary subjects' (Plutarch, c. 100 A.D.).

With the gradual lessening of this conservative influence, women experienced increasing emancipation from the strict control of the *pater familias*, eventually reaching full social and legal equality. Women were considered both the equal of men and their rivals. Women, as well as men, were easily able to obtain divorces. Many women chose to reject the maternal role, often imitating their husbands' pursuits. Other women chose to reject marriage altogether. These combined factors contributed to the dissolution of family ties. In fact, in order to encourage marriage, Augustus in 9 A.D. passed a law which levied extra taxation on bachelors and spinsters. This dissolution, in contrast to the family solidarity of Classical Greece, may well have left many women alone in their old age.

However, inspite of this 'liberated' role of women, later historians have recognized Roman matrons only for the accomplishment of being the mother of, e.g., Cornelia, the mother of the Gracchi, Aurealia, the mother of Julius Caesar, etc. (Langdon-Davies 1934).

The Middle Ages. As in previous historical periods, during the Middle Ages (c. 476–1500) references to aging women were infrequent. Those which did appear represented stereotypical views regarding aging women. Philosophical conceptions reflected two contradictory themes – (a) the inferiority of women, as revitalized by the Church, and (b) the superiority of women, as idealized by the doctrine of courtly love.

Neither conception however accurately reflected the actual position of women. Their position was more accurately described as 'rough and ready equality' (Power 1926, p. 410). Given the harshness of feudal life, women living under this system had to be totally self-sufficient in agricultural and domestic endeavors. Similarly, women of the merchant class, as portrayed by the Wife of Bath in Chaucer's *Canterbury Tales*, were frequently independent, high spirited, powerful individuals.

The plight of widows was made difficult by the exigencies of feudal life. While the Magna Carta (1215) attempted to protect the rights of widows, permitting them to remain in their homes forty days after the death of their husbands, in actuality the feudal lord exercised complete power over them. Widows were often forced to remarry for the economic advantage of the lord. In considering widowhood, it is interesting to note that it was during the Middle Ages that social organizations (the Church and the guilds) first attempted to provide for their poor and aged members. However, this care was usually inadequate. The old, female and male, were often reduced to beggary.

The Renaissance. During the Renaissance the combined influences of the humanist movement and the protestant reformation led to an increase in the value of education for all individuals – including women. But the ,appropriate' channels for self-expression open to women were also extermely limited. In short, Renaissance attitudes toward women changed little. This lack of change may be at least partially explained by the attempt of Renaissance writers to return to the ideals of Classical Greece and Rome, as well as to the original Christian ideals. Returning to these values inevitably placed restrictions upon 'appropriate' behavior for women. Women of refined society were again expected to display the feminine virtues of 'submission, sensibility, and solitude' (Holtby 1934, p. 40). These severe restraints of decorum inevitably led to the beginning of women's protests. The first protest against this subjugation of women's character was *The Vindication of the Rights of Women* (1792) written by Mary Wollstonecraft which has since been cited as the bible of the women's movement (Holtby, 1934).

Due to the extremely high value placed upon physical beauty, the glory of womanhood was short-lived. A woman was considered old at forty. At this time, we are told, it was necessary for her to forsake her sex and become an 'amiable man' (Goncourt 1928, p. 335). As an upper class woman entered old age, she was able to choose among a limited number of alternative life styles. These included a life of 'fashionable' religious devotion, entertaining in intellectual salons, engaging in court intrigue' or acceptance of old age (Goncourt 1928). This last alternative must have been extremely difficult for most women to accept since old age was generally viewed as a period of unhappiness.

Living conditions of the lower class women certainly did not improve with age. Young or old, they continued to work long hours under unsanitary conditions for little pay.

Colonial America to the beginnings of the women's rights movement. During the early history of this country, husbands and wives were mutually interdependent upon one another for their survival. However, women were once again considered both physically and intellectually inferior to men.

During these pre-industrial periods, the rigors of daily life made every family member integral to survival. Consequently, the rights of the old were protected within the extended family. Old women, however, did not directly share in the economic or political power afforded 'the old'. They merely assumed the ascribed status of their husbands since no women, either old or young, had any legal rights.

With industrialization, the old no longer controlled economic or political power. The security which the extended family system had provided for the old was diminished (Goode 1964). As early as 1841, editorials concerning the lack of respect for aged persons appeared in newspapers such as *The Ladies' Repository of Cincinnati* (Calhoun 1966).

At this time women began to speak out for social and political reform regarding the rights of women, but the writings of the movement did not address the particular problems of older women.

Psychological views. Now, we turn to attitudes toward aging women which have been expressed by psychologists. While many psychologists have expressed extremely antifeminist views, this section is limited to attitudes regarding women and aging. Our naive expectations might suggest that scientific 'inquiries into the nature of man' would improve the treatment of aging women. However, this is not the case. Given that Aristotle is regarded as the first psychologist (Watson 1968), the earliest foundations of psychology reflect the same negative views of aging women that have just been described. However, the significance of Aristotle's position lies not in his being the first psychologist but in the persistent influence that his ideas have exerted regarding aging women. For example, to quote Sigmund Freud:

'A man of about thirty seems a youthful, and in a sense, an incompletely developed individual, of whom we expect that he will be able to make good use of the possibilities of development ... But a woman of about the same age frequently staggers us by her psychological rigidity and unchangeability ...' (Freud 1933, p. 170).

The early foundations of psychology in the United States reflect this long pervasive history of prejudice toward women and aging. Like Aristotle, the first American psychologist, William James, maintained that women age more rapidly than men but never quite reach the full maturity attained by men. According to *The Principles of Psychology* (James 1890), a young woman of twenty has relatively fixed opinions and character which change little. On the other hand, the mind of a young man of the same age has not yet become fixed 'which insures that it shall ultimately become so much more efficient than the woman's'. From this, one would assume that nothing is to be gained from studying women past the age of twenty since little, if any, change will occur. Perhaps this implicit assumption has been at least partially responsible for the failure of social scientists to study women (cf. Carlson and Carlson 1960).

Even with the publication of G. Stanley Hall's renowned work *Senescence* (1922) the treatment of aging women did not improve. Although the reputed 'father' of psychogerontology, Hall showed no new understanding of or sensitivity to the problems of aging women. He merely repeated the same antifeminist views of his predecessors. Hall was particularly intrigued with what he described as 'the horror that girls have of growing old, which begins ... before the end of the twenties and prompts every kind of deception and disguise ...' (letter to Adler, in Ansbacher 1971, p. 341). Hall further noted the almost obsessional quality of a woman's reaction as she approaches forty. To support his belief that middle aged women are the 'unhappy victims' of the aging crisis, he quoted extensively from *The Dangerous Age* (1912) by Karin Michaëlis. For example, '... If men suspected what took place in a woman's life after forty, they would avoid us like the plague or knock us in the head like mad dogs'. Hall's choice of examples and descriptions of aging in women, with phrases such as 'her cult of the mirror', conveyed an almost supernatural quality to aging women.

Typically, Hall concluded that women enter middle age (senescence) earlier than men. While women must direct their energy to the struggle to maintain their youthful qualities, men may direct their energies to other endeavors. Woman, according to Hall, is 'older than man in the same sense that the child is older than the adult .... But she is also at the same time, younger than he in that she is less differentiated in tissues and traits ...' (Hall 1922, p. 389). Neither James nor Hall cited empirical evidence to support this beliefs concerning aging women. Their views were based upon impressions rather than scientific investigation.

More recent psychological endeavors also reflect this predictable bias in the treatment of aging women. Psychologists as well as historians seem to have been interested in maintaining the *status quo*. Once again, women outside their conventional roles, i.e., marriage and motherhood, have been ignored. Empirical attempts to study adult women have dealt primarily with married women during their childbearing years. While there were a few pioneer investigations dealing with older women, e.g., Cavan (1952), Cavan *et al.* (1949), and Neugarten's summary of the 1958 Kansas City study (1964), it has only been during the last decade that a substantial number of psychologists have turned their attention to married women in the last half of the marriage cycle (Troll 1971). They have not yet begun to study the effects of aging on single women (cf. Adams 1971).

More recent investigations concerning older women have studied marital satisfaction in the later years (Blood and Wolfe 1960; Pineo 1968; Stinnett *et al.*, 1972), the empty nest syndrome (Bart 1970, 1972) the effect of wife's employment in the post parental period (Powers 1971), sexual activity in the later years (Masters and Johnson 1968), menopause (Neugarten *et al.* 1968), widowhood (Lopata 1973), and retirement as a life change affecting both husband and wife (Kerckoff 1966a, 1966b).

These studies provide an initial step towards understanding aging in women. However, before carrying out further investigations, psychologists must re-evaluate the 'stories' (myths) concerning aging women which until now they have unquestionably accepted (Peters 1953). Besides being aware of their traditional biases, psychologists must also become sensitive to rapid changes occurring in the lives of women.

Psychologists have often blamed their failure to understand aging women on the 'unpredictability' of women rather than on their own stereotypes and lack of flexibility. They have either ignored women as viable subjects for empirical research or have blamed women for not responding in an 'appropriate' manner. This attitude is obvious in the question, 'Why can't a woman be more like a man?' (Birren 1971). But is it naive to ask, 'Why *should* a woman be more like a man?'

Present attitudes. Our society with its practices of ageism and sexism also adjudges aging women as inferior to aging men. The 'social judgment' which allows men to mature, while judging women to obsolesce quite accurately represents this discrimination (Moss 1970; Sontag 1972). Aging women are constantly placed at a disadvantage–socially, sexually, and economically.

A woman today can expect to live 25 years longer than a woman living during the 1900s (President's Commission on Women 1963). Unlike previous historical periods, motherhood is becoming a part-time occupation (Rossi 1964). A woman can expect to live 40 years after her last child enters school and 25 years after her last child marries (Bell 1970). Despite these drastic changes which have occurred in the lives of women during the past century, attitudes toward aging women have not changed.

The ultimate value which society places upon a woman's youthful beauty, loudly proclaimed by the mass media and multimillion dollar cosmetic industry, clearly denigrates the position of aging women. In fact, it not only serves to isolate aging women from society, but also to alienate her from her own body. As Susan Sontag (1972) has clearly discussed, the standards for female beauty do not allow women to age with dignity. While the standards for male attractiveness are natural, the standards for female attractiveness are not. Men are allowed a much wider range of possibilities which may be considered attractive, such as greying at the temples, a rugged look, and a variety of other characteristics which are signs of 'character' in men. Women, however, are not allowed this privilege.

Informal, yet explicit, social sanctions eliminate aging women as desirable companions. These social sanctions, as well as the larger number of aging females, deny most of these older women any opportunity for sexual fulfillment. Despite their increased time to engage in alternate roles and activities, actual opportunities afforded aging women are extremely limited. For instance, although middle-aged and older women are entering or re-entering the labor force, they continue to be relegated to low-paying, low-status jobs (Arrington 1972).

Women have come to dread painfully the 'crisis of aging'. Since an aging woman can neither escape the destiny of her sex nor the biological fact of aging, this planned obsolescence places her in a situation with seemingly no out. Unless women are prepared to reject the youthful stereotype which society has idealized for them, this double standard will continue.

While this discrimination is, or at least until now has been, the inevitable fate of all women if they live long enough, the Women's Liberation

Movement has not addressed itself to the problems of elderly women. Lewis and Butler (1972) provide an excellent discussion of the needs and potential of elderly women in the struggle for liberation. According to them, elderly women could not only serve as an inspiration for younger women but also provide political muscle to bring about necessary reform.

Conclusion. Despite the rapid cultural, technological, and scientific advances which our society has attained, attitudes toward aging women have remained relatively unchanged. While the historical information concerning aging women is scant and fragmentary, the information that does exist consistently expresses narrow, stereotypical portrayals of aging women. In addition, this general lack of information concerning aging women indicates the relative unimportance of aging women in the eyes of historians and philosophers.

Obviously, the references cited in this paper do not constitute a genuine history of aging women. Rather, they serve to expose the myths, stereotypes, and prejudices which, throughout history, have been written about aging women. Regrettably, this historical analysis does not provide us with actual information concerning the daily lives and accomplishments of aging women. Further attempts to reveal what, if any, historical information concerning these women exists must come from the diaries and autobiographies of older women. Perhaps this arduous process will bring us one step closer to discovering the heritage of aging women.

Yet beyond this goal, I wish to propose an even greater goal. I make the 'immodest proposal' (Rossi 1964) that all people may come to realize that this discrimination against aging women hurts not just women but all people. Until society can dispel the rigidly constrained roles which it has proposed for both women and men, any further chance for human growth or potential is eliminated. Before any liberation movement may be effective, both women and men, old and young alike, must abandon traditionally defined roles in favor of a wider range of human potential.

Formal models of development

A. ORGANIZATION AND TRANSFORMATION

by Leland D. Van den Daele, *Columbia University, New York*

The problem of development is a general concern in philosophy and science. It is another guise of the problem of change, the reconciliation of identity and continuity with transformation and difference.[1] The problem of development transcends the narrow boundaries of discipline or orientation.

Any general developmental formalism possesses implications for analysis in the physical, biological, and social sciences. The constructs of these sciences are 'content' to a general theory. A theory of development is a domain of General Systems Theory.

A formal theory of development summarizes the plausible modes of change from some initial to some final state. Given some organization, A, a theory of development describes the relation of that organization with some successor organization, B. The type of relation is linked to the permissible mechanisms of change, and the modes of analysis by which the process of change is understood.

Algorithms of decomposition and construction. Any state, stage, or organization may be decomposed into any number of components, aspects,

---

1. An excellent introduction to problems of change and transformation is found in Flavell's (1972) monograph *An Analysis of Cognitive-Developmental Sequences* and Riegel's (1972) *Time and Change in the Development of the Individual and Society.*

or differentia. The rules by which a whole is differentiated into its parts is an algorithm of decomposition, and the rules by which parts are placed into relation is an algorithm of construction. With reference to the same whole, algorithms of decomposition and construction are complementary.

The algorithms by which wholes are decomposed or constructed depend upon the domain of interest, the theory, and the endeavor, whether conceptual or practical. An anthropologist or historian concerns himself with cultures and roles; a psychologist, with cognitions and behaviors; an anatomist, with morphology and cellular structure; a biochemist, with molecular chains and interactions; a physicist, with energies and particles, and so on. Algorithms of decomposition and construction are conventions applied to a domain of interest.

Given some algorithm of decomposition or construction, any organization, stage, or state is a potential hierarchical structure (Figure 1). Whatever is content for a higher level is simultaneously form for a lower level. The distinction between content and form is a matter of perspective only.[2]

Figure 1. *Decomposition with transposition. In the example, an element, representing some stage, stage, or general organization, is decomposed into two components, the 'bs' at the second level of analysis. In turn, the 'bs' are differentiated into four 'cs' at the third level of analysis. The transposition to a linear hierarchical form is a notational convenience which simplifies subsequent representation in the figures which follow*

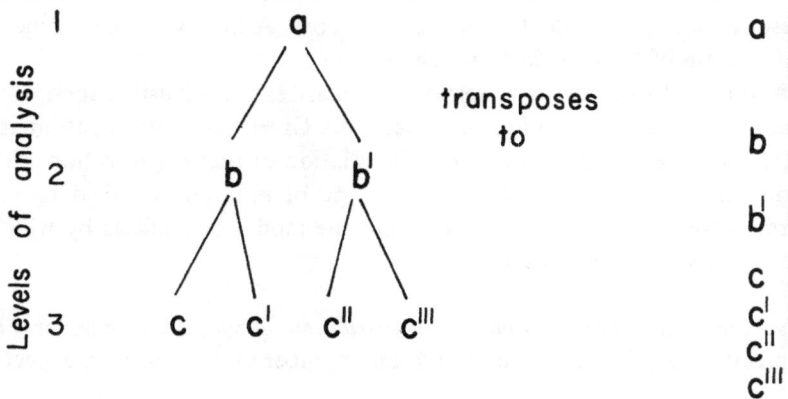

2. However, from the perspective of a consistent theory, the irreducible is content. It is, as it were, an ultimate content.

Consistency. A consistent algorithm is tautological. Its circularity defines an admissible class of form and content and, at the same time, excludes the inadmissible. For any consistent algorithm, there is a primitive content, a primitive language, and a primitive set of operations. Whatever is primitive is asserted. Whatever is asserted may be justified. Any justification may be justified, but finally all justifications are circular and possess their primitive contents, languages, and operations. Beyond the primitive is the unutterable.

Types of change. Qualitative change implies difference in the form or content of successive states in a developmental progression. Any qualitative change is derivable, nonderivable, or partially derivable. The types of change impose constraints on the successive organization of states. Organization and transformation are interdependent.

Derivable change. Derivable change implies common items in a state *A* and a state *B* which serve as 'continuity components' in transformation. Continuity components are identity elements which provide a common substrate in change. The successive states of a derivable progression, taken two at a time, are analogous to a set of balanced equations. Given any state in a derivable progression, its precursor or successor is obtainable, given some rule of transformation.

The states of a derivable progression are transformed in a simple sequence, a, b, c..., and correlatively transformed in a cumulative sequence (Van den Daele 1969; in press). The identity elements of a derivable progression may occur at the same level of analysis, at a lower level, or at a higher level. When identity elements occupy the same level, transformation is parallel. When identity elements occupy lower or higher levels, transformation is subordinate or emergent, respectively. Within any level of analysis, transformation is a correspondence when components are in one-to-one relation; a differentiation, when components are in a one-to-many relation; and an integration, when components are in a many-to-one relation (Figure 2).

The nomenclature of transformation is a description of the mapping relations between successive states of organization between and within levels of analysis. Subordination with differentiation implies that identity elements of an analysis are successively subordinated to other elements while the number of these elements within a level of analysis is increased. Emergence with integration implies that identity elements are successively

Figure 2. *Derivable transformations*

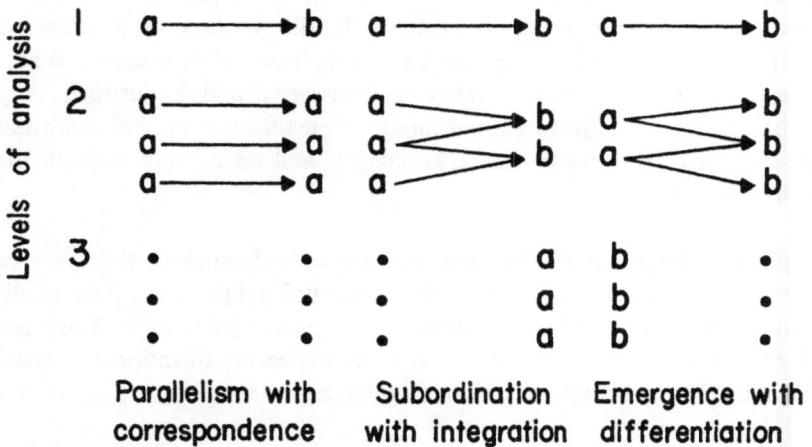

Parallelism with   Subordination   Emergence with
correspondence   with integration   differentiation

desubordinated while the number of elements within a level of analysis is decreased. The identification of the relations of successive organizations is the identification of the form of transformation.

A statement about the form of transformation is not only descriptive but also generative. Given some form, i.e., subordination with correspondence, and given some initial or final state, all successor or precursor states may be derived. Since a variety of states may be organized by the same rule of transformation, the statement of a transformation rule is a statement of general utility in developmental analysis.

Models of change in the physical and biological sciences typically are models of transformation. In traditional embryology, identity elements reside in cellular substrates; in chemistry, atomic elements serve as identity elements; in subatomic physics, when identity elements are not readily observable, they are invented. In these sciences, transformation occurs within a framework of conservation. Non-conservation is tantamount to incompleteness.

In psychological investigation, a derivable progression is examplified by Piaget's stages of cognitive development. Given a set of initial schema, an appropriate set of system conditions, and the operation of the system invariants, stages follow one another in a determinant way. Initial schema are successively subordinated to higher-order structures which derive through an integration of these schema. The schema serve as successive identity elements in transformation and link sensory-motor operations with formal operations.

Nonderivable change. Nonderivable change implies no common items in a state *A* or state *B* which serve as continuity components. States are incommensurable. Since there are no identity elements, there is no transformation to obtain one state from another. A transformation implies an implicit identity.

The states of a nonderivable progression are substituted in a simple sequence, *a*, *b*, *c*..., and added or deleted in a cumulative sequence, *a*, *ab*, *abc*.... A substitution is an addition with a deletion. The discrete elements of a nonderivable progression may occur at the same level of analysis or at successively lower or higher levels. When discrete elements occupy the same level, substitution is coplanar. When discrete elements occupy lower or higher levels, substitution is expanded or contracted respectively. Within a level of analysis, substitution is coincident when components are in one-to-one relation; augmented, when components are in one-to-many relation; and reduced, when components are in many-to-one relation (Figure 3).

Like the nomenclature of transformation, the nomenclature of substitution is a description of mapping relations between successive states of organization. Expansion with augmentation implies successive in-

Figure 3. *Nonderivable substitutions*

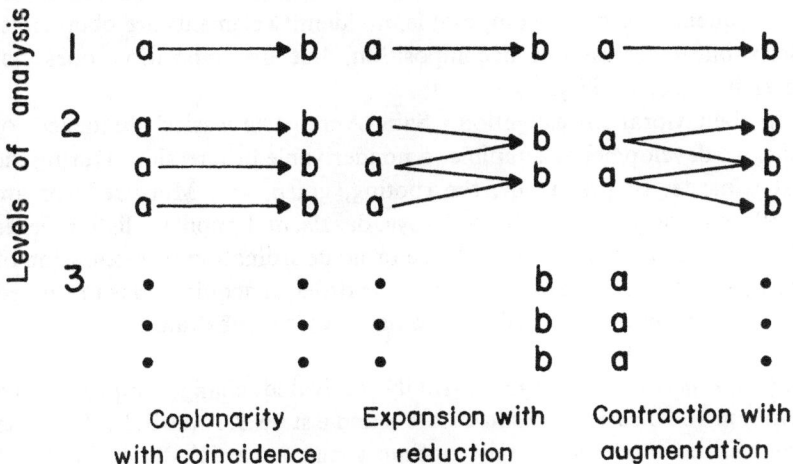

crements in the number of levels of analysis and the number of components within a level. Contraction with reduction implies successive decrements in the number of levels and number of components within a level. Since identity elements are absent or unspecified in a substitution sequence, the mapping of relations is often ambiguous.

Modes of transformation and substitution are isomorphic in mapping relations but discrete in content. The language of transformation implies continuity, and the language of substitution, discontinuity. The isomorphism of languages extends only to mappings not to the content of mappings.

Models of change in selected games and opportunisms are models of substitution, addition, or deletion. In various games, such as poker, cards are taken or discarded to secure an optimum set. In collections, such as stamps or coins, items are added or replaced to complete an array. These examples implicate an open system. Change results through exchange between the system of interest and some universe.

When the universe from which items are drawn is known and restrictions placed upon sample procedure, probabilities may be attached to specialized substitutions, additions, or deletions. The probability obtains unity when some rule of substitution, addition, or deletion, i.e., expansion with augmentation, strictly orders items in the universe from which items are drawn. In such a case, a rule of substitution, addition, or deletion is a rule of order which determines content.

Any sequence of discrete states which are not subject to decomposition are sequences of substitution, addition, or deletion. If the discrete states of a sequence are not decomposable, no identity elements are obtainable. Derivability necessitates decomposition, but decomposition does not necessitate derivability.

In behavioral investigation, Saint-Anne Dargassies' sequence of reflexive development exemplifies a nonderivable progression. During the last trimester of pregnancy, the rooting, grasp, and Moro reflexes are developmentally prior to the doll's eye, dazzle, and pupillary light reflexes (Saint-Anne Dargassies 1966). Little or no coordination or integration of successive reflexes is readily evident. The order of acquisition is presumed to reflect the maturation of discrete neurological substrates.

Partially derivable change. Partially derivable change implies some common and discrete items in a state *A* and a state *B*. A partially derivable progression implies a partial continuity and a partial discontinuity of identity elements. The successive states of a partially derivable progression, taken two at a time, yield a set of semi-balanced equations.

The states of a partially derivable progression are transformed with any substitution, addition, or deletion of identity elements between consecutive states. Any parallelism, subordination, or emergence may occur with any coplanarity, expansion, or contraction; and any correspondence, differentiation, or integration may occur with any coincidence, augmentation, or reduction.

The nomenclature of partially derivable transformation is potentially complicated since both the languages of transformation and substitution are applicable. Given this descriptive problem, a convenient method of description is an identification of the type of relation among identity elements with a statement about substitutions, additions, or deletions associated with the transformation. Parallelism with substitution implies at least one element of a set of elements at the same level of analysis is discrete. Subordination with deletion implies at least one element of a set of elements at a successive lower is eliminated, and so on (Figure 4).

Figure 4. *Partially derivable transformations*

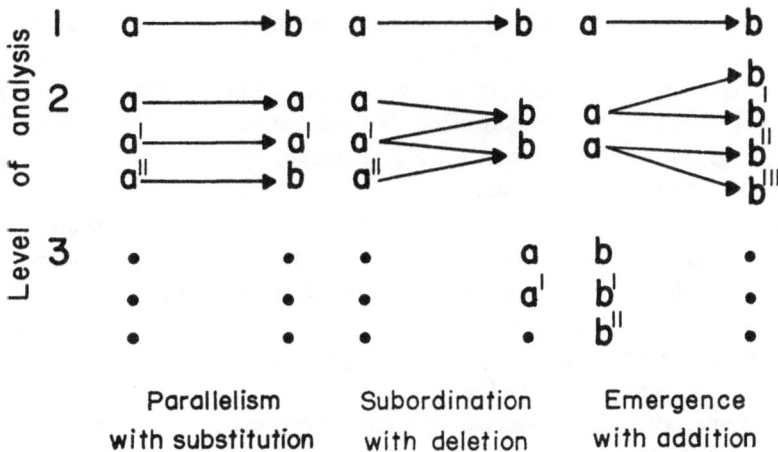

Models of change in cultural-historical studies are typically models of partially derivable transformation. Cultural analyses specify a thematic, valuative, linguistic, or social set of items which interact with innovations or inventions to yield changed patterns of belief or behavior. Historical analyses isolate the serendipitous and construct its consequences for individual and society. Nontrivial analyses identify the continuities as well as discontinuities in change.

In personality theory, a partially derivable progression is exemplified in Kohlberg's stages of moral judgment (Kohlberg 1969). Kohlberg relates the mechanism of stage organization and transition both to purely cognitive competencies, such as those described by Piaget, and to the occurrence of various 'role-taking' experiences. These role-taking experiences interact with cognitive organization to generate premises from which derive moral solutions. The development of moral judgment is not a simple function of cognitive stage but requires the introduction of new information associated with interpersonal experience.

Formal rules and conditional determinants. In a scientific theory of derivable transformation, the rules of transformation are expressed in the explicit assumptions and postulates of that theory. The transformation of gaseous hydrogen and oxygen into water is an integration with subordination, and the obverse transformation of water into gaseous hydrogen and oxygen is an emergence with differentiation. The language of chemical theory expresses this transformation in terms of atomic valances and changes in molecular structure. The general statement is a statement in the metalanguage of transformation, and the chemical statement is a statement in a specialized language of transformation. Both languages specify mappings of relationship between successive states. Neither language, insofar as the language is a statement of relationship, identifies the conditions of transformation.

In the metalanguage, the conditions of transformation are conceptually independent of forms of transformation. In all likelihood, a binding of conditions to forms of transformation would reduce the generality of the formulation. A binding of 'compression' to 'integration' might prove useful in the analysis of physical aggregations but unfortunate in the analysis of personality development.

In a specialized language, obvious advantages occur when some sort of binding between conditions and forms of transformation is specified. Yet potent difficulties to this endeavor arise. The difficulties are not primarily conceptual (although they are that as well) but empirical. While gaseous hydrogen and oxygen may combine under conditions of sufficient pressure and heat, other conditions of transformation apply to other materials. The introduction of catalysts may change the usual modes of combination in physically dramatic ways. This is not to argue that a theory of conditional transformation is not practical; it is only to assert it is difficult to construct, given the complexity of the world.

These problems with reference to a theory of conditional transformation seem particularly relevant to psychological analysis. Consider, for example, the myriad ways in which the intelligence of the adult may be influenced developmentally. Genetic factors, pre- and perinatal events, early experience, education, and so on, may be viewed as equipotent with reference to later intellectual competence. The investigator who wishes to identify the role of these variables in intellectual performance is confronted with an enormous task.

Strategically his task seems somewhat simplified if the formal aspects of organization and transformation are known, then empirical conditions correlated to transformation. The commonalities among various conditions of transformation might then suggest a conditional transformational theory in a specialized language. The task of developmental psychological investigation is rendered less arduous if the formal-descriptive and empirical-conditional aspects of change are rendered independent, at least provisionally.

Implicit metatheories and correlated characteristics. Psychological theories not only possess specialized languages but implicit theories of transformation. A derivable progression is state-determined under appropriate conditions while a nonderivable progression is nonstate-determined although potentially orderable when the universe from which states are sampled is itself ordered. A derivable progression is closed under transformation, and a nonderivable progression is open. A derivable progression implies continuity, and a nonderivable progression implies discontinuity. Distinct strategies and specialized languages of theory construction are associated with the respective points of view.

Theories of derivable transformation specify identity elements or the common components in a transformation. The relations of successive organizations are mapped, and some formulation of transformation is usual. These theories commonly employ a symbolism or a deductive or quasi-deductive logic. A concern with the empirical conditions of change often is subordinated to the description of organization and transformation. Theories of nonderivable change stress the discreteness and independence of successive states. The relations of successive organizations rarely are mapped with any explicitness. Empirical description dominates formal analysis, and description of organization and transformation is subordinated to evaluation of the empirical conditions of change. Theories of partially derivable transformation represent an intermediate case and share characteristics of theories of derivable transformation and non-derivable transformation (Table 1).

Table 1. *Representative theories by types*

Derivable transformation	Partially derivable transformation	Nonderivable transformation
Cunningham (1972)	Bridges (1932)	Bandura and Walters (1963)
McNeill (1966) Piaget (1970)	Brown (1972) Erikson (1966)	Loevinger (1966)
Witz (1971)	Kohlberg (1969)	Saint-Anne Dargassies (1966)

This collection of characteristics happens to correlate with contemporary theories of derivable and nonderivable transformation, but there is nothing necessary in the association of these characteristics. It is not difficult to imagine a theory of nonderivable transformation relatively abstract in language, or conversely, a theory of derivable transformation relatively empirical in language.

The characterization of theories of derivable and nonderivable transformation appears to resemble Reese and Overton's characterization of 'organic' and 'mechanistic' models respectively, but the resemblance is only superficial. Reese and Overton (1970) assert that organic theories are 'teleological' and 'irreducibly discontinuous' in formulation but theories of derivable transformation are neither teleological nor irreducibly discontinuous. In fact, these characteristics might better characterize some theories of nonderivable transformation. Are then theories of substitution mechanistic? Theories of substitution are mechanistic only if mechanistic theories possess teleological characteristics, but this contradicts the Reese-Overton classification. Characterizations of types which embrace content are utilitarian in the study of the history of ideas but doubtful in proscriptive contexts.

B. CONCEPTUALIZING BEHAVIORAL DEVELOPMENT

by Klaus Witz, *University of Illinois, Urbana*

I would like to discuss certain fundamental problems that arise when one tries to conceptualize the development of behavior in infants and small children. My task has been made much easier by the contribution to this symposium by Van den Daele. In his terminology, the question which I would like to ask is: What kinds of conceptualizations and models of infrastructure and transition am I led to if they are to include my own deepest insights about the organism and about behavior? I will begin from within the overall framework posed in Van den Daele's paper and go on to suggest that the kinds of conceptualizations required must ultimately lead outside this very framework.

States A → States B. The usual approach to the development of behavior is to consider the organism at successive periods of time and to try to explain how its state at one time, say state A, is related to, and changes into, its state at a later time, say state B. States A and B themselves are described using some system of theoretical constructs (Van den Daele's elements and infrastructural components and relationships), which together explicate what it is that the theorist believes to underlie behavior at the time in question. The change from state A to state B, then, is, in lowest terms, always described in terms of changes in certain aspects of A and the rise of new aspects in B, or in terms of relationships between aspects of A and B which the actual changes satisfy.

Within this overall framework, most of my own and my associates' research on small children can be very accurately located. We are studying natural behavior like object manipulation and play interactions with other persons, etc., and we try to deduce and model the multilevel, temporal, and dynamic organization of such behavior on a real time basis. Our basic constructs are cognitive structures similar to Piaget's sensory motor schemes (Piaget 1952, 1950, 1954). These structures are thought to 'exist in the child', to assimilate aspects of the environment, and to produce evidence in observable behavior that they currently are, or have just been, active. In addition they are thought to function in real time and are modelled explicitly as dynamical systems.

Let me give an example of a fragment of a state description in these terms by sketching a few aspects of the state of language production in a little girl, Laura, age $1^1/_2$. (The description is based on micro-analysis of a series of one-hour video tapes made in Laura's home, see Witz and Duchan (1973) and Witz (1973)) At that time Laura has about 50 words or morphemes. The great majority of her multi-morpheme utterances are two morpheme utterances, and almost 90% of the latter are pivot constructions in which the pivot occurs in first position and functions like a prefix, i.e., is separated from the second position morpheme by a gap of .2 seconds or so (*dadogi, dakuki, dabuk*; the prefix *da* is derived from 'that' and is used demonstratively). To start our state description, we assume that for each individual morpheme (*da, dogi, kuki, buk*) there is a particular structure, the *production structure* for that morpheme, which is responsible for the production (articulation) of the morpheme on different occasions. The production structure for morpheme x functions, or is active, when and only when the child utters x. Next consider *dadogi*. The fact that *dadogi* occurs repeatedly (10 times), always with short time lags between *da* and *dogi* (almost all around .1 second), and the fact that in many of the utterances of *dagogi* there is phonetic assimilation of the initial *da* to the *do* of *dogi*, indicates that production of *dadogi* is a highly integrated process, with production of *da* and of *dogi* as sub-processes and suggests that as such it is underlain by a larger structure, the production structure *dadogi*. This larger structure, then, is responsible for the production of *da* and *dogi* in sequence, as an integrated process; it functions normally whenever *dadogi* is produced in the normal fashion.

To model the *dadogi* structure with its two substructures as a simple dynamical system we use the concept of a node (Witz 1972). By definition, a node is an entity which at any moment of time can be at different levels of activation, indexed by numbers between 0 and 1, and which has the additional property that there is a constant $L > 0$ so that if the node is suddenly brought from its rest state to a positive activation level, then in the absence of any other influences it will remain at that activation level for L seconds and then decay. The *dadogi* structure as a whole can then be modelled by a dynamically interconnected complex of 3 nodes, one for *da*, one for *dogi* and a third representing integration of *da* and *dogi* into a single unit and guaranteeing the required sequential and short time lag operation of the two substructures by suitable dynamical coupling to these nodes (see Witz and Duchan 1973, and Witz 1972, for more details).

Other two morpheme sequences with prefix *da* are treated in the same way, and the same holds for other prefixes besides *da*. The system can be made to produce *dadedogi* and *daan*, just like Laura herself, because the node for *de*-integration and the production node for *an* are coupled dynamically to the nodes for *da* and *da*-integration in the same way as the node for *dogi*.

Of course, the production system functions only as part of, and embedded in, other structures, like structures concerned with object manipulation and other person interaction, including both motor patterns like reaching for an object or pointing, eye-head behavior, etc., and intentions, expectations, imaginal activity, etc, behind these motor patterns. As one illustration of such embedded functioning, let me consider a remarkable phenomenon called the beta 1 pattern. The pattern begins with a one or two word utterance xxx coordinated with a gross motor movement. This is followed by a pause of one second or so, during which the child drifts into something like a 'suspended state': there is an overall slowdown of all ongoing motor activity followed by an overall stationary attitude. The latter is finally terminated by a second sound segment (yyy, again coordinated with a gross motor movement). The overall impression is that yyy is an 'after thought'. The beta 1 pattern occurs on the order of 100 times on tapes 1 through 6. I have argued elsewhere (Witz 1973) that at least in a certain subclass of beta 1 occurrences, the beta 1 pattern should be modelled as being due to the 'motions' of a continuous scalar field into which are coupled motor structures concerned with pointing, holding out for showing, reaching, as well as the verbal production structures. More generally, in other beta 1 situations, this field functions somewhat like a buffer between the observable verbal and motor behavior on the one hand and changes of intent or interest (represented by activation in 'activity elements' elsewhere in the system) on the other.

The preceding sketch of a fragment of the state of Laura's language behavior on tapes 1 through 6, when she is 17 and 18 months old, may be compared with the state of affairs on tape 24, when she is 26 months old. (Let me state explicitly that whereas the picture at age 1-5 and 1-6 is supported by immense amounts of data, data-processing, and analysis, the picture for age 2-2 and its relationship to that at age 1-5 and 1-6 is only tentative.) At age 2-2 Laura produces fairly frequently strings of 4, 5, and 6 words which express complete actions and states of affairs (e.g., the equivalent of 'bird gets drink of water', 'that doggie bites hand'). In these utterances the individual words are separated by very short time lags of .1 or .2 seconds, and the words are produced evenly, with even intonation and often with a faint rhythm, until the last word or last two words of the utterance are reached. The latter are then always given the main stress as well as a change in intonation. The faint rhythmic aspect and the even manner of production give the impression, during the early portions of the utterance, that production proceeds as a single steady drive toward a predetermined event, namely the stress-intonation change at the end. In addition to long utterances, some of the prefix constructions common at age 1–6 are also present. The beta 1 phenomenon finally is as common as before except that the initial segment xxx may now be a 2 to 6 word utterance with much less coordination with gross motor movements.

In terms of the systems at age 1–6 that we have discussed, we can say that the verbal production system has become tremendously enlarged and that its functioning has become vastly more complex. We can try to model the new system by using larger and larger substructures which interpenetrate to a greater and greater extent. This would increase the depth of the system (considered as a partially ordered set) from 2 to 4 or 5. However, in the long utterances verbal rhythm and intonation play an active role in holding the utterance together in time. This suggests that the continuous verbal rhythm and intonation systems that exist as independently functioning entities at age 1–6 have invaded, and are now intrinsically functionally intertwined with, the upper regions of the enlarged verbal production system. It is quite unclear at the moment how to conceptualize this mixture, however.

Differences between Laura A and Laura B become still larger when we ask why it is the case that Laura produces words and phrases that are appropriate in the situation – why she says *dadogi* rather than something else. It can be shown that at age 1–6, the mechanisms and structures that are responsible differ almost completely from word to word. To give a simple example, *ma*, a prefix derived from 'my', has at that time a usage which can perhaps be summarized by the phrase 'in connection with this object here, I am a relevant person or agent'. Laura uses *ma* when she discovers or turns back to an object she has some interest in; in social situations, involving several people, when an object is the universal center of attention, to emphasize her own role, etc. Thus, in the verbal production system, the nodes for *ma* and *ma*-integration must be somehow dynamically connected with action systems and general social interaction structures. On the other hand words like *dogi*, *aek* (wet), and *au* (out, in the sense of out of, or of) involve perceptual elements and possibly imaginal activity specific to the word in question, but again each word presents a qualitatively different picture.

At age 2–2, however, Laura seems to have the ability to grasp complex external states of affairs and to keep them in her mind as units. For example, looking at a picture of a woman standing with a bucket near a bush she asks *(beinda)*, 'berries in that?' with equal stress on each syllable and rising intonation on *da*. It is tempting in many of these situations to postulate a new system, which corresponds to 'thinking, or holding in mind, a complex state of affairs as a single unit' and which in addition helps determine the exact sequence of words making up the utterance, perhaps even guiding it during its production. This would mean that most of the structures and mechanisms that are causally involved in initiating the production of a given word at age 1–6 have been superseded by a single more powerful system. And so on.

My aim in this section has been to illustrate what a description of the state of behavior at a given time might look like, and what kind of considerations a comparison of states at successive periods of time might lead to. State descriptions were envisaged exclusively in terms of structures functioning in real time, i.e., in terms of their nature and modes of inter-action as mathematical dynamical systems, and in terms of how their functioning in time is related to observable behavior and environment. By conceptualizing infrastructure and transition in this way, one is led to envisage numerous qualitatively different types of structures; one can trace in detail vast reorganization of existing systems (such as the reorganization of the production system above), as well as the genesis of totally new systems and of totally new modes of dynamical organization (e.g., the mechanisms necessary to initiate verbal production on the basis of mental images and long-term memory of persons, objects, or events, and the systems involved in comprehending a state of affairs that directs production of sentences expressing this state of affairs). Perhaps more important, by trying to recreate the multilevel, temporal organization of ongoing be-havior by means of underlying dynamical systems, we avoid having our constructs on infrastructure and transition tinged with 'content', with categories normally used in an external or objective analysis of subject matter, of a task, or of a piece of apparatus.

Micromodels for the emergence of new structure. Having insisted that, in general, my description of state A and state B should be in terms of dynamical systems corresponding to aspects of behavioral organization and having duly noted continuity and differences between the two states in these terms, however, it has also become obvious that I cannot make much progress on the problem of development in this way. For by simply comparing A and B, I have not explained why the change was to B rather than to some other state B' — I have not explained why development took this particular course. 'Modification of within-structure functioning' of certain structures and of the 'assimilatory characteristics' of certain others; 'growth by addition' of structures and 'reorganization of overall dynamic' (as in the verbal production system); and the 'emergence of completely new kinds of systems' (e.g., systems concerned with internal representation of whole states of affairs) – all these things are after all only superficial descriptions of the difference between state A and state B: they do not touch the springs of development. The very vocabulary used (modification, growth, emergence) is completely general and descriptive and shows no insight into why and how these specific kinds of changes occurred, or why such changes occur in general. More generally in a state A → state B approach, there is always a temptation to compare A and B, to formulate some important difference between A and B that can be read out from the full description of A and B, and then simply to declare the sources of development to be some abstract principle that produces the difference in question (*cf.* the list of principles at the beginning of Van den Daele's paper). Such a procedure would be descriptive, but not explanatory.

To achieve explanatory power, one can (explicitly) embed the organism as it exists in state A in an environment, and then try to show that under suitable long-term assumptions on the larger system consisting of the organism in state A and the environment, state A must indeed necessarily transform into state B, and the abstract principle must therefore indeed hold. This is done for example by Simon (1973) for the principle of increase in hierarchical structure. Now my own bias, and I think that it is also Piaget's, is to try to explain the potentiality of change toward state B that is inherent in the organism when it is in state A in terms of *intrinsic qualities of biological tissue* – the intrinsic ability of biological tissue to become organized into new functioning systems, regardless whether this tissue is unorganized substrate or whether it is part of the physical system underlying already existing organization of behavior. (This ability is not an absolute characteristic of any particular level of biological organization, e.g., the cell level, but must be seen anew and differently at many levels.) In terms of the approach mentioned at the beginning of this paragraph, therefore, my bias is to try to build conceptualizations and models which highlight this specific quality of biological tissue.

Although I am not very far along on these problems, let me at least illustrate what I have in mind with an abstract example, which I will dub 'micromodels of the emergence of new functioning'. Imagine a functioning system in the form a cylinder, with ends A and B, which normally functions as follows: Upon suitable stimulation at A, a plane wave of excitation travels slowly and with constant speed from A to B. In addition, after the wave front has passed a given point, excitation at that point will stay high for a second or so and then decay. Call this sytem M. We can think of M as a simplified version of a structure underlying a complex motor behavior pattern such as picking up an object and setting it somewhere else to have a better look at it. That is, M is really made up of several components that operate in a coordinated fashion (represented by the points inthe cylinder): Activity in the components progresses in an orderly way across the system as a whole, and each component operates for a period of about 1 second.

Now assume that M is embedded in a sea of 'micro-elements'. Each element is assumed to be small compared to M, and to have the property that, once excited, it will stay excited for L_0 seconds, where L_0 is small compared to 1. In addition, neighboring elements may interact, but no others. The system of micro-elements will be considered as a 'substrate' within which M operates and will be denoted by M^1. The (three-dimensional) space in which M and M^1 are embedded here, as well as the cylinder shape of M, are of course fictitious and are only used to suggest a functional connectivity in M and M^1.

Now depending on the kind of interaction envisaged, it is not too difficult to set down a simple set of axioms on how neighboring elements must be coupled so that the substrate of microelements as a whole, M^1, functions in the same way as M: That is, when stimulated near A, a wavefront will move with the same constant speed to B, and once it has passed a given micro-element, excitation in that element will stay high for a second or so and then decay. Given this neighbor-neighbor coupling scheme, call it S, one can then set up a second system of axioms, which spell out in what manner repeated operation of the system M is to slowly modify any existing coupling between the micro-elements in order to eventually produce S. Combining these two systems of axioms, then, one has a model for explaining how repeated functioning of M can organize an unstructured substrate M^1 in such a way that it begins to function like M.

The importance, in principle, of this kind of model is clear. M organizes an unstructured substrate M^1 so that it functions like M, and hence the combined system of axioms is in fact a model for the 'emergence of new functioning' (in the substrate). Further, this organizational act by M is possible only because of intrinsic biological properties of the substrate – the generic properties of individual micro-elements, the type of interaction permitted between neighboring elements, and the fact that the existing coupling can be slowly modified as time goes on. And finally, this kind of mechanism might explain many things. For example, because it functions like M, M^1 might be regarded as embodying a different representation of the same knowledge that is embodied in M. After M^1 has come into existence, it might start to operate independently, without M – a ghost or internalized version of M. In fact M itself might die away and its ghost remain. As a scientific approach, however, this kind of model is seriously flawed. The basic thinking in it is too spatial-mechanical. Perhaps as a result, it does not come to grips with the plasticity of development in general.

Long-term memory. In the preceding section I said that if in the study of the development of behavior we take as our basic aim to develop some understanding of the infinite ability of biological tissue to become organized or reorganized into new types of functioning systems, the state A $\rightarrow$ state B paradigm becomes much less important. There is a second set of considerations which suggest that an exclusively state A $\rightarrow$ state B based approach not only misses some really basic problems but may lead to a quite inadequate overall conception of development.

Let me begin with a deep fact about development which was first driven home to me by Shirk (1973). Shirk was studying in depth four beginning teachers (college sophomores doing practice teaching in an elementary school): how they conceived of teaching and of the role of the teacher, how they conceived of the subject matter (mathematics), how they handled children's questions or unexpected confusions in class, how they prepared their lessons, etc. Reading these case studies one cannot fail to be struck by the fact that in each person, innumerable behavior patterns at many different levels have subtle affinities for one another and coexist as if in some strange harmony. For example, one of the subjects, Tom, judging by term papers of his on 'what is mathematics' and on 'the essence of teaching,' conceives of mathematics as an ordered system of propositions and considers the basic role of the teacher to be to establish in his students belief in these propositions. This has affinities with his tendency to interpret a student's failure with a particular point as indicating a need for more explanations by the teacher on appropriate principles that had been covered earlier. It also has affinities with his tendency to keep on going over the previous principles persistently, and trying not to get sidetracked, until the student performs as he should. (For details, see the discussion of some specific classroom episodes on p. 45 ff. The term 'has affinity with' here is essential; alternatives such as 'is presupposed by' or 'implies' are misleading.) The impression one gets reading these case studies, then, is that the whole organism at the given time period is a gigantic stable organization, permeated by affinities through and through, and thus with an unbelievable cohesion. Each structure is in harmony with many others, so that on the one hand it is impossible to intervene and change a single one (it would be immediately regenerated by the remaining system), and on the other hand, even a small change propagates deeply into the whole system.

Now this picture of the total behavioral organization of the organism as being mysteriously 'in harmony' at any one time period must be understood in relation to 'long-term build up' and 'long-term memory'. Long-term continuous accumulation or build up is illustrated by the way a small child becomes accustomed to a room or to a new toy – by degrees, over a period of days or weeks. It is gauged by the way a child operates in the room, by the way he handles the toy, by the way in which he takes room or toy for granted, and by the gross time structure of this behavior over a period of days or weeks, and it is not assumed to involve conscious recall, or mental imagery, of features or aspects of the room or the toy. One often says that in long-term continuous accumulation, there is something which actually does accumulate or get built up, *viz.* an internal representation of the room, or of the toy. This way of speaking seems to be completely misleading.

It is clear that in very small children (age ≤ 2 years), a very large proportion of what one would call long-term memory implied in ordinary, everyday behavior comes in the form of long-term continuous accumulation – e.g. the long-term memory needed to operate in various spatial environments in and out of the house, the familiarity needed to participate in, and take for granted, various daily routines with the members of the family, etc. And we must assume that long-term continuous accumulation somehow affects and nourishes all the structures of intelligence, beginning with sensory motor schemes. J. McV. Hunt pointed out to me that almost all the breakthroughs in problem solving that are reported in *The Origins of Intelligence* occurred with very familiar objects, concerning which the infant had had plenty of opportunity to build up a 'long-term model'. This suggests not only that the sensory motor structures, modelled by dynamical systems as in the first section, function over a continuous background of long-term continuous accumulation, but that perhaps the very unfolding and emergence of these structures (the schema for removing obstacles, the schema of the stick) can only be understood as proceeding in a medium of long-term continuous accumulation perhaps at low and global perceptual and motor levels of organization. My view here is thus not that long-term memory is an end product of growth, a repository of all a person's knowledge about the world and that person's representation of the world, but instead that long-term memory in the form of long-term continuous accumulation is the very fabric of growth. As such, it cannot be approached in a state A → state B paradigm. Returning to Shirk's dissertation, the great harmony and cohesion of structures in an individual at each time must be viewed as being continuously achieved at each time within a process of long-term continuous accumulation. That is, if we try to think of the organism over a period of years as a single whole, we must think of it as a single object, a single substance which at each point is determined both by the possible modes of coexistence and interpenetration of diverse modes of organization and their embodiments (structures), and by long-term continuous accumulation. To comprehend the organism over time as a single whole is an object of epistemology. For that reason, the problems discussed in this and the preceding section are the same problems that Piaget has been trying to deal with under the name equilibration.

C. A VIEW OF COGNITION FROM A FORMALIST'S PERSPECTIVE

by Juan Pascual-Leone,* *York University, Toronto, Canada*

In its ordinary sense the word *cognition* refers to a specific capability of the psychological system, namely, the capacity to know and the structures and mechanisms underlying this function. That definition, however, loses some of its appealing clarity when we notice that other supposedly different aspects of the psychological system like learning, perception, and motivation, have also to do with knowledge and knowing in various ways. Indeed, as Rapaport (1959) pointed out some 15 years ago, the process of theorizing in psychology is such that specific functional aspects or capabilities of the psychological system are usually taken by theoreticians as the initial domain of inquiry and as a sufficient data base for the development of theories. These theories, however, exhibit a very strong expansionary tendency: While they start by being specific, i.e., by applying to perception, thinking, learning, or motivation, they rapidly grow into a motivational general theory of psychology, or a perceptual, problem-solving, or learning one. Examples of such reductionistic general theories are too well-known to be mentioned.

A better alternative to this reductionistic theorizing would be to attempt to formulate theories which are truly general from the start, i.e., which from the start contain a representation of the various aspects of the psychological system, such as problem solving, thinking, learning, perception, motivation, and cognitive development. Although detailed arguments cannot be provided here, a truly from-the-start general theory of this sort would have to be a constructive theory and have to maximally satisfy the list of requirements presented below. The constructive theory notion and its corresponding requirements are deeply rooted in the epistemological tradition of cognitive psychology.

The paper will present first the concept of a constructive theory followed by the corresponding requirements. Then three classes or types of

* I am grateful to my students J. Burits, G. Parkinson, S. Pulos, and R. Logan for their advice and assistance in the preparation of this paper. For her gracious last minute help I am grateful to D.A. Signori. I owe thanks for particularly thoughtful comments on an earlier version of the paper to J. Burtis, Dr. Robbie Case, Dr. E. Neimark, and Dr. G. Toussaint.

constructive general theories (i.e., purely structural, process structural, and organismic structural) will be presented and briefly discussed.

Requirements of any adequate general constructive theory in psychology. To be constructive the theory should function as a conceptual gadget capable of simulating the genesis in the subject of his performances, i.e., capable of deriving these data, by means of a 'rational reconstruction' (Carnap 1929) carried out on the theory's symbolic medium. A rational reconstruction explains the data by way of exhibiting the genesis of their construction. This notion of structural simulation of data genesis is the implicit kernel and criterion of success of the constructive method. Such a constructive definition of explanation, proposed by Carnap (1929) and well established in modern mathematics and physics, has only recently become explicit in psychology largely through the work of structuralists (.*cf* Piaget 1970a), or computer-simulation psychologists (e.g., Newell and Simon 1972; Newell 1972) and mathematical psychologists (e.g., Restle and Greeno 1970). A theory should be called constructive if and only if it aims at rational reconstructions of data on its symbolic medium. Constructive theories are contrasted by Piaget (1968, 1970a) with what he calls *reductionistic theories*, namely, theories which aim at empirical prediction of data based on analogic relations assumed to exist between the to-be-explained performance and some other well-known performances of the subject. An example of reductionistic theory is mediational learning theory which reduces the mental-processing performance of the subject to the empirical conditioning paradigm.

To get a concrete image of what a rational reconstruction is, you could think of Piaget's logical models, of the mathematical-learning models which follow the tradition of Estes and Restle, of Chomsky's grammars or of the computer-simulation models from the school of Newell and Simon.

To be adequate a general constructive theory must satisfy maximally the following ten requirements:

1. *A general constructive theory must reflect separately both the structure of the subject's psychological system (rather than the structure of the data itself) and the structure of the relevant situations as construed by the subject.* Indeed, the whole purpose of a constructive psychological theory is to model or reflect[1] the subject's internal functional organization

---

1. A scientific theory (or a mental structure) can be said to be semantically adequate when its structure actively *reflects* or models, up to a given pragmatically sufficient level,

(i.e., his psychological system) in order to rationally reconstruct the genesis of the subject's performance. Notice that to carry out this reconstruction the scientist also needs to have, or to have inferred, a description of the situation as construed by the subject's psychological system.

Since it is so central to constructive theorizing, I define a new term, metasubject (MS), for referring to the subject's psychological system, i.e., the internal functional organization – the psychological machinery of the subject. Using this new term, we can briefly state: A useful constructive theory must contain a description of the subject's MS and also a metasubjective representation or description of all the relevant tasks.

This requirement of constructive theories stands in contrast with the simpler requirement of reductionist theories (e.g., empiricist behaviorism). Reductionist theories need not and usually do not describe the structure of the metasubject or the metasubjective task structure; they describe in a generalized, more or less formal, manner the structure of the task and the structure of the subject's performance as viewed by the scientist observer. This observer's description is carried out by means of empirical constructs, concrete (concepts) or abstract (rules), and leads to the creation of situation-specific theories, more or less general. The constructive theories must use purely theoretical constructs in addition to the empirical ones in order to represent the MS system. However, if they are successful the constructive theories turn out to be invariant across situations because the subject's MS system is invariant this way. As a consequence of the different methods of theory building two very different ways of making predictions ensue. The reductionist theories base their predictions mainly on empirical generalizations of earlier data because the theories themselves are but formalized empirical abstractions

---

the structure of the reality for which it stands. This notion of active reflection has been emphasized by early logical semanticists (e.g., Frege– see Walker 1965; Carnap 1929, 1953) and Marxists, by Piaget with the concept of reflective abstraction (Beth and Piaget 1961; Piaget 1970b, 1970c) and by 'cognitive' epistemologists (e.g., Polanyi 1958; Watanabe 1969; Ullmo 1958; Quine 1972; Bunge 1972).

Acceptance of the epistemological notion of active reflection (reflective abstraction) does not commit the scientist to any metaphysical assumption regarding the structure of reality, beyond a weak form of materialism (i.e., the acceptance of the existence of reality constraints). Indeed, imagine an ideal observer who could foresee the structure of the ultimately valid theory or theories. For this ideal observer the principle of active reflection would merely say that a theory is true (can yield valid predictions) to the extent that its structure approximates the structure of the to-be-discovered ultimately valid theory or theories. Thus formulated the metaphysical assumptions disappear.

from the data; the mechanism of their predictions is therefore the instantiation of a logical class (a new object or datum is recognized as being a member of the old class – the empirical construct). The mechanism of prediction in constructive theories on the other hand approximates more closely the derivation of a theorem in an axiomatic system or, even better, the determination of the output of some mechanical cybernetic device.

For this reason, a constructive theory which produces valid rational reconstructions can do so only because it reflects the underlying relevant processes of the MS which generated the data. Also, in order to set up what corresponds to the initial conditions on which the mechanical device operates, the constructive theory must reflect the relevant aspects of the situation where the data was produced (*cf.* Carnap 1929; Beth and Piaget 1961; Newell and Simon 1972; Minsky and Papert 1972; Papert 1973; Bunge 1972). Thus a constructive theory must reflect the structure of the relevant situation as represented by the metasubject.

The part of the theory which reflects the structure of the subject's MS is called the general model; the part of the theory which reflects the relevant situation as construed by the subject's MS is the specific model (in that it is specific to the given situation).

2. *The theory should be invariant across situations for a given type of subject.* This requirement means that the theory, i.e., the general model, should be capable of representing and deriving the relevant data regularities or invariances found in the performance of subjects across different situations, i.e., across different specific models. Which data regularities are relevant for a theoretical derivation is, of course, a function of the intended use or implicit purpose of the to-be-developed theory. This requirement explicitly holds only for a given type of subject in order to allow the possibility of a general model which reflects individual differences, i.e., which changes according to the subject's type.

3. *As the constructive theory has to be a theory of human psychology it must be general enough to apply in principle to any human being.* By virtue of requirements 1 and 2, it follows that the theory should be capable of constructively deriving human individual differences such as age differences, cognitive styles, learning capabilities, affective and personality factors, etc. This derivation should be carried out by means of general constructs or metaconstructs presenting different concrete instantiations or different parameter values. This notion that a general theory would have to account for individual differences was pointed out by Lewin

(1951) and by Tolman (1932, 1961) and has been emphasized ever since by various people (e.g., Cronbach 1957).

4. *As the structure of the general constructive theory must reflect the structure of the subject's MS (requirement 1) and as the theory must be applicable to all human beings (3), the theory must reflect the MS of the scientist himself.* The scientist's MS includes his knowing processes. It follows that the dynamic structure of the theory must be interpretable as a valid epistemology. That is, when thus interpreted it must provide possible guidelines for a scientific methodology. This link between a constructive psychology and epistemology was pointed out by Lewin and Piaget and has more recently been suggested by various epistemologists and logicians (e.g., Polanyi 1958; Ullmo 1958; Quine 1972; Rozeboom 1973). Furthermore, if the scientist's knowing processes are a reflection of his metasubjective structures then some syntactical structures of formal systems reflect the metasubject.

5. *If the constructive theory is to be explicitly stated or formalized, then the technical language used for describing the explicit theory cannot be chosen arbitrarily because the structure of this linguistic description must, in its relevant aspects, be isomorphic with the very structure of the MS which the theory is meant to reflect.* Since a constructive theory is a theory about the MS (see 1), I will call the technical language in which such a theory is expressed the MS language. The requirement states that the structure of the MS language and the structure of the MS itself must be isomorphic. This is a general requirement for any language designed to optimally reflect a given subject matter. Such requirement of structural reflection was stated by Frege (Walker 1965; Geach and Black 1966) and by the early Carnap (1929) and has been emphasized by a good number of epistemologists and philosophers of science (Polanyi 1958; Ullmo 1958; Carnap 1958; Quine 1960, 1972; Bunge 1972; Hanson 1970; Feyerabend 1970, etc.). In the context of mathematics this structural-reflection aspect of representation has been emphasized by modern measurement theory (Krantz and Tversky 1971; Krantz, Luce, Suppes and Tversky 1971) and by the modern theory of induction (Polya 1957; Watanabe 1969, among others). In the context of psychology it was clearly sensed by Lewin (1951), Tolman (1932) and perhaps the early Skinner (1938); it has been explicitly stated by Piaget (1968), by Brunswik (1956), and by Newell and Simon (1972; Newell 1973) among others.

6. Humans cannot keep in mind too many ideas or perform too many activities at the same time; their behavior and cognitive processes are

forced to become serially organized. It follows that *constructive theories must adopt an MS language which is capable of representing the step-by-step temporal unfolding of behavior and of the mental processes.* (Simon 1962; Newell 1972; Newell and Simon 1972).

Although Piaget and Chomsky have both pointed out the temporal character of behavior and its structural characteristics, they have chosen formal representations of it which violate the present requirement. This fact illustrates the difficulties involved in developing a time-sensitive, i.e., process-structural psychological formalism.

7. *As the structures of a valid constructive theory must be reflected in the structure of the language used to express the theory (requirement 5), the assumption may be made that some of the general syntactical characteristics shared by all constructive theories are nothing but reflections of basic structural characteristics shared by all MSs.* The structural characteristics referred to are, for example, the existence of arguments, of predicates, and of transformation operators. This assumption amounts to the idea that these logical syntactical features are in fact psychological universals. This idea was introduced in modern psychology by Piaget (1953) using a different terminology. The idea, however, in a much stronger version, has been made popular by Chomsky (1968) and others (*cf.* Bever 1970) who independently proposed it in the context of language.

8. *A truly general constructive theory which is consistent must be capable of explaining the production of truly novel behavior* – behavior which is neither mere transfer of learning or novel integration of pre-existent learned units, nor innately determined. This capacity to explain truly novel behavior is necessary in order to avoid what could be called the learning paradox, namely: (a) The subject's production of a given acquired behavior is frequently attributed to previous learning even though (i) the behavior in question has never before been produced by the MS, (ii) such a behavior is complex and improbable enough not to have been produced by 'chance'. (b) Yet all learning theories agree that a behavior cannot be learned by a subject before he has ever had the opportunity to produce a simple instance of it. To say otherwise (this is the learning paradox) is to imply that learning can take place without experience. This paradox can be resolved by concluding that truly novel behavior does exist and that it is produced by organismic factors different from learning. To be consistent, a general constructive theory must include a representation of organismic-structural factors other than learning to account for truly novel behavior.

9. *In a general constructive theory, the theoretical description of the MS should be, as much as possible, a structural description, with minimal reference to content.* There are at least three reasons for this requirement: (a) A theory which did not satisfy this requirement could not be invariant across situations, and across human subjects. (b) A desirable goal is for the explanations and predictions of the theory to be carried out, as far as possible, in a purely mechanical way, i.e., as if by someone who does not know anything about the subject matter of the theory but those aspects which the theory explicitly states. This type of explanation and prediction is only possible when the constructs are defined structurally rather than with reference to the content which they are meant to explain. (c) The theory can be properly communicated to other persons who are not already quite familiar with the content of the theory. Further clarification of this third reason will be provided below.

Although the scientist's aim is to seek structural formulations, the reader must notice that content cannot be given up entirely. Somewhere in the informational loop interconnecting the community of scientists with their object of inquiry, there must exist a point where an explicit reference to verifiable content, a point of contact with the concrete, is made (*cf.* Mandelbrot 1959; Quine 1960, 1972). This minimal reference to content (or to a protocol description shared by the community of scientists) appears in the language used among scientists for talking about the structural linguistic description which constitutes the explicit theory. Henceforth this language used will be called *U language* of the observer (Cury 1963).

If a theory T is being communicated by a scientist A to a scientist B and if T is new to B, B will *not* to able to understand T unless, in the very process of communication, the necessary cognitive structures are tacitly taught by A to B. Notice that there are two types of cognitive structures required: (a) The one representing the empirical content of the theory, i.e. its referential domains and the semantic features or criteria needed to use the constructs appropriately and (b) the deep meaning or network of relations interconnecting the constructs of T. The structural teaching of T in the communication process can take place only if three conditions are satisfied: (a) The theory must be, in the act of communication, formulated mainly in terms of structures because a structure (i.e., an invariant defined by a system of relations holding among token elements which is preserved when the specific set of elements is changed) is communicated independently of the speaker's and listener's private meanings for the linguistic token elements (i.e., the construct names) among which the structure holds. This independence would obviously not be preserved if the more traditional nominal formulations, i.e., formulations using non-relational lexical definitions and undefined names, were used in the communication process in lieu of the structural ones. (b) The total structure of the linguistic formulation of T must be similar to the structure of the deep meaning of T. The reason for this second condition is to ensure that the irrelevant structural constraints of an inadequate, arbitrarily chosen linguistic formulation do not interfere with the structural communication process. (c) B must go through a scientific empirical apprenticeship (*cf.* Polanyi 1958; Kuhn 1962) in order to acquire the content-structures of T.

The recent emphasis on structural representation in modern human sciences, the emphasis on 'procedures' and 'descriptions' in artificial intelligence research (Minsky and Papert 1972; Minsky 1973; Papert 1973) and Bunge's notion of 'model object' in the philosophy of science (1972) are but three examples illustrating how much modern cognitive-epistemological research is consistent with though not always aware of the structural principle given above.

10. *A general constructive theory satisfying all the requirements given above would have to have, within the same MS organization, two different structural systems: A situation-specific semantic-pragmatic 'automaton' by the system of schemes, superschemes, etc.* (i.e., the system of situation-specific subjective units or concrete constructs), *and a system of higher-order or deeper organismic factors organized according to little-known dialectic or context-sensitive laws.* The system of schemes is like an automaton because it seems to be syntactically stable, i.e., its structure and its generative properties are invariant across time for as long as learning or other deeper (higher-order) factors do not affect them. This syntactical stability makes the system of schemes come analogically closer to the formal notion of cybernetic automata. This cybernetic-like system should be a semantic-pragmatic one because each one of its situation-specific constructs or schemes must be constituted by a bundle of pragmatically relevant blueprints corresponding to percepts and/or beliefs and/or expectations and/or actions and/or plans and/or affects. For any scheme, the bundle of pragmatically relevant blueprints can be elicited by features of the input-features which confirm (as a semantic truth-function would) the scheme, in its propensity to activate and apply to determine performance.

The deeper organismic system is constituted by factors which could be called 'metaconstructs'. The function of these factors is to operate on the repertoire of subjective units or schemes in order to combine or *modify* their behavioral consequences. As the situation-specific schemes of the repertoire are concrete constructs and the organismic-structural factors which modify their manifestations are abstract, it seems appropriate to call the latter metaconstructs. One example of such a metaconstruct might be learning, and requirement (8) states that there must be at least one more metaconstruct, in order to explain truly novel behavior. Requirement (3) also explicitly states the necessity for the deeper system of metaconstructs.

In contrast to the automaton-like system of schemes, the deep dialectic or context-sensitive system of metaconstructs may well be syntactically unstable or at least structurally so complex as to make impossible the detailed formalization of its generative properties. This complexity exists because the external context (the input and/or the internal context (the current state of the constellation of schemes and other organismic factors) can affect the system's output, i.e., the system's influence on the next current state of the subordinate scheme system. Perhaps the deep system of metaconstructs may only *at present* be represented as a 'dialectic' or 'extra-logical' process (Riegel 1973; Watanabe 1973), or by means of equivalently useful but obscure formulations such as Freud's principle of unconscious overdetermination of behavior, Tolman's performance vectors and schematic sowbug (1932, 1961), Gestaltist principles of structuration, Piaget's equilibration principle, or theories of cognitive consistency (Abelson, Aronson, McGuire, *et al.* 1968).[2]

A classification of constructive theories. Call metasubjective a theory which attempts to satisfy the ten requirements given above. Only such a theory could hope to reflect adequately the functional structure of the MS. No present-day constructive theory in the psychological literature is metasubjective. Modern constructive theories satisfy, however, some of the

2. In logic semantics studies the relations between symbols and their meanings, which psychologically interpreted correspond to the relations between the constructs (schemes) and their 'meaning', i.e., the network of other constructs with which they are related (Riegel 1970; Lindsay and Norman 1972). Pragmatics studies the relations between the symbols and the humans using them; thus, psychologically, pragmatics corresponds to the relations between the schemes of a subject and the expectations vis-à-vis the environment, which the subject can produce by virtue of these schemes, including the process of human communications (Hass 1974).

requirements given above. Depending upon which requirements they satisfy, and to what extent, theories can be classified in different types. Consider the following three nonexclusive classes of constructive theories: purely structural, process-structural, and organismic-structural. A constructive theory is *purely structural* if it violates requirement (6) (and possibly some others as well); i.e., its MS language is incapable of explicitly representing the step-by-step temporal unfolding of the subject's (mental or overt) behavior. Most of the available structural theories are of this type. Piaget's models, say of conservation, or of concrete/formal logic, are of this type because they define the child's competence and yet they never analyze this problem-solving process in a step-by-step manner. Chomsky's psycholinguistic models and even many recent models of structural semantics belong also to this type. A constructive theory is *process-structural (cf.* Simon 1962; Newell 1972) if it requirements (1) and (6) and satisfies in part requirement (9) (and possibly some others as well). Such a theory can attempt to simulate in its MS language the step-by-step process underlying the unfolding of behavior. The literature offers excellent examples of process-structural models in the work of Newell, Simon, and their followers (Newell and Simon 1972; Klahr and Wallace 1970, 1972, 1973; Klahr 1973; Baylor, Gascon, Lemoyne and Pothier 1973). Finally a constructive theory is *organismic-structural* if it satisfies requirement (1) and satisfies in part requirements (9) and (10) and possibly others. The aspect of (10) which must be satisfied is the representation in its MS language of at least some metaconstructs in addition to the theory's subjective units or constructs. Concepts such as 'habit strength', 'drive', 'composition of vectors', 'autochthonous field forces', 'adaptation level', 'intelligence', 'problem space', 'central processor', etc., are all metaconstructs.

A constructive theory is metasubjective if it aims to maximally satisfy the whole ten requirements. A metasubjective theory is at the same time process-structural and organismic-structural.

The followers of Piaget at Geneva, led by Professor Inhelder, seem by now to be aware of the purely structural character of Piaget's classic formulations; they are seeking to develop what Inhelder calls 'dynamic models' i.e., process-structural ones to complement Piaget's formulations (*cf.* Inhelder 1972; Céllérier 1972). Likewise, psycholinguists seem by now to be aware of the limitations of Chomsky's and other purely linguistic models (e.g., Bever 1970; Bransford and Johnson 1973; Trabasso 1973).

Computer-simulation and artificial-intelligence investigators however frequently write as if they believe that their models are metasubjective (Klahr and Wallace 1972; Klahr 1973; Minsky and Papert 1972; Papert 1973). Such optimism is understandable given their impressive recent achievements. To introduce some more clarity, consider briefly some arguments suggesting that neither the MIT researchers, inspired by Minsky and Papert, nor the Carnegie-Mellon school led by Simon and Newell, have yet reached the level of MS theorizing. In the first case (Minsky and Papert 1972; Papert 1973) their description-manipulating procedures, and structural descriptions, together with the many concrete programs based on these ideas, provide profound observer's analyses of central processes in perception, learning, and problem-solving. These process-structural models cannot however be considered metasubjective in the light of the following three arguments:

(a) These models (i.e., their programming systems) do not contain a representation of the discrete, relatively autonomous and highly active, metasubjective units of information which psychology has found necessary to posit (e.g., habits, traces, forces, operants, IRM/action patterns, unconscious wishes, schemes, chunks, etc.). To the extent that this tradition of psychology is valid, the MIT work is still lacking. Newell and Simon are superior in this regard because their recent programing system is based on productions – a programing concept which represents well the metasubjective unit of information. Newell and Simon (1972, p. 804) offer thoughtful arguments in support of this notion. (b) The work of the MIT group leaves unanswered the issue of how the psychological system comes to develop the procedures and descriptions it needs to perceive, learn, and problem-solve. As hierarchical control structures are needed to monitor the 'learning processes' they describe, the issue of the emergence of these structures remains unsolved. In other words, truly novel behavior is not explained by the MIT group. (c) The constraints of other organismic factors such as short-term memory, motivation, and development are not represented in their work.

Consider now briefly the models of the Carnegie-Mellon school. To see why these models cannot at present be considered properly metasubjective it suffices to notice the following : (a) Perceptual or representative processes, learning, affective processes, and development, i.e., aspects of the human data which reflect organismic constructs, are not included in the theory. (b) The main theoretical notions in addition to that of the long-term memory, are: (i) the notion of a production which corresponds to the Piagetian concept of scheme (*cf.* Pascual-Leone and Smith 1969; Pascual-

Leone 1970); (ii) the notion of a production system which corresponds to a task-specific repertoire of schemes which is organized or monitored by a goal-system. The goal-system corresponds to a Piagetian (or neo-Piagetian) system of operational or 'executive' schemes; (iii) the notion of a short-term memory which serves the double function of production releaser and of short-term store of the output of previous productions. Short-term memory is supposed to contain data structures which stand for the unknown perceptual and representational processes; the productions are conceived as operators which operate on the data structures to test and to modify them. Of these notions only short-term memory in its function as storing device can be considered to be an organismic factor or metaconstruct. (c) Yet there are clear symptoms in the limitations of the theory suggesting that more metaconstructs are needed. In addition to (a) the most important of these symptoms may be the theory's inability to account for the emergence of new productions. That is, truly novel behavior in the sense described in requirement (8) cannot be explained at present by the Carnegie-Mellon theory. This deficiency suggests a lack of necessary metaconstructs and leads the theory to fall under the learning-paradox contradiction.

D. SOME INGREDIENTS FOR CONSTRUCTING DEVELOPMENTAL MODELS*

by Roy Freedle, *Educational Testing Service, Princeton*

We can become profoundly discouraged by our inability to describe not only the necessary and sufficient conditions for development to occur, but also our inability to give a detailed account of the process itself by which this transformation from one stage to another is carried out. It is some relief to note that several older sciences are plagued by similar limitations. Thus we find that evolutionists cannot predict *when* a new species will emerge nor *what* it will look like when it does emerge; also they cannot tell us *how* new species manage to arise almost instantaneously. In a related vein, chemists are now struggling to describe the minute steps by which high-speed chemical changes occur. The chemists probably can state necessary and sufficient conditions for their reactions to occur but they are still hard at work describing the minute *processes* by which the substeps are carried out. I mention these presumed facts only to remind us that there is nothing peculiar about our state of ignorance in describing developmental change nor is there any reason to be embarrassed by wide-ranging speculations about the kinds of models we think may be important in guiding our thinking on developmental change. What I shall outline below are three broad concerns that I find important in discussing development: (a) whether developmental theory has a need for probabilistic aspects in model construction or not; (b) whether developmental theory should be sensitive to situational constraints; and (c) whether there is a need for a separate analysis of task requirements and another analysis of the developing organism's ability to meet the obligatory features of the task.

Probabilistic considerations. Implicit in the above comments about necessary and sufficient conditions for change to occur is the philosophic problem of scientific determinism. If we frame our developmental model so that we require *all* uncertainty of change to be accounted for by stating algebraic conditions for transitions to occur, then we have, whether we realize it or not, committed ourselves to a nonprobabilistic model of

* I would like to thank Irving Sigel for a critical reading of this paper.

development. This may or may not be correct. If probabilistic indeterminacy is present in some developmental changes, then allowing for this possibility will alter the kinds of models that we attempt to construct. Indeed, some months ago I planned to present a stochastic Markov process model so as to account for moral development data. My quantitative focus just that brief time ago stemmed from a belief in the correctness of a probabilistic viewpoint for explaining much developmental data. While I now seek to question this viewpoint there is a sense in which uncertainty always enters into developmental data – it has to do with errors of measurement. For example errors in assigning a child to one of several developmental stages will, if we get fussy enough, force us to graft onto any algebraic (all-or-none) model a probabilistic process that accounts for errors in assigning subjects to stages. There are other levels of a developmental model that may or may not require probabilistic mechanisms to operate – for example, accounting for why the same person in repeated presentations will sometimes be correct and sometimes incorrect in responding to what is (or what seems to be) an identical situation. This type of uncertainty *within* the individual being tested or observed has occurred often enough that other theorists have given it a name – decalage. Do we wish to explain this variance by introducing probabilistic assumptions somewhere in our developmental model or do we wish to explain it by invoking algebraic criteria by which we attempt to capture what was unique about each response which the subject made? It's a hard choice to make, and it's a critical choice since it will affect the ways we theorize about developmental transformations. I will touch upon this issue again later.

Let me return to the Markovian model so as to give you a taste of why I began to question whether this type of modelling necessarily clarifies developmental transformations. To make a long story short I got what can be regarded as a good fit of model to data. The data incidentally were Kohlberg's (1971) data on moral development obtained for the U.S. and Great Britain for several socioeconomic and age levels. The only piece of this model that I wish to comment on at this time is the use of a construct of a 'critical moral event' which I was forced to invent so as to explicate the psychological significance of taking the Markovian transition matrix of probabilities to higher 'powers'. (See Freedle and Lewis 1971 for examples of Markovian theory.) With the passage of time the number of critical 'events' had to increase; this was reflected in the fact that older groups of subjects required a higher power of the matrix to fit their data than did younger groups of subjects. This assumption plus another probabilistic one allowed me to fit most of the data reported by Kohlberg for the two countries and the several socioeconomic and age groups. The singularly important question though is what did I learn about the developmental process of moral development from having applied this stochastic theory to group data? The sad truth is that I learned very little, or more accurately, I learned that from fitting grouped data I could say nothing important about the *internal* mechanisms and their transformations which elevated the *individual* from one stage to a higher stage. Looking at this from another point of view, I can now say that while it may be appropriate to postulate probabilistic mechanisms so as to account for the properties of grouped data, and while knowing the parameters of populations may have its uses, one should not confuse this type of modeling group data with an explication of the cognitive processes within an individual that undergo change. This is not to say that other quantitative theorists should eschew Markovian models in developmental theory – it only means that my particular use of Markovian theory for the moral development data had a very restricted outcome with respect to clarifying individual development. This realization led me to become more cautious in acceptance of probabilistic models of development.

To sum up the first point, developmental theorists implicitly or explicitly commit themselves to a choice between determinacy in developmental description as opposed to indeterminacy. Given the latter choice, there are at least three 'levels' at which indeterminacy can operate: (a) measurement errors in classifying responses by their stage characteristics; (b) variation in responses under experimentally 'identical' conditions; and (c) distributional variation resulting from considering the group characteristics of individuals classified by age, sex, etc. A particular probabilistic model may implicate any or all of these three levels.

Situational constraints. A second major issue for consideration in developmental theory construction is the following: How much of the situational setting in which behavior occurs must be taken into account before the experimenter or theorist assigns the observed person to a developmental stage; and, in related fashion, how much of the current situational setting influences the subject's current behavior?

The second part of this issue may sound redundant but it isn't, as I shall attempt to show. Before doing so, let's first consider why it may be important to study situational setting. This concept has been used increasingly in various developmental accounts. For example, Lois Bloom (1970) has argued that immediate context is necessary to separate out the several meanings of what seems on the surface to be the same utterance of a child. Situational setting has been shown by Lewis and Freedle (1973) to influence the transitional probability of mother-infant vocalization interactions when the infant is only 3 months old. Aebli (1973) has employed situational context in experimental settings to account for decalage effects in general developmental theory.

If one grants that the concept of the situation has explanatory value, one must at the same time admit to a certain inadequacy in defining just what is meant by a situation. Let's examine this problem. Suppose I ask you to give a situational description of what's happening right now in this conference room. Someone may define the situation by the following description: (a) a talk is being delivered; or (b) a developmental talk is being delivered by one person in the morning to an audience of *n* persons; or (c) a segment of a developmental talk is being given at the University of Michigan by one person with *k* other potential speakers listening in while a group of *n* persons in the audience shift about in restive fashion, and so on. These examples, while arranged in order of increasing specificity (both with regard to the mentioning of supposedly important features of time, place, and momentary composition of social structure) need not have been so ordered. The fact that all of them may be correct descriptions of the 'situation' raises the issue of how much of the setting and how long a duration of time needs to be implicated in trying to define any situational setting. Perhaps the answer is: the definition is *relative* to what one's scientific purposes are and *relative* to what the subject's momentary goals are. Thus if one's theory says that discrimination among situations *x*, *y*, and *z* are the only important discriminations, then an adequate situational definition with respect to such a theory would be one which allows for an unambiguous categorization with respect to alternatives *x*, *y*, and *z*. Some other theory which requires a different categorization system may find the same definitions inadequate. This way of looking at the problem suggests that there is no single way to completely define a 'situation' since the same objectively recorded behaviors may simultaneously satisfy many different definitions.

The related problem of trying to define how the experimental subject perceives the situation is of course closely tied to which categories a particular theorist thinks are relevant; but the subject's own situational perception carries a subtle problem along with it that carries us back to the first problem area, namely, that of probabilistic indeterminacy. Let me clarify this.

Recent accounts of human perception suggest that perception is not a passive consequence of stimulus input but rather an active reconstructive process that may employ cognitive strategies (see Neisser 1967; for an account of perceptual strategies in linguistic perception see Bever, 1970). We can speculate that the subject's perception of what *situation* it finds itself in may also depend upon active reconstruction based upon past experience. The particular cognitive strategies one employs to recognize a current situation may be either probabilistically chosen or algebraically determined. The choice a theorist makes will again affect the whole conception of developmental changes in situational perception.

But if we grant the importance of situational context as one contributor to clarifying our understanding of development, we still need to analyze the notion of 'situation' to distinguish possibly different classes of features which in turn lead to different categories of situations. I shall attempt to sketch one such framework below. The reader is forewarned, however, that it is a highly fanciful conception but I hope will contain enough grains of truth to be considered of heuristic value.

Consider the following ways in which the environment is structured, and then note that the restrictions on how the environment is structured carry import for the possible identification of features which we as theorists may use to recognize and help define situational settings. The earth and its physical environment into which we are born, grow up, and die is far from random. Indeed, for many phenomena, a remarkable periodicity constrains and relates one moment to the next. This is important to note because it is a sure bet that the evolution of life in the midst of these profound cyclic phenomena has been molded and is itself constrained by these external regularities. We seem so accustomed to these cycles that it seems necessary to force them back into conscious awareness by explicit mentioning.

Here are some of the physically determined cycles: day and night; fall, winter, spring, summer; rainy and dry seasons; high and low temperature periods. Each of the above has its immediate effects on behavior: day and night is correlated with brightness and darkness and also with warmth and cold. Seasons of the year are correlated again with warmth and cold and probably with degree of physical activity. Rainy and dry seasons influence not only our immediate individual responses but can in a larger sense be the nucleus around which elaborate cultural ceremonies are performed – as in the Mayan religious ceremonies. But to implicate cultural patterns is to get too far ahead of ourselves at the moment.

A list of biological rhythms can also be mentioned which appear to be correlated with or influenced by some of the cyclic physical phenomena: being awake versus being asleep is cyclic; birth, life, and death is cyclic; then there is the monthly menstrual cycle in women; cyclic eating periods, periods of sexual arousal, breathing – all have a cyclic rhythm.

To return now to the cultural import of cycles, there are a number of cyclic social phenomena which may have been instigated by or had their inspiration from modeling after rhythms discovered in nature. Some of them are weekend rest periods; summer vacations; elections every four years rather than randomly selected times; yearly scheduled professional meetings; and on a more serious note, it has even been suggested that there seems to be a periodicity to the occurrence of war and peace.

A number of the above events may not be a simple function of time, but a good number are. Be that as it may, you may ask, what has all this to do with the particulars of infant growth and the particulars of perceiving situational contexts? I think it may have a great deal to do with it. In addition to the effects of the large-grained events mentioned above, it appears that a very fine-grained cyclic schedule is set up in many homes which varies in its pattern from household to household and also varies as a function of the age and number of children in the household. Some mothers may establish a highly rigid schedule of *daily* activities into which the infant or child becomes enmeshed. She may get up and wash at a certain hour, fix breakfast at a certain time, wash dishes, iron, etc., all the while carting the infant or child about with her for many of these activities. This schedule may repeat day in and day out with minor variations. Other mothers or primary caretakers may establish a weekly routine so that the cycle clearly repeats only at weekly intervals. What effect does this great regularity have for the developing infant? It must form the backdrop of security and predictability that become preconditions for manipulating the objects around himself and venturing out on this own. A highly unpredictable world (both physically and socially) would hardly be conducive to encouraging a frail infant to become adventuresome. Regularly repeating events tend to induce not only a sense of security but also a sense of boredom, and this in turn can provide the impetus for active exploration of the immediate environment.

Situational contexts may, in this regular cyclic world, become consciously perceived through the occurrence of minor variations in format that occur in the daily or weekly schedule of events. That is to say, minor violations of expectancy help to focus attention on the source of the disturbance and in so doing provide a precondition for forming conscious schema of situational occurrences. It is known that expectancies can be set up quite quickly even in young infants (see especially Freedle 1971; Lewis and Baumel 1970); these same studies also indicate that violations of these expectancies lead to increased attention. What is being suggested here is that similar kinds of expectancies operate outside the controlled laboratory setting, and this is especially true for those expectancies which have a cyclic patterned basis, be they physically or socially determined. When such violations in expectation occur I further speculate that in addition to the increased immediate attention which the organism pays to its immediate surroundings, the necessary conditions have also been established for the discovery of an integrated entity called 'situation'. Let me give an example. Suppose that in household x the grandmother typically stops by at one o'clock for a daily chat. This social situation (visit by grandmother) begins with an explicitly marked entry point – the grandmother knocks on the door and calls out 'It's me'. (Many socially defined situations have explicitly marked entry and exit cues precisely because these situations are under the direct control of knowledgeable humans – situations which depend upon physical cycles may not have such clear-cut entry and exit cues.) Further suppose that the grandmother picks up the infant, drinks a cup of coffee, and then leaves. This is the typical flow of events which define the situation 'visit by grandmother'. Suppose the infant has 'learned' a certain expectancy about this flow of events and suddenly one day the grandmother arrives, bursts into the room, has an argument with the mother, and then leaves. This violation of expectancy has at least two consequences for the infant: His heightened attention signals to him that something new has occurred and at the same time provides him with information that something old has been violated; it further provides him with information relevant to defining the beginnings and endings of a recognizable situation because the regular cyclic episodes in his 'typical' day have been violated only at a certain point in time (the point in time when the grandmother burst into the room) and ceased to be violated at another point in time (when the grandmother finally left). If the above reasoning is correct, then the expectancies that grow out of the experiencing of cyclic events also form the fabric out of which one segments the salient features of a situation – this latter segmentation being facilitated by experiencing violations in the typical flow of events.

As the infant gets older and moves into environments beyond the confines of his household he develops a somewhat different set of expectancies and a more complex set of situational settings especially in the social realm of school settings, business settings, political settings, etc. In a wider sense, as one experiences the culturally permissible variations as to which situations can substitute for each other, then one's earlier schemata may accommodate to these sets of variants so as to reconceptualize at a more flexible level the critical features of situations. From a developmental perspective, there is probably survival value in being able to increasingly conceptualize the flood of detail of experience at a more general level – that of situations. Perceiving the world as a sequence of situations, some of which run their expected course while others get interrupted momentarily, helps to chunk and integrate the millions of pieces of raw data into manageable cognitive portions.

To summarize this second point, developmental theory should attempt to incorporate the perceptual and dynamic aspects of situational recognition as an important and previously neglected aspect of developmental theorizing. In addition, a straightforward mechanistic approach to defining situations and their perception must be modulated by a consideration of what the organism's momentary goals and purposes are. Thus the notion about having specific 'knowledge' of situations as one develops and moves into new environments must be modulated by considerations of a more dynamic system which parses and identifies relevant aspects of situations as a function of current momentary goals.

Task requirements and subject capabilities. A third major ingredient of developmental theory should be one which attempts to define the obligatory and optional features of some externally defined task – such as tasks found in experiments, or tasks which a parent poses for his child, or errands or household duties that the parent requires the child to do. Notice that in talking about 'tasks' one should allow for some task to be totally optional in its requirements in the sense that the child may define for himself what he wants to do with some object. It should also be pointed out that the requirements of a task are flexible and subject to redefinition as a function of the situation in which the task is performed. Thus if a child is alone he may impose no obligatory features on what he does with the task; similarly, if the child is playing with an object in the vicinity of an *inattentive* adult, no obligatory features may be imposed on manipulating the object. However, if the adult suddenly gets interested in what the child is doing, the manipulation of the object may acquire some obligatory features due to the insistent monitoring of the attentive adult. As another example an inquisitive scientist may impose many more obligatory or challenging features to the manipulation of the same object than any attentive parent might think of. I mention this simply to point out that there is always a dynamic and flexible set of criteria which are to be discerned in trying to characterize what the obligatory and optional features of task performance are – clearly, the set of obligatory and optional features is or can be a function of the social and situational setting.

After a task description and task requirements have been settled upon for a given circumstance, we also wish to delimit how these requirements mesh with the child's information-processing capabilities. How many relational structures can he hold in memory so as to unite them into a resultant? How many dimensions can he 'sample' at one time and is this adequate to the demands of the task? How many 'actions' can he perform together or in sequence and are these limitations within an acceptable range to get a correct score on the task? If his capabilities fall just short of the current task requirements, do we wish to invoke some probability ideas to indicate how many times out of 100 he will get the task correct? Some of these questions can be approached in a more systematic fashion by assuming that a certain subset of tasks consists of dimensionalized features with one or more values on each of the dimensions. One can then inquire which dimensions the child is capable of processing and interpreting as he gets older; presumably, the number of dimensions that one can process increases as one matures, and also, the number of these dimensions that can be dealt with simultaneously (in multiplicative fashion) increases with maturity. To introduce situational context, one can speculate that the dimensions of a task that are likely to be sampled (i.e., that are regarded as obligatory by the subject) and processed may be a function of the context. Thus if asked to find novel uses for a toy, we may examine dimensions of the toy that we otherwise would ignore.

One can see that at the level of task description and subject capabilities, the three themes of this paper come together: obligatory and optional features of tasks are viewed as functions of the immediate contextual situation; furthermore, probabilistic aspects of success in task completion may enter in when a mismatch between a subject's dimensional capabilities and task requirements occur.

A more formal theory which weaves these ingredients into a detailed account of cognitive capabilities and cognitive perceptions which have testable consequences may eventually take the form of an elaborate computer program much in the spirit of Newell and Simon's (1972) theory. Thus one can well envisage a master program that consists of 'task' goals as a function of situational indices which serve to integrate and motivate complex sequences of behaviors towards some concrete objective – remember, we allow for the possibility that for young children, objective may totally consist of optional features. The master program would also contain information regarding structural changes which occur as the child matures through interaction with his social and physical environment. These structural changes might be at the level of relational knowledges which the child has acquired, for example, through discovery of situational invariances. As the dimensional sampling capability of the child increases, the rate at which situational invariances can be discovered may increase. Similarly as dimensional capacity increases the ability of the subject to hold fast to a situational goal may improve – thus, the probability of distractibility from some momentary goal may decrease with age simply because the subject now has sufficient dimensional 'computer space' so that he seldom loses track of this relevant piece of information in guiding his more molecular subroutines of behavior. Another aspect to this overall master program may incorporate assumptions regarding the degree to which conscious monitoring of molecular behaviors occurs as a function of maturity levels. Thus a young child who may be said to be in a sensorimotor stage may use all his available conscious 'computer space' for sequencing his motor movements in interaction with the environment. Later in learning, the subroutine which handles sensorimotor coordinations may not be consciously monitored, with the consequence that the 'computer space' previously taken up by monitoring these more molecular behaviors is free now to deal with bigger chunks of the environment, such as monitoring the situational network and closeness to the total task goals. The ambitiousness of the above enterprise suggests that we may be quite far from a true theory of development which cannot only provide detailed and accurate description of current behaviors of a child at various age levels, but at the same time, can make interesting and perhaps startling predictions about observable behaviors of which we were not previously aware. At least, a good theory should be capable of doing this. For the moment, we may have to content ourselves with less ambitious theories until such time as we can agree upon a small but combinatorially productive set of developmental axioms out of which a more inclusive theory can be constructed.

SECTION II

Cognitivists' and socialists' inquiries into human development

The concept of development and the genetic approach in psychological theory of the Soviet Union and other socialist countries

A. PHILOSOPHY AND PSYCHOLOGY IN THE SOVIET UNION

by Levy Rahmani, *Harvard University, Cambridge*

The average Western psychologist interested in the studies his Russian counterpart has been doing avoids publications dealing with philosophical mattres. He finds them difficult to understand and wonders how relevant they are for specific topics. Readers of *Soviet Psychology*, a journal which provides information about current developments in Soviet psychology mainly through translations, tend to complain that there is too much philosophy even in articles concerned with specific issues. It is certainly true that Soviet authors have often given the impression that their writing on philosophical topics is a matter of lip service. It is also true that one can grasp the empirical content of Soviet works and get some insight into what Russian investigators are looking into without paying much attention to their philosophical statements.

Yet a deeper understanding of the current scene, of the formation of contemporary Soviet psychology, and of its attitude toward Western schools of thought requires familiarization with the basic Soviet positions. One should realize that over and above the differences between Soviet schools, which are significant indeed, they share fundamental positions which make Soviet psychology as a whole a distinctive school (Rahmani 1973). There are basic concepts underlying specific studies, so that the comprehension of Soviet approaches to mental processes requires going beyond the possible analogy with Western schools. Not only are issues such as the brain-mind relationship, or the relation between the physiology of the nervous system and social environment, frequent topics of articles in *Voprosy Filosofii*, *Voprosy Psikhologii* and *Sovetskaya Pedagogi-*, *ka* but debates on these topics have been initiated by the editorial boards of these publications. It is the purpose of this paper to show, through a number of illustrations, the close relationship between philosophy and psychology in the Soviet Union.

Behavior theories. The history of Soviet psychology has been marked by an endeavor to implement two tenets of the Marxist theory of knowledge: (1) human mind represents the functioning of the brain, the most highly organized form of matter; (2) man's psychology is the expression of the economic structure of the society in which he lives and of his position vis-à-vis the means of production. The Soviet students of mind have not been satisfied with a division of psychology into explanatory and comprehensive physiological, and social, etc. Vygotsky (1956) was critical of such divisions and so is now his disciple Leontyev (1965). The development of Soviet psychology since 1917 could be regarded as a chain of attempts to attain a synthesis on a Marxist basis. Experimental psychologists and philosophers have joined their efforts – not without conflict – to rebuild psychology on the ground of dialectical materialism. This has been an ideological task and has involved political publications. The fate of important schools, particularly in the early phases of Soviet psychology, has been decided by how close they came to achieving a unitary psychology. The acceptance of their *empirical* findings has been contingent upon their interpretation and contribution to a Marxist psychology. The rise and fall of reflexology and reactology are cases in point.

Bekhterev (1918), a reputed neuroanatomist, endeavored to study the effect of physical, biological and psychological factors on psychological functioning in a strictly objective manner. Among his contributions were the motor-associative procedure, the introduction of the conditioned-reflex method to the study of the sensory-motor reactions, the discovery that each sensory apparatus contains both afferent and efferent components, and the initiation of an experimental study of collective psychology (he called it collective reflexology). But Bekhterev pointed out that his study of associative-reflex activity did not relate to a direct study of the functioning of the brain, contrary to Pavlov's belief. He accepted self-observation as a necessary method. He speculated that matter and mind are identical and reduced all phenomena to mechanical laws.

In 1928, a special panel was set up in Leningrad to reorient reflexology on the basis of dialectical materialism. The next year, an extensive conference was held on the topic 'reflexology or psychology'. It concluded that reflexological propositions were incompatible with Marxism. In the same year, the Second All-Union Conference of Marxist-Leninist Research Institutes concluded that reflexology was a revisionist trend that deviated from the true Marxist-Leninist position. This marked the end of reflexology as a dominant school in the Soviet psychology of the 1920s.

Reactology was another attempt in the Soviet psychology of the 1920s to develop a Marxist psychology, by bringing together the biological and social factors determining human psyche. Kornilov (1930), who made a strong plea for the application of the dialectical method in psychology and had the support of the Soviet authorities who appointed him director of the Moscow Institute of Psychology, saw 'reaction' as a dialectical concept: the subjective state is the thesis, the reflexes are the antithesis, and reaction is the synthesis. He regarded reaction as a phenomenon which has a biological side and an introspective expression. Kornilov thought that the study of human behavior as an assembly of reactions was fully compatible with the methodological tenets of dialectical materialism: continuous variability of nature, connections among phenomena, determinism, development by leaps with transition from quantity to quality. On this line, Kornilov made an extensive study of the relationship between speed of reaction and nature of the task, as well as between its intensity and the kind of activity performed by the subject.

But Kornilov failed to see the cognitive role of man's mental activity and its regulatory function for his behavior. Sensations, to which contemporary Soviet psychology, following Lenin, ascribes an important cognitive function, were omitted from Kornilov's works. Kornilov stated that in man instincts are masked by social reactions; he did not speak about their transformation. His reaction theory was seen as an eclectic combination of Marxist principles. A discussion initiated by the Communist Cell of the Moscow Institute of Psychology, in 1931, concluded that reactology was an anti-Marxist theory.

Development theories. The most conspicuous case of so to speak philosophical shaping of a psychological theory is that of the conception of the child's mental development. This could be illustrated by the work of Blonsky (1935) and Vygotsky. Blonsky, a contemporary of Vygotsky, thought to substantiate the dialectical-materialistic principle of development in pedology – a multidisciplinary study of the child. He wrote: 'The most important task of pedology is to study on a Marxist basis the child's connections with his environment, the child's development in the context of concrete social relations specific for a given period ...'. Blonsky endeavored to tackle the genesis of a mental function on a threefold plan: evolutionary, historical, and genetic. He applied this approach to the study of memory.

Blonsky distinguished four types of memory: motor, affective, pictorial, and verbal-logical. He regarded them as both phylo- and ontogenetic stages and linked them to different levels of the nervous system: visceral, subcortical, and cortical. The affective and motor memory appeared in the early stages of animal development. For the understanding of the development of memory at the human level, two factors have to be considered: man's historical development and his ontogenesis. The development of verbal communication has changed the character of memory. Memory was transformed from an involuntary reproduction of events to a voluntary recall. The verbal-logical memory has become the leading type of memory. It turned indeed into the motive force of human development. Thus, memory as a natural property has contributed to the growth of thinking and language and has been transformed itself under the influence of thinking and language. Verbal memory is qualitatively different from pictorial memory by its social character, since it is based on communication between people. Due to its verbal form, an individual's memory becomes available to other people. The social character of memory is manifest in the individual's interests – which are socially determined – and in the society's demands toward the individual. Blonsky concluded that the content as well as the ways of remembering are determined by the interests of the social group, that different social groups, in different historical periods, have different ways of remembering.

Blonsky's contribution to the understanding of the development of the relationship between memory and thinking – he relied on extensive empirical findings in both ethnography and child psychology – is currently recognized in the Soviet Union. A selection of his works was published in recent years. But in his lifetime, Blonsky was labeled 'pedologist', an advocate of fatalistic views on the child's development.

Let us turn to Vygotsky's case. Vygotsky made the most elaborate attempt to find a Marxist solution to the contradiction between the general line of biological evolution and the specific line of human development. His theory of the development of higher mental functions, or his 'cultural-historical' theory, went through several variations from his joint work with Luria in 1930, *Essays on the History of Behavior*, to his well-known volume *Thought and Language* published after his death in 1934.

Taking as a starting point Engels' proposition that the use of tools is what makes human activity different from animal behavior, Vygostky assumed that labor, which basically changed man's adaptation to his environment, led to a transformation of his behavior. The development from animal to man is not limited to a mere complication of the relation between stimuli and reactions. Vygotsky felt that a mediator developed between them. Along with the production of tools directed toward external objects, there has been a development of 'tools of mental production'; that is, language, signs, symbols, diagrams, etc. These are psychological implements that first occurred as necessary means of communication between people engaged in a collective work and gradually became means of the social conditioning of the individual's behavior. Thus, the stimuli-symbols mediate the mental processes and change their structure. Originally, symbols have the form of external stimuli, then they are internalized. To Vygotsky, any mental function is a social relation between two people before becoming an inner mental function; the means of influencing oneself are initially means of influencing others.

Vygotskii's book was suppressed two years after its publication. It was said to be anti-Marxist. He was blamed – as was Kornilov – for his uncritical acceptance of Hegel's triad, for his admittedly contradictory analysis of the relation between higher and lower mental functions. The role of signs, or symbols, was thought to leave the door open for idealism. They appeared as a direct expression of an individual's inner experience rather than being determined by the 'material practice'. Finally, the role of the social factor for the child's mental growth was said to have been confined to an interaction between adult and child. The philosophical-ideological problems raised by Vygotsky's theory are currently the focus of an extensive debate between two schools of thought: Leontyev's and Rubinstein's.

On internalization. Leontyev (1965) developed Vygotsky's 'internalization' theory in an attempt to eliminate the conjectures thought to be incompatible with the Marxist philosophy. He first advanced his views in 1945 and 1947 and subsequently revised them, taking into acount their criticism in 1948 (Maslina 1948) and 1955 (Editorial 1955). Leontyev's current position is that a theory of the social determinism of mind should take as a starting point Marx's statement that the mastering of a certain class of tools is tantamount to the development of a certain group of abilities. Man lives in a world of objects which incorporate human abilities developed in the course of social-historical practice. An individual is exposed during the course of his development to this world of objects. It is reasonable to assume, the argument goes on, that he has assimilated the mental processes and abilities embodied in the world of objects. Thus, psychical phenomena exist in a twofold manner: in man himself and in the material and the spiritual objective products of human activity. The development of mind consists in the internalization of the latter. This process of acquisition had developed through numerous generations. Leontyev speaks about a 'mechanism of social heredity'.

Leontyev makes a distinction between two types of abilities. The first type is that of natural or biological abilities such as the ability to form and differentiate quickly conditioned reflexes. Some abilities are common to humans and animals. They are directly linked to innate inclinations and develop in the course of man's activity. The second type of abilities is specifically human, such as linguistic, musical, and constructive capacities. The initial internal conditions of the organism, in particular the hereditary disposition, does not play any significant role in the development of these abilities. That means that this type of ability is determined exclusively by external factors and is related solely to the forms of human activity, developed in the course of history. They are assumed by Leontyev to be new mental properties developed during the individual development and not a manifestation of what he has received by heredity.

Vygotsky-Leontyev's internalization theory has been the target of constant criticism by Rubinstein (1959) until his death in 1960. Since 1934, when he published a paper about problems of psychology in Marx's works, Rubinstein took a different approach to the problem of the way in which mind reflects the external reality. He accepted the proposition that a theoretical activity originates in a practical activity. He also admitted that man's development is essentially different from that of animals, that the results of human activity are incorporated in its objective products which consolidate the continuity of the development of mankind and mediate the individual development. But Rubinstein opposed the distinction between natural and human abilities and their different determinism. He rejected the proposition that man possesses both human and non-human abilities. Furthermore, to Rubinstein any concrete act involving an object already involves mental components. He assumed the existence of a process of transformation of the mental component of a material act into a mental phenomenon existing independently of a concrete act; in other words, the transformation of one form of activity into another. To Rubinstein, 'internalization' is not the mechanism by which this transformation is achieved, but its result, the direction of the transformation. Rubinstein felt that Leontyev misinterpreted Marx's statement about the formation of human abilities. In his view, what Marx really meant was that after the elimination of private property and the establishment of a collective property of the means of production, the assimilation of these means will be tantamount to the development of corresponding skills.

Studies on thinking and perception. The internalization theory has been implemented in concrete investigations in Galperin's (1966) work on learning and in El'konin's (1960) and Zaporozhets' (1964) work on the cognitive development of the child. Galperin had initially advanced, in 1952, a theory of learning in young children and then expanded it in a general theory of the child's mental development. He accepted Vygotsky's view that the origin of higher mental functions resides in an external reality which is internalized. He also adopted Vygotskii's contention that the forms of verbal communication are transformed into the individual's verbal thinking. But Galperin felt that this process of transformation of 'external' into 'internal' had not been thoroughly studied and the manner in which the forms of communication become forms of mental activity remained an unsolved problem. Furthermore, he took issue with a basic aspect of Vygotsky's theory, that which was mainly responsible for its being labeled 'anti-marxist': the view that symbols are 'tools' of mental activity. Galperin felt that Vygotsky's assumption that the development of the meaning of words represents the most important factor of the child's mental development led him to 'intellectualism' which Vygotsky himself had opposed. Galperin stressed instead the role of the child's activity and formulated the hypothesis of the formation of intellectual operations by stages. This aspect of Galperin's work is better known and will not be discussed here in detail. The main point is that a concept is formed when the underlying action has passed through several stages each of which represents a different reflection of this material action. Perceptions and representations are formed in similar ways. Mental processes are thus identified with ideal actions.

Hence, Galperin's empirical studies have aimed to show that a mental function is the final product of the acquisition of a certain type of action in the course of solving certain types of problems. Orginally, these operations are practical and concrete and have to be mastered as such. After the accumulation of experience, the further development of these operations may start from the level already attained. The formation of mental functions always starts with the formation of corresponding external operations. If it turns out that a certain function has not been sufficiently or properly formed, its correction has to start with the return to its initial, external, and concrete form and go through the various stages. So mental development, its genesis and content, cannot be separated from the pedagogical process.

Galperin's theory has not been free of criticism, again in terms of Marxist tenets. It was said to imply a separation of practical and mental acts. Critics have pointed out that Galperin overlooked the fact that even the most developed mental or intellectual act is still contingent upon its connection with a practical activity, that there are no pure thoughts. It was remarked that Galperin regards man's mind as a reflection of his own activity and not of the external reality impinging on his sense organs.

Rubinstein, who was among the critics, tackled the process of thinking in his own way. He thought to apply the dialectical-materialisic principle of determinism according to which external causes act on a body, phenomenon, or process through their internal conditions. The external causes imply assemblies of factors or situations, whereas by internal conditions Rubinstein meant the specific nature and logic of development of that body, phenomenon, or process. He regarded thinking as a process of continuous interaction between the thinking individual and the object to be known. This interaction involves the inclusion of the results of each act in the subsequent course of problem solving. Thus, the object of knowledge does not act as a mere trigger, but each of the thinking processes leads to a change in the object and in turn determines the next step until the problem is solved. In Rubinshtein's view, the study of thinking should disclose the processes of analysis, synthesis, and generalization manifest in the course of solving a problem. As for the methodological problem, Rubinstein and his school (Slavskaya 1968) assumed that varying the external conditions, for instance by presenting the subject with cues or an auxiliary problem at different stages of solving the original problem, would help to discover the role of the internal conditions.

The study of perception in Soviet psychology has also been under the influence of the antagonism between the two philosophical positions. There has been an extension of Vygotsky's theory to the investigation of perception, in particular visual perception. Zaporozhets (1967) and Zinchenko (1967) have followed this line. They assume that a perceptual act is genetically linked to external, practical operations and, similarly to them, it transforms a concrete situation, this time not on a material but on an ideal plane. An image is formed during the process of attunement of the effector components of the reception apparata to the perceived objects. Such components are the movements of the head, touching an object, the eye movements following the contour of an object and the movements of the vocal chords reproducing heard sounds.

Ananev's (1968) school has taken a different position following Rubinstein's line of reasoning. Sensory images, perceptions, and representations are seen not so much as a reproduction of the subject's activity, although they are admitted to be formed in the course of an activity, as they are a reflection of the external reality itself. Perception is seen by Ananev's school as an interaction between the nature of the object and the structure of the subject. The operations performed in the course of knowing objects are reflected only in relation to objects. Ananev's developmental studies, in particular the studies on the development of perceptual constancy, have followed this line.

B. THE SOVIET CONCEPT OF DEVELOPMENT AND THE PROBLEM OF ACTIVITY

by Thomas Kussmann, *Federal Institute for East European and International Studies, Cologne, Germany*

Kostyuk, the outstanding Soviet psychologist from Kiev who is mainly active in the field of child psychology, stated in 1969: 'The genetic method for studying psychic phenomena cannot be separated from the theory of development on which it is based. The genetic method cannot be separated from the relevant general concept of development, which dictated the course for research endeavours, including those in the experimental field.... The research endeavours will have little effect if development is considered to be a growth process, an increase or decrease of psychic functions or a repetition. The endeavors of the psychologist are similarly unsuccessful if development is reduced to isolated changes of a (quantitative or) qualitative nature, or if the conditions and the motive powers of development are understood unilaterally, incomprehensively.' The genetic method of study means that the object in question is examined from the point of view of its genesis, i.e., the process is investigated in which the object has become what it actually is.

Let us first of all take a look at the philosophical, but not specifically psychological, explanation of the dialectical-materialistic concept of development. We can see that the qualitative aspects of development are given special emphasis. Furthermore, we find that modern Soviet explanations of the development process are inspired by system theory approaches which could be traced back in the field of psychology to Köhler's gestalt psychology. (The basic assumption is that the whole is 'more' than the sum of its elements. Three isolated notes, for example, sound different than a chord.)

Philosophical aspects: The primacy of quality. In the Moscow *Philosophical Encyclopaedia*, Grushin (1967) – a sociologist – says: 'Development is defined as the transition from one quality to another. Development presupposes the existence of an object which develops or of a structure which changes in quality. A distinction must be made between sources, forms and directions of development. Developments can be observed in inorganic and organic material, in society and in the formation of the forms of consciousness.'

Dialectical materialism distinguishes between two forms of development: evolution and revolution. Evolution is the gradual quantitative change in a structure, whilst revolution is defined as the sudden 'jump' to a new quality. Each new quality in an object or system is followed over a certain length of time by gradual quantitative changes which may be called evolutive, until a qualitative change in the whole system suddenly occurs once more. Soviet and East European psychologists illustrate this move from quantity to quality by way of Sander's 'actual genesis' and refer to Heinz Werner (Schmidt 1970).

Therefore, each development process should be considered as being a dialectical entity consisting of continuity and discontinuity or as the transition from quantitative to qualitative changes. It may be assumed that there is, in this principle, a theoretical necessity for supposing the existence of a stage principle in ontogeny.

Thus we can already recognise one essential feature of the dialectical concept of development, which is the primacy of quality, i.e., each increase or decrease in quantities is a change. However, there can be no talk of a development unless a qualitative change in a structure can be observed. A qualitative change in the development process is identified as the transition from one structure to another structure with another quality.

Development is related to time. The structure of an object, a subject or a system at the beginning of a development and its structure at the end of a development are states which are determined by time, i.e., they are historical states. The development process is thus a series of historical states.

In this context the idea of a 'lapse of time' is not the same as the idea of a 'development process'. For example, it can happen that there are no qualitative changes during a specific period of time: or, various objects may assume different states in the same period of time. In other words, the development of this or that object is not a function of a time span which can be measured physically but is rather a function of the life activity of the object itself according to the Soviet philosophers. Used in this sense of self-movement, the idea of development is thus an immanent process whose origin is to be found in the developing object itself. The sources of self-development are inner conflicts or inner tendencies of a contradictory nature, which stem from internalized outer impulses. The outer impulses always have an indirect effect and never a direct one.

The Soviet concept of development is teleological: The transition from one state to another in an object is not a circular movement or an endless repetition of the past, although the later stages of any development include quite a few characteristics of previous stages. Development can be progressive or regressive. On the whole, however, the Soviet philosophers believe that development is directed towards perfection. Development takes the form of an endless movement on an ascending spiral.

In summarising the contents which link Soviet Marxism and the concept of development, we can say that the development process is a dialectical entity consisting of continuous changes of a quantitative nature and discontinuous changes of a qualitative nature, which can be pinpointed in the life history of individual subjects or groups of subjects. The quantitative changes pave the way for the qualitative changes, with the qualitative changes being decisive. Development is made possible by the interaction between inner tendencies and outer impulses. Due to the repetition of similar qualitative changes at similar intervals, development leads to an ever progressing perfection as on an ascending spiral. Development as a dialectical self-movement implies an active shaping of the self and is directed at the realisation of values.

Psychological aspects: The primacy of activity. Let us now turn to the concept of development of Soviet psychology. In the twenties and at the beginning of the fifties, Soviet psychology was supposed to be turned towards a causal-mechanistic concept of development, similar to that of Darwin's. Darwin merely saw the quantitative differences between the mental processes in animals and man, and he depicted the behavior of animals in an anthropomorphising manner (Darwin 1872). Pavlov's 'objective' physiology was directed against the 'subjective' anthropomorphising interpretation of animal behavior. The other well-known idea of 'objectivity' was Pavlov's assumption that the highest mental processes in man must function along the same lines as the submental processes, since both emerge through the same nervous substratum. A few pupils and interpreters of Pavlov applied Darwin's quantitative concept of development in Pavlov's 'objectivised' form to the interpretation of ontogeny for man's behavior.

The move away from this biological quantitative concept of development was due in the first place to biologists; in the West, this included Adolf Portmann in Switzerland. Portmann and others ascertained that the control of vital processes starts on the highest level of the hierarchy of these processes in the organism and is continued down through the various stages to the inanimate level. A level high up in the hierarchy always directs another level further down the scale. Thus, any study must also progress from 'top' to 'bottom'. For the same reason, we must look backwards into history when studying a development.

The same thought was developed in the Soviet Union by the biologist and mathematician Bernshteyn in his *Physiology of Activity*. Bernshteyn understands development as being a permanent process of self-organization in the organism, guided by contradictory inner tendencies and outer impulses and constantly directed at new targets related to the present moment. This idea of development favored by Soviet psycho-physiologists differs from the rigid concept of homeostasis: The organism itself must disturb the homeostasis, since this is the only way in which new quality can be added to vital processes. The rigid concept of homeostasis merely leaves room for the continuation of a quantity and quality already attained and does not allow for any development (Kostyuk 1969).

Clarification of this problem enabled psychologists to emphasize the qualitative difference between human beings and animals. The ultimate aim of animal behavior is a better adaptation to the environment, whilst the ultimate aim of human behavior is the active self-shaping in a changing world. The biologist Adolf Portmann feels than an animal merely 'lives' its life, whilst a human being 'controls' his life. Karl Marx, the philosopher, also said: 'An animal does not behave at all', by which he means that an animal has no conscious relationship to its material and 'social' environment. For this reason there is a belief in the Soviet Union that the psychologist cannot learn anything from ethnologists or behaviorists.

When the psychologist refers back to phylogeny, he can see that nothing relating to human behavior can be deduced from animal behavior. The 'recapitulation of phylogeny in ontogeny' ended some time prior to the birth of the human being if, that is, it is certain that he will not reappear on Earth as a fishlike monster. Thus, it must be supposed that human beings have a special biological constitution (Leontyev 1972).

On the other hand, the psychologist can study the history of civilisation and find examples which show that the development of the human individual depends on the social and material situation in the society in which he lives. Moreover, if the general situation changes, the human individual changes as well. At the same time, human beings have an influence on their situation. The human individual is entirely, but not exclusively, determined by the history of culture: he is open to change (Vygotsky 1934; Leontyev 1972; Antzyferova 1970).

Every psychologist working on human development studies must come to terms with two hypotheses, which can be formulated as questions. Firstly, is ontogeny determined in a decisive manner by structures or organizational principles which are preformed since birth? And secondly, does individual development pass through a number of stages which must be overcome step by step as if in accordance with a law of nature? Soviet psychology refuses to accept either of these hypotheses because of fundamental considerations.

The existence of hereditary factors, i.e., every form of behavioral genetics, is quite radically rejected as well. As regards stage theory, a more flexible attitude has come to the fore. Only a few experts in the field of pedagogic psychology (e.g., Lyublinskaya 1971, in Leningrad) would like to abide by a rigid sequence of stages. Perhaps this has something to do with the specific aspects of the pedagogue's work.

Activity and heredity. What is the Soviet alternative to the preformistic concept of development? The Soviet psychologists assume that all internal structures and organizational principles are acquired during the development process. All that can be said about a newborn baby is that potentially it has the power to act in the world as a human being. Therefore, the development process is not determined by inborn predispositions but rather by a general characteristic of man to play an active role in the world. The development process is realized and facilitated by the activity of man. (Activity is the translation of the idea *Tätigkeit* as used by Karl Marx. Activity is the general term for everything which an individual does).

Leontyev, the Dean of the Faculty of Psychology at Moscow University, defines activity as follows: 'Activity is a molar non-additive unit in the life of a physical subject. On the psychological level, activity is a unit of life which is mediated by psychic reflection [of the relations in the social and material world]. The real function of reflection [an active cognitive process] is that it orients the subject in the outer world. In other words, activity is not a reaction or a system of reaction – activity is a system which is characterised by a special [acquired] build-up, special inner transitions and changes and a special development' (1972a, p. 98; additions mine).

According to Leontyev, whatever man does depends on a complex hierarchical system of activities, actions, and operations. A study of this system must proceed from 'top' to 'bottom' from the general to the particular, from higher to lower qualities, since the lower qualities can only be understood in the light of the higher qualities. A distinction must be made between activity, actions, and operations.

Activity is a global process in which the individual structures and organises his relations to his social and material environment. At the same time the active individual is forming itself, forms his own self. 'We call action a process which depends on the result which is to be attained, i.e., a process which depends on a conscious aim' (Leontyev). Activity is directed by general motivations and realized by specific actionsl Actions are directed at the realization of secondary aims within a genera. activity. Operations are mini-units in the realizations of a general activity. One and the same activity can be realized by various actions and operations. When analysing the actual behavior of a person, it is interesting to discover which actions and operations have been selected. Individuals differ not only by showing different preferences for certain actions and operations. These differences do not acquire a significance and become understandable unless the dominant aims and motivations of an individual are known. In the first place, it is important to know how a human experiences his situation in his family, at work, or in society, in short, in his world as a whole.

The Soviet psychologists believe that any form of behaviorism reduces behavior to correlations between muscular movements. They reject the behavioristic concept of behavior because it reduces human development to a history of reinforcements. The specific quality of development as human development is the permanent search for personal meaning to individual life. Thus it can be said that development means an active shaping of the self.

We now know that Soviet psychology rejects the assumption that development is determined by inborn predispositions, and we must thus ask what, in fact, decides the development of activity. The Soviet reply to this question is that the development of human activity is determined by the contents which are conveyed in processes of interiorization and exteriorization. The developing individual interiorizes the rational and emotional relations which he finds in his environment. The interiorized relations then acquire a subjectively changed form. They are not isomorphous with the environment. The structure of these interiorized relations must also be permanently adjusted to the relations which exist apart from the subject, though this 'adaptation' is no passive reaction. The developing subject attempts to bring about certain changes in the environment himself, and at the same time the results of these attempts also rebound on the subject to effect the development of his inner tendencies. Thus we have a state of interaction between changing inner tendencies and changing outer situations. Activity is stimulated from within and without simultaneously.

Activity and stages. This brings us to the problem of developmental stages. The 'magic' emotional relationship between the child and his world has a quality different from that of the rational relationship between adult and his material and social world. Must it be assumed that the development between these two states progresses in strictly defined stages?

There are Soviet psychologists, though in particular pedagogues, who wish to abide by a rigid sequence of stages. In contrast, the pupils of Vygotsky and Leontyev in particular are endeavouring to win support for a flexible periodization for the development process. They believe that individual development must be studied with a view to seeing which type of activity is dominant at a particular instant in ontogeny. One specific group of activities dominates mainly because they are demanded by the educational habits which are customary in a certain civilization. (Even the social and economic status of the parents and the completeness or incompleteness of the family, etc., are naturally of importance.)

El'konin, for example, makes a distinction between different groups of child activities in the sequence in which they play a leading role for behavior:
1st epoch: early childhood (infants and small children)
    1st group: direct emotional communication
    2nd group: manipulatory activity with objects
2nd epoch: childhood (pre-school children and younger school-children)
    1st group: assumption of roles at play
    2nd group: learning activity (school)
3rd epoch: adolescence (older school-children and young people receiving vocational training)
    1st group: intimate personal communication
    2nd group: learning activity (job).

El'konin thus makes a distinction between three epochs in ontogeny (early childhood, childhood, adolescence). Each epoch is divided into two periods, and it is also supposed to be possible to subdivide each period into two further phases.

Hitherto, nobody knows what happens at the 'transitions' (e.g., between childhood and adolescence) and where these transitions can be precisely located. This has induced Soviet authors to investigate the possibilities of accelerating or retarding development. Gal'perin, for example, discovered that careful training makes it possible to acquire specific intellectual capabilities at a much earlier stage than Piaget's stage theory of intellectual development would lead one to expect. This and similar results are taken to disprove the existence of the preformed inner tendencies which Piaget's stage theory of intellectual development presupposes.

El'konin's model is based on the dominant child activities at a certain instant. These activities depend on typical situations and functions, which can be pinpointed in certain periods of life. El'konin and the Soviet psychologists consider situations in life and not preformed dispositions to be the motive powers for the fact that a certain activity is dominant at a certain stage. El'konin wants to (a) get away from the intellectualized stage theories, i.e., see the motivational and the intellectual development as a dialectical entity embracing both of these aspects in the developing personality; (b) visualize the development process not as a straight line but as a recurrence of similar events at similar intervals, i.e., as an ascending spiral; (c) attempt to see the functional significance of the preceding period or epoch for the one that follows. In doing this, he wants to proceed from activities and situations in life and not presuppose any biological or logical laws of development.

Conclusion. In concluding, the most important hypothesis for the Soviet psychology of development is the rejection of inborn predispositions. The developing individual acquires the structures of his activity himself in processes of interiorization and exteriorization. The Soviet model of development is that of the ascending spiral, i.e., the recurrence of similar quantitative and qualitative changes at similar intervals, with a trend toward higher and more complex qualities. The Soviet psychologists have a more flexible attitude towards stage theory models. This attitude is confirmed by numerous studies of the relations between quantitative and qualitative changes in the development process. The results of these studies support the assumption that periodic changes in the speed of development, synchronicity and asynchronicity, and differentiation and integration can all be observed simultaneously in various areas of the developing behavior structure. In the Soviet Union, development is understood as being a process of active self-shaping, as the individual comes to terms with changing inner and outer situations (Leontyev 1966, 1972; see also Thomae 1968).

There are many formal similarities between Piaget's theory of development and the Soviet interpretation of the concept of development. The similarity between Piaget's ideas on processes such as accommodation and assimilation and Vygotsky's ideas on interiorization and exteriorization could be taken as an example. But the differences in content and interpretation are fundamental (Wozniak, in press). If you asked me to briefly characterize the Soviet concept of development, I would say that the Soviets believe that individual development is far less determined by given logical or biological laws than Piaget supposes and somewhat more determined by events in the history of society and the individual than G.W. Allport maintains.

C. CONDITIONS AND DETERMINANTS OF CHILD DEVELOPMENT IN CONTEMPORARY POLISH PSYCHOLOGY

by Maria Przetacznikowa, *University of Krakow, Poland*

Concept of development. The aim of this paper is to present some theoretical conceptions found in Polish psychology of the last twenty years. We would like to give especially a conditional and causal analysis of factors influencing child development. This will be preceded by some remarks about the concept of ontogenesis and its stages. Contemporary Polish ideas present many theoretical issues. These have been derived from the native traditions of the Polish pioneers of child psychology such as Dawid, Szuman, and Baley, and enriched by the attainments of world psychology. The actual viewpoints of our psychologists are influenced by different psychological currents, in particular, the Marxist theory of development. Polish developmental psychology, in cooperation with world science, elaborated its own original concepts of some questions. These concepts will be discussed.

Contemporary Polish developmental psychology accepts as the development of the individual the dynamic process which leads to quantitative and qualitative changes in all psychic functions and actions, as well as in the respective components of human behavior. The changes in development are progressive, directed toward attaining the higher forms of regulation by the individual of his relationships with the external world.

The most important qualitative changes, i.e., the most essential transformations in the behavior of the individual and in his consciousness, decide his transition to the next stage of development, the new phase separate from the preceding period of his life. Therefore we accept the model of stage development, the model of successive phases. The division of the course of life into periods does not serve, in our opinion, only the technical and practical purposes of ordering developmental phenomena in time, and facilitating the teaching and the directing of human behavior. We consider the periods or stages, marked by the basic developmental changes, as well as the phases differentiated in their course by the smaller changes, to be the real psychological facts. The stages and the phases form the basic structural links of human development; the typical qualitative changes follow each other in the same order, although the limits of the periods fluctuate because of the individual's rate and rhythm.

Stages of development. Polish psychologists are particularly interested in the development of children and adolescents. They are also interested in the stages in which the progressive character of development manifests itself. The periodization of childhood and youth, established in Poland by Zebrowska (1966) in connection with the earlier suggestions of Baley and Szuman, consists of the six following periods from birth to maturity: (1) infancy (first year of life); (2) post-infant period (from 1 to 3); (3) pre-school period (from 3 to 7 years); (4) early school period (from 7 to 11–12 years); (5) puberty or mid-adolescence (from 12–13 to 17–18 years); (6) late adolescence (from 18 to 24 years). These stages are distinct and subordinate approximately to the definite years of life on the basis of three criteria, namely (1) the manner and the level of cognition and the knowledge of the surrounding reality; (2) the dominant type of the child's activity, and (3) the specific form and method of educational influences (Zebrowska 1966).

The first criterion means that in each of these periods there are essential changes in the child's consciousness, i.e., in the way of perceiving different objects and phenomena of the world, in the forms of perception, memorising, thinking, etc. The second criterion emphasizes that in each period important changes take place in the child's activity: the child undertakes new kinds of activity and these new actions transform its whole behavior. The third criterion states that in each period the different forms and methods which influence the child can be observed. In spite of the continuity of influence in some educational environments, for example, the family or the school, with increasing age the breadth and the character of the information stimulating cognitive development change and the instruments for the formation of the child's and adolescent's personality are different. Of course these three criteria are considered together because the changes in consciousness arise through education accompanied by the changes in the child's activity. Therefore in each stage the unity of the specific characteristics of age appears. They are manifested in the individual as an unrepeatable form in each child.

The description of the developmental stages of childhood and youth, elaborated by Polish psychologists on the basis of empirical studies, cross-sectional and longitudinal, is derived from the above-mentioned assumptions and criteria of the developmental periodization. The most exhausting and synthetic elaboration is contained in the works of Zebrowska (1966) and Przetacznikowa (1967), as well as in monographs concerning the development and the education of the child during different ages (Spionek 1967; Landy, Kwiatowska, Topińska 1970; Wołszynowa; 1967 Przetacznikowa 1971).

Four factors in the child's development. The task realized by Polish psychologists is not limited to the description of developmental phenomena. They also try to answer the questions: 'In which conditions and under which influences does the child's activity arise and meaningful actions develop? Which laws rule the child's development and the perfection of its consciousness and behaviour?' (Zebrowska 1966).

During the inquiry into the solution of the problem of developmental determinants Polish psychologists adopted the concept of four factors, taken from the Marxist theory of ontogenesis. According to this concept individual growth and development is influenced by four factors: (1) the innate organic equipment, above all the traits of the nervous system; (2) the self-activity; (3) the environment; (4) education and teaching. Szuman (1964) suggested some modification and at the same time some tentative ordering and classification of these factors. He differentiated between the internal (biological) and the external factors of development. The first group contains the anatomical and physiological equipment and the maturation of the child's organism as well as the needs, tendencies, and aspirations becoming the issues of self-activity. The second group comprises the stimuli and influences of the environment determining and realizing the development of children and adolescents, the intentional, suitable formation of the personality through teaching and education.

Besides the undoubtable resemblances and analogies of Szuman's point of view to the concept of the above 'four factors' and with the thesis of Rubinstein, that 'the external causes act through the internal conditions' (1961, p. 305), there are some differences in the interpretation of the particular factors and in the comprehension of the mutual relationships and of the specific role of each of them. Therefore Szuman traces the self-activity to the active satisfaction of the child's needs and innate tendencies. These biological endogenous needs are, in Szuman's opinion, the basis of the impulsive, spontaneous, with increasing age more independent, actions which determine the essence of the child's self-activity (Szuman 1964, pp. 56–57). The older adolescents express their spontaneity in the activity of self-training and self-education. Concerning the mutual relationship of the four factors and their relative role in development, many psychologists who were drawn to materialism recognize the dominance of teaching and education in development; on the contrary, Szuman emphasizes that each of the factors has equal significance, although in the different stages of development one or another factor may be moved to a primary or secondary position.

Conditions and causes of growth. In my opinion (Przetacznikowa 1973) the question concerning conditions and factors which form the child's behavior is at the same time the question about the basic mechanism of the individual's development – about his dynamic forces and drives. The answer to this question demands a conditional and causal analysis of ontogenesis. The first type of analysis consists of an investigation of the conditions in which the human being develops in its childhood and youth (conditional analysis), the second consists of the differentiation in the developmental process of the links between causes and effects (causal analysis). Many controversies arising during the exploration of this problem consist of the usage and the varying significance of such psychological terms as factors, conditions, and mechanisms of development. One does not distinguish the causal relationships from the others, for example, time relations, etc. It may be useful to differentiate between the conditions and the causes of developmental changes based on the following principles, according to the dialectic concept of determinism. Or, the psychological growth of any organism is the process which occurs in definite conditions. These conditions determine the developmental changes in the sense that upon them depends the appearance of the phenomenon or the maintenance of a factual state. The condition is not synonymous or identified with the cause, which may be found in the whole complex of conditions and in their mutual interaction. The cause is a specific type of condition; it occurs when the definite factual state (event, phenomenon) arises from other states and when this relation is not reciprocal. The causal relationships in human growth are joined to the conditions and factors which accompany the developmental changes. These conditions at once mediate the developmental process and also accomplish the auxiliary, instrumental function of the detection of essential causes of the given phenomenon of growth.

In psychology one applies the name of developmental factors to the external as well as internal conditions of growth. We shall proceed to suggest the distinction between the *conditions* of an individual's development and its *determinants*. For this purpose the conditional and causal analysis will be useful. By genetic conditions of development we often mean those factors which are connected with the organic equipment of the individual. It is necessary to pay attention to the distinction between the innate heredity traits and the traits which appear at the moment of birth. The innate traits can be partly a result of early experiences acquired in the prenatal period. The Polish anthropologist Wolański (1972) proposes another distinction. He isolates two groups of inner factors: (1) the endogenous genetic factors, i.e., determiners (set of genes or the genotype), and (2) the endogenous paragenic factors, i.e., stimulators (protoplasmic extrachromosomal structures). The above mentioned conditions of development are the subject of genetics. Ecology, however, deals with a third group of factors – with the exogenous external factors, i.e., the modifiers. Then, by the ecological factors of the child's development we can understand the external conditions of the environment in which the child grows.

Interaction takes place between the genetic and ecological factors, i.e., the character and breadth of the influence of one factor depends on the participation of the others. Then, the influence of heredity on a given psychic property is not a constant value but changes according to different environmental conditions. Analogous to this is the role of the environment in the growth of definite traits which change in relation to the different hereditary conditioning. It is necessary to emphasize the indirectness of the influence of these factors on developmental changes. This element is discussed by some American psychologists, who propose the notion 'continuum of indirectness' in the case of the analysis of genetic influences, and the notion 'continuum of breadth' in the case of environmental influences (Anastasi 1958).

If the conditional analysis consists of the detection and the presentation of all the internal and external conditions in which an individual's development takes place, the causal analysis aims mainly at answering the following question: Why, how, and by what mechanism do the developmental changes occur? This approach allows not only the explanation of the course of the developmental processes and the discovery of definite principles and laws of ontogenesis but also the prediction of some changes which may be of both theoretical and practical value. Through the causal analysis of the complex of conditions and factors we can detect those which have specific functions in development, which are its source and reason. We call them the determinants of development.

The term 'determinants' has been used in Polish psychology by Gerstmann (1966). This author distinguishes between the primary determinants (e.g., biological environment, system of external situations, orientational and controlling functions of conscious processes, experience) and the secondary determinants (active and latent attitudes formed on the basis of neurodynamic activity schemas). In our approach the term 'determinants' is used slightly differently from Gerstmann's work, more specifically as the indispensable factors determining psychic processes of an individual's activity involved in the whole of the external and internal conditions of his life and in the complex system of genetic and ecological factors. In the dynamic causal analysis of the determinants of development influencing an individual in the various stages of ontogenesis, mainly in childhood and youth, we can discover the functional mechanisms of some developmental phenomena, i.e., of definite changes and laws in psychic growth.

Self-activity as a determinant of development. Among the most important determinants of a child's development is his own activity and education which steers the child towards the formation of his consciousness and personality. These are the higher mechanisms of adaptation and regulation of behavior.

The activity is a typical state and a basic attribute of each living organism. It causes this organism to regulate in an active manner its relationships with the external world. Analogous to movement, which is the indispensable attribute of matter, is the activity which forms a capacity, for all living beings, to incessantly transform itself and its actions. The growth of the regulation of human interactions with the environment consists therefore of adaptive changes in the individual organism and psyche, as well as the evocation of changes in the surrounding world by the subject. The activity conceived in such a manner is not only a state but also a process and is manifested in the form of concrete actions undertaken by the individual from his early childhood. The actions and behavioral acts are then the expressions of the activity.

According to the suggestion of Tomaszewski, accepted in Polish psychology (Tomaszewski 1963), the actions, in which the self-activity of a human being is manifested, are the processes directed into something tending to any goal or result. These processes have their own organization and structure. From this point of view they may be considered as the *sui generis* structural and functional elements which would be, in the stream of human activity, well distinguished, described, and classified. This forms amongst others the basis for the analysis of the developmental changes which occur in this domain. Furthermore the actions and acts are essential units of human behavior; this is not without significance for the studies of child development because the behavior is observable in natural or experimental conditions.

The difference between these two notions is a rather conventional question. It seems that if we would consider in a multilateral way the regulatory processes in human ontogenesis we are obliged to introduce as the basic notion the concept of action. By action we understand first of all the form of regulatory activity which consists of the transformation of reality by the individual, the evocation of changes in the environment in order to adapt it for the satisfaction of the individual's needs. The child executes from birth many actions: gradually it learns to act, i.e., to affect its environment. In Polish psychology this is emphasized by Szuman, who states that the essence of the active process consists of the influence on objects, of their transformation and possession, i.e., their subordination to the control of the active person (Szuman 1955). Then, it may be admitted that during the child's development the actions transform themselves into complex acts which are functional units in point of view of their breadth and level of their organization. These complex acts are composed of particular homogenous or heterogenous actions. The various actions form the definite types of human behavior.

The self-activity of the child has this specific characteristic, that being a determinant of psychic development, it becomes a subject of transformation and perfection with increasing age. The progressive character of human activity is that during a course of life, areas of actions become wider and wider, and the different actions executed by the subject become more effective. Furthermore the individual changes the repertory of his actions when his needs increase with the growing complexity of his environment. The child elaborates the new kinds and types of actions, which assure and facilitate the optimal regulation of his relationships with the external world. This plasticity in the domain of self-activity, meaning the capacity to produce new forms of actions or to transform them, or to give them another direction, is greatest in the early stages of development – in childhood and youth. That does not mean that later, in adulthood, the individual can not learn other actions or modify the manner of activities earlier acquired.

Changes in human actions. The principal directions of changes which occur in human actions form the pair of reciprocally complementary processes of development and are as follows: (1) the differentiation and the integration of actions, i.e., their passage from the global activity of the subject to specific actions integrated into the greater functional complex, into the whole of the hierarchical systems; (2) the interiorization and exteriorization of actions; the passage from the external actions executed on real objects (things) to the internal, mental operations and reciprocally the growing possibility of the concretization of these last operations in the form of real acts; (3) the growth of the role of the consciousness in goal-directed actions and the parallel automatization of many actions determining their perfection; (4) the socialization and individualization of the actions; the passage from individual to group actions, the formation of the particular style of activity.

The child's self-activity is not only an immanent 'force', preformed in an unchangeable shape from the beginning of life, but is the dynamic determinant of the individual's development. This thesis is confirmed by the continuous growth of the structure of particular actions which manifest this capacity of active regulation of relationships between the organism and the external world. Many examples from the developmental, empirical studies in child psychology prove that with increasing age one can observe more and more differentiation of definite actions, distinguished by the total behavior in some situations as well as an increase in the level of the inner organization of the activity which is the most essential structural trait of action. The research done until now, although not complete or exhaustive, gives an outline of the development of the activity's structures and presents the main directions of actions in some domains of development, e.g., in the area of cognitive operations. This outline is as follows. The individual proceeds: (1) from the actions of simple structure to the actions of complex structure (we consider here the quantity and quality of the structural links, components, elements, and relations between them); (2) from the actions of the incomplete structures – i.e., the breaches in surface and time between these elements and the deformations in the mutual relationships between them – to complete and full actions; (3)

from ineffective actions to effective actions, the structure of which leads directly to the result; (4) from the actions of the uneconomical structure which contains the elements too much extended on the surface or in time to the actions structurally economical, i.e., containing only the elements necessary in respect to the result they lead to; (5) from the actions of the discontinuous structure to the actions which are logically close and complete. The specific features of chaotic and stereotypic actions which occur often in early childhood may show the immature forms of the structure and functioning of activity (Przetacznikowa 1971).

Thanks to the inner organization of elements, which compose the psychophysical organism of a human individual, this organism becomes an isolated system which differs from its environment and at the same time enters into relations with it. When these contacts with the external world develop, the inner ordering of this system increases. The individual's activity becomes more and more structured and organized, and nearly all developmental changes in it extend and have a progressive character. If we consider development as a process of self-organisation we must think about the formation of new experiences which consists of consolidation in the nervous system of the functional changes under the influence of the environment. The psychophysical self-organisation occurs at the cost of the surroundings, i.e., for the structurization of the activity's schemas (patterns of behavior) the various stimuli of the environment are necessary. They have an informative character and are ordered in a specific manner. The general principles of this process of self-organisation elaborated by cybernetics facilitate the interpretation of many phenomena observed in the course of a child's growth. This has been shown in our institute in Krakow by two young psychologists, Kaiser and Niemczyński (1970), who consider in such a way the relationships between the organism and its environment in connection with the concept of ontogenesis given by Piaget. The authors presented examples of behavior in early stages of childhood which proved the restructurization of the schemas of activity, in circumstances where the mobility and diversity of the stimuli (information) exceeded the possibilities of adaptation elaborated by the child's behavioral pattern.

Educational influences on development. The formation of the psyche during ontogenesis does not consist of the accidental contact of the child with various elements of the social environment, or with the causal interaction of the individual with events and phenomena which are produced by social life. This interaction is consciously directed by educators and teachers of the child, as well as by the different institutions which are engaged in the organization of the educational process or which aid the parents in their tutelary functions.

The educational environment such as the family, kindergarten, boarding establishments, etc., may be considered as one of the components of the conditions of a child's life, and thus as an ecological factor of development. The process of education is regarded as the planned and suitable influence on the pupil's behavior tending to the formation of his personality in a definite manner. Therefore besides activity the latter determinant of human development is education. This process is historically changeable; it depends on the level of the economy and culture, on the social and political system and on many other factors. The role and function of education changes also in the course of an individual's development: the goals, methods, and educational instruments are always adapted to the stage of the child's growth, to the age and to the individual attributes of the pupil. Education, similarly to teaching, exceeds however the limits marked by the actual level of development. This is a 'developing education', according to the thesis of Vygothsky. Such education influences are effective that precede the child's development and are directed towards immature features of the personality.

In spite of the diversity and inconsistency of the educational influences, furthermore because education as a system of influence is a plastic complex of stimuli and situations which one can manipulate in realizing definite goals, it plays a great role in human development. The force of education as a determinant of development grows greater because it does not have the character of the isolated, personal influence on the child – although the personal pattern and the direct modeling of the pupil's behavior by the parents, teachers, or other significant people has undoubted importance in the formation of the different aspects of the personality. Education is a social affair, a process consciously organized by the society. The total society is interested in the effects and results of education.

Naturally, education as the determinant of the child's development is connected to learning and teaching; they are inseparable processes. In the formation of the child's personality we assume therefore that we should give the pupil a necessary set of information which permits an adequate orientation to the environment, facilittaes the estimation of the values of different phenomena and as a consequence causes effective action and permits some influence on the world. The compact but not rigid system of concepts and information is the condition of the constant enrichment of the child's knowledge about reality, and the increasing orientation to the world forms assumptions for emotional engagement in the changes directed to the progress of a social life.

Soviet developmental study of verbal self-regulation

A. RECENT DEVELOPMENTS IN SOVIET RESEARCH ON THE VERBAL CONTROL OF VOLUNTARY MOTOR BEHAVIOUR*

by Larry Wilder, *University of Wisconsin, Madison*

While this paper parallels Wozniak's in purpose, two major differences in approach should be underscored. First, Wozniak goes to great lengths to explain the Soviet ideology of dialectical materialism. While this subject is interesting in its own right, and while it surely does affect Soviet psychological theory, the present paper emphasizes the psychological theory (primarily that of Pavlov and Vygotsky) as it relates to the verbal control of behavior. Second, a different interpretation of 'voluntary behavior' is advanced in the present paper. Wozniak states that voluntary behavior is '... behavior which is organized via the imposition of "artificial" (i.e., psychological) stimuli between physical simulation in the world and response to that stimulation. Such artificial stimuli are usually, but need not necessarily be, speech signals. Thus voluntary behavior is typically "verbally-controlled" behavior' (1972, p. 15). It will be argued presently that voluntary behavior is only that behavior which is verbally controlled. It is precisely this fact which distinguishes the

* Published by the Wisconsin Research and Development Center for Cognitive Learniug, supported in part as a research and development center by funds from the National Institue of Education. The opinions expressed herein do not necessarily reflect the position or policy of the National Institute of Education and no official endorsement by the National Institute of Education should be inferred. Center No. NE-C-00-3-0065.

verbal control of behavior (either external or internal) from other forms of control. While these lower forms of control may behave according to the same general laws, they lack the strength, mobility, and generalizability of verbal stimuli.

General theoretical background. In 1950, the Joint Session of the Soviet Academy of Pedagogical Sciences convened for the explicit purpose of Pavlovianizing psychology (Cole and Maltzman 1969). While such political pressure had unfortunate consequence for many areas of psychological inquiry (e.g., heredity or mental testing), the study of verbal behavior flourished within a Pavlovian framework. Pavlov characterized language as a higher order or secondary system of signals:

'This supplement is the speech function, the last new principle in the activity of the cerebral hemispheres. If our sensations and concepts relating to the surrounding world are for us the primary signals of reality, the concrete signals, then the speech, chiefly the kinesthetic stimulations flowing into the cortex from the speech organs, are the secondary signals, the signals of signals. They represent in themselves abstractions of reality and permit of generalizations, which indeed makes up our special human mentality...' (1941, p. 43).

With the emergence of the 'second signal system', or language, Pavlov speculated that qualitatively unique 'higher nervous activity' results. However, it was Ivanov-Smolenskii, chairman of the 1950 Joint Session, who developed the major technique for studying on the second signal system.

While Pavlov's speculations motivated much of the early research on language, a less powerful influence at that time came from outside formal psychological circles. Vygotsky, a contemporary of Pavlov's, had a broad background in literature and philosophy and began intensive research on the origins of consciousness in children around 1934. Just ten years later Vygotsky died of tuberculosis, leaving behind a considerable amount of writing in various stages of completion, and a dedicated group of active psychologists such as Luria, Leontyev, and Zaporozhets.

Vygotsky (1962), who was quite skilled at applying the laws of dialectical materialism to developmental psychology,[1] considered a word to be

---

1. In an interesting and otherwise carefully thought out essay, Fodor (1973) naively assumes that Vygotsky wanted to '... pursue a straightforward "scientific" investigation of the relation between talking and thinking: one which adopted no philosophical preconceptions whatever and no generalizations except those dictated by experimental results'. For an excellent treatment of Vygotsky's dialectical approach, see Berg (1970).

'a microcosm of human consciousness', a product of social human history. Language is not a product of thought, according to Vygotsky, it is dynamically interrelated with it. In contrast to Piaget and other Cartesian 'idealist' psychologists, Vygotsky argued that language evolves as a function of the speech communication experiences of a child within society. During the course of human development, interpersonal speech communication internalizes and becomes a system of intrapersonal verbal communication. The result of this internalization process is that man becomes, in Pavlovian terminology, the highest self-regulating system.

Vygotsky's view of language differs from the more traditional Western psycholinguistic position in two major ways. First, the materialist view posits no internal language mechanisms which are genetically transmitted. The child talks with his culture before he can talk with himself. This view leads to the second point that speech is viewed as more than a convenient vehicle for transmitting language in all its internal, intricate splendor. Rather, it is a dynamic action system which is in a constant state of reciprocal transformation with thought.

Both Pavlov and Vygotsky believed that language transforms the individual into the highest self-regulating system. Because of language, behavior transcends direct dependence upon external stimuli. 'Voluntary behavior' implies that verbal planning precedes overt action. In addition to this theoretical contribution, Vygotsky placed the problem squarely in the arena of developmental psychology.

Soviet research on the verbal control of behavior. In 1958 the Soviet Academy of Pedagogical Sciences published Volume II of *Problems of the Higher Nervous Activity of Normal and Abnormal Children* edited by Luria. The volume contains the results of an extensive research program on speech and the development of voluntary movements in normal children, and deviations from such development in the mentally retarded. Luria's chapter, which integrates the lengthy technical reports into the Vygotsky perspective, was the basis for his 1957 Special Lectures at the University of London (Luria 1961), his 1958 paper delivered to the 15th International Congress of Psychology (Luria 1958) and his 1960 participation in the Third Macy Conferences on the Central Nervous System and Behavior (Luria 1960). However, the reports of Tikhomirov (1958) and Yakovleva (1958) provide the necessary detail which is understandably lacking in the Luria overview.

The apparatus for the study of the verbal control of behavior, developed by Ivanov-Smolensky, is quite simple. The subject sits immediately in front of a display panel containing a single stimulus light which can vary in duration from a quick flash to a long interval. The color of the stimulus light can also vary. The subject continuously holds a rubber response bulb attached to an event recorder which records all squeezing action as well as the onset and duration of the stimulus light. For the sake of clarity, let us also keep the experimental procedures simple. A child is instructed to perform a simple action such as 'squeeze the ball when you see the light come on'.

The degree to which the young child adapts his action to the required instruction determines the level of his voluntary behavior. To quote Tikhomirov (1958): 'The specific stimulus which evokes voluntary movement is the word, which doesn't simply replace the direct signal, but facilitates the abstraction and generalization of direct signals.' However, very young children (up to 2½ years) often press more than once (perseveration), press when there is no light at all, or press in strict coordination with the duration of the stimulus light. Yakovleva (1958) describes this finding in the following manner:

'We explained all these peculiarities of mastering and carrying out preparatory instructions by pre-school children in terms of the inadequate development in these children of the forms of synthetic activity which are realized on the level of the second signal system and by the fact that in our experimental set-up the connections of the second signal system had still not acquired a dominant meaning and reactions largely continued to be structured by the direct stimuli (by kinesthetic stimuli coming from the hand held balloon, and by the light stimuli coming from the flashing lamp, which evoked a strong orienting reaction). The diffuseness of nervous processes characteristic for a child of this age led to the fact that the excitation evoked by each of these direct stimuli irradiated, which led to diffuse reactions that were difficult to regulate.'

Luria (personal communication) has recently termed such unstable behavior stereotypic; that is, the instruction to press only once conflicts with the child's own movements.

When spoken instructions fail to mediate naturally, the situation can be altered in order to bring about the desired effect. First, instructions can be continuously repeated in order to assume significance over the natural tendency to squeeze impulsively. The child can also receive continuous verbal reinforcement concerning the correctness of his response to each stimulus. Third, nonverbal reinforcement (such as changing the flashing light so that it remains on until the hand squeeze occurs, or a bell rings after the response) can be used only if this additional signal is supplemented with meaningful instructions to the subject (e.g., 'turn the light off by squeezing the bulb'). Without meaningful instructions the additional signal causes even more extra-signal squeezing to occur.[2]

Instead of stabilizing the child's responses by means of meaningful verbal instructions, speech can also have a more direct motor effect on the child. The instructions to vocalize a single syllable (e.g., 'go' or a nonsense syllable) in response to the light produce less impulsive hand squeezes, and this self-regulatory speech is motorically based. In Tikhomirov's words: 'We view the word as a complex stimulus having a two-fold influence. The word can have a direct influence *in virtue of its pronunciation*, and a mediating influence *in virtue of the system of selective connections,* which is actualized under the influence of the word.'

Another finding by Tikhomirov, which was not mentioned by Luria, helps to explain the facilitative effects of overt pronunciation. Tikhomirov's data clearly show that a child's hand squeeze is faster than his ability to vocalize 'go' to a stimulus light when the two actions are measured independently. However, when the two responses are combined, and the vocalization follows the hand-squeeze, the hand-squeeze *takes longer* than it did when the vocalization was omitted.

Tikhomirov (1958) summarizes the ages and stages in the development of the verbal control of behavior quite succinctly:

'In the first stage, where we basically find pre pre-school children and only occasionally three-year-olds, there simply exists no regulatory influence of the connections which stand behind the word. The impulsive influence of the word stands in the front rank. Regulation of positive motor reactions by means of a speech impulse is hindered by the difficulty in creating a system of speech-motor reactions. In the second stage, with children of age 3–4 years, a clear regulation of motor reactions is formed with the aid of an auxiliary speech impulse. The word, which forms the signal meaning of the stimulus, acts not selectively but impulsively, and hence regulates the motor reactions only when the impulsive and selective influences are of the same sign. When they are of opposite sign, the impulsive influence of the word dominates, and for this reason adding the

2. Wozniak (1973) and I (Wilder, 1969) have both mistakenly assumed that speech signals were replaced by the additional external signal. However, Tikhomirov emphasizes the speech-based nature of this manipulation by reporting that some children immediately became timid and refused to play the game when they were not informed of the additional signal.

response "must not" to an inhibitory signal leads to an inhibition of a delayed motor reaction.[3]

'In the third stage, with five-year-olds, movement regulation is effected by the system of selective connections actualized by the word. Even when the impulsive and selective influences of the word come into conflict, the specifically selective influence of the word predominates, which organizes the realization of the motor reactions in the execution of the instruction.

'Subsequent development presumably consists of an ever increasing selective influence of speech, but no longer in the form of external pronunciation, but in the form of inner speech or of the traces of connections which are set up in accordance with the preparatory instruction and which become so solid that it is unnecessary to present them in external speech.'

Another form of conflict is aroused when the verbal instructions conflict with the child's immediate perception, and echopraxic behavior is the result. One of Luria's students, Subbotsky, has recently completed a series of experiments which analyze echopraxia. Subbotsky's experiments (1972a) involved giving children of various ages a rattle and a small furry dog. The experimenter also had the same objects, and the child was asked to hold up the dog when the experimenter held up the rattle, and vice versa (reverse association). Second, the children were tested on their ability to hold up the dog when the experimenter pointed to his watch, and to hold up the rattle when shown a pencil (simple association). Third, the children were instructed to perform the reverse association when the experimenter pointed to the dog, and vice versa. Children under three could not do the reverse association, although they easily mastered the simple association. Subbotsky reasoned that the regulatory function of speech was operative since children could perform the simple association, but that the conflict between immediate perception and the instructions hindered performance in the conflict situation. Further, since the children produced even more errors when the experimenter pointed during the reverse association, it was concluded that the child's dependence upon his perception was not imitative or 'echoic'. In another series of experiments, Subbotsky (1972b) asked children who performed either the simple association or the reverse association to judge the correctness of a peer's performance. It was found that the children under three could not

3. Here the Soviet jargon is somewhat confusing. 'Inhibition of a delayed motor reaction' means that the child fails to delay his response, or incorrectly presses the bulb.

recognize incorrect performance in peers, which suggests that the ability to adapt one's own behavior to a verbal request precedes the ability to perceive it in others.

Thus Soviet research on the verbal control of behavior involves the careful analysis of the child's ability to subordinate his behavior to verbal instructions when such instructions conflict with the immediate environment. When the conflict is with the child's own movements stereotypic behavior results; when the conflict is with perception echopraxia is produced.

It should be emphasized that nonverbal conditioning procedures could be implemented to reduce perseveration or teach reverse associations in young children. However, such procedures would tell us nothing about the origins of the verbal control of behavior. It is presumed that verbal self-control is truly human behavior, and to study its processes is to study the genesis of higher mental processes in a social environment.

Non-Soviet research. In the United States, the Soviet study of the verbal control of behavior is usually associated with young children saying 'go' and squeezing response bulbs. The finding that such vocalizations facilitate performance appears to be quite similar, at first glance, to the Kendlers' (1961) finding that relevant overt verbalization is superior to silent performance (especially in younger children), or to the Meichenbaum and Goodman (1969) finding that overt verbalization of 'faster' and 'slower' produced desired effects on finger tapping. It should be emphasized that such overt verbalization effects are different in two major respects from those reported in the verbal control of behavior research. First, the vocalization must precede the response in the above studies, and it follows the bulb-squeeze response. Second, the vocalization reinforces the semantic aspect of the utterance in the learning and conditioning research, while the motor component is significant in the Soviet research. Clearly, then, the 'mediation' involved in vocalizing 'go' is of a different form than response-produced stimuli. As was pointed out earlier, the vocalization increases the latency of the hand squeeze response which precedes it, which suggests some type of central nervous system mediation.

The studies which were aimed at direct replication of the motor component of verbal self-regulation (Jarvis 1968; Wilder 1969; Miller, Shelton and Flavell 1970) all utilized procedures derived from American experimental learning research. In a characteristically sterile atmosphere, therefore, the effect was randomly eliminated, and comparatively little attention was paid to the processes involved. Wozniak (1972) has criticized every conceivable deviation from the appropriate procedures, and only the replication itself remains to be done.

In conclusion, the Soviet research on the verbal control of behavior cannot be explained in traditional Western psychological terminology. It is a combination of physiological and social theory. Perhaps this research doesn't answer many questions of interest to Western researchers. But, then, it wasn't meant to.

B. SPEECH-FOR-SELF AS A MULTIPLY REAFFERENT HUMAN ACTION SYSTEM

by Robert H. Wozniak, *University of Minnesota, Minneapolis*

Although the cultural and psychological importance of speech as a medium of social communication is obvious, assessment of its value for personal communication, for communicating with oneself, has been a surprisingly intractable problem. The nature of the problem is summed up rather well in what might be called the 'language and thought' paradox, namely, speech, in order to affect a listener (in this case the speaker-as-listener) must be decoded to have meaning; but meaning is determined by knowledge structures which the listener already possesses and (in the case of the speaker-as-listener) by the self-same knowledge structures which produce the meaningful utterance to begin with. In other words, the problem is one of how we can tell ourselves something which we don't already know. How can speech-for-self play anything but an epiphenomenal role in cognitive process?

Speech as human action. One answer to this problem, at least, is that it stems from a wrong-headed conception of speech. It thinks of speech as consisting simply of a representational system for the encoding of what is already known, as a sort of totally passive receiver of content imparted to it from deep within some system of knowledge. A potentially more productive position is to think of speech as an action system, similar in many ways to the other action systems which the human organism possesses, such as walking, reaching, grasping, etc., but with perhaps a few additional special characteristics. When speech is considered as an action system, the thought-language paradox seems to vanish. For example, asking how we tell ourselves something we don't already know should be potentially no more puzzling than asking ourselves how we walk somewhere we don't already know how to walk to. The answer is that action is a self-corrective process, that the expression of knowledge in action feeds back continuously to alter the very knowledge system which is producing the activity and to allow for an infinite variety of novel actions. Speech action should be no exception.

Furthermore, as an action system, speech may be united with other human action systems in a hierarchy responsible for the self-regulatory nature of human behavior. Here, 'self-regulation' is meant to imply the dynamic capability of adaptive functioning operating through a number of distinct subsystems interrelated via a system of reafferent interconnections. Speech, as one such subsystem, must feed back not only on itself but on a variety of other response systems which in turn possess reafferent interconnections to speech. It is by inclusion in such a multiply reafferent structure that speech can participate in the self-regulatory process which ensures the adaptive control of human behavior.

When one phrases the question of the importance of speech as a medium of self-communication in this way, the problem areas then become the three empirically more tractable ones of describing the nature and development of speech as an action system, of investigating the developing regulatory intercoordinations which exist between speech and other human action systems, and of determining the characteristics of both the process and the products of cognitive change as a function of the actualization of knowledge in speech. Unfortunately, despite the growing wealth of information regarding certain aspects of the speech feedback system (as, for example, in the investigation of speech perception and articulatory phenomena), and the heavy emphasis in some quarters on the nature of the linguistic system (as, for example, in work on syntactic and now semantic development), there have been almost no systematic attempts to achieve the objective of the first of these three problem areas, *viz.*, a description of the characteristics of the nature and development of speech action as action – as the actualization of what is known in the production of hierarchically integrated, meaningful, reafferent speech acts. What little information we have to have comes to us only mediately, through research which has had as its primary focus the clarification of questions which have arisen in the second problem area, *viz.*, the investigation of interactions and intercoordinations between speech and other action systems in man. Unfortunately, even in this area, what we have gathered to date is only a quantity of descriptive information about a multiplicity of changes in performance in a huge variety of tasks, which appear in ways rarely meaningfully related to one another to be correlated with either the development or use of speech. The question of whether or not speech has this or that effect has been asked a multitude of times, and with a multitude of task-dependent answers. The question of how one system could be designed such that it might produce these various effects, the question of the implications of this data on speech-non-speech intercoordinations for a theory of the nature of the speech action system itself and of its role in the self-regulatory process, has barely begun to be articulated. It is hardly surprising, therefore, that the last of the three problem areas, that of delineating the characteristics of both the process and the products of cognitive change as a function of the actualization of knowledge in speech, has yet to be tackled in any substantive manner.

With this in mind, I would like to review the data on the effects of speech on other response systems, pointing out two major reasons why so little in the way of a coherent picture of these effects (let alone a theory of the nature of the speech action system itself) has emerged. Then I would like to outline the major characteristics which must describe speech as a human action system.

Intercoordinations of speech and other response systems. A question which must occur to many when they initially confront the wide array of investigations of the effect of speech on other response systems is why no consistent picture has emerged from this research. The first and most obvious reason for this failure (see Slamecka 1968; Stevenson 1972) is that procedural differences among studies all purporting to investigate speech interactions have certainly out-numbered procedural similarities. Even the operational nature of that which investigators have considered to be participation of the speech system has varied from verbal maturity through electromyographic tracings to overt vocalization; and, as will become evident shortly, there is no particular reason to assume that the effects of speech on other response systems in such varied instances should be parallel.

A second major reason for our inability to construct an organized picture of the results of studies of speech intercoordinations is what might be termed the 'conceptual overgeneralization problem'. This refers to an apparent inability or unwillingness among workers studying the effects of speech-for-self to discriminate clearly among a number of possible, distinct mechanisms by which the speech system can exert regulatory control over other forms of response. Not totally facetiously I would like to suggest that this lack of discrimination, or equivalence, has been mediated at least in part by the term 'verbal mediation', and that this term, despite (or perhaps because of) its venerable history and link to our theoretical past, is now so nonspecific as to be meaningless.

In order to bolster this contention and in the hope of arriving at a few tentative suggestions about the nature of speech as an action system, I would like to enumerate a number of distinct regulatory mechanisms almost all of which have, at one time or another, been referred to as instances of 'verbal mediation', and in so doing highlight a number of sources of our information concerning speech intercoordinations.

Lexical, syntactic, and phonetic regulations. The first such regulatory mechanism might be termed 'lexical regulation'. This refers to a semantic regulation which is carried by the core meaning which accrues to a particular word. Thus it is the word, as a word, as a meaningful symbol, which serves to regulate response. It does this either by helping the subject to abstract the significant dimension of stimulation as, for example, in the dimensional mediators investigated in studies of children's discrimination shift behavior Kendler and (Kendler 1961), or in the relational mediators assumed to be operative in far transposition (Kuenne 1946; Marsh and Sherman 1966) and in solution of the intermediate size problem (Reese 1966); or it mediates by increasing or decreasing the likelihood of a response as a function of prior association as in classical paired associate studies (Norcross and Spiker 1958; Boat and Clifton 1968; Davis 1966; Palermo 1962; Nikkel and Palermo 1965) and studies of the effects of associative strength on paired-associate learning (Castaneda, Fahel, and Odom 1961; Wicklund, Palermo and Jenkins 1964).

A second mechanism might be referred to as 'syntactic regulation'. This refers to a semantic regulation which is carried out by the syntactic relationships between two or more words which themselves may be serving as lexical regulators. This regulation, often paired with 'lexical regulation', has been investigated in studies of the effects of different syntactic relationships on the recall of paired associates (Reese 1965; Davidson 1964; Jensen and Rohwer 1965; Rohwer, Lynch, Suzuki and Levin 1967), in the modification through verbal self-instruction of behavior ranging from category sorting in the elderly to conceptual tempo in children (Meichenbaum and Goodman 1971; Wozniak and Nuechterein 1973), and in at least one investigation of the use of verbal description of complex social settings to facilitate observational learning of the components of those settings (Coates and Hartup 1969).

A third mechanism, 'phonetic rehearsal', is a non-semantic regulation which is carried out through the repetition and consequent maintenance of a phonetic pattern over time. This regulation is attributed to overt or sub-vocal acoustic rehearsal in short-term memory tasks (e.g. Flavell, Beach and Chinsky 1966; Keeney, Canizzo and Flavel 1967; Hagen and Kingsley 1968).

A fourth mechanism, 'phonetic cue-addition', is a non-semantic regulation which is carried out during initial discrimination learning by the addition of cues to components of the stimulus complex as a function of the verbalization of either distinctive or highly similar names for these components (Norcross and Spiker 1957; Norcross 1958; Katz 1963). This notion is embodied in the hypothesis of acquired distinctiveness or equivalence of cues. In this instance, as in the case of verbal rehearsal, it is not the verbal component of speech, i.e., meaning, but the vocal or phonetic-articulatory aspect of the spoken word which is essential to the regulation of response.

Orienting-acoustic and orienting-motor regulations. Two further and quite different regulatory intercoordinations have recently come to light in a study which we carried out to establish at least prima-facie evidence that the effective mechanism in the Soviet investigations of the verbal inhibition of motoric perseveration (i.e., bulb-squeeze) could be an external inhibition induced through the subject's orienting to his own vocalization (Wozniak 1972). Briefly, orienting reactions are non-modality specific sensitizations of receptor systems, generalized attending responses, which occur with sudden changes in the level of input energy to some receptor. The occurrence of the centrally mediated orienting reaction is signaled by changes in skin conductance and finger blood volume; and these changes typically habituate with the repetition of the eliciting stimulus over time.

In our study (Wozniak, Acredolo and Peterson 1973), adult female subjects were asked to listen to a series of tones, after being instructed that following each tone they were to count silently from 1 to 20 and then, depending on the condition, either silently mouth the word 'Go' or vocalize 'Go' out loud. In addition, a group of control subjects was similarly instructed with the exception that they were asked to say 'Go' silently after counting to 20 rather than either to mouth or vocalize the word.

Alterations in skin conductance and digital vasoconstriction were recorded; the results for the two measures were similar and fairly startling. Subjects in the 'think "Go" only' control group gave evidence of orienting to the initial tones only and gave no clear indication of orientation to the internal stimulation they had been requested to produce. Subjects in both the mouthing and the vocalization conditions, however, all gave skin conductance and finger blood volume responses during the initial trials to both the tone and the overt response (i.e., mouthing or vocalization) with typically flat response tracings between the tone and the overt response. In addition, as was to be expected if these measures were reflecting the occurrence of an OR, response did habituate for almost all subjects within at least 40 trials and for most subjects in many fewer trials; and, what is most interesting, the median number of trials to habituation (with a habituation criterion of three consecutive trials of no response) was 7 for subjects in the mouthing condition and 17.5 for subjects in the vocalization conditions.

This indicates that not just one but two orienting response mechanisms are operative in any overt vocalization. The first is an orienting reaction to the kinesthetic feedback arising from the vocalization as a speech-motor response; the second is an orienting reaction to the auditory feedback arising from the vocalization as a discrete acoustic stimulus. Orienting to an overt vocalization takes longer to habituate than orienting to a speech-motor mouthing response because both of the components are operative in the former case and only one in the latter.

On the basis of this study (and preliminary data from a replication with 7-year-old girls), we feel reasonably safe in positing at least semi-independent regulatory connections between both the phonetic output and the articulatory movements of speech and the central arousal mechanism responsible for production of the orienting response. These intercoordinations might then be termed the 'orienting-acoustic' and 'orienting-motor' regulations respectively.

This extends our list of distinct regulatory mechanisms to six. There is strong reason to believe, however, that this list, far from being exhaustive, only begins to identify the speech-non-speech intercoordinations which contribute to self-regulation. This is particularly obvious in view of the fact that all of the reafferent interconnections so far mentioned are directed from speech to some other response system. It may be that a variety of return connections from other action systems to speech also play important roles in self-regulation.

Rhythmic regulation. Before moving on I would like to touch on one additional regulatory mechanism with implications for a theory of speech as human action somewhat different from those of all but perhaps one of the mechanisms reviewed so far. This is the form of regulation which is discussed in more detail by Harris, namely, the temporal organization of non-speech action through a superimposition of the rhythmicity of speech action on the non-speech system.

Although data on 'rhythmic regulation' is still fairly sketchy, the relative accent and timing of articulatory movements which underlie meter, intonation, and stress at the level of the sound pattern may be capable of exerting a reafferent, and hence, regulatory control over other action systems. This control, however, unlike the regulation achieved through the previously discussed interconnections, consists in a reorganization of the temporal character of non-speech action as it unfolds over time rather than in the initiation, direction, or inhibition of that action. If this reorganization is achieved by the timing of reafference from elements of the unfolding preorganized speech act to the subordinate system, then this is indeed a case of regulation par excellence since the notion of a self-regulated system is precisely that of a dynamic organization whose behavior unfolds over time, generated and corrected by processes within the system. On the other hand, if the rhythmic intercoordination of speech and non-speech action is brought about by the assimilation of the non-speech action to a common central organizational structure which, for the sake of economy, preprograms both activities in such a way that their relative accents and timing match, then rhythmic regulation is not regulation at all, since it is not reafferent connection from speech action to non-speech action which induces the temporal match.

Speech as a multi-level process: Movement, sound, and meaning. According to the regulatory mechanisms just reviewed speech has three aspects, all or only some of which may be present in any given speech action. At the lowest level and common to all overt and many covert speech actions, speech is essentially a motor response with all the attendant kinesthetic reafference that accompanies any motor response. At the next highest level, speech, when overt, is the production of sound with concomittant acoustic feedback. When covert, speech is also accompanied by feedback but from a little understood source, namely the acoustic image. However, acoustic imagery is not functionally identical to physical acoustic reafference. If this were not the case, no difference in habituation of the orienting response to the mouthing and vocalization conditions of our study should have been found. Furthermore although acoustic imagery can exist in independence of measurable speech-motor movements, the reverse is not the case, that is, the speech movements of the vocal apparatus are seemingly inevitably accompanied by acoustic images.

At the third level, the speech act is generally, although not always, the representation of meaning, that is, is often a word, a phrase, etc. The production of a meaningful speech act must be accompanied by either physical acoustic reafference or an acoustic image and in the case of all overt and much covert speech by motor-kinesthetic reafference as well. However, the reverse is not the case. Speech-motor movements and the production of acoustic signals and images can be completely devoid of meaning.

When speech is considered in this way, statements to the effect that 'speech has or does not have some effect X' on an individual's behavior are hopelessly imprecise. Speech is not one but many things, and questions about speech effects must specify what the operative components of speech are in the given context.

Speech as a structured system of movement. The notion that the speech action system exists at combinations of three levels is not, however, the only characteristic of the speech system implied by the results of work on speech-non-speech intercoordination. Both syntactic regulation and rhythmic regulation call attention to another important aspect of speech as human action which, though discussed in some quarters for many years (Bernstein 1935; Jakobson 1941; Chomsky 1957), has until recently had only a negligible effect on psychologists investigating speech inter-coordinations (*cf.* Rohwer, Lynch, Suzuki and Levin 1967; Locke and Fehr 1970; and Meacham, Harris and Blaschko 1973). This characteristic of speech action, although it unfolds over time, is not and cannot be considered a series of concatenated events, a serial chain. Rather, beneath each of the phenomenal levels, i.e., the levels of movement, of sound, and of meaning, lie integrated, atemporal, wholistic structures which pre-organize action. The existence of such structures as a necessary central condition for any integrated, rhythmic peripheral motor act was perhaps first pointed out by Bernstein (1935), a pioneer of Soviet motor physiology and bio-mechanics. Bernstein argued from data on the regularity of motor acts such as walking and running that such movements could never be understood as produced through the repetition of identical successions of single impulses to individual muscles involved in the act. Such chains, he argued, would produce only rigidly stereotyped movements incapable of adapting to events at the periphery. Rather, coordinated action must be understood as the result of the 'simultaneous cooperative operation of whole systems of impulses' (p. 36) organized in a structural schema. Furthermore, in order to be properly activated in time to produce the temporal regularities of molar movement, such as the time intervals between successive coordinations (i.e., tempo) and the quantitative relationships in their duration (i.e., rhythm), these schemas themselves must in turn be controlled by a higher-order schema for which Bernstein uses the term 'engram'. The engram must contain an atemporal state, the precise form of the movement as it will unfold at the periphery over its entire course in time. This is because the essential function of the central engram is to coordinate impulses so as to produce a homogenous and regular movement at the periphery on every repetition despite the fact that change in the external force field may require that the pattern of efferent impulses over time vary considerably from one repetition of the action to another; and hence, these impulses cannot themselves reflect the peripheral form of the molar movement. This form must be latent in the engram which consequently constitutes the structure of the movement.

At the level of the articulatory-speech system, structures similar to those described by Bernstein for gross motor movements must exist; and it is of considerable interest that a view remarkably in line with this supposition has recently been set out by MacNeilage (1970), who hypothesizes the existence of an 'internalized space coordinate system which specifies invariant (articulatory) "targets" which (exert a closed-loop) control (on) the generation of necessarily context-dependent movement patterns ... (thereby achieving) relatively invariant motor goals from varying origins' (p. 182).

Speech as a structured sound system. In addition to this form of structure in the articulatory system, there is also structure in speech at the level of sound, in the relationships which underlie the perception and discrimination of phonemes as in the structure of distinctive features of Jakobson (1941). Since this phonemic structure is assumed to be the result of general perceptual principles, it need not necessarily be identical to the articulatory structures which underlie sound production. Similarly, because the reafferent pathways from speech-as-articulation and speech-as-sound are different (i.e., namely, motor and acoustic feedback respectively), there is no reason to suppose that their coordinations should be the same. On the other hand, evidence has been accumulated by Liberman and his co-workers (Liberman, Cooper, Shankweiler and Studdert-Kennedy 1967) which indicates a marked lack of correspondence between particular acoustic forms and perceived phonemes. This evidence argues for the necessary participation of the articulatory system in the perception and discrimination of phonemes. If this is the case, articulatory structures may be identifical to the structures underlying the organization of sound as speech-sound; and acoustic reafference from speech-for-self may serve only to reinforce the more basic motor-articulatory reafference. Given this interpretation, the slower habituation of the orienting reaction to vocalization than to mouthing, in the study summarized earlier could have been due to an increased strength in the reafference which elicited the orientation.

Speech as a structured system of meaning. The third level of speech, the level of meaning, is also supported by structures – grammatical structures from which lexical features are derived which determine the logical connections between words (McNeill 1970) and semantic structures from which lexical features are derived which determine the psychological connections between words. In addition, these linguistic structures may (Sinclair de Zwart 1968) or may not (McNeill 1970) be determined by prior cognitive structures; or they may be co-determined with cognitive structures by a still more general higher-order system of organizing principles or procedures for constructing structures.[1] The status of any such relationship is at this time a completely open question.

In summary, speech is a multi-level process, existing as movement, sound, and meaning, all of which unfold over time in a highly organized fashion which must be underlaid by structural representations which contain within themselves the course of the action over its duration. There is nothing startling about this interpretation. We have been aware of it for a long time; but taken in conjunction with a view of speech as an action system participating in a complex, self-regulatory network of reafferent interconnections with other non-speech systems, it provides a fresh perspective from which to approach the study of speech as a medium of self-communication. To succeed in this task, we need to know much more about the nature of speech as human action. We need to become able to conceptualize within a single cognitive structure a much wider variety of speech coordination effects than is now possible; and we need to tackle the more difficult but potentially productive problem of the utilization of speech-for-self in the facilitation of cognitive change. By approaching the age-old 'thought-language' problem from this triple perspective, we may be able to shed some light on what has so far managed to remain quite dark.

1. Such a system might correspond to whatever structure is responsible for what Piaget (1952) has termed the 'functional invariant of organization'.

C. DEVELOPMENTAL ASPECTS OF RHYTHM IN SELF-REGULATION

by Gail Zivin, *University of Pennsylvania, Philadelphia*

Soviet developmental psychologists emphasize that under age five the motor system of speech creates unwanted manual motor pulses. However such contagion of speech to motor impulses may actually be useful. One of the functions of private speech or 'speech-for-self' may be that it can impose its rhythm on accompanying motor acts and thus structure these acts into units. These units should be easier to process and require less monitoring by focal attention than a string of non-structured acts. Ease of processing should contribute to the mastery of the act.

Lashley hinted this in his germinal suggestion that a central timing mechanism organizes complex performance needing little monitoring during execution. He suggested contagion of rhythm from a central pacer. Such temporal mechanisms are implicit in current work, noted below, in skill, cognition, and psycholingustics. One of the most explicit suggestions that some general timing mechanism facilitates mastery comes from Schmidt (1968): 'The complex task (was) superior to the sum of the parts . . . in that timing of both responses was guided by the same timing mechanism' (p. 642). He suggests economy in the number of mechanisms required for control of a complex task. Most feedback theorists do not consider restructuring of one component of the task by the rhythm of another. Such restructuring has been hypothesized by Meacham, Harris, and Blaschko (1973), Wozniak (1973), and myself (Zivin 1973). This paper argues for the existence of this rhythmic restructuring by speech on other motor systems.

My argument has clear boundaries. First, it is only argued that speech rhythm can organize motor acts, not that it must. Further the only motor acts under consideration are repeated sequences of components like bicycle riding and material sorting. Finally, it is not claimed that other motor systems never impose rhythm on accompanying speech.

There are two steps to the argument: (a) To demonstrate that rhythm from speech-for-self can set a rhythm in other simultaneous action, and (b) to demonstrate that this rhythmic coordination can facilitate mastery of the accompanying action. After these two general points, the paper will emphasize relevant developmental data, predominantly that younger children illustrate more rhythmic coordination than do older.

Several definitions are needed. Acquisition of mastery is synonymous with 'internalization and abbreviation' in the Soviet literature and learning of 'motor programs' in the literature on skill acquisition. This synonomy implies no explicit agreement on an explanation of mastery. Martin's (1972) definition of rhythmic pattern in terms of its surface structure is useful in agreeing on what a rhythm looks like.

'Rhythmic patterns are defined as event sequences in which some events (elements) are marked from others, for example, loud ... sound ... versus soft ... sound ... call the marked elements "accents". The accents occur with some regularity regardless of tempo ... or tempo changes within the pattern' (pp. 489–490).

The term 'coordination' on the other hand, implies neither presence nor absence of rhythm. It merely denotes coincidence of action in two or more responses. If a coordination has a rhythmic pattern, the phrase 'rhythmic coordination' is used to emphasize the presence of one simultaneous rhythm in two or more responses.

It is useful to seek the point that rhythm from speech-for-self can set a rhythm in accompanying motor acts in two steps. The first is to review neuropsychological literature supporting mutual communication and influence between afferent and efferent components of one or more response systems. The second is to indicate that this influence is more likely to be from speech to other motor systems than vice versa.

Neuropsychological evidence of intersystem commerce. There appears to be a central timing mechanism to coordinate actions. Lenneberg (1966) estimates the frequency of a central timer for speech production at 6/sec. Keele (1968) reports 6/sec. and 8/sec. as two estimates of minimal time needed to process kinesthetic feedback. He notes Bryan as finding the same frequency as a natural rate of finger tapping and Travis as reporting about 8/sec. as the frequency on which finger taps are carried by natural tremors. The coincidence of these estimates over various response systems strongly hints at a central timer.

Soviet theorists have elaborated upon a reafferenting (continuously output-modified) feedback system to control acts. Their component which compares feedback input against desired goals is alternately called the 'acceptor of action' or the 'acceptor of effect'. It examines neurological traces from any sensory modality (or 'analyser') and adjusts neuro-dynamic inhibitions and excitations accordingly. Similar models which emphasize frequent reading of proprioceptive feedback abound in the American skill and perception literatures.

Soviet researchers agree on neurophysiological data which indicate the probability of communication between response systems, especially if the systems share an 'acceptor of effect'. Summarizing this work from Pavlov through Luria, Sokolov (1972) gives this description of the intimate cellular connections between afferent and efferent processes: 'The nerve cells of all analysers are connected with the efferent motor cells, with the result that any afferent stimulus can produce a corresponding movement' (p. 240). Luria's study of pathologies further shows that at least five cortical areas are necessary for the act of writing, including the primary and secondary segments of the auditory cortex (p. 243).

Smith (1973) argues for a new feedback-providing role of metabolic energy levels in the muscles of organic and skeletal effectors. He provocatively suggests that voluntary (but subliminal) control of respiration can pace motor actions. He presents data that suggests that breathing reliably paces rhythmic coordination in such diverse responses as manual and visual tracking. Further, he found that breathing tracked a visual target more accurately than did hand movements. Breathing could be a most natural link to contagious speech rhythms as intonation units (up to seven syllables) often correspond to breath groups. Smith's (1973) and Harris' (1973) suggestion that breath may pace both speech and other motor systems must be explored. Speech, however, could be a major transmitter of paces originating in respiration.

Speech pacing of other systems: Data. Soviet developmental work provides most of the evidence that speech paces other motor systems rather than having other systems pace it. Additionally, Shapiro (1973) shows that overt repetition of the nonsense syllable, 'veb', or overt counting reduced reaction time errors for 5 and 8 year-olds. It would thus seem that even nonsensical but repeated utterances give time-keeping, if not rhythm-making, influence to manual responses.

Shapiro's findings resemble the bulk of Soviet literature supporting the initial motor influence and later (from age $4^1/_2$ on) semantic influence of the speech system upon other motor systems (e.g., Galperin 1969; Luria 1969; Tikhomirov, in press). Their empirical support is usually of the following form. Under $4^1/_2$ the mere presence of a vocal pulse, such as a nonsense syllable from the child, will usually cause a coordinated manual pulse, even if the child knows the manual pulse should be inhibited. Such errors occur in older children only when the rate is increased to 2 or 3 per second (Tikhomrov, in press).

To explain the one-way influence from speech to action, Soviet theory emphasizes the greater 'mobility and concentration' of the verbal system (Luria 1961, p. 75). Main evidence for these qualities is that the child's own speech differentiates responses (e.g. 'press' and 'don't press' to two different lights) at an earlier age than does his manual system. Between ages 3 and $4^1/_2$ mobility and concentration are expressed in the 'impulse aspect' of speech which is neurological irradiation from the speech system. After $4^1/_2$ the 'semantic aspect' also shows these properties of mobility and concentration.

Data supporting direct excitatory communication from speech to other muscles comes from Sukhanova (1961) who reports that during speech in 4 to 7 year-olds, higher potentials were found in muscles closer to the speech apparatus. Potentials were measured in the thigh, biceps, gastrocnesmius, finger extensors, triceps, and sternhyoid muscles.

Two sets of data examine whether voice or hand led when starts were nearly simultaneous. Meacham, Harris, and Blaschko (1973) observed that some 7 to 8 year-old children uttered a cue word so that 'the word was said before the hand began moving to the button'. Because the word was sometimes irrelevant, they speculated that this prior vocalization led the manual, again suggesting the same direction of influence regardless of semantic content.

My own work includes an analysis on 3 to 5 year-olds of whether hand or voice led when there was spontaneous utterance and a sudden change of direction in a finger maze. Examining all vocal-manual coordinations, the percentage of leading was compared for voice and finger. While the bulk of the cases showed simultaneous starts, vocal leading was conconsistently more frequent than manual leading. Manual leading stayed around 0% and always below 6%. Vocal leading was 9.5% at about 3-6, rose precipitously to 46% at about 3-10, and leveled off to 33% at 4-2 and 4-7. The low manual percentage is more evidence that at the impulse level the major direction of influence is from speech to non-speech acts.

Speech pacing of other systems: Aid in mastery. Consider that if rhythmic organization exists, it can aid processing by virtue of its structure. Any reduction in the number of units to be processed obviously makes an act more economical to master. Rhythm could impose reduced structure on the flow of component acts. When this occurs there is the motor analogue to Miller's 'magic number' reduction into 'chunks' of knowledge that are denser but fewer for easier processing.

Keele (1968) concludes that some motoric chunking mechanism exists, noting that 'consecutive movements, in contrast to simultaneous ones, result in substantial slowing' (p. 394) or loss of precision. Martin's (1972) comprehensive article makes a strong case that such rhythmic chunking is demonstrated in studies of speech production and comprehension. For example, it is easy to predict the placement of high information words from accent contours alone. Martin views rhythmic organization of speech as necessary to economize production, ease recognition, and aid retention and suggests these benefits of rhythmic organization characterize all response systems.

Recall the neurophysiological evidence giving substrata for the rhythmic organizations whose necessity Martin urges. If, as argued above, speech rhythm can impose rhythm on other response systems, rhythmically created economy should characterize processing in these systems. Martin's rhythmic 'chunks' appear to provide organized inputs required by such mechanisms as Keele's (1968) learnable 'motor programs', and Gal'perin's (1969) 'abbrevited and internalized' acts.

Overt rhythms and coordinations: Greater prevalence in younger children. It must now be demonstrated that rhythmic coordination of voice and action is sufficiently prevalent in young children to justify claiming it as a route to motor mastery and as one reason why people, especially children, make noises to themselves.

The relevant data on children and rhythm deal with spontaneous emission of rhythms. Clear cases of prevalent rhythmic coordination between the child's own speech and manual acts appear in experiments requiring a child to coordinate his speech and bulb-presses with the onset of a signal light. Tikhomirov (in press) noted in passing that for children up to 5 years there may be rhythm in unusually long presses while the light continued to shine and after the child's speech ('press twice') had ended. Luria cites some similarly extended presses without noticing rhythm. He claims it is coordination of long speech ('I shall press twice!') with long action (1961, p. 86) and notes the relative immaturity of this response. Tikhomirov noticed only one clear instance of rhythmic coordination. In one particular experiment children of 4 and younger segmented their vocalizations into thirds ('two/times/squeeze'), thus creating three coordinated presses. The identical error is reported by

Bronckart for children up to $4^1/_2$. 'Je/pousse/deux fois' yielded three presses (1970).

Excepting the Tikhomirov observations, the Soviets do not point out rhythm. It has been left to others (e.g., Bronckart 1970) to note that speech-hand rhythm may be so predominant as to confound some bulb-press experiments. There are 15 new records from the Tikhomirov manuscript to be added to the 4 relevant ones previously available in Luria's 1961 book. The prevalence of spontaneous rhythmic coordinations is impressive. Eighty-seven percent of all presses showed them.

Tikhomirov's records are clearer than Luria's and will supply two illustrations. There are two ways rhythmic coordinations appear in these records: (a) When presses and vocalizations are simultaneous. These cases are most convincing when the coincidence is due to manual errors mirroring correct vocal responses. (b) When any vocal-manual coordinations have internal accentuations breaking them into rhythmic patterns. The first type is so common that the following illustrations will emphasize the second. The recording apparatus recorded duration and amplitude of manual presses but only presence or absence of each word. Multiple word utterances will therefore be judged as vocal accentuation; lack of accentuation will be seen as single word utterances. The contrast in these illustrations is between single and multiple word utterances.

Martin's (1972) definition of rhythm tells one to look for generally repeated patterns where some elements receive stress and others do not. He does not require that maintaining absolutely invariable patterns, absolute timing, or identical accent markers be criteria of rhythm.

Figure 1. *The subject Yura B., age 3 years, 4 months*

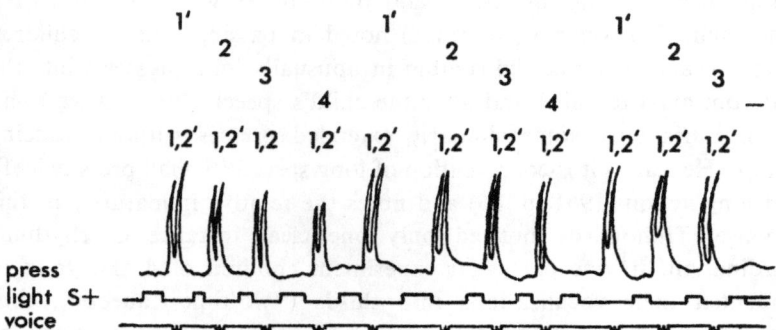

These two illustrations are typical of the majority of all 19 records. In the first illustration the vocal act is repetition of 'to to' and the manual act is a pair of presses. This coordinated vocal-manual act is cued by a single light flash each time. This record has two interesting features: (a) The rhythmic patterns are indicated by amplitude differences of the actions. (b) There is rhythm inside a rhythm. Each pair of beats, 1–2', 1–2', etc., gets greater amplitude on '2''. There are also three sets of four pairs with each set having a simple descending pattern: 1'–2–3–4, with the last pair of the last set anticipated but not published in the available record. The absolute timing of the first press per pair is controlled by the flashing light. However, Yura's record shows spontaneous imposition of accent patterns upon correctly timed responses.

Figure 2. *The subject Gena P., age 3 years, 7 months*

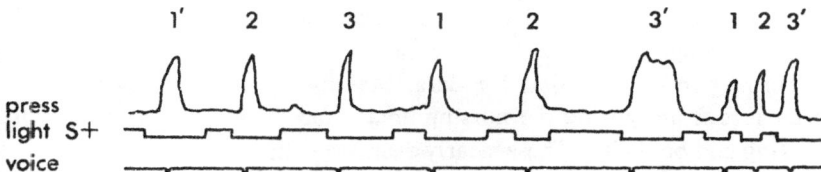

In the second example the child says 'must' for a light (S+) signalling a correct press and 'must not' for a light signalling inhibition (S–) of a press. Because the inhibitory part of the task has the vocal accentuation of two words it is not surprising that 'must not' is incorrectly accompanied by presses and that they are of higher amplitude. They are the accented last elements in the pattern 1–2–3', 1–2–3–4', 1–2–3'. In its last two triplets this record shows manual patterning (1–2–3') during vocalizations that appear of equal stress, perhaps as maintenance of the preceding rhythm. Recall that there is no accurate record of vocal stress beyond one versus two word utterances. But in the last triplet, composed of two word utterances, all presses are higher than in the preceding triplet of one word utterances.

The last example has the child say the nonsense word 'to' to signal a press. Its interest lies in illustrating duration, not amplitude, as the stress marker. Note how much longer are the first presses in the first set of three (creating 1'–2–3) and the last presses of the last two sets of three (creating 1–2–3').

Figure 3. *The subject Valya S., age 4 years, 4 months*

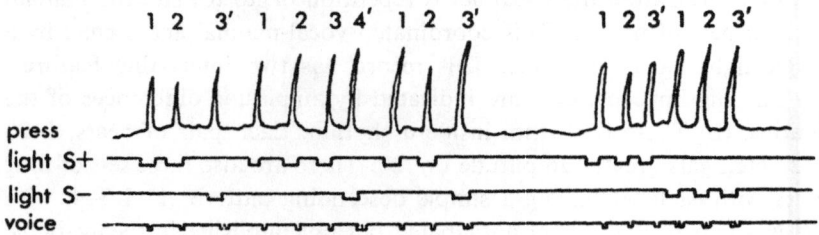

The bulk of the spontaneous rhythm and coordination data indicates that frequency of overt displays declines with age. In the 19 Soviet records one finds 100% of the Ss showing some rhythmic coordination but a general decrease in its frequency. Divided into four-month intervals from 3-2 to 5-10, the drop averages .75 presses per group, with the largest drop between 3-1 to 4-6. The coordinations do not, however, disappear even at the age of 5-10.

Turning to other realms for data, Meerloo (1961) cited an array of behaviors from pawing the nursing breast and sucking to spontaneous rocking and bouncing. These clearly decrease with age but may be evoked in adults in conditions of pathology, relaxation, and mass participation. Gilles (1971) noted that the complexity and number of rhythmic motor sequences in spontaneous play is inversely proportional to age between 6 to 10 years.

In two of my own studies there is decrease with age of vocal-manual coordinations during spontaneous activity. The first study examines only coordinated onsets of discrete acts, not parallels within rhythm patterns. The second study does look at rhythmic coordinations. However, the same phenomenon is demonstrated: joint accents on a homogeneous background. This is created by mutual presence and absence of voice and movement.

Thirty-eight children from 3-4 to 3-9 vocalized while working finger mazes unblindfolded (Zivin 1973). An event recorder recorded when, where, and for how long children moved their fingers and/or vocalized. 'Pulses' of vocal and finger synchrony could be computed by counting the frequency with which the onset of a vocalization was accompanied (within .5 sec.) by the onset of a sharp reversal of finger direction (a 'U-turn' in a dead end). This count as a percent of vocalizations shows the rapid decline over age: 5.3%, 2.5% 3.1%, and 3.1% for the 5, 5, 10, and

12 children who fell into the four sets of months from 3-4 to 4-9. Standard deviations are 4.14, 3.51, 3.89, and 3.59, respectively. The coordination between speech and action, if present in older children, is more difficult to notice.

A second set of data comes from video-taped observations of free play by 5 to 7 year-olds (Zivin in press). Children played alone in a laboratory playroom, with three toys in full access: a pile of 30 styrofoam worms, 13 lettered dice, and a magnet board having 12 pieces for making pictures. The criterion of rhythmic coordination was the easy appearance of speech accents and actions coinciding. These vocalizations usually were sing-songing a story about what was being built, counting, saying the alphabet, or repeating a few nonsense words over and over. Concurrent manual activity could look like rolling a dice over and over, waving a toy, or lifting and placing pieces.

Of 24 children in each age group, 5, 6, and 7 years, video records of 4, 3, and 5 children, respectively, were randomly selected for observation. Martin's (1972) definition was used to recognize rhythm. For each child there was stop-watch timing ($\pm$ .5 sec.) of the amount of vocal-manual rhythmic coordination. This time was divided by total play time, giving the proportion of play activity having joint rhythm in voice and body. For the three age groups, this proportion is 17.3%, 8.6%, and 5.6% with standard deviations of 11.69, 1.44, and 3.35, respectively. The appearance of rhythmic pacing of constructive and exploratory activity by speech drops drastically over the period from 5 to 8 years.

Although the dominance of rhythmic coordinations declines with age, one can find its presence in older children and adults. In an experiment where rhythm was purposely provided by chanting the jingle 'one potato two potato', Meacham, Harris, and Blaschko (1973) noticed that all adults and most children (7 to 8 years old) broke up the jingle so as to press while uttering a word. Both adults and these children have developed strategies to break away from antagonistic verbal rhythm while still remaining sensitive to it. One strategy was to spontaneously segment the vocalization in a non-antagonistic way. Another, used by the children, was to say the jingle less frequently. Neither strategy would be needed if the vocal rhythm were not internally contagious for both children and adults. The adults seem simply to have better techniques to lessen interference from conflicting vocal rhythms.

These developmental data have indicated the decline with age of easily observable rhythmic coordinations. In overt form they are 'primitive':

readily visible in young children, seeming to disappear with age, and seen in adults during mild stress and pathology.

Primitiveness hints fundamentality. It suggests rhythmic coordination to be a basic mechanism – a mechanism facilitating reduction and hence mastery of complex but repetitive tasks – and that the rhythm is often generated (or at least carried) by speech-for-self. Current knowledge cannot determine whether the origin of pacing rhythms is a central timer, breath, speech itself, or some combination of these candidates. It also cannot tell us whether breath and/or speech carry rhythms originating in each other and in a central timer.

Several factors may contribute to the age disappearance of rhythmic coordinations. Young children have yet to reach mastery of trivial automatizations. Their elders have developed new strategies to aid mastery. They also have found strategies to avoid interference from conflicting rhythms. Finally, as the Soviets emphasize, elders have clearer neural differentiation easing inhibition of unwanted responses. These factors must account for some part of the disappearance of overt rhythmic coordinations in older children and adults. The inverse relation between age and appearance of rhythmic coordinations tells only that adults have less frequent need to use more subtle and controllable forms of the same mechanism. Surely the well-documented phenomenon of adult inner speech and how it hinders mental acts (Sokolov 1972) suggests that rhythmic coordinations of speech and action could function for adults in aiding mastery when needed.

Summary. Response systems are in close neurophysiological commerce and therefore may be organized so as to allow the rhythm of one to pace rhythm in others. This would give the accompanying motor behavior internal structure for economic processing. Despite breath and a central timer being possible origins of rhythm, overt speech-for-self presently seems most likely to carry rhythm in this economizing function. Finally, the dominance in younger years of rhythmic coordinations indicates their primitiveness or fundamentality as mechanisms useful to the organism. The disappearance of overt rhythmic coordinations between vocal and motor systems need not persuade us that adults do not employ rhythmic coordinations. Inner speech research shows that mental and physical acts are hindered by mechanical preclusion of inner speech movements of the tongue. This points up the plausibility of adults simply using sophisticated covert strategies to aid organized processing when facilitation is needed. The remaining time they function efficiently without such strategies – partially because as children they drew heavily upon overt speech-action rhythms to develop these beginning masteries.

D. THE FUNCTION OF SPEECH RHYTHMS IN THE REGULATION OF NON-SPEECH ACTIVITY

by Adrienne E. Harris, *Glendon College, York University, Toronto, Canada*

A central assumption in Soviet investigations of language is that speech-for-self can be an effective regulator of other non-speech behaviors. Language is hypothesized to facilitate the planning, production, and maintenance of a variety of nonverbal activities. In considering how language might function in support of nonverbal activity, Luria (1959) has identified two properties of speech – motoric and semantic – tied in a developmental sequence in which the impulsive effects precede the semantic. Wozniak (1973) also suggests that speech has a multiply reafferent nature and proposes six regulatory mechanisms which capitalize on semantic, syntactic, acoustic, and motoric features of speech. Here, using Wozniak's context, I am suggesting that speech rhythms can also be regulators for noverbal systems. Regulation refers to the capacity of the organism to use features of some or possibly many subsystems (such as language) in a process of reafference and reactive calibration to adapt and monitor ongoing activity.

This paper has three aims. First, I wish to identify levels of rhythm in speech and action. Secondly, evidence will be reviewed to suggest how such rhythms in language may affect non-speech activities. Finally, the claim that rhythm plays a verbal regulatory role requires the successful demonstration that rhythmic properties arise in and are specific to the language system. If sequences of speech appear to organize and pace motor activity, while both in fact are driven by some central generating mechanism, such a rhythm is not a mechanism for 'verbal' regulation, as it is conventionally defined.

Levels of rhythm in speech and action. This analysis of rhythm begins with a specification of a variety of temporal relationships between elements. Rhythm refers to the relative arrangement of pulses, beats, or accents within some coherent structure in complex motor or linguistic activity. Within this very general definition, four distinct categories or levels of rhythm are hypothesized to have some involvement in the production of natural language.

Central pacer. A number of researchers have distinguished rhythm at the level of nervous activity and primary sensory processing (Lenneberg 1966). This rhythm is generally identified as a rapid, fairly regular and periodically structured beat, being variously termed pacer or rhythm generator. Allport (1966), among others, identifies the alpha rhythm as the base unit of time operative in 'the programming of events in the central nervous system'. In a number of psychophysical studies and in some work on skilled performance (Michon 1967; Posner 1967; Travis 1929) there is evidence which points to the primacy or saliency of some pacer or temporal quantizer operating at approximately ten beats per second. A pacer which Lenneberg suggests would be cortical in origin would act as a reference point or background in the processing of sensory information or the timed execution of smooth and overlearned motor patterns.

The importance of some high-speed timing device is suggested in Bernstein's (1967) model for motor movement. Bernstein's hypothesis is that in complex, learned action sequences, a high degree of variability in the action sequence leads to specific and nonvariant goals. Reafference, which is based on some abstract and structured engram or action schema, allows the organism to moniter and adapt ongoing activity and thus replicate the learned action sequence. Reference to some central counter or pacer is an essential feature of such a theory. A pacer provides coherence in complex serial activity by preserving the relative internal temporal relationships.

McNeilage (1972) and Lieberman (1969) would mount a similar argument with regard to speech production in which the integration of complex motor activity occurs at a particularly rapid pace. The case for a high speed pacer in speech production is also argued by Lenneberg, who cites evidence from studies of delayed feedback, dichotic listening and syllable production rate.

Stress. There is a rhythm or organization of beats in speech manifested in the production of single words or compound noun phrases. Stress patterns, at the perceptual level, are perceived variations in loudness and possibly pitch. Halle and Keyser (1971) derived a series of rules for the placement of stress in English, arguing that these rules represent tacit assumptions of competent speakers and listeners. Unlike the pacer rhythm, stress is not a highly regularized structure of beats, but rather, at the acoustic level, alterations in perceived amplitude employed and decoded on the basis of language-specific rules. Stressed syllables in

English are consistently correlated with an increase in subglottal air pressure (Ladefoged 1967).

Intonation. Rhythm can also be identified at the level of constituent structure or sentence. Within these units, variations in fundamental frequency and amplitude are organized to provide characteristic intonation patterns for particular utterances and particular languages. Lieberman (1967) defines intonation in terms of two distinct features, characterized by the articulatory process involved in their production. 'Breath-group' is a basic, archetypal, suprasegmental feature involving a pattern of motor activity in which subglottal, laryngeal, and supraglottal structures are coordinated during one expiration. The second feature of intonation identified by Lieberman is prominence, a segmental feature, to distinguish relative loudness within constituent structures.

Breath-groups can delimit entire utterances or constituents. Thus, although it is a phonological feature, intonation carries syntactic and, at some level, sematic information. For example, breath-groups will allow disambiguation of certain sentences. Shifts in intonation can signal alternative readings or crucial distinctions at the level of phrase markers.

Meter. Rules of rhythm or meter can also be distinguished in the structure of utterances. Meter is more akin structurally to the pacer rhythm than either stress or intonation, in that it is a highly regularized, periodically organized beat, although it can have quite complex arrangements of strong and weak elements. Halle and Keyser (1971) define meter simply as an abstract pattern of pulses which can be combined with a set of correspondence rules and mapped to phonological properties of utterances.

Rhythm and non-speech activity. Having delineated four levels of speech rhythm – pacer, stress, intonation, and meter – I want to consider these rhythms as potential regulators for non-speech activity. First, it seems doubtful that a pacer rhythm is language-specific. In fact, all the evidence points in the other direction, that is, to considering a central pacing rhythm as available and implicated in a variety of action systems, sensory and motoric. Lenneberg (1966) and Martin (1973) view a pacer as central in origin acting as a generator for language. It is possible that the production of overt speech both capitalizes on such a generator and also acts as a 'primer' for other action systems. Spoken language would alter the conditions of arousal, creating in the speaker an organismic climate whose conditions favor or facilitate the execution of other noncompetitive activity. There is, perhaps, a 'crosstalk' between neural systems, based on those components the systems hold in common. It should be pointed out that this function of a pacing rhythm in language is better described as 'priming' than as 'regulating', the emphasis being on alterations in conditions of arousal or orientation rather than in the restructuring of activity in concert with pacing rhythms. Wozniak's (1973) study of discrete verbal responses after silent counting is evidence in support of the view that overt self-generated language alters the conditions of arousal, creating conditions of reaffereance which promote generalized responses of orienting and attending. By extension, ongoing, speech might in a fashion similar to the discrete responses recorded by Wozniak, sustain awareness and sharpen response systems in concurrent serial motor activity. Limited evidence can be offered in this connection. In a combined motor and verbal response task (Harris and Meacham 1972), we asked elderly subjects to sort cards manually and in some conditions to accompany the card sorting with verbalizations. In one non-verbal condition, an elderly subject suddenly began to verbalize spontaneously, as she sorted, producing on that trial her fastest time. Other elderly subjects in our study produced faster motor performance times when asked to perform specific verbalizations. Among the possible explanations for such a finding, I would like to include the hypothesis that engaging in the language system per se might through the activation or priming of central pacing rhythms facilitate the execution of other activities served by the same pacer. Note that this effect would be independent of either the semantic or syntactic directives in the speech message.

Stress and intonation present special problems as potential regulators for action, for these rhythms perform complex functions in speech. Working from Lieberman's (1967) account of the physiological and motoric process involved in the production of stress variations and intonation, we have defined these rhythms in terms of articulatory mechanisms. Therefore, on the one hand, rhythm might well be a source of motoric and acoustic regulation. On the other hand, intonation carries syntactic information. Intonation delimits constituent structures, and stress patterns allow speaker and listener to distinguish among morphemic classes. In this sense, stress and intonation may be included among those linguistic features through which lexical or syntactic regulation takes place.

Returning to the motoric and articulatory features of stress and intonation, these rhythms may also provide orienting acoustic and orienting motoric regulation which is specifically useful to sustain serial motor activity. Bronckart's (1970) analysis of the confounding effects of rhythm in the Luria bulb-press experiment provides an ex ample. The rhythmic patterning of three presses is combined with four linguistic elements 'je/pousse/deux fois', and the language which is structuring the bulb presses is itself rhythmically structured. Stress is applied at particular focal points, and it is these stress elements in the utterance which appear to offer the structuring beat for the manual activity.

A preliminary study done by Meacham, Harris, and Blaschko (1973) can provide some data, primarily for speculation, on the issue of metric rhythm regulation. Subjects were asked to perform a motor and verbal response in a task in which the children's rhyme 'one potato, two potato' was recited aloud while cards were sorted manually according to color. We had predicted that the presence of a strong metric pattern in the speech system could organize the periodic structure of ongoing motor activity. We found instead that the condition in which subjects rhymed and sorted took a longer total time than conditions in which subjects spoke single congruent color or irrelevent words and sorted cards. After analyzing the meter of both the motor and verbal task, we concluded that the coordination of the two activities in that task required what was essentially an exercise in counterpoint. Although no direct confirmation of a facilitative regulatory role for metric rhythm is found, the difficulty in integrating the rhyme 'one potato, two potato' and the particular motor sequence in our study may speak indirectly to the strength of the effect of metric patterns in speech upon non-speech patterns.

A clear demonstration that these are reliable and persistent effects waits further study. Research on this problem will need to measure facilitation, not only in terms of increased speed, but increased economy of movement and regularization of tempo in continuous motor activity. A highly regularized, stereotyped rhythm in speech would lead to greater economy of movement by reducing variability in the motor sequence. Rhythm would thus operate as an ongoing structure in which serial motor acts might be embedded, thus obviating the need for elaborate mechanisms of surveillance or attention as the act unfolded. Rhythm would allow activity to unfold as though on 'automatic pilot' the complex sequence of acts held in place by the persistent structure of the speech rhythm.

There are other instances where rhythmic features of language may be serving a process of regulation. Glossolalia (speaking in tongues), hypnotic induction, chanting, and some yogic phenomena, are all linguistic activities with a strong component of rhythm, in the sense of meter, which I would propose as sources of regulation. Orne's (1959) account of hypnotism represents a safe and conservative framework for analyzing these phenomena. His view is that almost all of the hypnotic experience is due to the voluntary response of the subject to the demand characteristics of the experimental situation. That is, 'successfully' hypnotized subjects are suggestible, responding to explicit and implicit demands for cooperation and obedience. Hypnotic induction is thus a kind of syntactic or semantic regulation where the content of the verbal instructions operates to structure and maintain subsequent behavior by the subject. Samarin's (1972) study of speaking in tongues also points to the essentially voluntary, non-trance nature of that phenomena.

Without invoking any explanation dependent on trance induction, both glossolalia and hypnosis may be instances of rhythmic regulation in which the systematic, overt, metered verbal activity is used to alter the focus of attention and possibly to affect the arousal characteristics of the subject and sustain ensuing activity.

Descriptions of hypnotic induction methods usually endow a great importance to rhythm. A review of some typical induction methods (Barber 1969; Friedlander and Sarbin 1938) indicates that it is the rhythmic feature we have described as meter which is employed. Instructions are always given in low, measured tones and often synchronized to some strobe-like light or metronome. The verbal meter may be strengthened or driven by visual or auditory stimuli. The level of suggestibility can apparently be intensified simply by the additional application of verbally transmitted metric pattern.

There are few studies of glossolalia which have performed a quantitative or metric analysis on the verbal output. However, Goodman's (1969) analysis of glossolalia in four different cultural settings produced sound spectographs of the language samples. Interestingly, the meter in her samples was remarkably similar across the four distinct languages. In this case, meter dominated and appears to have diminished the usual stress and intonation unique to the different language communities.

To be quite speculative about evidence from these studies, I would suggest that rhythmic elements in speech, specifically meter, may facilitate and regulate activity for three different reasons. Overt production of continuous patterned speech may orient Ss to some stream of continuously unfolding stimuli – motoric or otherwise. The speech thus facilitates the maintenance of attention over some ongoing task, in which serial non-speech events are restructured to match serial patterned rhymed speech. Wozniak has defined orienting acoustic and orienting motoric reafference in discrete response situations. Metric speech rhythms could provide ongoing reafference suitable for the maintenance of continuous serial activity. Metric speech rhythms would allow the formation of ongoing regulatory connections between the speech producing mechanisms, auditory feedback from self-produced vocalizations, and centrally managed arousal or orienting mechanisms. It is probably important, as Zivin (1973) has suggested, that the potential for connections between speech and motor systems be distinguished from the problem of facilitation. Reafference from the speech system, as the manipulation with the 'one potato, two potato' rhyme indicates, may not always be facilitative.

If metric rhythm makes available to the subject some stable, regularized and easily programed structure which allows the monitoring and management of serial activity, this would involve an expansion of Wozniak's list to include rhythm as a mechanism for 'structural regulation'. Essentially, linguistic meter would act as the spine for motor activity. This strikes me as a very primitive tool for the management of non-verbal activity, for it requires the persistence of the speech system as an accompaniment to unfolding serial action.

Specifically, I would propose that rhythm as a regulator of activity is facilitative for immature and developing organisms, in situations of stress, or situations where disease, organic deficits, and interference of some speech function is suspected. Meter and possibly other rhythms in speech might thus be particularly effective in shoring up or sustaining a defective system. This view is consistent with some Russian evidence on the interaction of the two signalling systems. Luria (1959) has data showing the supportive function of overt self-instruction upon motor acts in subjects with organic damage. This speculation also allows an interpretive bridge between our data on the performance of elderly subjects in combined verbal and motor tasks and general findings (Welford 1951) on the performance of the elderly which suggest that verbal skills decay or diminish more slowly than certain sensory-motor skills. That is, the adults in our study showed no speed-up with the addition of verbal responses, while for the elderly, who were already slower than younger adults in the motor task, the introduction of a series of verbal responses produced faster motor responses.

Rhythm as language specific. The final question to be addressed here concerns the specificity of the rhythms outlined in this paper to the language system. One rationale for distinguishing between pacer, stress, intonation, and meter is the possibility that this question has to be answered differently for different rhythms. Speech rhythm is a motor phenomenon. It is a by-product of particular articulatory and pulmonary motor movements which produce speech. Thus it would be unlikely that the mechanisms involved in the maintenance or production of rhythm would share no common characteristics with non-speech motor activities. This certainly seems to be the case with regard to a pacing rhythm. Most of the evidence concerning pacemakers or generators in a sensory processing or motor movement model speaks to the central origin of such a system.

Stress and intonation have, in my view, quite a different status than pacing rhythms. It may finally be demonstrated that such rhythms are based on, or in harmony with, a central pacing rhythm as Martin (1973) suggests. They are nonetheless linguistic features particular to ongoing human speech, though no doubt highly variable in different languages. The question is really whether motor systems, manual or pulmonary, for example, can produce or take over all the regulatory mechanisms available through stress or intonation patterns. This is, of course, possible and should be put to some empirical test. However, I think it is important to reiterate a concern for language to which both the Russians and the French structuralist school have always been highly sensitive. Language is a rich and highly elaborate system, a system of differences yielding up complex sets and networks of relationships. Even where other action systems can provide patterns of reafference which regulate activity, such patterns may be more easily accessible, more easily mastered, and structurally more rich when elaborated in the speech system.

The case for meter as functionally specific to language is much more difficult to decide. There is not sufficient evidence to judge the parameters and limitations of metric properties arising in the speech system as organizers of other serial motor activity. The efficacy of metric patterns in specialized settings (such as hypnosis, glossolalia, and chanting) and for special populations (such as the elderly) has been proposed. The question is what other human systems might substitute for language rhythms in this regard.

Breathing and speech production share some of the same apparatus. If breath patterns or particular breath rate should prove to be a mechanism for regulation, the case for a special regulatory role exclusive to metric rhythms in speech would be substantially weakened. A pacing role for breathing in a variety of sensory-motor tasks has been proposed by Smith (1973). One researcher on glossolalia (Goodman 1969) notes that the glossa she analyzed bore great similarity to curative breathing rituals. Natural childbirth employs a system of metered or paced breathing which reportedly alters the focus of attention and possibly sensory threshold for its adepts.

The disturbing possibility arises that in a number of instances in which speech is proposed to play a regulatory role on the basis of motoric reafference, the overt vocalization is only artifactually the mechanism for regulation. If breathing rhythms can structure activity as competently and efficiently as overt speech, this would minimize the importance of acoustic reafferent *per se* and strengthen the case for motoric reafference (not neccessarily vocal) as an important agent for regulation.

The appropriate test of a regulatory role specific to and originating in the speech system would compare the effect of verbal sequences with that of other non-linguistic or non-verbal response systems. If a sequence of vocally produced clicks and hisses, breathing rhythms, or metric patterns of hand or foot tapping can alter or modify motor activity, then speech rhythms are perhaps only one member of a set of response systems whose features may be used to control and regulate activity.

In conclusion, speech rhythms present an intriguing problem for researchers in the area of verbal control. At one level, rhythm is a very primitive phenomenon. In dance, in poetry, in ritual, in a wide range of skilled activities, rhythm can be a potent organizing spine or structure. Yet although rhythm must be considered in terms of its motoric and acoustic character, it is also a subtle mechanism for signalling both syntactic and semantic distinctions. In short, rhythm is one of those curious linguistic hybrids – a phonological, motoric component of language which bears syntactic and semantic information. Rhythm thus appears to cut across the categories of verbal regulation which Wozniak (1973) has identified, for he distinguished between motoric, phonetic, and syntactico-semantic regulation. Language rhythms are thus provocative features of the speech system in which to examine the limits of our definitions of verbal regulation and the specificity of certain regulatory mechanisms to the speech system.

E. SOVIET RESEARCH IN THE PSYCHOPHYSIOLOGY OF INDIVIDUAL DIFFERENCES

by Luciano Mecacci, *National Research Council, Rome, Italy*

In a psychophysiological experiment, according to the classical definition of Stern (1964), independent variables are represented by psychological states or processes (attention, emotion, conditioning, etc.) and dependent variables by physiological processes (electroencephalogram, electrocardiogram, psychogalvanic reflex, etc.). Even though there are general patterns following which a certain physiological response can be correlated with a psychological process (for example, the blocking of the alpha rhythm at the appearance of the conditioned stimulus in a conditioning process), in different individuals a large variability exists in the characteristics of physiological response (for example, in the amplitude and in the latency of the electroencophalographic response).

This problem is known to all psychophysiologists. It has been faced systematically in the Soviet Union by the Pavlovian school and by the school of Teplov and Nebylitsyn; in the Western countries it has been studied only by a very few psychophysiologists.

Pavlov's theory. Right from the first research on conditioned reflexes in dogs, Pavlov and his collaborators noted the existence of individual differences in conditioned responses. Their attention was drawn at first to the global behavior of the animal before and during the experiment (general motor activity, restlessness, drowsiness, etc.). Later on, more and more specific research was carried out on single physiological responses and on particular aspects of the processes of conditioning (speed of formation and extinction of the conditioned reaction, effect of the intensity and duration of the conditioned stimulus, etc.). The research was analysed by Pavlov in numerous articles whose theoretical conclusions were often reviewed and re-elaborated (Teplov 1956). In the 1935 article entitled 'General types of animal and human higher nervous activity' (Pavlov 1957, pp. 313–342), we have the last version of Pavlov's conception of the individual psychophysiological conception, a conception known as the 'typology of higher nervous activity'.

The conceptual principles of the theory are three: the properties of the nervous system, the experimental indices, and the types of the nervous system. The properties of the nervous system are the principal parameters of the functional organization of the nervous system; they regulate the fundamental processes of the nervous system: the excitatory process and the inhibitory process. According to Pavlov, the properties are three: the strength of the excitatory and inhibitory processes, the mobility of the same processes, and the equilibrium between the excitatory and the inhibitory processes. In short, the strength is definable, in Pavlov's terms, as the 'working capacity of the cerebral cells', the capacity to react to the repeated and concentrated action of a stimulus without entering in an inhibitory state; *equilibrium* indicates the relation between the excitatory process and the inhibitory process, that is, whether or not there exists the same capacity in the elaboration of positive and negative (inhibitory) conditioned reflexes; mobility indicates the capacity to react rapidly to changes in the environment, passing from the formation of a certain conditioned reflex to that of another according to the demands of the environment. For the evaluation of the properties, specific experimental indices are adopted. The three properties, however, appear in a different degree in the various subjects (for example, in one subject the excitatory process and the inhibitory process can have equal value; in another the excitatory process prevails on the inhibitory one, etc.). The type is precisely the total of the three properties in the measure in which they appear in a certain subject. Pavlov distinguished four fundamental types for whose denomination he often made recourse also to classical hippocratean typology.

The school of Teplov and Nebylitsyn. The typological Pavlovian conception has been further re-elaborated by various Soviet authors like Ivanov-Smolensky (1954), Kradusky (1971), Fedorov (1969) and Troshikin (1971) The more important re-elaboration, however, is that of the school of Teplov and Nebylitsyn, conducted within the past twenty years at the Institute of Psychology of Moscow on the basis of experiments carried out on human subjects (Teplov 1956–1967; Nebylitsyn 1966, 1969, 1971; Nebylitsyn and Gray 1972).

Among the main general critical observations raised by the school of Teplov and Nebylitsyn against the Pavlovian typology, we want to remember two: (a) A typological classification is premature. One has to first of all examine deeper the functional characteristics of the various properties of the nervous system and the relation between those same properties. It is not excluded that future research will lead us to identify other properties unknown today. (b) The concept of property itself has to be revised. A property has not a general functional value for every sensorial modality. In the same person the strength of the excitatory process in relation to a visual stimulus can have values different from those of strength in relation to an acoustic stimulus. According to Nebylitsyn (1956, 1971) we must distinguish between 'partial properties' of the nervous sytem of a subject and the 'general properties'. The partial properties are those that are concerned with the single cortical analyzers. From the experiments conducted so far, it appears that in about twenty percent of human beings the strength of the excitatory process has different values in the same subject depending on the cortical analyzer that is directly concerned from time to time in the conditioned reflex. The general properties, instead, are those that are concerned with the functional characteristics of the activity of the whole brain. Nebylitsyn, on the basis of the analysis of the experimental literature, retains that this general pattern of functioning is mediated by the frontal area, the subcortical structures, and the reticular formation. Of course the interindividual differences in general properties considerably influence the eventual intraindividual differences in the partial properties. The general properties in fact represent functions like the regulation and the coordination of behavioral programes (frontal areas), the activation levels (reticular formation), etc. – functions having general characteristics such that the intraindividual differences on the level of the single analyzers usually assume a secondary role in differentiating one individual from another.

One of the most important contributions of this Soviet school to the clarifying of the relations between the properties of the nervous system was in distinguishing the strength of the nervous system from another property introduced by Nebylitsyn, dynamism. In the Pavlovian formulation, strong dogs distinguish themselves from the weak ones by the rapidity of the formation of their conditioned reflexes. In his last article on typology, Pavlov writes: 'In the first case [that is, strong dogs] the conditioned reflexes developed rapidly after the application of two or three combinations; they quickly reached considerable strength and remained constant, no matter how complicated the system of reflexes. In the second case [that is, weak dogs], on the contrary, the conditioned reflexes were formed very slowly, after many repetitions (about ten) their strength increases at very slow rate, and they never acquired stability, being sometimes even at zero, no matter how considerably their system was simplified' (Pavlov 1957, p. 316).

Various research conducted on animals in the last twenty years, particularly in the Laboratory of Genetics of Higher Nervous Activity of the Institute of Physiology at Koltushi (Fedorov 1969; Krasusky and Fedorov 1971), has demonstrated that between the results obtained in the test for the evaluation of the strength of the excitatory processes and those for rapidity of the formation of the conditioned reflexes there does not exist any correlation whatsoever. The speed of the formation of the conditioned reflexes has been denoted by Nebylitsyn as 'dynamism of the nervous system'. Strength and dynamism are two distinct properties of the nervous system. The subjects classified according to the strength as 'strong' or 'weak' are not directly estimable as 'more dynamic' or 'less dynamic'.

Gray's theory: Introversion-extraversion and arousal. The approach of the school of Teplov and Nebylitsyn to the study of individual psychophysiological differences became known in the Western countries through Gray's book *Pavlov's Typology* (1964). Among the many contributions of this scholar we will remember that of having compared the 'strong/weak' classification of the Soviet school with the 'extraverts/introverts' classification of Eysenck.

According to Eysenck, at least in the first period of his research, the extravert subjects form conditioned reflexes with difficulty, and once formed these very easily die away because in these subjects the process of inhibition prevails; the introvert subjects, on the contrary, form conditioned reflexes easily and their extinction is slower because the process of excitation prevails. The problem of the relation between conditioning and introversion/extraversion has constitued an obscure and contradictory point in the experimental literature. The reason why not a few experimental results contradicted Eysenck's hypothesis or were not in accord among themselves depends on not having adequately distinguished the property of strength from the property of dynamism in the process of conditioning. On that depended also the terminological confusion for which, according to the parameter on which it was based, the extravert subjects were considered at one time strong, at another weak, and the introvert subjects at one time weak, at another strong.

To clarify this problem, one needs to consider the interpretation that Gray made both of the concept of strength (Gray 1964) and of the physiological bases of introversion/extraversion (Gray 1970; Passingham 1970). The concept of intensity of the excitatory process which we measure with the indices of strength is assimilable to the concept of arousal level elaborated by the theory of activation (Malmo 1959). Individual differences, according to the property of strength, correspond to individual differences in the arousal level that Gray calls 'arousability'. The basic difference between extraverts and introverts is not in a different degree of conditionability, but in a different degree of arousability. In this sense, joining the two reinterpretations of Gray, the difference between introverts and extraverts corresponds to that between the weak and the strong subjects, the two differences both having as a common parameter of physiological differentiation the degree of arousability. This coincidence has been demonstrated by the various researches of Mangan (White and Mangan 1972) and of Zhorof and Yermolaeva-Tomina (1972). All the same, exactly as in an experiment of Eysenck (Eysenck and Levey 1972), the result was that the difference in the level of conditioning between extraverts and introverts is not unidirectional and is obtained only in certain conditions. If low intensity stimuli are used (and one works therefore on the property of strength or on the arousal level of the subject), a difference in the conditioning level is obtained in favor of introverts; if, on the other hand, high intensity stimuli are used, the difference results in favor of the extraverts.

Conclusion. Now let us summarize all that we have dealt with so far. By means of some experimental indices of strength, one can distinguish the strong subjects and the weak subjects. The neurophysiological processes that mediate this differentiation depend on the processes of arousal and on the structures indicated by Gray as the reticular formation, the septal area, the hippocampus, and the frontal areas. They would seem to be, therefore, the same structures that Nebylitsyn considers as the mediators of the general properties of the nervous system. Strength, meant as arousability, would seem therefore a general property of the nervous system having in some persons (twenty percent of the samples examined) differences on the level of the cortical analyzers. The influence of strength on behavioral performance, like the acquisition of conditioned responses, varies from person to person, depending on the experimental procedures that are used (for example, the intensity level of the stimuli) and on the individual arousability.

  In an experiment that intends to evaluate the differences in the degree of conditioning, one needs to proceed in the way we propose: (a) Evaluate the subjects on the basis of the tests of strength and divide them in two groups – strong subjects and weak subjects. (b) Consider separately each group and analyze the differences in the degree of conditioning with the indices of dynamism. In this way one would eliminate, at least in a large part, the influence on conditioning due to substantial differences in arousability. The eventual differences in conditioning would depend on other neurophysiological processes different from those that mediate the arousal level. According to Konorski (1973), the formation of the conditioned reflexes depends on the degree of 'transmittability of the synapses linking the neurons belonging to each of these centres [of the conditioned stimulus and of the unconditioned stimulus]'. These connections are formed in the interaction of animals and men with their environment during their ontogenetic development, and their 'quantity' and 'quality' depend on the type of interaction itself. Arousability, as Eysenck (1968) supposes, would seem, instead, a mainly hereditary process.

The problem of psychophysiological differences is therefore strictly linked with that of the ontogenetic development of physiological variables, a research theme that Stern (1968) calls 'developmental psychophysiology'. The psychophysiologist cannot consider abstractly and statically the physiological variable and then correlate it with a psychological variable. The physiological variable is the result of innate and acquired processes. Often, instead, it has been considered a 'pure' and essentially innate process, to be correlated to a psychological process, such that it would act as an index of the innate character of the psychological process. An example of such an approach are the experiments of Ertl (1969; see the critical notes of Vernon 1970) on the correlation between evoked potentials latency and intelligente quotient.

Even if the problem of the relation between the innate and the acquired is one of the most intricate in psychology, one cannot depend for the solution of this problem on the use of physiological variables. To resolve the complexity of the psychological processes with the supposed but not real simplicity of the physiological processes does not indicate an anti-dualistic approach; on the contrary, it hides the most dangerous dualism.

F. LIFE-SPAN COGNITIVE DEVELOPMENT AND THE SOVIET THEORY OF SELF-REGULATION

by Howard C. Eisner, *Duke University, Durham*

Throughout much of its history, cognitive development has generally been equated with developmental changes in the growing child. Recently, a few investigators have begun to examine the concept of development from a life-span perspective (see, for example, Baltes 1973; Goulet and Baltes 1970; Nesselroade and Reese 1973). Two general developmental models of cognitive growth across the life-span have been proposed.

Models of development. The continuity model views the development of human cognition in a purely mechanistic manner as nothing more than a steady quantitative rise (and subsequent fall in senescence) in the number of S-R bonds, habits, informational units, or amount of information processing capacity available to the developing organism. On the neurophysiological level, this implies that human capacities are a direct function of the number of fully operative neural conduction fibers.

A discontinuity model of development, on the other hand, identifies changes in the ontogenetic process as more than merely the accumulation of neuronal units or increases in speed, accuracy, or efficiency in processing information. The meaning of development is instead limited to:

'... changes which are are not merely irreversible, or which yield only a greater numerical complexity; those changes must in addition eventuate in modes of organization not previously manifested in the history of the developing system.... The connotation of development thus involves two essential components: the notion of a system possessing a definite structure and a definite set of pre-existing capacities; and the notion of a sequential set of changes in the system, *yielding relatively permanent but novel increments not only in its structure but in its modes of operation as well*' (Nagel 1957, pp. 16–17, italics added).

The continuous, neo-behavioristic, mechanistic model and the discrete, discontinuous, organismic approach have usually been classed as diametrically opposed word views (Nagel 1957; Overton and Reese 1973; Reese and Overton 1970; Zigler 1963). The former has been described by Reese and Overton (1970) as implying that complex behavior is completely predictable from more elementary concepts and can be understood in terms of cause and effect and the total history of the organism. The organism is viewed as a reactive collection of elements; and development is nothing more than a continuous change in the status of this set of components as well as being at least potentially amenable to precise mathematical description.

By way of contrast, the organismic viewpoint proposes that the organism is an organized totalitly, one which changes in novel and not wholly predictable ways. The organismic conception depicts an active organism whose behavior is not reducible to cause and effect and whose developmental history is a discontinuous one with frequent reorganization and the emergence of qualitatively new behavioral forms.

The benefits of considering these models by a developmental psychologist, particularly one interested in describing life-span cognitive development, lie in the ability of a model to delimit and organize those features of human behavior which are the essential aspects of ontogenetic cognitive growth. An increasing number of cognitive theorists have selected the qualitative, change-in-function model because it is felt that this type of model provides just these benefits. Certainly those adherents to Piaget's developmental system have been attracted to his model for just this reason. What I would like to suggest is that another discontinuity model which stresses developmental changes in the regulatory or planning functions, especially with regard to speech, may be an even more powerful tool for structuring and explaining observed cognitive performance changes across the life-span.

Verbal self-regulation. The discontinuity model being proposed is one associated primarily with Russian theorists such as Vygotsky (1962) and Luria (1961). The Soviets have continually placed great stress on the regulatory role of language in child development. Several discrete stages in the verbal control of behavior have been identified, beginning with a period when the speech sound is little more than one of many equivalent components of a multi-faceted cue-possessing stimulus. Speech then progresses to a stage where adult verbalization can impel or initiate behavior as through the command 'Give me the ball!' There follows next a stage where self-verbalization acquires directive, impulsive control of a child's movements as in the command 'Press!' accompanied by a squeezing response. And then finally speech reaches a full significative, semantic stage at which time it acts as the mature regulator and planner of the whole stream of human activities. In this most advanced stage, a child or adult can use covert verbalization to regulate an activity or to inhibit one ongoing activity and replace it with some other action. Speech at this point is viewed as serving a master planning function in controlling all human activities.

Developmental changes in childhood and old age. The focus of the remainder of this paper will be a demonstration that the self-regulatory model of cognitive growth is a fruitful technique for describing and explaining cognitive change at all stages of the life-span. At the early stages of the life-span a considerable amount of evidence has already been collected to support such a position. Luria, for example, has demonstrated how, with the introduction of self-regulating speech into the child's repertoire, activities are formulated before they are carried out; and a specific goal and plan of attack are established. Whether it be play activity or problem solving, the introduction of verbal control indicates a shift in cognitive behavior from mere describing of the past to a verbal elaboration of future objectives and possible solutions. A course of action can be outlined which goes well beyond the limits of the environment (Luria and Yudovich 1959).

Sheldon White (1965) has done a masterful job of summarizing the literature on the many changes occurring in the age range from $4^1/_2$ to 7 years – the time when the mature aspects of the speech control function finally are becoming realized. The many studies he cites support the proposed discontinuity position. The idea that emerges from his review is that at some point between the age of $4^1/_2$ and 7, language becomes pre-eminent in directing and regulating the form of a child's cognition. At this time the child learns to label, compare, plan, and hypothesize. He learns to use his covert verbalizations in uniquely different ways to direct his behavior. To give only two of many possible representative examples, training young children to respond relationally to one pair of stimuli will generalize only to other pairs of stimuli which are similar along the specified dimension. In older children, relational responding is found on both near and far tests of transposition (Kuenne 1946). The Kendlers have documented in numerous studies the transition in children from initially better performance on nonreversal shifts to a later age period when subjects do better on reversal problems (see, for example, Kendler and Kendler 1962). This transition has been further shown to coincide with the productive use of language in the problem situation (Kendler and Kendler 1961).

Now, what about the elderly? Do ideas about verbal control or the regulation of behavior apply to the elderly as well? I think they do. It seems to me that cognitive and performance deficits at the upper end of the age range can often be understood and successfully explained in terms of deficiencies in self-regulatory control or planning mechanisms (for a more complete expansion of this position see Wozniak and Eisner 1972). It can be argued that in the same way that children progress through advancing levels of verbal regulatory control of their behavior, the elderly may be going into decline because of inadequacies in this same set of regulatory and planning mechanisms.

This does not necessarily mean, however, that during the declining period of the life-span the individual simply goes backward through the same stages he progressed through on the way to mature cognitive development. One compelling reason for believing that this is not the case is that, except in the case of organic brain damage or advanced senility, the older individual does not lose his language capabilities. Deficits in elderly cognitive performance would not, therefore, seem to be directly attributable to a constriction in the phenotypic representation of the language system *per se*. What instead appears to be happening is that the older individual loses the capability of effectively utilizing language in its capacity for verbal self-instruction. This, in addition to changes in the discriminative character of stimuli from the environment, may account for much of the observed decline in the elderly with regard to effective mechanisms for controlling concurrent activities as well as planning future actions.

An analogy to computers similar to an idea suggested by Rabbitt (1968) may prove useful in putting these ideas into perspective. The young child may be seen as an under-programed system. The child does not have the information, experience, or the verbal facility to plan and direct his behavior. Behavioral development implies adding instructions, programs, or subroutines to the young organism's repertoire such that he can effectively handle the situations of everyday life. Adolescence and later periods merely add to the effective number of programs in the repertoire, so that self-produced and environmentally interposed cues can set off effective cognitive strategies for productive behavior.

What may well be a significant aspect of performance deficits in the elderly is that the machine gets too well programed. The older individual has many programs available, but he becomes inflexible in his selection and evaluation of how to operate on his environment through the utilization of these previously learned programs. The aged person may be too effectively controlled by his past experience, his verbal self-instructions, as well as environmental cues. The result is that a self-produced or environmentally supplied cue may select a highly practiced behavioral program for the accomplishment of a desired goal. The difficulty is that the wrong subroutine or program may be selected on the basis of incomplete or inappropriate information, and the elderly person may continue to use this program without ever evaluating whether it is the most efficient or even an appropriate mechanism for accomplishing this goal.

The conclusion thus drawn is that maturity and old age is a time when the individual has overdeveloped rather narrowly directed behavioral algorithms. Whatever the actual stage of cognitive performance the older person is in, he has developed a highly practiced way of using his experience, as well as verbal self-instruction and environmentally supplied cues, to direct his everyday affairs and professional life. Piaget (1972) has recently alluded to the same point. In his paper, Piaget looks at how the individual develops intellectually from adolescence to adulthood. He makes the point that the rate of development for different individuals may vary because of cultural factors. He further states that while all normal subjects will eventually reach the stage of formal operations '...they reach this stage in different areas according to their aptitudes and their professional specializations...: the way in which these formal structures are used, however, is not necessarily the same in all cases' (p. 10).

The conclusion which once again can be made from this is that there is a defect in the individual's control mechanisms. Experience may become so overly specific that it interferes with the capability of the organism to utilize certain concrete or formal operations in other than very narrowly circumscribed situations. The carpenter may effectively use cognitive operations in his work; but at the same time he may be losing, or at least be unable to apply these same principles in a non-carpentry situation. Such an explanation may also help to account for reports by Kominski and Coppinger (1968), Papalia (1972), and Sanders, Laurendeau, and Bergeron (1966) of failures of the elderly in conservation tasks. It may be the case that the elderly are simply unable to take algorithms they do possess in the real world and transfer them to unusual or unfamiliar situations. Older subjects may simply not be familiar with or interested in test problems involving cows grazing in a field. On the other hand, if the same problem is restated in terms of experiences where they have well defined operational systems already developed and highly practiced, performance might turn out quite differently.

Let me now briefly cite some other evidence which can be interpreted as indicating changes in the control process and/or the narrowed focus and lack of flexibility in plans of action in the elderly. Because of space limitations, examples have been selected primarily from the human performance literature, but the same reasoning could as easily be applied to studies from perception, problem solving, or any other area of cognition. Rabbitt (1968) has reviewed a whole set of studies which looked at the ability of young and old subjects to utilize regularities in signal information. Older subjects were found to be both less able to take advantage of predictable foreperiods in reaction time tasks and also more hindered by an occasional irregular or unexpected foreperiod. Here, what seems to be happening is that older subjects do indeed appear to be controlled by external signals. They also seem well able to formulate strategies about what is happening and programs of what it is they are expected to do. The controlling aspects of the stimuli and the behavioral algorithm seem, if anything, to have become overly predominant so that the elderly subjects must continually check on the signal value of each and every stimulus. This need to over-examine signals and run completely through a pre-programed course of action to confirm expectancies would explain the behavioral slowing seen in both tasks. It may also be the explanation for the finding by Rabbitt and Birren (1967) that older subjects were faster at recognizing discontinuities in a repetitive pattern of signals (a program set up to carefully examine every signal would, of course, be effective in early identification of an unusual signal).

In a similar manner the over-programing of behavior and need to check the validity of each step in a behavioral chain may explain the observation of Szafran (1955) that older workers tended to look more at each step of what they were doing even after a considerable amount of practice. A similar explanation could account for the related finding by Singleton (1954) that slowing in older subjects was particulary noticeable when the appropriateness of a motor movement was indicated not only by kinesthetic cues but also by redundant confirmatory external light signals. It appears that far from being unable to take advantage of internal and external controls, older subjects are unable to ignore the signal value of redundant or confirmatory inputs. Finally, similar interpretations can be placed on the finding that older individuals showed the most susceptibility to set on tasks such as the Luchins' Water Jars Test (Heglin 1956) and the report of a decreasing ability in older subjects to disregard the initial percept in Boring's ambiguous wife or mother-in-law figure in terms of their ability to reorganize the same stimulus into a second percept once the initial alternative has been identified (Botwinick, Robbin and Brinley 1959). In all of these cases, once an initial program has been selected by the individual he rigidly adheres to this mode of operation. The result is behavioral slowing, inefficiency, or limited success in detecting alternatives or correct solutions in the specified task.

Determinants of cognitive growth. It has been suggested that one of the primary determinants of cognitive growth and decline across the life-span is the functional level of the regulatory mechanisms possessed by the individual at any one point in development. A goal of the cognitive psychologist should be to assess those processes and cues which are maximally effective in producing skilled behavior in a particular age range. Looking first at early development, Flavell and Bem have both analyzed the failures of the young child to respond accurately in various memory tasks or problem-solving situations. Flavell has expanded on the original mediational deficiency position (Reese 1962). He has suggested a production deficiency hypothesis according to which some performance failures in children are due to the child's failure to spontaneously produce appropriate verbal mediators (Flavell, Beach and Chinsky 1966). A subsequent serial recall study (Keeney, Cannizzo and Flavell 1967) demonstrated that teaching young children who are normally non-rehearsers to rehearse raised the performance of these subjects to a level equivalent to that of children who did spontaneously rehearse the items. Bem (1968) has additionally suggested that failures in some tasks are due to the child not generating a description of the task and what it is he is supposed to achieve. Bem has reported successfully teaching the child to comprehend the task which, in turn, has led to successful problem solutions. This seems to be a case of increasing the control value of the critical stimuli as well as a way of compensating for inadequately programed strategies in young children.

Baer (1970) has gone a step further and suggested that the control of behavior need not be viewed as related to the age variable at all. Although not subscribing to an organismic view of behavior, Baer recognizes that different environmental or self-produced cues may be more or less effective at different points in development. He thus makes the important observation that cognitive development can be facilitated, not merely by growing older (see also Wohlwill 1970), but by understanding what are the effective controlling stimuli at any particular time in the organism's history. This is the same point made in a study by Zaporozhets (1961). Here it was found that the effective cuing features for successful orientation to an unfamiliar environment or problem change from tactile to visual and finally to verbal as the child passes through the age range from 4 to 8.

Determinants of cognitive decline. Turning to later maturity and old age, the material reported earlier has indicated the kinds of deficits observable when cognitive functioning begins to decline. Many workers in human aging see such deficits in the aged as the inexorable and irremediable concomitants of the aging process. Much of this type of thinking seems tied to mechanistic views of aging as accumulated losses in neuronal functioning or information processing capacity. Alternatively, one could adopt the model suggested above that aging involves certain changes in the control value of internally or externally produced stimuli. Adopting such a position leads to a conclusion that even if certain systems are no longer fully effective, attempts should be made to identify other intact functional systems which could partly or even fully compensate for what are most frequently viewed as inalterably lost skills.

One obvious place to look for such a compensatory mechanism is within some part of the verbal regulatory system. It has been suggested that in aging the control value of stimuli may be qualitatively altered. It may well also be true that the individual becomes overly influenced by external signals or too narrowly focused by his own previously formulated verbal strategies. What needs to be determined are ways of using the older individual's already highly organized verbal skills to regulate his behavior.

Crovitz (1966) has argued that the elderly are less effective than the young adult in using verbal mediators for devising effective strategies in problem-solving tasks. She trained older subjects to verbalize the critical aspects of stimulus cards in a visual discrimination task. Whereas almost half of the older subjects in the non-training group failed to learn the discrimination problem, all of the subjects who had been trained to use their own verbalization to describe the stimulus features solved the discrimination problem in the test situation.

Brinley and Fichter (1970) have shown that when aged subjects are provided with step by step information concurrent with their performance on a set of simple arithmetic and letter cancellation problems, performance is improved over a situation where instructions were given prior to performance. In comparison with younger subjects, the elderly seemed to benefit more from external signals as a mechanism for regulating rapid, efficient performance.

In the area of memory, there is evidence available which demonstrates that both verbal and visual imagery cues can facilitate retrieval in elderly subjects. Laurence (1967) presented young and old subjects with a 36 word list comprised of six different categories of six words each. Providing category cues prior to list presentation had no effect on retrieval. If, however, the category cues were provided just prior to retrieval, older subjects were especially benefited; and their performance improved to a level equal to that of a younger group. Hulicka and Grossman (1967), using a paired-associate task, found that instructions in the use of verbal and visual mediators facilitated performance. Although both young and old subjects were aided by instructions to use mediators, the older subjects did show relatively greater improvement from such training.

The results obtained in the preceding set of studies point to the possibility of a production deficiency in the elderly resembling that found in the very young. Both groups are ineffective in employing verbal self-regulation. However, since the elderly do possess a highly developed linguistic repertoire, it seems that they should especially benefit from training in the more effective utilzation of their own verbalizations to regulate behavior. Meichenbaum (1973) has devised just such a self-instructional training program. Through a series of stages including experimenter-produced models of correct behavior, performance of activities by the subject as directed by instructions from the trainer, and self-initiated instructions by the subject, both hyperactive children and adult hospitalized schizophrenics have been taught to use their own verbalizations to produce more acceptable forms of behavior. It seems likely that such training could have equally beneficial effects on preserving and even extending the cognitive potential of the aged. Since their verbal lexicon is intact, the older individual should be an especially suitable subject for training in the use of verbal self-instruction as a way of programing effective behavior.

The conceptual framework developed in this paper leads to certain conclusions regarding strategies for investigating life-span cognitive development. Insofar as the proposed self-regulatory model is an appropriate one, investigators will gain understanding and descriptive power from the search for qualitatively demonstrable changes in cognitive functions, especially linguistically regulated functions, across the entire life-span. But, at the same time, adherence to this or any other model should not be a deterrent from the more basic goal of maximally employing all of the cognitive potential which is available to an individual at any point in time, regardless of how closely that performance may fit the particular developmental model under consideration. So, for example, even if some form of organismic model such as the one proposed is most effective in organizing and explaining the changes in cognitive development across the life-span, let us not hesitate to employ mechanistic procedures of the type suggested by Baer (1970) and Meichenbaum (1973) if they are successful in maximizing the life enjoyment of people at all points along the age range.

Cognitive development through life: Research based on Piaget's system

A SENSORIMOTOR PERIOD: THE SOURCE OF INTELLECTUAL DEVELOPMENT

by Gene C. Anderson,* *University of Illinois, Medical Center, Chicago*

Scientists are looking ever earlier into the life-span in an effort to get a 'Head Start' on problems of behavioral development. The realization that the infancy period required study was not originally looked upon with relish. Infants, not to mention newborns, had been traditionally viewed as unknowing, uneducable, unmeasurable, and therefore uninteresting, and hopefully unimportant precursors of humanity. The burgeoning, and sometimes startling, infancy literature attests to the fact that this traditional view can no longer be upheld. Amazing perceptual and cognitive capacities have been documented in some infants and under certain conditions. The naturally delivered transitional newborn, free of obstetrical medication (*cf.* Brazelton 1961), is a case in point. The behavior of the very young human clearly changes with his experiences during the first months, days, and even hours, of life. Defined in this broad sense, it can be said that newborns and infants have the capacity to learn.

Piaget's theory. Piaget (1952, 1954) transformed the study of infancy

* The author wishes to thank Professor Frank H. Hooper, University of Wisconsin. Madison, for his critical comments and support during the preparation of this manuscript.

irreversibly when he introduced his unique conceptualization of the human infant. He views the developing newborn and infant as an active organism who constructs his own reality as he engages in intimate inter-action with his environment. The infant, through this activity, quickly learns to distinguish among various features of the immediate environment and to modify his behavior appropriately. For Piaget, such adaptation to reality reveals the origins of intelligence.

According to Piaget, an invariant sequence of six stages characterizes the qualitatively different general levels of intellectual development within the sensorimotor period. He emphasizes the process by which the infant masters these stages. This process involves the elaboration and extension of action schemes, through their progressive intercoordination. This occurs for each content domain. The gradual internalization of schemes, in the form of schemata, marks the beginning of representation. The sensorimotor period reaches functional maturity when these schemata can be used to deductively infer new means for achieving desired goals. These goals are then achieved through action upon directly perceived objects.

The development of schemes may be viewed in two ways. The first considers the progressive intercoordination of the various sensorimotor abilities themselves, e.g., vision and prehension. The second view considers the levels of progressive intercoordination as abstractions. This latter view provides a very useful taxonomic device, designated by Ginsburg and Opper (1969) as the theory of each stage.

Piaget's theory also emphasizes the continuity which is present across the stages and major periods. The functional invariants help to provide this continuity, for they are present across the life-span and function the same from the physiological to the formal level of analysis. They are subsumed by the equilibration process, through which the organism reaches progressively more effective states of equilibrium. The equili-bration process itself, as a whole, might be considered a functional invariant of a higher order. From this higher order-perspective, the equilibration model also appears to organize and subsume the six stages of infancy.

The notion of overt sensorimotor precursors adds considerable im-portance to the infancy period. Intellectual activity occurs during infancy in the form of sensorimotor action schemes. These action schemes are analogous to, and the functional precursors of, the mental schemes of the later concrete and formal operations periods. From this view, analogies can be drawn between schemes of action and thought. One profound importance of the action schemes may be that their progressive inter-cocrdination occurs in overt and thus observable form throughout most of the sensorimotor period. The gradual internalization of these processes is also observable. The progressive intercoordination of the mental schemes generally occurs internally, however, and is relatively inaccessible for study. Analogies carefully drawn should therefore be useful in understanding the usually covert processes whereby intelligence develops during these later periods. Herein may lie one of Piaget's major contributions. For it is in following the processes that an understanding of cognitive development will be achieved. It seems likely that actions, at least sensorimotor actions, do indeed speak louder than words.

Literature review. This review's main focus was upon evaluating the very active research issues of within-major-period invariant sequence and correspondence. You will no doubt recall Wohlwill's (1963) amusing description of Winnie-the-Pooh and Piglet, who were going around and around in a big circle. They were not quite sure what they were hunting, but they called it 'woozle'. They continued to follow the woozle's tracks until Christopher Robin happened along and kindly pointed out their folly. Indeed, the tracks they were following turned out to be only their very own. Wohlwill intended this as an analogue to developmental psychologists, who were busily conducting Piagetian replication research, but who were not testing Piaget's theory, *per se*. Wohlwill felt these replication studies, however valuable in their own right, did not recognize explicitly the essence of the Piagetian system. He offered suggestions, which might be viewed as aliment to help Pooh and Piglet out of their 'circular reaction' rut. In particular, he posed two empirical questions, which he felt would evaluate the validity of Piaget's theory and would be testable: '(1) Do the steps marking the development of a concept appear according to a fixed, orderly progression? (2) Do responses to tasks which differ but which, according to the system, are based on the same mental operations, develop simultaneously, i.e., in phase with one another?' (Wohlwill 1963, p. 254). The first question refers to invariant sequence, the second to correspondence.

Within-major-period invariant sequence appears generally established, at least for infants of Western culture. However, Corman and Escalona (1969) found this was so only for first emergence of skills (vertical progression). Within-stage invariant sequence and the rate of vertical progression evidence greater variability both within and between subjects and across content domains. Still greater variability is evidenced for the postulate of within-major-period correspondence. Such variation is usually attributed to status variables and environmental influences such as test setting, task dimensions, relevant prior experience, and testing errors. The same general conclusions hold true in studies of special populations. Ordinal scales developed by Corman and Escalona and by Uzgiris and Hunt have been invaluable as dependent measures in such studies, and the trend toward their increasing usage promises to continue. Uzgiris and Hunt (1972) offer a comprehensive discussion of this area, gleaned from their decade of scale construction endeavors. Enrichment studies (e.g., Eppink 1969; Kravitz and Boehm 1971; Ourth and Brown 1961; Watson and Ramey 1972; White 1971) have demonstrated the considerable plasticity of the young human infant to environmental influences. Wachs, Uzgiris and Hunt (1971) present data revealing deficiencies in performance in Negro and white lower SES American infants as early as seven months. This may be the beginning expression of an ever increasing deficit in consolidation. This deficit does not noticeably hamper vertical progression but appears to undermine subsequent over-all intellectual development.

Exercise and practice appear to be important quantitative components of the developmental process, which ultimately results in qualitative change. Slow motion films demonstrate unforgettably the process of sensorimotor skill development (Bruner and May 1972; Bruner, May, and Koslowski 1972). Hunt's (1965) important work on intrinsic motivation reiterates, and elaborates upon, Piaget's principle of moderate novelty. This area is just beginning to receive the attention it deserves. Support for Piaget's postulate of disequilibrium may be found in a general principle of conflict demonstrated by Bower, Broughton and Moore (1971) and elaborated upon by Bower (1973). They found that earlier skills seem to temporarily disappear in service of the development of a new skill. This phenomenon appears to precede, and be necessary for, qualitative change. Bower is now subjecting this principle to further testing through longitudinal training studies in cooperation with Inhelder and Piaget.

Smillie (1972) has recently set forth a most heuristic theoretical exploration of Piaget's infant observations and interpretations. Serafica and Uzgiris (1971) present evidence suggesting that person permanence and object permanence develop in reciprocal fashion. Bell (1970) reports that person permanence precedes object permanence when quality of maternal-infant attachment is high, whereas object permanence precedes person permanence when attachment quality is low. Charlesworth (1969) offers theoretical and empirical justification for the validity of the surprise reaction as evidence that the infant possesses a particular expectancy. When the infant's expectancy is violated through a rearrangement technique, he reacts with surprise (e.g., LeCompte and Gratch 1972).

Piaget observed that his own newborns possessed congenitally organized patterns of behavior such as sucking, looking (*cf.* Kessen 1967), hearing, grasping and phonation. These behaviors were present, however tenuously, prior to any opportunities for extrauterine learning. Possession of inter-sensory coordinations and complex perceptual abilities has now been documented in at least some newborns and in many young infants (e.g., Bower, Broughton and Moore 1970). The ability of these young humans to learn now seems established beyond question (Lipsitt 1970). To match their limited processing capacities, however, stimuli must be carefully chosen (e.g., Ramey and Ourth 1971).

To sum, the current outlook amongst developmental psychologists seems to include an increasing appreciation for (1) the ability of young infants, and even newborns, to learn from and adapt to their environment; (2) the significance the sensorimotor period may have for cognitive development; (3) the complexities inherent in the process of cognitive development; and (4) the need to test for causal relationships.

The potential role of training research[1]. The use of theoretically based training research during the infancy period has barely begun. The first intentional, systematic, and longitudinal sensorimotor training studies in press may be those of Bower and his colleagues (1973). Bower considers such studies 'the only way to test the causal processes of development' (see also Hooper 1973). Wohlwill's questions deal essentially with causal relationships. To adequately test these questions, the various types of training research are necessary. Uzgiris captures the essence of training research as it relates to the invariant sequence assumption. She writes:

'... only manipulation of particular steps in the sequence probably

---

1. Any study which provides or permits increased usage of the sensorimotor schemes might be considered an enrichment study or a potential sensorimotor training study, from this author's perspective. Recall that, for Piaget, use is the aliment of the scheme. To test Wohlwill's question, the dependent variables must be chosen and measured specifically for this purpose.

through modification of well-defined environmental circumstances, will show whether the ordinal sequence represents a requisite hierarchy' (Uzgiris 1967, p. 333).

Piaget's postulate of correspondence can be evaluated through transfer of training designs. Hooper discusses an interesting dichotomy found in his own research of the concrete operations period, and also in the studies reviewed by Hooper, Goldman, Storck, and Burke (1971).

'All six of the studies ... which failed to find nonspecific or far-transfer, utilized a *single*, relatively unitary training procedure for any particular experimental treatment condition. In contrast, the six studies which showed significant far-transfer, employed *multiple* training strategies for any treatment group' (Hooper 1973, p. 313).

Hooper concurs with Wohlwill (1970), who feels that the use of multiple training strategies in experimental formats probably offers a closer approximation to the generalized life experiences found in typical natural settings or as revealed in longitudinal ecological analysis.

The prime source of current confusion seems to be Piaget's postulate of horizontal decalage, which is closely related to that of both invariant sequence and correspondence. A horizontal *décalage* also constitutes a sequence, though one more subject to the influence of environmental, task, and status variables. At the same time, a horizontal *décalage* embodies elements akin to correspondence. It too occurs within a major period and does not involve qualitative change, at least so far as concepts are concerned. Pinard and Laurendeau (1969) underscore a current methodological pitfall. They assert the notion of horizontal *décalage* '... should immediately become the object of systematic experimental studies rather than serve as a magic passkey to the post hoc explanation of observed asynchronisms'. Inhelder (1968) feels that we can further our understanding of horizontal *décalage* through training research of a special sort. It should consist of longitudinal learning experiments, which analyze in great detail the qualitative transformations of each subject's behavior in the successive phases of training procedures.

It is safe to say that life would be simpler, particularly for developmental psychologists, if the strong version of Piaget's stage theory would only conform to developmental reality. It seems equally safe to say Piaget's theory is considerably more complex than most had originally imagined (Uzgiris 1972). Some cases of correspondence are theoretically necessary, whether or not they occur. Yet some apparent correspondence is probably only coincidental, with no base in Piaget's theory whatsoever. In short, it seems necessary to question how many of us can tell a real *décalage* from a pseudo*décalage*. This may be an example of what Overton (1973) meant when he pointed out that it is quite possible for a theory to seem wrong, when in reality the failure may be only in errors of translation.

Ten years have passed since Wohlwill's gentle chiding began the trend toward experimental validation research, yet I must reluctantly conclude that Winnie-the-Pooh and Piglet are still hunting 'something' in circular fashion. I fear if you were to ask old Pooh-Bear how things were going, he would give you his well known disgruntled response: 'Not very how!' I am more optimistic than this, however. The experimental and theoretical endeavors resulting from Wohlwill's suggestions have certainly revealed additional and bewildering complexities. But some of these endeavors (e.g., the taxonomic contributions of Flavell 1971, 1972; Flavell and Wohlwill 1969; Pinard and Laurendeau 1969) have also led us to better understand the nature of the beast we are seeking. This beast, then, is no longer such a 'woozley' figment of Piaget's hypothetico-deductive imagination. It seems to me that Pooh and Piglet have already begun to glance beyond their beaten path of circular reaction and are about to break loose into relatively untrod territory. In fact, if you were to listen closely, perhaps you would hear them saying, 'Will the *real décalages* please stand up?'

The need for a baseline. The preceding paragraph brings this article to a reasonable conclusion. Perhaps well enough should be left alone, but I believe (Anderson 1972) that our current scientific endeavors are being conducted under the influence of a pervasive handicap, i.e., the absence of a scientifically established baseline of normality for the human organism. What justifies our assumption that the typical western culture newborn and infant is really normal? What if this putatively normal organism represents, instead, an artifact of culturally imposed (*cf.* Riegel 1972, 1973) birth traditions? I refer to such traditions as obstetrical medication, cord clamping, and mother-newborn separation for 12–24 hours post birth. These were routine experiences for the infant populations studied by Gesell (1925).

Studies which find no differences between African and Western culture infants find neither group to be precocious. When precocity is found, it is found in the African infants (*cf.* Warren 1972). As near as can be discerned, studies finding no precocity have been with infants born and/or cared for in ways resembling Western culture tradition. This does not appear to be the case for those African infants adjudged precocious. Yet Warren's review appears to have rendered the dependent variable of infant precocity a dead issue. I wish to suggest, in rebuttal, that differing levels of a complex independent variable may vary the degree of precocity found. This complex variable, which is denoted by the acronym SMYLI, is self-regulatory mother-young longitudinal (uninterrupted by birth) interaction.

Recall that Piaget's newborn and infant subjects represent only Western culture. Hopefully Piaget and others will supplement his detailed observations of his own three infants with similar observations of infants, both white and African, who have been born in truly natural fashion.

'At present, we know very little about the major factors and variables which, in the routine life experiences of human organisms, determine the course of cognitive growth. An understanding of these factors clearly requires an ecological analysis concerning the spontaneous activities of children *in natural situations*' (Hooper 1973, pp. 388–309, emphasis added).

Three basic facts are relevant here. SMYLI was once virtually a universal life experience for the human organism. Deprivation of such ongoing interaction (ASMYLI), through cultural imposition in the form of Western culture birth tradition, is now more generally the case (Eppink 1969). The transitional newborn period is recognized to be a critical one, physiologically.

Four possibilities are being raised for consideration: (1) The transitional newborn period may also be a critical one in the psycho-socio-emotional sense; (2) the availability of SMYLI may provide ideal stimulation, particularly well-suited to the transitional newborn's limited processing capacities. Such opportunity for interaction may amount to a naturally occurring sensorimotor multiple training strategy (see footnote 1); (3) ASMYLI may be creating a generally unsuspected but controllable, as well as preventable, status variable; and (4) such deprivation may negatively affect human ontogenesis at several levels of analysis.

Let me close with just one brief example at the cognitive-emotional levels of analysis. A precocious infant would surely have more successful problem-solving experiences. Thus his contingency awareness (Watson and Ramey 1972) and his expectancy of effectiveness (Lewis and Goldberg 1969), i.e., of competency (Bruner 1971; Huntington 1971; Yarrow, Rubenstein and Pedersen 1971), would be enhanced. So also would his intrinsic motivation (*cf.* Hunt 1965). Precocity may be the real norm while the average putatively normal Western culture newborn may be only common. The time has come for experimental evaluation of these possibilities. Such experimental evaluation is possible, and I feel the responsibility to mention this.

B. THE ROLE OF STRUCTURES IN EXPLAINING BEHAVIORAL DEVELOPMENT.*

by Charles J. Brainerd, *University of Alberta, Edmonton, Canada*

Every modern science springs from certain common sense observations about reality which Russell (1948) has termed 'ostensively defined' concepts. In view of this fact, we are confronted with the task of ascertaining those attributes of sciences by virtue of which they may be clearly distinguished from their common sense foundations. Perhaps the characteristics of science most frequently mentioned in this regard are description and prediction. It is frequently maintained that the methods of science allow one to describe reality systematically and to predict empirical phenomena with relatively little error. However, a little reflection shows that neither systematic description nor precise prediction suffice to draw the boundary between science and common sense. Consider the following example from astronomy. The rise of the modern science of astronomy occured in the late Renaissance. It is only since the late sixteenth century that man has possessed a true science of astronomy. Now, consider a member of the large class of common sense celestrial observations which fall within the province of astronomy, *viz.* lunar eclipses. If description and prediction are the criteria by which sciences are to be distinguished from their common sensical roots, then we have a right to expect that the advent of systematic descriptions and precise predictions of lunar eclipses should coincide with the advent of astronomy. However, man has been able both to describe lunar eclipses and predict them with tolerable reliability for roughly 4000 years. The increases in descriptive systematicity and predictive power which have accrued from modern astronomy are, pragmatically speaking, miniscule. The point that this example illustrates is a simple but fundamental one: Description and prediction are well within the bounds of common sense.

* The questions discussed in this paper belong to a class of issues whose intension is perhaps best specified by the phrase 'the conceptual foundations of development'. I am painfully aware that this class of issues is not one with which working developmental psychologists tend to concern themselves overly. However, the mere fact of indifference does not, in my opinion, make these issues any the less important or interesting. I should like to express my sincere thanks to Professors Hooper and Papalia for providing a forum in which these somewhat recondite matters could be examined.

What is it, then, that serves to differentiate science from common sense? The most likely criterion appears to be the unrelenting emphasis on systematic and testable explanations that characterizes modern science. This emphasis is widely acknowledged as the *sine qua non* of science by most contemporary philosopers of science (*cf.* Hempel and Oppenheim 1948; Hempel 1965, 1966; Nagel 1961). A science, so the argument goes, seeks to develop comprehensive explanations of phenomena which can be confirmed or infirmed by simple empirical tests. According to this view, testable explanations are the unique by-products of the scientific method; common sense can describe and predict, but only science can explain.

Scientific explanation schemata. Since the publication of Ernest Nagel's seminal work on the logic of scientific explanation a little over a decade ago, it has been widely conceded that modern sciences treat of two generic forms of explanation: (*a*) explanation by sufficient conditions, and (*b*) explanation by necessary conditions. There is only one distinguishable case of explanation by sufficient conditions in modern science, *viz.* the deductive explanatory schema. There are not less than three distinguishable methods of explanation by necessary conditions, *viz.* the probabilistic schema, the teleological schema, and the historical schema. We shall briefly review each of these four schemata and consider a concrete instance of each. We shall see that 'developmental explanation' traditionally has involved only two of the four categories. Of these latter two, one seems to be clearly preferrable.

To date, only one schema that purports to set down sufficient conditions for the occurrence of referent phenomena has been employed: the so-called deductive schema, which has been routinely used in the physical sciences since the publication of Newton's *Principia*. Whenever a deductive explanation is advanced, the explanation itself takes the form of truth-functional entailment. That is, the explanation is worded in such a manner that the occurrence of the to-be-explained event is logically guaranteed by the conditions stated in the explanation. The rub is that either we must assume that the stated conditions are true *a priori* or we must have experimental evidence for their truth. The assumption of *a priori* truth (or 'self-evidence') is no longer as fashionable as it was in Newton's time. Today, experimental evidence for sufficient explanatory conditions is deemed essential. Of the four schemata we shall review, the deductive schema is by far the most prestigous. Most philosophers of science view it as the ultimate goal to which scientific explanations should aspire.

Let us consider a brief illustration of deductive explanation. Suppose we are asked to explain why it is that a piece of lead shot invariably sinks to the bottom of a glass of water at sea level. The explanation of anyone who has studied physics would contain statements about the following conditions: (*a*) the density of lead in gm/cm^3; (*b*) the density of water in gm/cm^3; (*c*) Archimedes' law about the buoyant force exerted by water. The important point to note is that the event is logically guaranteed by conditions *a*, *b*, and *c*: Given that lead shot has a specific gravity greater than 1.0 and given Archimedes law, any piece of lead shot always will sink in a glass of water at sea level.

There are three schemata which purport to explain phenomena by stating necessary conditions in their realization: the probabilistic, teleological, and historical schemata. Unlike the deductive schema, these explanations never take the form of truth-functional entailment.

The probabilistic schema bears a *prima facie* resemblance to the deductive schema. Although the conditions stated in such an explanations, are not sufficient to guarantee phenomena on logical grounds, the conditions make the occurrence of the phenomena very probable. The probabilistic schema is in operation whenever one or more of the stated conditions is a statistical assumption about some class of occurrences, while the to-be-explained phenomenon is a single occurrence from that class. To illustrate, consider explanations of the riots in Black residential areas of Detroit during the summer of 1967. The conditions usually stated include: (*a*) awareness of economic and social injustices precipitated by educational campaigns; (*b*) increased militancy as a result of the civil rights successes of the late 1950s and early 1960s; (*c*) a generalized belief that destruction of property is the only effective means of fomenting change. Conditions such as *a*, *b*, and *c* – as well as others which we could name – quite obviously are insufficient to insure the occurrence of the 1967 Detroit riot. Their insufficiency is apparent from two well-known facts. First, no one maintains that all or perhaps even a majority of Black Detroit residents who satisfy conditions *a*, *b*, and *c* were riot participants. The conditions only moved some people to action. Second, there were other cities in which precisely the same conditions existed during the summer of 1967 which were not torn by riots. Thus, the most that we may legitimately say about our explanation is that it makes the event in question very probable.

The teleological schema is employed primarily in biology and, to a lesser extent, in psychology. Its principal feature is the invocation of functions that phenomena serve as a means of explaining them. Generally speaking, the conditions stated in any teleological explanation are the (assumed) functions that a phenomenon serves in maintaining the progress of a system (almost always a living system) toward the attainment of some aim or end-state. Thus, a teleological explanation always mentions (or implicitly assumes) some end-state and the functions by which it is achieved. Teleological explanations fall into two categories: (*a*) explanations of specific phenomena occurring at specific times in the history of a system, and (*b*) explanations of phenomena occuring at all times in the history of a system. Concerning *a*, suppose we are asked to explain why creative intelligence chose to manifest itself primarily through painting, architecture, and sculpture during the Renaissance. An explanation might stipulate that, for whatever reasons, creative intelligence aimed primarily at the construction of products which have concrete visual expressions during this era. Having said this, it is apparent that painting, architecture, and sculpture all can be construed as maintaining the concrete-visual aims of creative intelligence. Concerning *b*, suppose we are asked to explain why humans have eyes. A teleological explanation probably would mention a human goal that remains constant across the life span: biological survival. Given the present environments in which we find human beings, eyes make food gathering, avoidance of predation, and other survival-related behavioral capacities less difficult. These examples illustrate another important point about the teleological schema, *viz.* it is quite obviously future-oriented. Present and past phenomena are explained in terms of where the system is going rather than in terms of where it has been.

Finally, let us turn to the historical schema. As 'historical' no doubt suggests, this explanatory mode has evolved in the developmental branches of the sciences. The aim of any historical explanation is to set down as conditions for some present state of a system the various phases (or 'stage') by which some earlier state was transformed into the present states. As was the case for the teleological schema, the phenomenon to be explained is a present state of some system (again, usually biological); however, the conditions contained in the explanations are past states rather than future goals. A final point to consider is that historical explanations are as clearly past-oriented as teleological explanations are future-oriented.

To illustrate the historical schema, consider the concept of object permanence. By object permanence, we shall understand the human belief that objects and their attributes continue to exist independent of our experience of them. Suppose we are asked to explain an instance of the adult-state concept of object permanence. The fact that large majority of adults would answer 'yes' to the question 'If a tree falls and there is no one around to hear, would there still be a noise?' is a well-known instance of adult object permanence. Piaget's work (e.g., Piaget 1967; Piaget and Inhelder 1969) provides an excellent example of how one might set about explaining this fact historically. According to Piaget, the organism passes through several states during infancy which are relevant to object permanence. The infant gradually builds up the first definite behavioral examples of object permanance in the form of the knowledge that objects continue to exist independent of the sensorimotor actions that can be performed upon them. Next, during the preschool years, object permanence is broadened to include all-or-none-qualities of the objects such as sex and generic indentity. The next improvement occurs during middle-childhood when the concept is further broadened to include conservation of so-called (Brainerd 1970; Brainerd and Allen 1971) 'first-order' quantitative properties (e.g., length, number, weight, area, height). Finally, during adolescence, object permanence comes to include the conservation of object properties in purely hypothetical situations. At this time, 'yes' answers to the aforementioned question become possible.

Only the teleological and historical schemata have been influential in developmental psychology. Of these latter two, psychologists overwhelmingly have prefered to explain behavioral development historically since the time of G. Stanley Hall. Hence, developmental research and historical explanation have been virtually synonymous. Most of the 'classic' pieces of developmental research we learned about as students (e.g., Hall's work on social development, Gesell's work on mental development, Bridges' work on emotional development) are instances of historical explanation as I have defined the term. This statement also holds for research conducted under the aegis of the dominant theoretical orientation of the late-1950s/early-1960s, S-R theory, and research conducted under the aegis of the dominant theoretical orientation of the late-1960s-early-1970s, Piagetian theory. As is usually his wont on fundamental issues, Piaget has not taken a definite stance on whether behavioral development is to be explained historically or teleologically. There are certainly aspects of his grand meta-theory which have a teleological flavor (e.g., the functional invariants of organization and adaption).

However, Piaget (1971) has very explicitly eschewed the more extreme forms of teleology (finalism). Moreover, vague meta-theoretical propositions aside, it is clear that most of Piaget's empirical work (e.g., the studies of object permanence mentioned earlier) fit the historical schema. S-R developmental psychology also is mainly historical. S-R theory explains present psychological states in terms of the prior operation of forces such as reinforcement contingencies. The Piagetian and S-R frameworks therefore do not appear to differ in principle on the question of how behavioral development is to be explained. The real difference between the two is over the comparatively minor point of what specific conditions must be incorporated in given historical explanations.

Historical explanation has not been so universal in other developmental branches of the sciences. Although historical explanations have been the rule in other developmental sciences, certain minority schools of thought maintain that teleological explanations are to be preferred over historical ones. Of these dissenting viewpoints, the so-called organismic school of developmental biology is the best-known. The late Ludwig von Bertalanffy (e.g., 1933) has been perhaps the most vocal member of this school. A central tenet of the organismic position is that the development of biological structures can only be understood with reference to the vital functions they serve in maintaining the 'system property' of life. Historical explanations are assigned the status of hindsight (*cf.* Kaplan 1967). In the organismic view, it is more crucial to know where an organism is going than where it has been.

There is one theoretical position in developmental psychology, which rivals the S-R and Piagetian formulations in scope, that is a staunch advocate of teleology: Wernerian theory (e.g., Werner 1948, 1956; Kaplan 1967). Werner's thinking has had no appreciable impact on the broad spectrum of working developmental psychologists – despite the fact that the theory has been around for about three decades. White (1970) has speculated that this lack of interest can be traced to the fact that the theory is just too metaphysical for most of our tastes. However, there are signs that attitudes toward the theory may be thawing: learning-oriented developmentalists are beginning to discuss Werner's views seriously (e.g., White 1970); the most recent revision of the *Manual of child psychology* (Mussen 1970) contains a full chapter on Werner's theory; Werner-oriented developmental research has been appearing with greater frequency in recent years. If this trend continues, it is only a matter of time until the question of whether behavioral development is to be explained teleologically or historically becomes an important issue.

Before passing on to structural analysis, a few brief words should be said about precisely why it is that historical explanations traditionally have been preferred over teleological ones. Implicit in these remarks is a value judgment which favors historical explanation and suggests that it is not without reason or through mere force of ingrained habit that developmentalists have shunned teleology. Although the objections raised by organismically oriented writers are of sufficient manitude that we cannot assert the preferability of historical explanation with absolute certainty, the problems that I shall mention indicate that those who advocate teleology have a considerable amount of work to do before they can hope to bring the working developmentalist around to their position.

Teleological explanations entail three logical problems which neither the 'organismic viewpoint' nor any other pro-teleology viewpoint has been able to resolve. First, a teleological explanation always seems to pre-suppose a reversal of the familiar cause-effect paradigm. Causes normally are regarded as events that precede effects. In teleological formulations, however, effects appear to precede causes: The cause is some end the system is tending toward, while the effect is the here-and-now state. How, the question usually runs, can something that presumably does not yet exist exert a pull on a present phenomenon? Second, teleological ex-planations invariably assign to the organism a degree of purposiveness and willfulness that most working scientists find difficult to countenance- – even if they are not Skinner. Metaphysicians and theologians seem to be able to produce appropriate amounts of will and purpose upon demand, but not scientists. The final problem is the most fundamental of the three. It has been persuasively argued by Nagel (1961) and others that, organ-ismic arguments to the contrary notwithstanding, teleology does not even constitute a distinct explanatory schema. Nagel argues that, instead, all and every teleological explanation can be translated into an equivalent nonteleological explanation without any loss of meaning whatsoever. But Nagel will speak for himself on this matter: 'a teleological statement of the form "The function of A in a system S with organization C is to enable S in environment E to engage in process P" can be formulated more explicitly by: Every system S with organization C and in environment E engages in process P; if S with organization C and in environment E does not have A, then S does not engage in P; hence, S with organization C must have A' (Nagel 1961, p. 403).

The concept of structure and structural analysis. There is another issue which must be dealt with before we may arrive at a precise formulation of the relation between positing structures and the problem of how development is to be explained: the meaning of the word 'structure' or, what amounts to the same thing, what it means to 'do' structural analysis. Having a clear grasp of what, generally speaking, is involved in the structural analysis of phenomena is essential if we are to understand what it means to analyze behavior structurally. If a precise formulation of the principles of structural analysis already existed in the psychological literature, then the present remarks would be unnecessary. Somewhat surprisingly, however, structural psychologists have not seen fit to formulate the relevant analytic principles. Instead, they seem to be content to identify structural analysis with certain controversial tenets of the personal philosophies of leading members (mainly, continental European members) of the so-called 'structuralist movement' in contemporary psychology. Among the most frequently mentioned of these tenets are holism, anti-reductionism, emergent evolution, and Hegel's dialectics (*cf.* Looft and Svoboda 1973, for a review). Vague philosophical tenets are entirely unsatisfactory for our purposes.

The present formulation was developed around 1910 by Bertrand Russell and Alfred North Whitehead (Bell 1940). It was the culmination of almost a century of work by foundationally-oriented mathematicians. Structural analysis first became important in mathematics during the 1820s/1830s as a result of the work of Evariste Galois and Niels Abel. Galois and Abel each developed an important mathematical structure whose properties are well-known today. However, scrutiny of the Galois-Abel work revealed a serious flaw: The question 'What *is* a structure?' had not been answered. Galois and Abel did not bother to specify what sort of operations were involved in a structural analysis. They chose to operate with an intuitive formulation which they presumed was sufficiently valid so as not to introduce blatant inconsistencies. Mathematicians therefore were confronted with a serious foundational problem: Abundant evidence existed to the effect that mathematical structures were of vital importance, but no one was certain precisely what was involved in positing a structure.

The Russell/Whitehead definition has been widely accepted in mathematics, logic, philosophy of science, and the physical sciences (both basic and applied) but has not yet been widely disseminated in the biological and social sciences. The biological and social sciences currently seem to be operating at about the same level of definitional precision *vis-à-vis* structure that Galois and Abel operated at a century and one-half ago. The version of the Russell/Whitehead definition that I shall present was one of Russell's last and it may be found in Part Four of *Human knowledge: its scope and limits.*

The cardinal point about structure is that *it is a purely logical notion.* We must not, on pain of imprecision, confuse the concept itself with its various representations in given domains of study (e.g., 'mathematical' structure, syntactical structure, 'chemical' structure). The adjectives which we attach to 'structure' by virtue of our particular academic discipline cannot serve to define structure; they can only modify whatever general definition is formulated. 'Structure' is a composite of two (and only two) primitive logical notions: *element* and *relation.* A structure must always have both elements and relations. To posit a structure for a given domain of study – that is, to 'do' structural analysis in that domain – is first to stipulate certain elementary (i.e., undefined) phenomena which belong to that domain and then to stipulate the manner in which these elementary phenomena are related to each other. By 'structural analysis', we shall understand the carrying out of these operations in some specific domain of study. The *field* of a structural relation is that specific subset of the elementary phenomena which stand in that relation to each other. A structure may involve more than one relation, and more than one structure may be posited for a given domain. Muscle anatomy provides an excellent illustration of these points: First, the various muscles of the body are identified and then the spatial relations between them are specified. Atomic structure provides another excellent illustration: First, three elementary particles ('electron', 'positron', 'neutron') are posited and then spatial relations between them are specified.

In science and mathematics, structural analysis usually has a sequential character. That is, the analysis of the structure of some empirical or mathematical domain usually goes through a series of successive approximations to the 'true' structure of the domain. Those entities which are posited as elementary phenomena in the early phases of the analysis are themselves subsequently analyzed and their structure exhibited. We may return to atomic physics for an illustration of this point. Two centuries ago, *whole atoms* were taken to be elementary phenomena of matter. The structure of matter therefore was viewed as synonymous with atoms standing in certain spatial relations to each other. This was called the 'billiard ball' theory. A century later the atom was no longer viewed as irreducible. It had been analyzed into electrons, protons, and neutrons standing in certain energistic relations to each other (e.g., the Bohr model for hydrogen). Evidence collected during the past few decades suggests that electrons, protons, and neutrons also should not be regarded as elementary. Subatomic particle research indicates that protons, neutrons, and electrons also have complex structures of their own.

The course of structural analysis in those sciences where it has been extensively employed has been one of successive penetration to ever more fundamental levels of analysis. One posits certain elementary phenomena and certain relations; the structure of these elementary phenomena is exhibited at some later date; still later the structure of what were taken as elementary phenomena in the second phase is exhibited; etc. This fact is one of the main reasons why structural analysis has proved to be so fruitful to date. It provides us with a *modus operandi* for coming nearer and nearer to the elementary aspects of any field of study. There is an important methodological conclusion which follows from the sequential quality of structural analysis: It is patently unwise to regard any currently accepted structure for some domain as ultimate or final. The elementary phenomena of that structure could, at any moment, be found to be resolvable into more basic elements and relations without any loss of meaning. This conclusion should be borne in mind by structurally oriented psychologists. It is quite obviously inconsistent with the 'holism' and 'anti-reductionism' of certain leading figures in the structuralist movement (e.g., Piaget).

Another important aspect of structural analysis is structural isomorphism. It is possible to group various domains of study together by virtue of their structure. Domains of study which have the same structure, though the ostensive meanings of their respective elements and relations are quite different, are said to be structurally isomorphic. Let us consider a simple illustration from abstract algebra, *vtz.* the group structure. A group structure is an arbitrary set of elements together with an arbitrary relation which satisfy four basic properties (closure, associativity, identity, inversion). Now, the following very different collections of numbers can all be shown to be characterized by a group structure: (*a*) the set of all rational numbers under addition; (*b*) the real numbers under addition; (*c*) the complex numbers under addtion; (*d*) the non-zero rational numbers, the non-zero real numbers, and the non-zero complex numbers under multiplication. It even has speculated (e.g., Inhelder and Piaget 1958) that adult reasoning may be characterized by a group structure.

The crucial point that I wish to make about structural isomorphism is this. Structural analysis, by virtue of the property of structural isomorphism, frequently allows us to establish the underlying identity of domains which bear virtually no *prima facie* resemblance to each other (e.g., a phonograph record and a printed sheet of music; a city and a two-dimensional map of that city). Once structural isomorphism has been established for two domains, another great benefit of structural analysis accrues: All the statements we can make about one domain which we can verify as either true or false and which depend only on the structure of the first domain, we can also make in the second domain; moreover, each statement in the second domain will be true only if its counterpart in the first domain is true and false only if its counterpart in the first domain is false. This is a very substantial benefit indeed. It means that if we have a collection of domains of study which have been shown to be structurally isomorphic, we can know a very great deal about each and every one of them by studying only one of their number. I need not comment on the obvious efficiency and economy of such a procedure.

As an illustration of the preceding fact about structural analysis, let us return to the example of the group structure. Suppose that, in line with Inhelder and Piaget's (1958) conjectures, it could be established that the group structure is a satisfactory representation of adult reasoning. Basically, this would involve establishing that the principal group axioms also describe the way adult reasoning works. Having done this much, we would then know an enormous amount about adult reasoning and could make literally an infinite number of specific empirical predictions (which would all be subject to verification of course). The things that we would know and the predictions that we would make would correspond to well-known number theorems which are derived from the group axioms under suitable 'cognitive' interpretations. With the theorems arranged before us, we could set about our empirical studies of adult reasoning with precision and systematicity. We would be very certain of the empirical questions we wanted to ask, the order in which we wanted to ask them, and, when the data were in, what sort of answers they provide.

Structure and developmental explanations. We may now return to the question with which we began: What sorts of explanations of behavioral development do structural models entail? It will be recalled that only two of the four explanatory schemata discussed earlier (history and teleology) have been influential in developmental psychology and that there exist some grounds for dispute over which of the two should be invoked when explaining behavioral development. The crux of the dispute may be formulated as follows. First, we have some behavioral state N that we wish to explain. The historical position is that the target state N should be explained in terms of the preceding state N — 1 by showing how the behaviors of N — 1 are transformed into those of N. [N — 1 then is explained in terms of N — 2 and so on until N = 1.] The teleological position is exactly the reverse. Each target state N is explained in terms of the succeeding state N + 1 by specifying the function (or functions) served by N *vis-à-vis* the attainment of N + 1.

The general relationship between structure and developmental explanation seems to be as follows. Structural analysis and structural models for specific states are important constituents of any really thorough historical explanation. There are some obvious reasons why this relationship obtains that are easily seen when we consider the general task of historical explanation in developmental psychology. To illustrate, let us consider the limited task of explaining middle-childhood cognition in terms of early-childhood cognition. Now it is unreasonable to expect that we ever will be able to exhibit each and every early-childhood cognitive behavior from which each and every middle-childhood cognitive behavior derives. In the first place, we simply would not be able to obtain universal agreement on what categories of behavior are and are not cognitive. Even if such an agreement could be reached, we have to confront the fact that any cognitive-behavioral catalogue for any developmental state will be necessarily incomplete because the set of specific cognitive behaviors for such a state is always potentially infinite. If we cannot list specific behaviors, then what can be done about explaining middle-childhood cognition? The answer is that we can try to do two things: (*a*) formulate the structure of early-childhood cognition and verify it empirically, and (*b*) formulate the structure of middle-childhood cognition and verify it empirically. Although we cannot hope to agree on what behaviors comprise 'cognition' and although we cannot hope to list all the cognitive behaviors of either period, it might be possible to agree on structural models for both periods and to verify that early-childhood and middle-childhood cognition obeys the laws of their respective structural models. Having done this, it would not be necessary to show how each early-childhood cognitive behavior is translated into its middle-childhood counterpart. It would only be necessary to show how the early-childhood structure may be transformed into the middle-

childhood structure. If the structures happen to be behavioral representations of mathematical structures whose properties are well-known, the
translation of one structure into another becomes purely mechanical.

What I have just said is illustrated in the following example. Suppose
a structural analysis of what we know about early-childhood cognition
leads us to suspect that the algebraic ring is an appropriate structural
representation of cognitive behavior at this level; where an algebraic ring
is defined as a set R of elements, together with the operations $+$ and $\times$,
which obey the following laws: closure for addition; associativity for
addition; right identity for addition; right inverse for addition; com-
mutativity for addition; closure for multiplication; associativity for
multiplication; left distributive law; right distributive law. Suppose we
had reason to believe that cognitive development normally proceeds
from general to specific. This would lead us to posit specialized versions
of the ring structure, such as Boolean rings (rings in which every element
is idempotent), as structural models for middle-childhood cognition.
Assume that independent experimental evidence verified both models.
In view of the fact that the properties of both the ring and the Boolean
ring are well-known, it is a simple matter to demonstrate the translation
of the former into the latter. Thus, by positing structural models for
early- and middle-childhood cognition, we arrive at a formulation which
satisfies the earlier description of historical explanation.

In contrast with what has been said up to this point, teleological
explanations of middle-childhood cognition (or any other aspect of
behavioral development) do not involve structural analysis to any notable
degree. The structures of states N and N $+$ 1 cannot be compared the
way the structures of N and N $-$ 1 can because N $+$ 1 does not yet
exist and therefore cannot be analyzed directly. The relationship between
N and N $+$ 1 therefore must be one of function rather than structure.
Hence, the heart of a teleological explanation of middle-childhood cognition, to continue our example, would be a statement of the functions
it serves in the realization of adolescent cognition.

There is a final point of general psychological interest which can be
drawn out of the relationship between structure and developmental
explanation. The disagreement over whether behavioral development is
to be explained historically or teleologically can, in principle be reduced,
to the longstanding structure-function dispute that William James introduced. If we opt for history, then we come down on the side of structure
(for the limited case of developmental psychology). If we opt for teleology,
then we came down on the side of function.

C. LIFE-SPAN ANALYSES OF PIAGETIAN CONCEPT TASKS: THE SEARCH FOR NONTRIVIAL QUALITATIVE CHANGE*

by Frank H. Hooper, *University of Wisconsin, Madison*

Initially, I will take this opportunity to respond to certain recent criticisms of Piagetian theory and related research which deny the utility of the Genevan views for a viable life-span approach in today's (and yesterday's, and tomorrow's) ever-changing sociocultural milieu. I hope to demonstrate to you that only one of these putative weaknesses in the Piagetian system, i.e., the lack of a comprehensive acknowledgment of development beyond the adolescent years, is a genuine deficiency. Following this, I shall briefly discuss some of the issues raised by the complementary juxtaposition of an organismic viewpoint (i.e., Piaget's or Werner's developmental theories) with an interest in life-span cognitive development. It is my contention that a whole-hearted commitment to the latter subject area demands a collateral acceptance of the Piagetian-type of developmental world view (*cf.* Hooper 1973; Overton and Reese 1973; Reese and Overton 1970).

Piaget and his system are alive and well – and not only in Geneva. While it is distinctly presumptuous of me to assume the role of defender of the 'Piagetian Faith', I feel that certain recent critics of Piaget's theory have been singularly unfair and/or misinformed in their criticisms – thus I would like to make a few points on Piaget's behalf. The majority of these recent criticisms of Piaget's system discuss one or more of the following 'deficiencies': (*a*) that Piaget's single-minded pursuit of the dominant characteristics and determinants of a structural approach to *logical* reasoning has culminated in a sterile automaton model of cognitive functioning devoid of concern for the individual person's needs, goals, and related idiosyncrasies (e.g., Looft and Svoboda 1973); (*b*) that in his views regarding the interactive pattern of hereditary, maturational,

* I would like to acknowledge continuing 'dialectical' conversations with Nancy Sheehan, Gene C. Anderson, Judy Hooper, Jane Goldman, and Stephen Kerst of the University of Wisconsin, Charles Brainerd of the University of Alberta, William R. Looft of the Pennsylvania State University, and the members of a proseminar on cognitive functioning across the lifes-pan held during 1972–1973 at the University of Wisconsin for many of the more worthwhile ideas discussed in this paper.

and socioexperential factors, Piaget has not sufficiently recognized the salient role of the latter component, especially in regard to changing historico-generational conditions (e.g., Looft 1973; Riegel 1973a, 1973b) or to the role of the individual as a potential source of change upon the surrounding environment (e.g., Riegel 1973a, 1973c); (*c*) that Piaget's inordinate emphasis upon a biologically constrained 'unfolding' of cognitive structure, relatively impervious to environmental variation, denotes genetic preprograming (Beilin 1971a) or, by implication at least, acceptance of a Kantian variety of apriorism (Riegel 1973b), (points *b* and *c* are obviously closely related); (*d*) that the Piagetian system (particularly the equilibration processes), with all its reverence for an active constructionist view of man's cognitive growth, is not really 'dynamic' enough in comparison to the neo-Hegelian dialectical approach of Rubinstein (*cf.* Payne 1968, as cited in Riegel 1973a, 1973c; and Wozniak 1973); (*e*) that the interrelationship *among* the major Piagetian periods or stages of cognitive development and their respective behavioral archetypes (sensorimotor, concrete, and formal operational), especially following maturity, do not adequately characterize normal human functioning with its inherent blending of affective, motoric, iconic, and symbolic aspects. This criticism usually involves the stipulation of optional, multilevel operations (Riegel 1973b; Werner and Kaplan 1963) or claims that the progressive elaboration toward formal operational thought carries with it a systematic *alienation* of earlier modes of dealing with the 'real' world (Riegel 1973b), and related to this point; (f) that Piaget and his collaborators have paid insufficient attention to development during and beyond the years of cognitive 'maturity', especially to the aging years, and that consequently many interesting changes of both a progressive and regressive variety (perhaps of a genuine qualitative nature) have been ignored (e.g., Hooper 1973; Hooper, Fitzgerald and Papalia 1971; Looft 1972, 1973; Looft and Svoboda 1973; Riegel 1973a, 1973b, 1973c; and Wozniak 1973).

I believe the initial criticism concerns a natural outcome of the progressive elaboration and increased formalization which has characterized the growth of Piaget's theorization attempts. The answer to 'Where have all the people gone?' (Looft and Svoboda 1973, p. 15) is quite straightforward – the individual cognizer is still there, but he is now encapsulated in a highly abstract formal *model* of logical problem-solving and associated ratiocination. As Van den Daele (1969) has recently pointed out, developmental stage theorists engage in a three-phase evolutionary process in 'constructing' their theories. Brainerd (1973b) has discussed this three-step sequence in terms of general typologies. In the initial phase, mutually exclusive behavioral traits which clearly differentiate certain developmental levels are selected under logical and/or empirical criteria.

'During the second phase, the potential groupings are refined. Redundant traits and inconsistent traits are eliminated from the intensional complement of each stage ... During the final phase, the typology is translated into an abstract symbolism of some sort. Each stage is assigned a symbolic representation that facilitates description and explanation' (Brainerd 1973b, p. 7).

It is clear that Piaget's theorizing has 'progressed' to the final abstract model stage (somehow it seems most appropriate to describe Piaget's scholarly endeavors themselves in stage terms!). In so doing, the original emphases (on unique individual persons with age-related particularistic thought processes, for example) are not lost; they are merely subsumed under the higher-order abstract mechanisms or constructs, e.g., the logical *groupements* which cover classificatory and relational concepts during the middle-childhood period. Of course, one could argue that Piaget has never paid enough attention to individual difference variables (unlike his American psychometric counterparts), but this is *not* a result of his recent model building endeavors which stress the formal analogies between systems of logic and behavioral patterns (e.g., Piaget 1970c, 1972a), but rather stem from his bias toward behavioral uniformities and generalities (which we all know are the hallmark of any dedicated stage theorist).

The second criticism dealing with the supposedly minor role accorded to social or general experiential factors may be valid for secondary interpretations of Piagetian theory, but it clearly is not true of Piaget's own later writing. He has consistently (e.g., Inhelder and Piaget 1964, pp. 293–294; Piaget 1952b, pp. 18–20, 1962a, pp. 290–291, 1966, pp. 156–166, 1967, pp. 117–120, 1970a, pp. 721–722, 1970c, pp. 61–62; and Piaget and Inhelder 1969, pp. 152–159) assigned a necessary (but not sufficient) 'causative' role to socioexperiential determinants. Moreover, he distinguishes between logicomathematical, physical, and social experiences, all of which are essential to normative development (Piaget 1970a, pp. 719–722; Piaget and Inhelder 1969, pp. 155–156). For Piaget

'maturation ... is undoubtedly never independent of a certain functional exercise where experience plays a role ... the maturation of the nervous system simply opens up a series of possibilities ... without giving rise to an immediate actualization of these possibilities so long as the conditions of material experience or social interaction do not *bring about* this actualization ... This actualization presupposes certain conditions of physical experience such as the manipulation of objects, etc., which is also essential for logic, and certain social conditions such as the regulated exchange of information, mutual control, etc.' (Piaget 1967, pp. 119–120, emphasis added).

There are no possible grounds for misinterpretation here if one is willing to accept Piaget's defining criterion for accommodation – one conceptual part of the dynamic duo (the counterpart being assimilation, of course) which together make up the functional invariant of adaptation. The Piagetian organism does alter his cognitive makeup as a consequence of repeated encounters with his environmental surround.

Piaget does deny that *specific* directed teaching is apt to produce genuine (i.e., those changes which demonstrate long-term stability, increased operational and functional complexity, and which involve nonspecific transfer) cognitive modifications (*cf.* Hooper 1972, 1973; Piaget 1964, 1970a, pp. 713–117) or should be the guiding focus of our educational endeavors (*cf.* Furth 1970; Piaget 1970b) at least insofar as the sensorimotor, pre-operational, and concrete operational child is concerned. Didactic approaches are appropriate for older individuals who have reached the formal operational level.

While it could be maintained that Piaget has neglected the *outward directed* results of operative thought, i.e., assimilation modifies environmental inputs but there is little *formal* treatment of the organism's influence *on* the surrounding milieu (*cf.* Riegel 1973a, p. 15), the obvious implication of Piaget's comments upon the role of optimal educational programing (Piaget 1964, 1970b, pp. 178–180) and the type of individual required in modern society show a distinct concern for man as a creative innovator, thus as a *source* of potential change. Misunderstandings may arise over this issue because Piaget uses the equilibration process model both to describe the internal organizing factors which underlie sensorimotor schemes or higher-level representational schemas and their respective intercoordinations (Langer 1969), and as a mediator of the macro-level interchanges between the active organism and the active environment (*cf.* Klausmeier and Hooper 1974).

Piaget's interest in long-term historico-generational changes in our past cultural heritage is evidenced in a number of instances (e.g., see Kaplan 1971; Piaget 1950, 1957 as reviewed in Flavell 1963, pp. 255–261;

and Piaget 1970c, pp. 97–119). His major concern with the historico-developmental approach to the analysis of particular knowledge forms certainly qualifies Piaget as one interested in long-term change.

'For a structuralism of this sort, structure and function, genesis and history, individual subject and society are – once the instruments of analysis have been refined – inseparable, the more so the more it perfects its analytic tools' (Piaget, 1970c, p. 128)

Specialized assessment strategies designed to generate developmental norms nonconfounded by cohort or generational biases (*cf.* Baltes 1968) are of little import, but methodological considerations such as these have never seemed to trouble the Genevan researchers (they have always been much more preoccupied with what you *do* with your observational data rather than *how* you obtained it – provided, of course, that the integrity of the *methode clinique* is not at issue).

The assertion (point *c* above) that Piagetian theory implicitly accepts a form of Kantian apriorism is directly contrary to the explicit statements found in Piaget's writings (e.g., 1952b, pp. 376–395, 1966, pp. 14–17, and 1970c, pp. 55–60). As is the case with Werner's theory (*cf.* Kaplan 1967; Werner and Kaplan 1963), the innate categories of reasoning are the focal topics for developmental analysis, but Kant's *a*genetic thesis is not accepted.

'Moreover, recourse to innate factors never resolves problems; it merely passes them on to biology, and as long as the fundamental question of acquired characteristics is not definitively resolved, it may always be supposed that modification resulting from environmental influence will be found at the origin of an innate mechanism' (Piaget, 1967, p. 117)

As the comments under point *b* imply, Piaget also denies that his theory necessarily requires '... that the mechanism by which thought processes develop is under the control of species-specific genetic programming ...' (Beilin, 1971a, p. 99.) The commonly observed systematic regularities (one is tempted to use the term cultural universals) observed across markedly varied sociocultural settings for the concrete operational period concepts, for example, could also be determined by functionally uniform or ecologically equivalent life experiences (*cf.* Wohlwill 1966, 1970). Piaget would probably assert that these cross-cultural consistencies follow from the fact that all significant cognitive growth is governed, in the final analysis, by the equilibration dynamics which all men share as biological entities.

Point *d* is perhaps harder to deal with in the present brief (and sometimes cavalier) fashion, but it is refreshing in a way to speak to the contention that Piaget's conceptions are not dynamic enough![1] In my reading of the Piagetian literature, I have always been impressed with the relativistic nature of the slowly evolving knowledge forms. The external world, the cognizing self, and, of equal importance, the awareness of the self/world differentiation process, could never be orthogonally defined without consideration of the interrelationships *among* these components. The description of this process, whether in terms of the organization-adaptation (assimilation and accommodation dyad) invariants or in terms of the equilibrium model, has always appeared to me as distinctly *dialectical* in nature. This formation-dissolution-reformation process includes within period and across period developmental phenomena. Moreover, the dialectical nature of the equilibration processes is highlighted by the dynamic aspects of these systems; they are never completely stable or balanced but ever changing throughout life. Other writers (e.g., Elkind 1967, pp. xii-xiii; Overton and Reese 1973, pp. 77–82; Reese and Overton 1970, p. 135; Hamlyn 1971, p. 15; and Riegel 1973b, pp. 8–9) have noted the close affinity of Piaget's views to a dialectical position. As will be shown below, certain writers (e.g., Looft; Riegel; and Wozniak)[2] apparently feel that the dialectical process aspects of Piaget's system are 'lost' during the adulthood and aging years. Piaget's recent

1. In comparison to the operational looseness of Piaget's system, it is interesting that a wholehearted philosophical acceptance of the neo-Hegelian dialectical position may result in a methodologically indefensible state of affairs (Overton and Reese 1973). Riegel's dualistic dialectic (soma/psyche and self/external world) in which *all* components are rapidly changing over cultural *and* ontogenetic time presents a formidable task indeed for those of us concerned with eventual operational specification. A single bipolar interacting entity is hard enough to specify and 'anchor' without qualifying the values of each polar aspect *vis-à-vis* another dialectical system's pertubation and regulations. The operational complexities inherent in a truly representative dualistic dialectical design strain the imagination.

2. In fairness to Riegel, it should be pointed out that he has directed his criticisms of Piagetian theory to that writing typified by such works as *The Psychology of Intelligence* (1966) and *The Origins of Intelligence in Children* (1952b). Thus, the earlier phase of Piaget's research and the most recent writings, represented by the overview volume, *Structuralism*, would not appear to be at issue (see Riegel 1973b, footnote 4, pp. 35–36). However, in fairness to Piaget, it does not seem completely equitable to ignore his more recent writings (i.e., Piaget 1970a, 1970b, 1970c) when building a case for conceptual inadequacies. As mentioned earlier, other critics (Looft and Svoboda 1973) have attacked the recent Piagetian formulations as contrasted with 'vintage' Piaget. Piaget's theory must be considered as an organic entity which itself has undergone change over time. I certainly concur with Riegel and with Looft in urging that a genetic analysis of Piaget's evolving theoretical views would be a genuinely worthwhile undertaking (*cf.* Looft and Svoboda 1973, pp. 11–12; Riegel 1973b, p. 35; 1973c, pp. 30–31).

views belie these misgivings. For example, he concludes as follows:

'Just as the structuralism of the Bourbaki has already expanded into a movement calling for more dynamic structures (the categories with their functional emphasis), so the other current forms of structuralism are no doubt big with future developments. And since an *immanent diclectic* is here at work, we can be sure that the denials, devaluations, and restrictions with which certain structuralists today meet positions which they regard as incompatible with their own will one day be recognized to mark those crucial points where new *syntheses* overtake *antitheses*' (Piaget 1970c, p. 143, emphases added).

One of the possible distinctions between the views and emphases of Piaget compared to Werner (as representative spokesman for the organismic world view) concerns cognitive functioning following maturity (points *e* and *f* above). Piaget is, of course, primarily a cognitive theorist; moreover, by choice, one rather exclusively concerned with *logical* reasoning and related problem solving. He thus pays little attention to imagination, reverie, dream states, creative expression in non-abstract media, or to many aspects of affective functioning (more exactly – he doesn't ignore them [see Piaget 1962b, pp. 167–175]; he simply subordinates these phenomena to logical thought processes or views cognition/affect patterns as indissociably fused, *cf.* Flavell 1963, pp. 78–82). Werner's views, in contrast, are much more global and all encompassing, concerning the variety of human behaviors which undergo genuine developmental transformation (Kaplan 1967; Langer 1969, 1970). In addition, a wider range of information sources dealing with comparative analyses, i.e., cross-species, cross-cultural, cross-generational, normal/pathogenetic, and micro-genetic, in addition to the focal ontogenetic changes are *explicitly* admissable as developmental data in Werner's approach. Most importantly for our present concerns, Werner at least discusses the possibility of bidirectional developmental change (Roberton 1972), raising the possibility of short-term functional regression under special conditions during the mature years, and general *de*differentiation and decreased hierarchic integration during the aging years.

A case could be argued therefore that Werner's position is a more veridical reflection of normal adult life (and a more sympathetic one for those of us who find it difficult to function at the formal operational level for extended time periods). Still, *both* Piaget and Werner would strongly disagree with the contention that the acquisition of formal operational thought or symbolic reasoning denies the continued utilization of earlier knowledge forms based upon motoric or iconic modes. They certainly would deny that the acquisition of higher (from their vantage point) thought processes *removes* the individual from contact with the real world and results in a perverse form of cognitive *alienation* from concrete reality (Riegel 1973b; Wozniak 1973).

It must be remembered that Werner's levels, and Piaget's stages, of cognitive development are, first and foremost, hierarchically organized systems in which the earlier (lower?) forms of dominant functioning are superseded by the subsequent forms, but are never lost (Langer 1970; Piaget 1960; Werner and Kaplan 1963). Thus the motoric and perceptual aspects may be functionally subordinate to the more abstract contemplative modes of 'knowing' our world, but they continue to operate and to undergo further development and specialization. In a normal individual, all forms or modes of contact with the surrounding environment exist in an organized system. Moreover, the various modes of knowing our world, of organizing our daily activities, and of mediating our intercourse with other persons are commingled in the distinctly human activities of art, mythology, language, warfare, unrequited love, etc. What mode is dominant at any given point in time depends upon the affective/conative context; the same symbol may denote markedly different meanings depending upon the shared context as the studies of word magic (Cassirer 1946; Langer 1951) have shown.

Now it is quite true that Piaget and Werner rank order, so to speak, the degree of absolute development or relative complexity of motoric, perceptual, and symbolic-representational (formal operational period for Piaget) levels, reserving the highest position to the latter contemplative-abstract level. But man as a symbol maker and user does not lose contact with reality as a consequence of this developmental process (although some would argue that neuroses are one uniquely human outcome). Rather, he acquires the ability to transform and transcend concrete reality if he so chooses. As Cassirer (1946) has made clear, reflective or contemplative abstractions, especially with regard to language forms, are the ultimate links between men as social organisms and the world about them – thus permitting a view of reality never possible through enactive or iconic modes alone. Finally, contrary to the contentions of Wozniak (1973, p. 16), it is indeed the abstract contemplative mode of cognitive functioning, as exemplified in Piaget's formal level hypothetico-deductive reasoning, which permits men to 'construct' theories like Piaget's and, not incidently, to engage in academic discourse concerning the correct interpretation of these theories once conceived (*cf.* Kaplan 1967, p. 81)

Insofar as the general issue of adult functioning is concerned, it appears that some very important cognitive advancements are indeed accomplished following the flowering of adolescence. In this regard, Piagetian theory is not very informative (Hooper, Fitzgerald and Papalia 1971; Looft and Svoboda 1973; Riegel 1973b). What little that has been written, from the Genevan viewpoint, concerning possible changes during the adult and aging years (Flavell 1970; Piaget 1972b, Smedslund 1963) has emphasized experentially based (e.g., occupational status, years of formal schooling, etc.) specialization and diversification of an essentially *non*qualitative nature. In contrast, Riegel (1973b) has proposed a fifth stage of cognitive development characterized by 'dialectical operations' and denoting qualitative progression during adulthood.

What empirical findings are available concerning the possible changes following adolescence may be briefly summarized. Initially, it must be acknowledged that we really know very little about the typical congitive competencies of normal adults as they are confronted with Piagetian concept tasks. A few studies have shown that criterial formal operations performances appear later than Piaget has originally contended and, in some instances, have been notably *absent* in mature subjects (e.g., Elkind 1962; Piaget 1972b; Smedslund 1963).

There are a somewhat larger number of studies that have administered Piagetian tasks to aged subjects (and in some cases compared these normative patterns to those of younger subjects). In almost every instance, these cross-sectional assessment studies have found marked *differences* favoring the mature adults, *similarities* between the young children and aged subject sub-samples' performances, and/or apparent *decrements* in the performances of the elderly persons on the Piagetian tasks. It is particularly interesting that in the elderly subject samples, the relative item difficulties for the formal/concrete task comparisons and the concrete operations inter-task analyses, i.e., the well-known horizontal *décalages* and the within-stage item concurrences or correspondences, parellel those found for samples of younger subjects aged 5 to 15 years. This has led to the intriguing speculation that longitudinal assessments could detect a regression sequence in reverse order to that associated with the child's normative acquisition sequence.

The fundamental questions at issue here concern: (a) Whether the performances of normal adults from a representative sampling of socio-cultural and occupational groups on formal reasoning tasks merit the use

of stage designation to the same extent (i.e., in terms of cultural univer-
salism and relatively minor interindividual and intraindividual variability) as that accorded to the earlier developmental stages; and, assuming
the answer to the initial question is affirmative, (b) whether the performance difficulties of the elderly subjects on formal, concrete, and sensorimotor tasks denote competence deficits (Flavell and Wohlwill 1969) and
hence merit the appellation of qualitative regression. Insofar as the second
is concerned, while it is indeed true that the Genevan researchers have
conducted some extremely interesting assessments on elderly persons,
they have not, as yet, systematically incorporated these findings into a
life-span model of cognitive development.

The relationship of organismic theory and life-span developmental research.
As recently as 1963, Bayley felt obligated to make a special plea for the
necessity of the life-span approach to developmental analysis. Today, I
think it is fairly safe to say that a general life-span orientation has been
accepted by a large number of developmental investigators (the present
conference is eloquent testimony to this state of affairs; see also Baltes
1973). I should like to ask: How many of these enthusiastic promoters of a
life-span *Zeitgeist* realize exactly what they are getting themselves into?
If one accepts the provisional definition 'Human life-span developmental
psychology is concerned with the description and explication of ontogenetic (age-related) behavioral change from birth to death' (Baltes and
Goulet 1970, p. 12), and if one wishes to add potential modification as a
long-range objective (Baltes 1973), then we do indeed have a formidable
task ahead of us. This follows as a natural consequence of the fact that *all*
of the conceptual and methodological problems germane to an age-
specific developmental analysis, e.g., infancy or the aging years, are the
natural preoccupation of a true life-span developmentalist. Now even if
you restrict your attention to a single relatively circumscribed behavioral
domain (and most life-span researchers are too zealously 'holistic' to do
this), the resultant assessment-interpretation task is enormously complex.
Initially, when I contemplate the considerable controversy and disagreement among researchers in a relatively restricted content domain/age
range, i.e., cognitive development during the years of middle childhood
– the topic area with which I am most familiar –, I must confess the pros-
pects for a viable life-span research program are dismally pessimistic.

Most of this initial pessimism concerns the considerable methodological
problems associated with life-span assessments (*cf.* Nesselroade and Reese

1973). These usually involve three interrelated prerequisites: (1) the provision of an array of task or measurement settings demonstrating equivalent reliability and validity (of a psychometric and ecological variety); (2) the provision of general assessment designs (normative measurement and experimental manipulation) which permit unbiased estimates of developmental changes; and (3) the provision of statistical analysis procedures which can accommodate multiple independent and multiple dependent variables. Assuming consensual operational agreement regarding the target cognitive behaviors, an explicit answer to a quest for specifying nontrivial qualitative change probably awaits the provision of these methodological essentials.

However, before we lapse into premature despair, I should like to point out that all problems of life-span psychology which are distinctly methodological in nature are *in principle* ultimately resolvable. In essence, the methodological and general research design requirements of life-span ontogenetic assessment are analogous to those in any area of comparative analysis (e.g., phylogenetic, pathogenetic, or ethnogenatic comparisons). It follows, therefore, that since workers in these related comparative disciplines are not beset with any noticeable methodological despair, we too have reason to be optimistic. It also follows that we could gain much by familiarizing ourselves with the methodological innovations and safeguards employed in these other comparative areas. Many of the proposed solutions to problems of data comparability as approached in cross-cultural research (*cf.* Eckensberger 1973, pp. 46–61), for example, are appropriate to life-span assessment applications.

Major advances in life-span assessment design and related statistical analyses (points 2 and 3 above) have recently been discussed by Baltes and Nesselroade (1973). In the present context, the availability of these improved techniques in conjunction with the fact that many Piagetian task formats have a most obvious face validity (at least when compared with many intelligence test items commonly employed in life-span research) is reason for genuine optimism. This will be particularly true if the reservations concerning the application of parametric statistical techniques (e.g., the linear additivity assumptions of parametric ANOVA models) to behavioral domains derived from organismic theory prove to be groundless (Overton and Reese 1973, p. 84).

In our initial attempts to conduct Piagetian research in a life-span framework, it is probably advisable to confine our endeavors to those task formats which have undergone thorough preliminary analysis with the original age-appropriate samples. The understanding of classificatory relationships as assessed in the class inclusion task, for example, has been extensively and intensively investigated, and the determinants of success-ful performance are reasonably clearcut (e.g., Brainerd and Kazor 1973; Klahr and Wallace 1972); its relationship to other Piagetian tasks has been demonstrated (e.g., Brainerd 1973a; Hooper, Sipple and Gold-man 1973); and the influence of instructional programming on criterial performance has been studied (e.g., Beilin 1971b; Klausmeier and Hooper 1974). In the employment of class inclusion tasks (or any tasks, for that matter) in a life-span assessment design, it is extremely important to provide comparable motivational attractiveness and appropriate instruc-tional sets for *all* the age sub-samples under examination. In discussing memory research paradigms, Meacham has stated:

'... If the child does not have an adequate understanding of the problem, then it should come as no surprise that the child does not engage in ac-tivities appropriate to solution of the problem... (and further) ... Ob-viously the question of whether adequate performance at this task is dependent upon comprehension of the end-state or is simply dependent upon heightened motivation must be carefully considered, but it can at least be suggested that experimenters often do not exact optimal per-formance from their younger subjects' (Meacham 1972, pp. 211–212).

Similar admonitions for researchers using class inclusion tasks have been engagingly suggested by Hayes (1972), and I would maintain that these caveats are equally relevant to assessment research with elderly persons. We simply cannot assume that since the fundamental task requirements are self-evident to us (as task designers or task administrators) they are equally obvious to any individual 'fortunate' enough to be drawn into our subject sample.

By way of conclusion, let us presume that we do indeed possess all the methodological armament essential to conducting life-span analyses of Piagetian conceptual abilities. Even if we had a series of absolutely equi-valent tasks, an infallible assessment research design and associated analytic techniques, and a 'normal' subject who was willing to have us follow and observe his activities from birth onward – there would still be something missing. I contend that there is something over and above a methodological sophistication, a penchant for model building, and ready access to subjects at widely disparate age levels which is the crucial defining criterion for a true life-span developmental investigator. Acceptance of the life-span orientation demands an awareness of certain process/product distinctions as potentially present throughout all our investigations. At the general level this implies that we discard the traditional notions that all developmental phenomena from birth to adulthood are necessarily progressive in nature and that all the interesting changes during the aging years are primarily decremental in nature. More specifically it means that we must recognize that the *same* absolute performance levels (quantitative and qualitative criteria) for differing age groups may be mediated by different process mechanisms (Turiel 1969; Wapner 1969; Werner 1937), or may involve multiple distinctive problem solving strategies or learning skills only some of which are age-specific (Goulet 1973), or that differential environmental conditions and related concurrent factors may be operative The same reservations, of course, may apply to observed performance *differences* across age groups.

The possibility that differential processes may be involved in supposedly congruent focal task performances may be briefly illustrated. A number of recent theorists have posited a close relationship between Piagetian task performances and memory factors as represented in information processing approaches (*cf.* Klahr and Wallace 1970; Neimark 1970; Pascual-Leone and Smith 1969). Many of the Piagetian task formats such as transitive inference and conservation have a memory requirement as an essential component. In discussing the possible interactive role of memory and operational factors, Piaget has stated that... 'the most likely hypothesis is that the memory code itself depends upon the subject's operations, and therefore this code is modified during development, and depends at any given moment on the subjects operational level' (Piaget 1968, p. 2).

Tentative support for memory variables as partial determinants of young children's success on Piagetian concept tasks has been offered (Roodin and Gruen 1970), and the development of memory strategies appear to parallel the growth of operational thought (Meacham 1972; Neimark, Slotnick and Ulrich 1971). In contrast to these findings with children, memory ability disturbances do not appear to be closely linked to the operational deficits observed in the elderly (e.g., Ajuriaguerra, Kluser, Velghe and Tissot 1965; Ajuriaguerra, Richard, Rodriguez and Tissot 1966). Thus, the possibility exists that the concept task performance pattern similarities shown in comparisons of young children and the elderly are not based on identical process mechanisms.

It is obvious that life-span assessments which involve an emphasis upon process distinctions such as these require *multiple measurement* settings. But, in reality, it requires more than just sophisticated measurement strategies with closely matched analytic procedures; it requires adherence to a world view which openly tolerates intraindividual and interindividual differences and which accepts *multiple causation* of developmental phenomena as a logical and natural outcome. This emphasis on an appreciation of individuality highlights the fact that we are, in the final analysis, concerned with people – thus a fundamental humanistic philosophy is essential. We must not attempt to impose our particular form of adult logic upon the preschool child, or the resident of the old age home, or the member of another 'different' subculture. Normative behavior from the life-span perspective must forever be a relative term.

As you no doubt have surmised, I feel that the organismic world view ideally meets these requirements. I shall even contend that anyone who openly accepts my criteria for a viable life-span developmental discipline is, implicitly at least, accepting the organismic world view of Werner and Piaget. In a previous paper (Hooper 1973), I have claimed that an investigator's world view or basic philosophy of man is the primary determinant of what he expects to find as he examines life-span phenomena, effectively constrains what behavioral alterations will be designated as developmental in nature, and, to a great extent, determines the methodological strategies to be employed. From this position, there is no possibility of acquiring so-called 'pure' objective data concerning life-span functioning. Any empirical observations are a product of the psychologist-observer's theoretical predispositions and his complex interactions with the system undergoing examination. As Boulding has stated: 'All scientists are participant-observers in their own systems... Hence the system changes as it is studied and *because* it is studied. There can be no myth of an unchanging universe with the scientist acquiring abstract knowledge about it' (Boulding 1967, as quoted in Riegel 1973a, p. 16). The most commonly discussed contrasting world views are, of course, the organismic and the behaviorist (Looft 1973; Reese and Overton 1973). While acceptance of the organismic approach may not guarantee that the quest for nontrivial qualitative change will find an empirical resolution, this acceptance at least acknowledges the question of qualitative change as an issue worthy of research and subsequent theory development. Few of our behaviorist colleagues would make that statement.

Theoretical viewpoints in perceptual development: The illusion as paradigm

A. ILLUSIONS AND PERCEPTUAL DEVELOPMENT: A TACHIS-TOSCOPIC PSYCHOPHYSICAL APPROACH

by Robert H. Pollack, *University of Georgia, Athens*

My interest in using optico-geometrical illusions as vehicles for studying perceptual development originates from two distinct sources – Piaget's research in perception and my own work in figural aftereffects. In two early papers (Piaget *et al.* 1942; Piaget and Lambercier 1944), Piaget set out his basic typology of illusions, dividing them into primary – those which declined with age and were based on field forces – and secondary – those which increased with age and were dependent on operations of comparison across time and space. He proposed a single set of mechanisms to account for the ontogenesis of both types (Piaget 1967, 1969) during the course of an extended research program that began with Piatet *et al.* (1942) and ended with the original French version of *Mechanisms of Perception* (Piaget 1961).

Piaget based his explanation on the mode of viewing used by the subject (centration vs. decentration) and some relatively primitive cognitive operations. He argued that early in life the child's attention is held by the dominant organization of a figure on its ground and that he centers on the details which produce maximal distortion. The child takes relatively few separate looks at the display, and these are concentrated upon the givens of the gestalt before him. As he grows older he decentrates, taking multiple looks at various parts of the figure and making comparisons. Thus by experiencing numerous 'encounters' with various parts of the figure and 'couplings' of one with the other, he is able to analyze the figural organization sufficiently to cut down on the illusory distortions produced by that organization. This shift from relatively passive perception or 'field forces' to perceptual activity supposedly accounts for the ontogenetic decline in the magnitude of primary illusions which leads to greater perceptual accuracy. Contrariwise, this same developmental shift to a higher level of perceptual functioning is proposed as the cause for the apparently paradoxical increase in secondary illusions. The mode of decentration is built into the presentation of these illusions (e.g., a discrete succession of figural stimuli). The inducing figures whose organization produces distortion are not functionally present in perception when the test figures are to be compared. The child, therefore, must make a successive comparison of the inducing with the test figures in order to experience the illusion. To the extent that he is better able to make such comparisons as he grows older, the magnitude of the secondary illusion increases. It is clear, then, that for Piaget the same mechanism which produces increasing veridicality in the perception of primary illusions leads to decreasing veridicality in the perception of secondary illusions.

Figural aftereffects. My own work on figural aftereffects began with an attempt to isolate some of the variables which affect the magnitude of contour displacements in the aftereffect situation. After examining the role of contrast level of the inspection or inducing figure and interfigural distance (Pollack 1958), I noted with my colleagues (Day, Pollack, and Seagrim 1959) a similarity among illusions, aftereffects, and the adaptational phenomena studied by the adherents of sensoritonic theory. There followed a series of five studies designed to account for aftereffect phenomena in sensoritonic terms (Pollack 1961; Pollack and Chaplin 1962; Pollack 1963a, b, c,). At the same time my reading of Piaget *et al.* (1942) and Piaget and Lambercier (1944) and close examination of the Koehler and Wallach monograph (1944) led to some testable expectations if there were a similarity between fixation effects and primary illusions on the one hand and between aftereffects and secondary illusions on the other hand. A study on the size effect using concentric squares was carried out (Pollack 1963d) which showed an attraction effect similar to that of the Delboeuf illusion when inscribed and circumscribed squares were presented simultaneously during prolonged fixations. These mutual attraction effects on the squares were just like those obtained by Ogasawara (1952) with the Delboeuf circles. Successive presentations of the squares in the traditional Koehler aftereffect manner produced the classical repulsion effects identical with those obtained by Piaget and Lambercier (1944) for the Usnadze effect or successive Delboeuf. The experiment demonstrated, in adults at least, an equivalence between primary illusions and fixation effects as well as an equivalence between secondary illusions and after-effects. Ikeda and Obonai (1955), first, and Adam (1966), later, showed that varying the onset time of the test figure produced a shift from an attraction to a repulsion effect if the delay became greater than 200 msec. In this fashion, the factor of a perceived succession of events was introduced as the key to the difference between primary and secondary illusions.

Despite the apparent congruence of illusions and prolonged viewing situations, a theoretical dilemma arose in my mind with respect to secondary phenomena. Under prolonged viewing conditions, Koehler and Wallach (1944), Graham (1961) and Pollack (1958) had shown that the magnitude of aftereffects was a function of the figure-ground contrast level of the inducing or inspection figure. In addition, Koehler and Wallach (1944) had argued that as the organism grows older a level of permanent adaptation or satiation builds up which acts as a resistor to the effects built up by situational prolonged viewing. Therefore, the magnitude and the frequency of figural aftereffects should decline through childhood. In contrast, Piagetian theory would expect an increase because of the improving ability with age to make successive comparions. If both theories were correct, and the mechanisms they proposed were perfectly reciprocal, no age change would be expected. An experiment (Pollack 1960) was designed to find out who was right. Both a displacement and a size effect were used. Fixation time was cut down to 10 seconds and frequency of occurrence of figural aftereffects was employed as a measure. In line with the Koehler-Wallach position, the frequency declined between ages 4 and 10 but rose again to adulthood in agreement with Piagetian theory. It seemed at that point that both notions were correct, but for reasons that were perhaps not in exact accord with those of the rival theorists. Given Koehler's notion of a highly sensitive receptor mechanism which adapts with age, one could argue that the 10 second inspection time was sufficient to produce a shrunken afterimage of the inspection figure which remained in view when the test figure was presented. Under such conditions the children would make a simultaneous comparison which would produce the usual repulsion displacement. The older children and adults, however, would respond with true successive comparisons which also produce the familiar repulsion effects. Fortunately, the two functions are not completely reciprocal in that the afterimage process declines before the successive comparison mechanism is well developed, thus producing the dip in the curve. These results suggested the possibility that ontogenetic changes in primary and secondary phenomena could be underlain by different mechanisms; Piaget's carefully worked out perceptual-cognitive mechanism so beautifully applicable to secondary phenomena might not be necessary to account for primary phenomena. It could well be that their ontogenetic decline is due to a loss in receptor sensitivity as a function of chronological age.

New approach to illusions. Before this new approach could be tested properly, certain methodological problems had to be solved. A situation had to be devised in which eye movements would be minimized, there would be no contamination due to prolonged viewing, and no adjustive response process to make exposure time variable. The obvious choice was a brief constant exposure time under fixation conditions with the subject responding dichotomously. Any other situation would allow for the entry of 'encounters' and 'couplings' into an explanation along with adaptation or satiation due to prolonged viewing.

The previous ontogenetic work carried out on illusions, comprehensively reported by Wohlwill (1960), shows some overall age trends, but there appear to be a number of contradictory findings. Many of these are due, probably, to the wide variety of experimental techniques and situations used. Many of the experiments on single phenomena are not comparable because such stimulus factors as illumination, contrast, size, presence or absence of head and eye movements are different, as are the psychophysical methods used to collect the data. Even worse is the high probability that such factors were not adequately controlled. Fortunately, this lack of concern for experimental variables has evaporated in recent years.

In sum, an attempt was made, using our methodology, to determine necessary as well as sufficient conditions for the occurrence, magnitude, and ontogenesis of illusions. I began by accepting, temporarily, that Piaget's explanation for primary or Type I phenomena was sufficient. Instead, I attacked its necessity by attempting to rule out and control experimentally those variables on which his theoretical mechanisms depend.

Historical development of the approach. It seemed to me that the proper way to begin was to do an outrageous experiment. If a negative correlation between the magnitude of a Type I illusion (Mueller-Lyer) and contour detection could be shown in a situation which minimized the conditions necessary for perceptual activity, as defined by Piaget, and which maintained the classical ontogenetic trend, then the effort needed to carry out parametric studies and to extend the theory to other phenomena would be worthwhile. Such results would indicate not only the plausibility of my aging hypothesis but would clearly show the lack of necessity of Piaget's explanation. To be brief, the threshold for the detection of a tachisto-scopically presented contour rose through childhood from ages 6–12 (Pollack 1963a). At the same time the magnitide of a tachistoscopically presented Mueller-Lyer illusion declined with age. The correlation between the two was −.49. In addition the small correlation between IQ and illusion magnitude was in a direction opposite to that expected by Piaget. Contour detection was not at all related to intelligence. In other words, a Type I illusion declined with chronological age under conditions of fixation, small visual angle (2°), and short exposure (200 msec.) using Piaget's own convergent method of limits. Its decline was independent of cognitive factors and related only to the threshold for detecting a contour.

This experiment was followed up by studies of hue detectibility as a function of age (Pollack 1965) and the limits of visual acuity as a function of hue (Skoff and Pollack 1969). Neither study showed any reliable age trends. These studies are important in that they show that the age course for detecting hues and contours produced by hue contrast in the absence of lightness are different from the detection of contours produced by lightness contrast. Up to this point, I had to be content merely to show that, although Piaget's explanation was not necessary, it could be sufficient. The data base was now present to show that his explanation was not sufficient as long as exposure times were brief and eye movements were minimal.

They key experiment involved simply presenting the Mueller-Lyer illusion tachistoscopically in the following five ways: red, yellow, green, and blue figures equated for lightness and saturation on neutral backgrounds of equal lightness, and a white figure on a black ground (Pollack 1970). Ages ranged from 8 to adult. If Piaget's explanation were sufficient, then all forms of the illusion should decline uniformly with age. Decentration accompanied by 'encounters' and 'couplings' should not depend on how contours are produced but merely on their visibility. If Piaget were wrong, then only the magnitude of the illusion produced by the white figure should decline with age. The latter is what occurred. The colored figures produced illusions which did not change with age.

Other studies. In the meantime, experiments were carried out to determine the general characteristics of Type I and Type II phenomena in order to determine their mutual border and to specify clearly the physical stimulus determinants of Type I phenomena. It was felt that these steps were necessary before the more exciting and more complicated determinants of Type II phenomena were examined in detail.

The first step was to repeat the transformation of a Type I illusion into a Type II illusion as Piaget had done (Piaget *et al.*, 1942; Piaget and Lambercier 1944) under our special conditions. This was accomplished using the Mueller-Lyer illusion, by separating in time the presentation of the oblique inducing lines and the test line. The subjects ranging in age from 8 through 11 perceived a reversal of the normal illusion whose magnitude increased rather than decreased with age. It was also noted that mental age was more highly correlated with this illusion than chronological age. This finding was just the reverse of that with the normal presentation used here as a control (Pollack, 1964).

Experimentation was extended to include such phenomena as backward figural masking and the dark interval threshold (Pollack 1965b, 1965c, Streicher and Pollack 1967; Pollack, Ptashne and Carter 1968, 1969). It was found that both of these fitted the Type I paradigm despite the fact that in physical terms they represented a succession of events. Apparently, succession must be perceived as such to produce a Type II phenomenon. This notion receives some support from the work of Ikeda and Obonai (1955) and Adam (1966) which showed a shift from Type I to Type II response to the Delboeuf illusion when test circle onset was delayed by 200 msec. My figural aftereffects study with children mentioned earlier (Pollack 1960) is also supportive. It seemed natural then to find another phenomenon which might delineate further the border between Type I and Type II. Apparent movement was chosen because it is produced by a succession of physical events and because it is experienced as a continuous shift in position through temporal interval. In two preliminary studies (Pollack 1966a, 1966b) it was found that the temporal range of interstimulus intervals which permitted the experience of movement was influenced by such typical Type I variables as figure-ground contrast level, contour orientation, and duration of exposure of the initial stimulus. As before, visual angle extent was kept under 3°, and the sequence of events was presented only once on each trial to prevent repetition effects. These findings led to the expectation that the temporal range of apparent movement would first decrease with age as these physical variables interacted with the aging visual system, but it might increase again as older children became better able to make successive comparisons and to integrate information through time. The expectation was confirmed with the inflection point at age 9 (Pollack 1966c). Additional evidence for the transition from Type I to Type II is the fact that the correlation between temporal range of movement and IQ was significantly higher in 10 and 11 year old children than it was in 7–9 year olds. It appears, therefore, that the inflection in the curve represents a true developmental shift from a dependence on an after-image-like stimulus persistence in the receptor system to the operation of a temporal integration process which makes use of the traces of preceding events compared and contrasted with ongoing stimulation.

Attack on Type II phenomenon. At this time, my colleagues and I thought it was safe and proper to begin to examine Type II phenomena to determine their characteristics and to see whether or not there is a single process underlying them. We began with an examination of intersensory phenomena because they must involve some central integration mechanism and because they should take place fairly early in life. In a series of experiments (Pollack 1967; Pollack and Carter 1967, 1968) dealing with the effect of prolonged fixation on apparent distance in the third dimension and the subjective median plane, we found that children between the ages of 7 and 8 changed the mode of interaction between muscle involvement stimuli and visually presented stimuli. For example, below age 7 children tend to judge the straight-ahead or subjective median plane as being displaced toward the side of muscular involvement produced by raising one arm (assimilation). Beyond age 8 they counteracted this stimulation judging the subjective median plane to be on the side opposite the muscular involvement. By age 9 there is no further change in the magnitude of the counteraction nor is there any relation to intelligence. Apparently the shift represents the end of egocentrism in that the organism becomes fully differentiated from the stimuli acting upon it and is able to counteract or compensate for their effects rather than assimilate to them passively. Such a shift appears to be at a fairly low level since no higher cognitive activities are correlated with it. If so, there are probably a number of Type II mechanisms which probably can be organized in a hierarchy.

Our next step was to return to the illusion as model. Carter (1970) manipulated both the exposure time of the inducing lines and the inter-stimulus interval of the successive Mueller-Lyer illusion. The object was to see whether or not increasing this exposure time could produce sufficient stimulus persistence to increase the illusion in younger children and perhaps to duplicate the curve obtained for figural aftereffects (Pollack 1960). This first attempt produced no clear age trend indicating that the durations chosen provided a perfect reciprocity between after-image and temporal integration processes. A second attempt (Carter-Seeman 1971) using an inducing stimulus duration of 1 sec. with a 500 msec. inter-stimulus interval reversed the age course. A 2 sec. ISI produced the usual increase with age expected of a Type II illusion. It was interesting that the illusion magnitude obtained with the 2 sec. ISI was smaller than that with the 500 msec. ISI in the youngest children, further strengthening the notion that different processes were at work. In a third study (Carter-Seeman 1972), the inducing lines were presented for 1.5 sec. with an ISI of 2 sec. Illusion magnitude declined from ages 4 to 12 and then appeared to increase at age 14. Further study will be necessary to show that the illusion will increase again as subjects approach adulthood. Other phenomena requiring temporal integration were studied as well including digit span forward and backward and Hearnshaw's (1956) spider-web matrix task. The latter required a subject to chose among a dot that never moved on successive presentations of a set of concentric circles intersected by 8 radii, a dot that moved systematically, and one that moved randomly. The subject is also required to anticipate the moves of the systematic dot.

The results showed that temporal integration tasks are organized hierarchically with digit span forward asymptoting by age 8, digit span backward by age 12, and no asymptote in sight at age 14 for the Hearnshaw task. The data showed also that the stimulus persistence indicated by the ontogenetic reversal of the successive Mueller-Lyer illusion could be a primitive but necessary analog of the developmentally superior mechanism of registering some sort of memory trace and integrating it with sub-sequent discrete presentation of additional information. Again the illusion presented under carefully controlled tachistoscopic conditions served as a tool for locating and characterizing developmental changes.

Recent work. All of the work discussed up to this point indicates a kind of steady progress from studying relatively simple Type I phenomena, their border with Type II, and finally the complexities of the latter. In actual fact this is not the case. We are in the midst of a fairly long regression in the service of our theoretical ego. The Type I phenomena we thought so simple at first have interesting facets which were bypassed earlier. Sjostrom and I (Sjostrom and Pollack 1971a, 1971b) attempted to simulate the aging factor of yellowing of the crystalline lens by placing a yellow filter between the subject and both the Delboeuf illusion and the Usnadze effect and found that we could reduce the former (Type I) but not the latter (Type II). We also found that the decrement produced was constant through childhood merely superimposing itself on the usual decline with age. The Usnadze effect was unaffected at all age levels. Sjostrom is now engaged in analyzing the figural stimulus components that comprise the Delboeuf figure such as circle shrinkage and parallel line attraction. A preliminary study showing circular shrinkage as a function of stimulus duration has been completed (Sjostrom and Pollack 1973).

Quina and I have analyzed the Ponzo illusion under our experimental conditions (Quina and Pollack 1971, 1972). This illusion never really classified by Piaget was thought to be a Type II illusion because of its increase with age (Leibowitz and Judisch 1967), but it was always presented as an extremely large figure, and the effects of its two test lines were never separated. We found that lines near the apex of the Ponzo wedge increase in length while those near the open end shrink. The age courses of the two effects differ as well. The growth of the apical line decreased from age 7 to age 12 and then rose slowly to adulthood. The shrinkage of the other line rose sharply to age 11 and then declined to adulthood. Summation of the two effects revealed an illusion which peaked at age 11. Needless to say, the illusion presented under our conditions is not a Type II. Quina is now dissecting the Poggendorff illusion under our conditions and thus far has found an attraction effect of the vertical parallels of the figure which varies with interline distance (Quina and Pollack 1973).

We have also been looking at the interaction of such variables as hue, saturation, lightness contrast, exposure duration, and fundus pigmentation on our old friend the Mueller-Lyer. In two early studies (Silvar and Pollack 1967; Pollack and Silvar 1967) we demonstrated population differences in fundus pigmentation and in illusion magnitude which were highly correlated. Ebert and Pollack (1972a, 1972b) have confirmed these findings within an all-white population showing that darkly pigmented individuals have significantly smaller Mueller-Lyer illusions at very brief

(500 msec.) exposures than lightly pigmented ones. All of these data have led us to question the view that cross-population studies of Type I illusions have shown differences dependent upon cultural factors (Segall, Campbell, and Herskovitz 1966). The argument presented states that many non-Western societies live in an 'uncarpentered' world or one which does not use right angles in the construction of dwellings, etc. Supposedly it is an inference of depth drawn from the experience of three dimensional right angles that underlies the distortions of the Mueller-Lyer illusion. It is strange, therefore, that Jahoda (1966) was unable to find difference among three Ghanian groups at different levels of carpenteredness. Indeed, Berry (1971) found that skin color was the most reliable single predictor of Mueller-Lyer illusion sensitivity in an analysis of data from ten widely varying societies. Recently Jahoda (1971) in comparing Scottish and Malawi architecture students found reduced sensitivity to a blue Mueller-Lyer figure on a neutral ground of equal lightness among Malawis but not among Scots. The Malawis also had difficulty in reading contour maps containing short wave hues but not those with long wave hues.

If we are correct in our thinking that biological factors due both to the aging process and to the genetic determination of optical pigmentation are the operative determinants of Type I phenomena, there are important consequences for early childhood education. This is especially so if after-image-like stimulus persistence processes are the primitive analogs of the developmentally higher-order processes of temporal integration. Our findings suggest that care will have to be taken to present appropriate materials under optimal lighting and viewing conditions and that population differences will have to be taken into account in choosing the colors of materials to be used. Our second outrageous experiment illustrates the point. Recently Mitchell and Pollack (1973) compared the performance of Black and white fifth graders in the WISC Block Design Subtest. When the standard red and white surfaces were used, differences in test performance were not significant. When the alternate blue and yellow surfaces were used, the performance of the Black children dropped significantly while that of the whites stayed the same. Apparently the Blacks' reduced sensitivity to blue blurred its border with the yellow and distorted the overall design making the task noticeably more difficult.

The prospect. Our methodology has provided us with an effective tool for studying perceptual development, and the illusion has remained as our most useful phenomenal tool in developing and testing our hypotheses. The work will continue in three major areas. First, our regression into Type I will continue until we isolate its variables completely so that we can resynthesize our findings within a more highly developed theory. Second, we shall continue our population studies using illusions in which we shall vary such key stimulus parameters as illumination intensity, lightness contrast, saturation, and hue contrast. Third, the work on delineating the levels of activity within Type II processes will continue both to determine their nature and to back our contentions that perception plays a key role at the highest level of cognitive functioning.

I would like to make a final theoretical speculation which may serve to integrate the papers by Coren and Leibowitz with my own. Let us conceive of the visual perceptual process as depending upon a neurophysiological system which operates on the principles of least effort and parsimony. If peripheral information is relatively complete and simultaneous, the higher interactional and organizational centers pass it on unchanged. To the extent that peripheral information is incomplete, disorganized, or broken up temporally, these higher centers will grudgingly organize and modify it so that the final product is rarely if ever chaotic. Additionally, the higher centers will operate if forced to do so by self or externally imposed instructional stimuli which may take the form of an *einstellung* effect produced by the mode of stimulus presentation. Whatever future research tells us about the underlying mechanisms, we find ourselves possessed of a concept of hierarchical organization which biologists have used fruitfully for the better part of a century.

B. PERCEPTUAL DEVELOPMENT: A DISTORTED VIEW

by Stanley Coren, *University of British Columbia, Vancouver, Canada,*
and Joan S. Girgus, *City University of New York**

In order to understand the conscious percept of any stimulus we must take into account at least two levels of processing of the information presented by the stimulus. The first depends upon the structural properties of the optical and nervous systems, and the second involves the cognitive components of the processing of visual information which occur in the higher centers. Many of the complications encountered in studying perception arise from the difficulty which a researcher has in separating the relative contribution of these two sources to any given perception. The problem becomes even greater when we consider perceptual development. It is clear that the organism is maturing and aging, and this results in changes in the efficiency of the various neural and optical structures. In addition, he is developing, revising, and amplifying his cognitive substrata of information processing strategies. Thus, it becomes clear that any developmental difference which is observed in perception could be due to either structural or processing changes, or to some combination of the two.

Visual geometric illusions have long fascinated workers in the field of perception. Figure 1 shows some of the standard configurations on which research frequently has been performed. Figure 1A is the Brentano form of the Mueller-Lyer illusion in which the horizontal line on the right is seen as shorter than the horizontal line on the left, although the two lines are identical in length. Figure 1B is called the Zoellner illusion, in which the vertical lines are, in fact, parallel, although they do not look it. Figure 1C is called the Poggendorff illusion; in this illusion, the transversal usually does not look like the ends of a single continuous line. Figure 1D shows the Ponzo illusion; the two horizontal lines are, in fact, the same length, although the one closer to the vertex of the angle tends to look longer. Figure 1E shows the Wundt-Hering illusion; the horizontal line in this configuration tends to look bowed when it is actually quite straight. Figure 1F shows the Oppel-Kundt or filled space-open space illusion;

* We would like to acknowledge the assistance of Richard Fraenkel in the collection of much of the data discussed in this paper.

Figure 1. *Some classical visual illusions (see text for explanation):*
A) *Mueller-Lyer (Brentano form); B) Zoellner;*
C) *Poggendorff; D) Ponzo; E) Wundt-Hering;*
F) *Oppel-Kundt; G) Ebbinghaus; H) Variant of Mueller-Lyer:*
I) *Variant of Mueller-Lyer (Coren's dot form)*

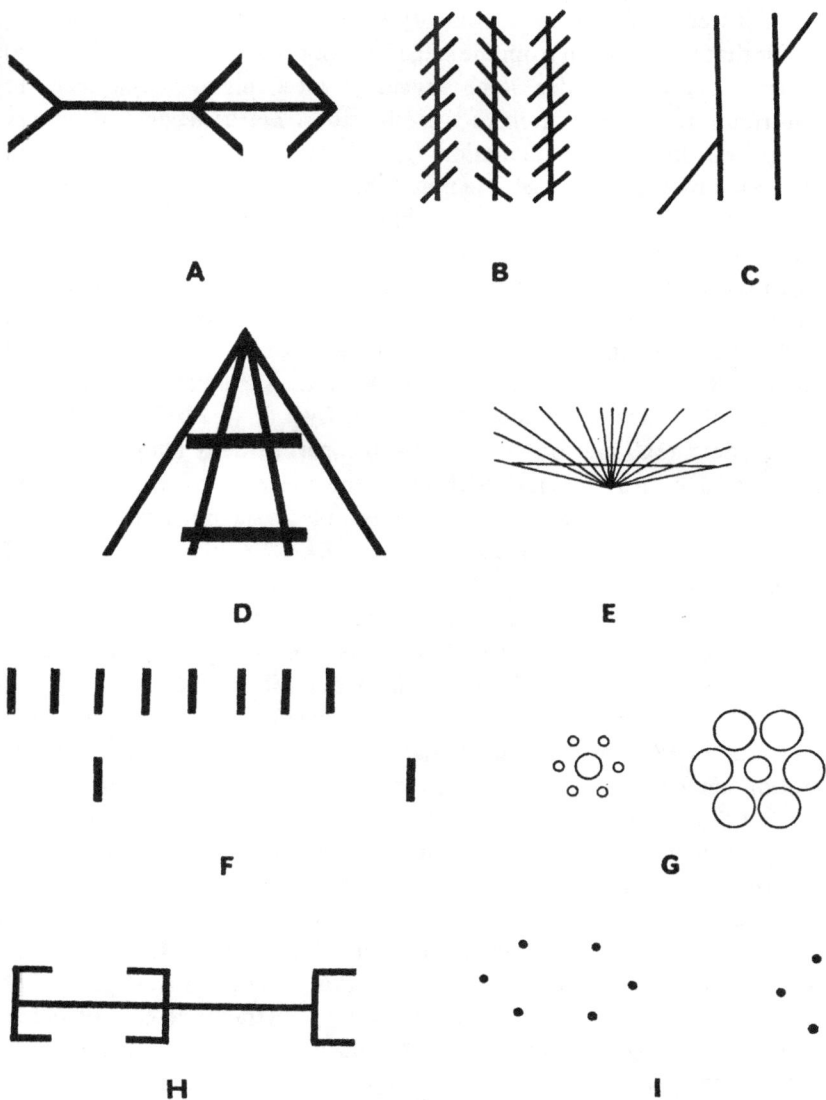

filled space tends to look larger than open space of the same extent. Figure 1G demonstrates the Ebbinghaus illusion (sometimes called the Titchener's circles illusion); the center circle surrounded by larger circles looks smaller than the center circle surrounded by smaller circles.

Sources of illusory distortion. Given such a variety of perceptual distortions, it seems unlikely that all illusory effects derive from the same source, or for that matter, even from the same level of processing within the visual system. Let us consider some suggested mechanisms which seem to contribute to the formation of these illusions. Let us begin with a very peripheral structural explanation for visual illusions which has been suggested by Chaing (1968). He noted that, during their passage through the pupil and the crystalline lens, light rays are somewhat defocussed and smeared, by diffraction at the pupillary aperture and by optical aberrations in the lens. As a result of this, by the time the image arrives at the retinal surface, there may be alterations in the pattern of stimulation such that the location of the vertex in acute angles seems to be displaced somewhat into the body of the angle. Such a mechanism can predict a number of illusions, including the Mueller-Lyer (1A), Zoellner (1B), and Poggendorff (1C) illusions. Coren (1969) experimentally manipulated the amount of optical aberration through the use of artificial pupils and narrow band chromatic filters and was able to demonstrate that this structural component can account for some 22% of the Poggendorff illusion, with the other 78% of the illusion presumably caused by other factors. In addition, it has been shown that density of the macular pigment, which might result in a similar stimulus degradation, contributes to the Mueller-Lyer illusion (Pollack and Silvar, 1967).

Another possible structural source has been suggested by Bekesy (1967) and Ganz (1966), who contend that lateral inhibitory interactions operating on converging or intersecting lines account for some of the perceived contour displacements. Coren (1970) has shown that removal of the converging line elements and replacement of them with dots reduces the magnitude of the illusory effect but does not completely eliminate it. This theory has also been tested through the use of binocular separation of test and inducing elements (Day 1961; Ohwaki 1960; Schiller and Weiner 1962; Springbett 1961). These investigators all reasoned that the required lateral inhibitory interactions cannot occur if the converging or intersecting contours do not appear on the same retina. The results from these studies agree with each other and with the data generated by Coren using dot forms of the illusion. The magnitude of the illusory distortion is reduced, but the distortion is not eliminated completely. This would seem to indicate that lateral inhibition plays a contributory role, but not the sole casual role, in illusion formation.

Another theory has proposed that the size of the illusion is a function of the eye movements used to scan the illusion figure (Festinger 1971; Festinger, White and Allyn 1968). These investigators have shown that saccades used to scan a Mueller-Lyer figure are erroneously long or short depending on which half on the configuration is being viewed.

Other investigators have proposed a variety of components, attributable to the cognitive processing of the perceptual inputs, as explanations for some illusory distortions. For example, Gregory (1963) and Gillam (1971) have shown that some aspects of certain classical illusion figures mimic perspective cues. Thus, the converging lines of the Ponzo (1D) illusion provide a stimulus array which inappropriately triggers the constancy scaling mechanism. This theory proposes that the subject receives the impression of a road or surface receding into the distance with the upper line thus farther away than the lower line. Since the retinal angles subtended by the two lines are, in fact, the same, the constancy scaling mechanism will, under these circumstances, compute the upper line as being physically longer than the lower, resulting in the perceived distortion.

There is also evidence that comparative judgmental processes, such as size contrast, play a part in illusion formation (Coren 1971; Girgus, Coren and Agdern 1972; Massaro and Anderson 1971; Restle and Merryman 1968). This explanation for illusory distortions was first proposed by Helmholtz (1962) who suggested that clearly perceived differences tend to be emphasized. This is the sort of judgmental effect which makes a Cocker Spaniel look very large when compared to a Yorkshire Terrier and very small when compared to a St. Bernard. Such effects have been quantitatively described by Helson (1964) in terms of his adaptation level theory.

One of the older process theories of illusion formation maintains that the distortion is caused by a confusion of the test with the inducing elements. On the Mueller-Lyer figure (1A), for example, the side with the outward turned wings is indeed longer in overall extent than the side with the inward turned wings. If the observer confuses the wings with the shaft in making his judgment, this would lead to an overestimation of the horizontal extent. This theory was first suggested by Mueller-Lyer himself and has since been restated by Benussi (1904) and Erlebacher and Sekuler (1969). Coren and Girgus (1972a) have shown that increasing the discriminability of the shaft and the wings, by making them different colors or by introducing a small spatial separation between them, leads to a reduction in illusion magnitude as would be predicted by this theory.

Separation of illusion components: With all of these possible sources of illusory distortion, the problem of separating the relative contribution of each becomes a veritable labyrinth. We have recently attempted to shed some light on this issue by using the fact that the magnitude of most illusions diminishes with continued viewing. This phenomenon, which is called illusion decrement, has been observed innumerable times since it was first reported by Heymans (1896) for the Mueller-Lyer configuration. Illusion decrement has also been found in the Poggendorff, the Zoellner, the Wundt-Hering, and the Oppel-Kundt illusion, as well as in the Mueller-Lyer (Coren and Girgus 1972b; Coren and Hoenig 1972). It seems unlikely that illusion decrement represents a change in the structural mechanisms which contribute to illusion magnitude, since it is improbable that the magnitude of optical aberrations from the lens or the operation of lateral inhibitory interactions would be affected by a few minutes spent inspecting the figure.

Instead the evidence seems to support the notion that illusion decrement is the result of changes in cognitive processing mechanisms. For instance, the diminution of the illusion has been shown to persist and to cumulate over days and weeks (Judd 1902). Decrement also seems to respond to traditional learning variables, such as the spacing of trials (Dewar 1968; Mountjoy 1961). The presence of saccadic eye movements, which may provide error information, facilitates the appearance of decrement (Burnham 1968; Coren and Hoenig 1972; Festinger, White and Allyn 1968). This implies that we should be able to use illusion decrement as a technique for separating the structural from the processing components in illusion formation. Since the amount of illusion that disappears during free inspection probably reflects changes in the organization and processing of the inputs, the rate and quantity of decrement should be a function of the more central processing components. On the other hand, the amount of illusion that remains after the decrement procedure should be predominantly a function of the structural components.

Girgus, Coren and Horowitz (1973) tested this formulation by using a variety of Mueller-Lyer configurations which were chosen so that they contained different amounts of converging or intersecting line elements. As we have noted above, converging contours provide the optimal stimulus arrangement for the operation of neural and optical mechanisms such as lateral inhibition and optical aberrations. The presence of structural components should result in a greater initial illusion for configurations such as 1A, but less for configurations such as 1H, which contains squared off wings and hence little opportunity for contour interactions, or 1I which contains no contours at all. Regardless of the initial amount of illusion, however, it might be expected that all of the configurations would decrement at the same rate. This expectation is based on the assumption that, since all are variants of the same illusion pattern (the Mueller-Lyer), they should contain common cognitive processing components which support the illusory distortion. The results which these workers obtained seem to be consistent with this mode of analysis. The initial illusion magnitude seems to reflect the structural contribution to the illusion, while the rate of decrement seems to be identical for all of the configurations, regardless of the original illusion strength. Such results support the idea of using illusion decrement as a method to separate the structural components from the more cognitive processing components of an illusion.

Perceptual development and visual illusions. Let us now consider the problem of perceptual development as it is reflected in visual illusions. Many investigators have presented various illusions to subjects of different ages. The resulting data indicate that some of these configurations, such as the Mueller-Lyer or the Poggendorff illusion, show a decrease in magnitude from childhood to adulthood (Binet 1895; Piaget, Maire and Privat 1954; Pollack 1964; Vurpillot 1957) while other figures, such as the Ebbinghaus or the Ponzo illusion, show an increase in illusion size with age (Leibowitz and Heisel 1958; Wapner and Werner 1957). It seems clear that these age changes might either be due to structural changes in the maturing optical and neural systems or to cognitive processing changes that reflect age changes in the ways in which organisms process information. Some theorists, such as Pollack (1969), have attributed some age changes in illusion magnitude to various structural changes in the visual receptor system, including the increasing pigmentation of the lens which has been shown to occur with age and which would tend to decrease the contrast of the stimulus (Coren and Girgus 1972c). Similarly, there are neural changes with age which decrease the sensitivity of the eye to contour processes and thus might reduce illusion magnitude (Pollack 1963). Other theorists might favor a more central processing interpretation of these age changes. For instance, a proponent of confusion theory might argue that the child has more trouble cognitively isolating the test element than does the adult and thus shows more illusion. It has already been shown that, for an adult, simple restriction of attention to the test element via instructions results in a reduction of illusion magnitude (Coren and Girgus 1972a). Similarly, Piaget's (1969) notion of decentration conveys the essence of a shift in processing strategy with age from a more passive global to a more active exploratory mode, which would also result in a diminution of some illusions, such as the Mueller-Lyer.

Deciding amongst these alternatives is not easy. However, one might start by attempting to alter the amount of peripheral structural involvement such as was done by Coren (1970) or Girgus, Coren, and Horowitz (1972). If structural components are responsible for the observed age trends in illusions, reduction of the relative structural contribution should reduce or eliminate any observable age trends. This is the strategy that we decided to adopt. The two forms of the Mueller-Lyer that we chose for this experiment were the Brentano (1A) and a dot form (1I) used by Coren (1970) in which all contours are removed from the figure and replaced by dots placed at the line ends and vertices. The Brentano form presents a maximum number of converging and intersecting line elements and thus is an optimal stimulus for optical and neural interactions, while the dot form presents no such opportunity for these sources of structural involvement. Each form of the illusion was presented to 20 subjects in each of four age groups: 6 year olds, 8 year olds, 10 year olds, and adults, and each subject was asked to set the two halves of the configuration to apparent equality.

The data for the illusion judgments are shown in Figure 2. It is clear that we have replicated the usual age trend for the Mueller-Lyer in the Brentano form. The decrease in illusion magnitude with age represents both a significant main effect and a significant linear decreasing trend. For the dot form, however, the effect of age is much weaker. For this configuration, the main effect for age is not significant, although the linear trend component shows a significant decrease in illusion magnitude with age. Not surprisingly, the interaction between age and illusion types is significant, indicating the differences in the developmental trends for these two configurations.

Figure 2. *Magnitude of two variants of the Mueller-Lyer illusion as a function of age*

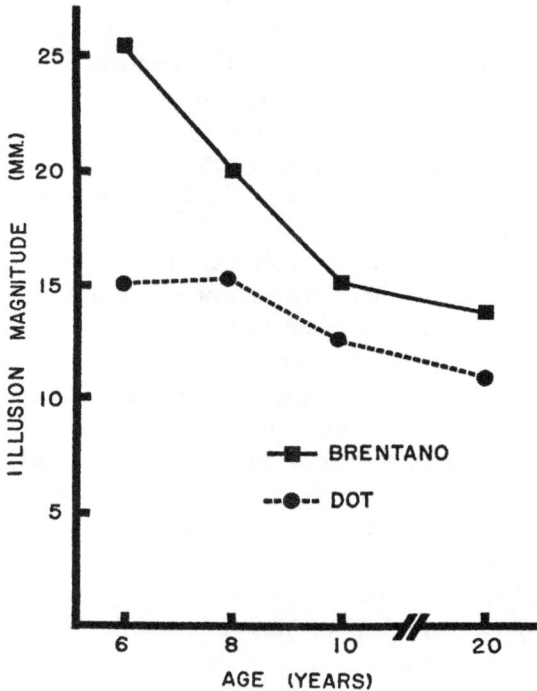

If one were to look at only these data, one might immediately conclude that structural mechanisms are largely responsible for age differences in the magnitude of the Mueller-Lyer illusion. This can be deduced from the fact that there are strong age trends for a configuration in which there is much opportunity for structural interactions (the Brentano form) while there are much weaker age trends for a configuration in which the possibilities for such contributions have been largely eliminated (the dot form). It must be noted, however, that in altering the stimulus configuration to eliminate the structural interactions we may have also affected some of the parameters which affect the way in which the stimulus is processed. For example, the subjectively constructed lines connecting the dots are surely less cogent stimuli than actually converging lines and angles for triggering the constancy scaling mechanisms which have been suggested by perspective theorists, such as Gregory, to account for the distortion. In addition, the dot form is highly differentiated since each dot is seen as a separate entity. This might lead to less confusion between test and inducing components and, hence, to less illusion. If children are more susceptible to such confusion effects than are adults, their perform-ance on the dot form of the illusion would show a particularly marked improvement in accuracy compared to the Brentano form and an inter-action between age and illusion form such as was found might be expected. Thus, it is clear that manipulations based upon alteration of the stimulus array contain a confounding of both structural and process variables. We cannot then isolate the source of the developmental trends on the basis of such data.

Since we were cognizant of this difficulty, we had not simply contented ourselves with a simple static assessment of illusion magnitude as a function of age. The data presented above only represent the first trial of testing on each subject. Each subject made a total of six judgments of apparent equality, spaced at 30 second intervals. Between settings, the two halves of the illusion configuration were set to actual equality and the subject was instructed to scan the figure. This procedure has been shown to result in an appreciable amount of illusion decrement (Coren and Girgus 1972a, 1972b; Girgus, Coren and Horowitz 1973).

This decrement should represent the modification of cognitive pro-cessing strategies, rather than any structural change, as we noted above. If our initial conclusion based on static assessment of illusion magnitude is correct, and the age differences are due to differences in neural and optical variables, we have no reason to expect any differences in rate or amount of decrement as a function of age. If the age trends derive from a structural source, we would expect the differences in illusion magnitude between the age groups to remain constant over the experimental session. On the other hand, any differences in the slope of the decrement curves would serve as evidence consistent with the hypothesis that age differences in illusions are due to changes in cognitive processing.

The complete results of this experiment are presented in Figure 3. As can be seen, for the Brentano form of the illusion, we find marked slope differences as a function of age. An analysis of variance performed on the regression slopes, computed individually for each subject, reveals a significant difference between the age groups in rate of decrement for the Brentano form (3A), but no significant difference between the age groups for the dot form (3B). Notice that after only two and a half minutes of inspection, the decrement curves have converged to the point where no significant age differences in illusion magnitude are found for either configuration. Certainly we have not altered lateral inhibition or the pigmentation of the crystalline lens over so short a period. The fact that we so rapidly reach a point where the age differences disappear would seem to contradict any hypothesis based solely on structural differences.

Figure 3. *Magnitude of two variants of the Mueller-Lyer illusion for various age groups measured as a function of viewing time: A) Brentano form; B) Dot form*

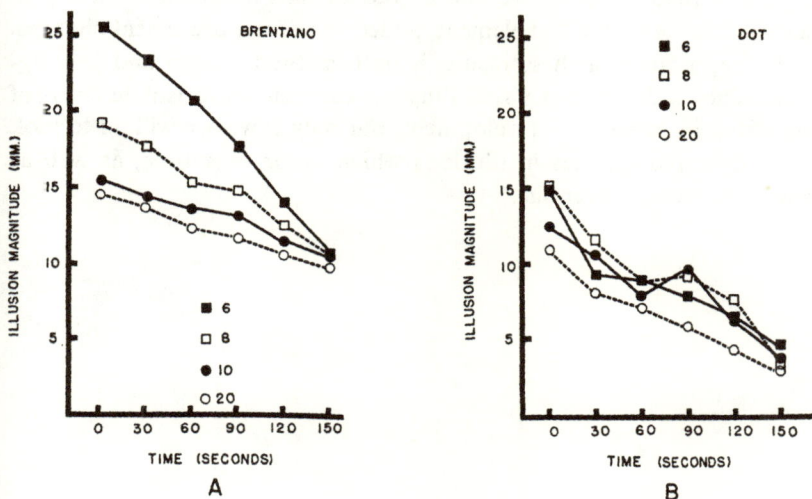

These data would seem to suggest that children initially view the Mueller-Lyer illusion in a somewhat different fashion than adults but quickly come to adopt the adult strategy. Although this experiment was not designed to isolate the specific nature of the processing differences as a function of age, some hints as to its nature emerge from the data. The weak initial age differences and the absence of slope differences for the dot form seem to provide a clue. This illusion form, in addition to reducing the amount of possible structural interaction, also presents a highly differentiated and disarticulated array. If the older subjects are utilizing a strategy which facilitates the gradually increasing isolation of particular parts of a continuous figure (in this case, the test extent), this would result in a reduction in the illusion magnitude as a function of age for the Brentano form. On the other hand, in a non-continuous configuration, such as the dot form in which the test extent is so clearly isolated, this strategy should have little effect, and the age differences should be greatly reduced. This would suggest that we might be looking at a shift in preference for wholistic versus partistic viewing with age or, alternatively, to the more efficient restriction of attention in the adult. Such an argument clearly reflects differences in perceptual strategies rather than differences in the basic ability to perceive. The steeper slopes of the decrement curves for the younger groups on the Brentano form of the illusion may thus be the result of two processes simultaneously taking place. For these subjects, we find a gradual shift in strategy, leading to increased focus on the test element, added to normal decrement changes.

The importance of these results is both methodological and paradigmatic. They indicate that visual illusions can help us to isolate levels of processing in perceptual development, but only if we are willing to look at the dynamic changes in illusions which occur over time, as well as those which occur over age.

C. CROSS-CULTURAL AND PERSONALITY FACTORS INFLU-ENCING THE PONZO PERSPECTIVE ILLUSION*

by Herschel W. Leibowitz, *Pennsylvania State University, University Park*

This presentation is divided into two separate parts, both concerned with factors influencing the magnitude of the Ponzo illusion and their methodological and theoretical implications. The first is based on the heuristic hypothesis that the Ponzo illusion is a manifestation of mon-ocular depth cues. The second part deals with an entirely new approach to the study of illusions, the effect of hypnotic susceptibility as a factor determining illusion magnitude.

The Ponzo illusion as a manifestation of monocular depth cues. One of the oldest explanations offered for the Ponzo illusion (Figure 1C) is that it represents the misapplication of depth cues which normally operate in three-dimensional visual space. According to this theory, originally alluded to by Helmholtz and further developed by Filehne (1898), Tausch (1954), Von Holst (1957), Gregory (1963), and Fisher (1968), the per-spective cues represented by the radiating lines of the figure are ordinarily associated with depth in three-dimensional space and are inappropriately activated while viewing the two-dimensional Ponzo figure. Since in our normal interaction with space we 'correct' for distant objects in the interest of size constancy, this same correction mechanism is misapplied in a two-dimensional presentation thereby producing an illusory enlarge-ment of the object located near the point of convergence of the figure.

Animal studies. There are a number of ways to test the plausibility of this hypothesis. An ideal technique would be to measure the illusion magnitude in animals, such as monkeys, whose visual and perceptual skills are similar to humans. By selectively exposing experimental animals to environments which are either rich or poor with respect to converging perspective lines, the effects of previous exposure history on illusion magnitude could be readily determined. A number of years ago William A. Mason and I unsuccessfully attempted such a study. While it was

* Supported by Grant MH08061 from the National Institute of Mental Health. The help of Dr. Robert J. Miller is gratefully acknowledged.

Figure 1. *The stimuli employed in the cross-cultural studies. In all cases, the horizontal lines have the same dimensions (From Leibowitz, Brislin, Permutter and Hennessy 1969)*

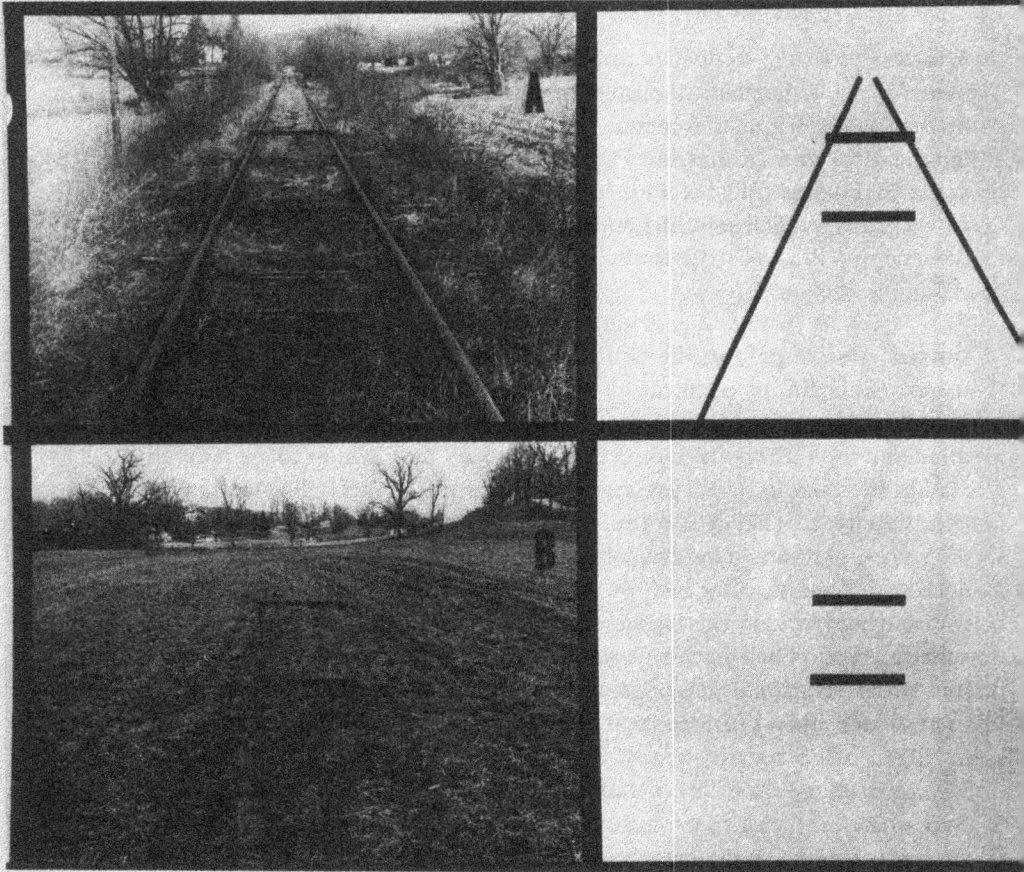

routine to train a rhesus monkey to discriminate the longer or shorter of two lines, the discrimination broke down completely when the enclosing lines were introduced. I have discussed this problem with a number of primate researchers all of whom are confident that the experiment could be satisfactorily completed. Perhaps some of the newer discrimination techniques, such as fading, might overcome our previous difficulty. In any event, this remains a potentially powerful, and to my knowledge unexploited, method for investigating the origin of the Ponzo (and other) illusions.

Developmental studies. A second approach, developmental in nature, has been more successful. It has been determined, and replicated, that both the Ponzo illusion (Leibowitz and Heisel 1958; Hanley and Zerbolio 1965; Leibowitz and Judisch 1967a; Farquar and Leibowitz 1971) and size constancy for distant objects (Zeigler and Leibowitz 1957; Leibowitz, Pollard and Dickson 1967a; Jenkin and Feallock 1960; Leibowitz 1961) increase as a function of chronological but not of mental age. If one is willing to accept the assumption that one of the monocular cues involved in size constancy is perspective, then it would follow that development of the strength of this cue is responsible, in terms of the misplaced constancy hypothesis, for the similar developmental trends in the Ponzo illusion and size constancy. This is not a logic-tight argument since we have established a correlation rather than unequivocal causation. One of the difficulties inherent in this approach is that size constancy is mediated by a number of mechanisms while the Ponzo illusion, at least to the extent that it is determined developmentally, would seem to be determined predominantly by a single cue, perspective. This may account for the observation that although the Ponzo illusion sometimes decreases in old age, size constancy does not (Leibowitz and Judisch 1967b). I would prefer to think that these data are suggestive, and that it is likely that the Ponzo illusion results at least in part from a depth cue which has been developmentally acquired by means of perceptual learning resulting from exposure to the environment. Obviously one needs more controls (such as, for example, might be available with experimental animals) to draw definitive conclusions.

The cross-cultural approach. The third approach is to investigate populations of human subjects whose history of exposure to perspective cues may be different from those found among our typical college populations.

This is the approach of the cross-cultural psychologist and is usually discussed in the context of the 'ecological hypothesis' (Segall, Campbell, and Herskovitz 1966; Miller 1973). Stated briefly, this hypothesis assumes that the stength of monocular depth cues depends on their frequency of exposure in a particular environment. With respect to the Ponzo illusion, it would follow that subjects reared in an environment with fewer converging lines would exhibit a reduced Ponzo illusion as compared with subjects whose environment presented many opportunities to associate converging lines with distance.

Several years ago we had an excellent opportunity to test this hypothesis on Guam. On this island, there are relatively fewer examples of perspective cues than is typically found in the continental U.S. In particular, there are no railroads (only a short spur line at the dock). The test consisted of four stimuli with increasing amounts of contextual cues. The first consisted of two horizontal lines on a white background (Figure 1D). This was instituted as a control for the observation, by William James, that the upper of two equal lines will appear larger, presumably because it is ordinarily farther away. The second stimulus consisted of the classical Ponzo figure with two enclosing lines (Figure 1C). The third was a photograph of horizontal 'lines', produced by boards, in a plowed field (Figure 1B). Naturally, we called this the 'Gibson' figure in honor of our psychologist colleague and friend who emphasized the role of texture in space perception. The fourth consisted of the same horizontal lines viewed on railroad tracks (Figure 1A). In all four cases, the physical dimensions of the horizontal lines were identical – only the context varied. The stimuli were presented to groups of college students at Penn State and in Guam using the same procedure.

As indicated in Figure 2, the results, as one might expect, indicated that the richer the context the larger the magnitude of the overestimation of the upper line (i.e., the illusion).

In the experiment with college students at Penn State, we were also able to include observation of the real scene both binocularly and monocularly. Monocular observation, with the field of view restricted to the same visual angle as obtained with the photograph of the railroad tracks, produces an illusion magnitude of more than 30 percent. We thought this large illusion magnitude was particularly interesting because it begins to approach the value of the overestimation obtained in size constancy situations, and it also has the same value for the photograph as for monocular observation of the actual scene.

Figure 2. *Illusion magnitude for the stimuli depicted for Figure 1 for Pennsylvania and Guam college students (Leibowitz, Brislin, Perlmutter and Hennessy 1969), and for college and rural Ugandans (Leibowitz and Pick 1972)*

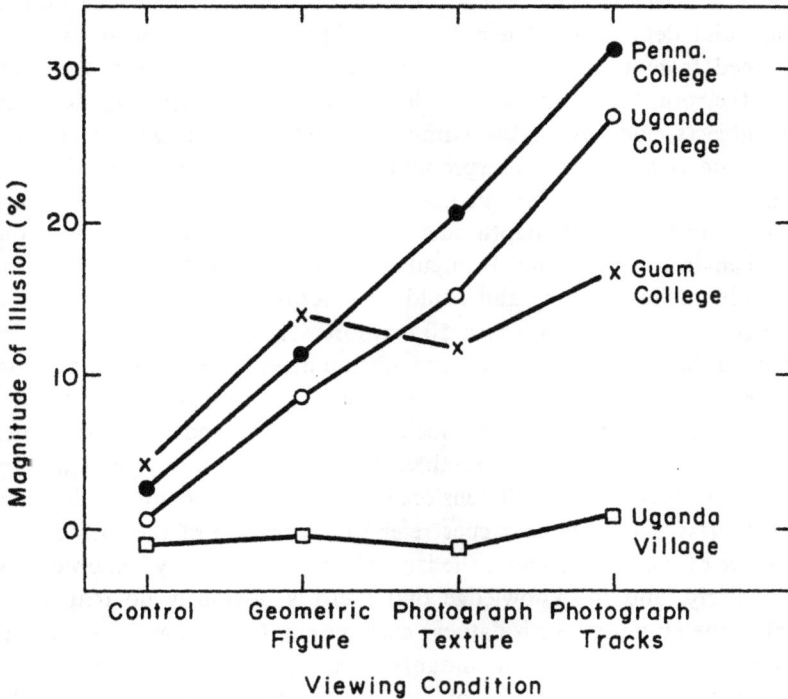

It is important to emphasize that the college students tested in Guam by Richard Brislin were fluent in English, as this removes a possible source of artifact resulting from demand characteristics and misinterpretations of language. The data indicated that the Guamanians, for the two photographic stimuli, produced significantly lower illusion magnitudes than did the Pennsylvania college students. Such results fit in nicely with the ecological hypothesis, in that the illusion magnitude reflects the relative exposure of the subjects to the monocular depth cues in the photograph. As a further test of this hypothesis, we presented the same stimuli to a different group of Pennsylvania subjects but with the figures rotated 90 and 180 degrees. This also produced a lowering of the illusion magnitude, a result consistent with the role of familiarity as a factor in the relative effectiveness of monocular depth cues (Leibowitz, Perlmutter, Brislin and Hennessy 1969).

The following year, Herbert Pick, during a sabbatical leave in Uganda, presented these same stimuli to two groups of Ugandans, college students and rural villagers. The college students lived in an urban area rich in monocular depth cues. Their data (see Figure 2) were similar to those obtained from the Pennsylvania college students. However, the data from the rural Ugandans were both unexpected and surprising. None of the subjects, for any of the stimuli, showed any illusion whatsoever. There are two possible interpretations of these results. One might be inclined to assume at first glance that their visual environments were deficient in monocular depth cues. This was quickly rejected since the visual environment in rural Kampala is not essentially different from that observed in this country and could be described as highly similar to a typical scene in rural America 50 or more years ago. Thus, it must be assumed that the failure to produce illusion magnitudes cannot be due to differences in the previous exposure history or strength of these cues.

A second interpretation is much more subtle, and perhaps rather speculative, but fortunately testable. As pointed out many years ago by Schlosberg (1941), a two-dimensional reproduction contains both depth and flatness cues. Flatness cues refer to the texture of the surface, the presence of the experimenter, the lack of retinal disparity when observing binocularly, and the knowledge that there is obviously no real depth behind the stimulus. Such flatness cues may not be ignored by subjects who have not had significant amounts of experience with two-dimensional representation. Another way of putting it is that subjects may not be able to perceive depth in pictorial representations unless they have learned to do so, as a direct result of experience with pictures (Miller 1973). We have conjectured that the failure of the rural Ugandans to show any illusion whatsoever is a result of the masking or inhibition of the depth cues by the flatness cues. The essence of the argument is that the college Guamanian, Pennsylvanian, and urban Ugandan subjects have had many more exposures to two-dimensional reproductions and thereby have learned to ignore or suppress the flatness cues. This is not the case for the rural Ugandans. Preliminary observations using college students at Penn State, in which the Ponzo illusion was shown to be greater when viewing transparencies monocularly in a black box, thereby eliminating flatness cues, lent encouragement to this hypothesis.

As of this writing, a replication and extension of the original study with Pick, as well as a test of the flatness cue hypothesis, has just been carried out in Uganda by Philip Kilbride. Dr. Kilbride is an anthropologist specializing in Uganda who speaks the native language and has access to populations whose previous exposure to two-dimensional stimuli is varied. The preliminary data favor a cognitive interpretation as opposed to one based on flatness cues. This tentative conclusion is based on the failure of elimination of flatness cues to produce marked changes in illusion magnitude among the Ugandans. However, a simple test devised by Dr. Kilbride appears to predict successfully whether any illusion will be produced by the photographs. The test included presentation of figure 1A which could be interpreted as a two-dimensional object (e.g., a ladder), or as a three-dimensional object (e.g., railroad tracks or a road). Based on responses to such stimuli the subjects can be classified as 'two-' or 'three-dimensional perceivers'. The two-dimensional perceivers produce illusions which resemble those in the first Ugandan study, while the data from the three-dimensional perceivers resemble those of the college students.

At this point, some general comments regarding the Ponzo illusion are in order. A number of studies, particularly those discussed by Robert Pollack, have shown that spatial factors are also important in the illusion. If one looks at the literature on illusions in general, or the Ponzo in particular, one has the impression that each investigator is concentrating on a single factor or class of factors. This is, of course, desirable from the experimental point of view, but it is obviously clear that a number of factors can influence the magnitude of apparently simple illusions. Indeed, illusions are 'illusory' in the sense that they would appear to have simple explanations. The experimental evidence, however, is that illusions, although perhaps not as complex as other phenomena, such as the constancies, are determined by a number of factors, some of which have developmental or learning components, and some of which depend upon interactions inherent in the nature of the stimulus *per se*. The wisdom of Boring's statement to the effect that illusions are special cases of the general laws of perception is certainly confirmed by the ever-expanding literature in this field.

Suggestibility as a factor in susceptibility to the Ponzo illusion. A second line of investigation stems from an entirely different theoretical background – hypnosis research. One of the more stable personality traits appears to be susceptibility to hypnotic suggestion. This can be assessed by a number of standard scales requiring the subject to respond to suggestions of varying degrees of difficulty. These scales are administered to a subject, and a quantitative score representing hypnotizability is determined by the number of suggestions to which the subject responds. These data are reliable and stable. However, one of the baffling aspects of this field of research is that such hypnotizability scores do not correlate well with other measures of personality, perception, or behavior. This is particularly curious in view of the fact that many of these scale items are perceptual in nature. As E. Hilgard (1965) has pointed out:

'Many conjectures about hypnosis are highly plausible, so that it is something of a shock to put them to the test only to find that practically none of the plausible conjectures can be proven to be true. There "ought" to be relationships to anxiety, to social desirability, to conforming tendencies, to social influencibility, to attention, and so on, but such relationships as we find are all very low and unstable, except the criterion of hypnotic susceptibility itself, which is remarkably stable' (339–340).

Recent data obtained by Robert Miller at Pennsylvania State University may help to explain the lack of correlation in previous studies (Miller, in press). Miller administered the Ponzo perspective illusion to a number of subjects for whom hypnotizability scores were also available. The data indicate that hypnotizability may indeed be a factor in determining the magnitude of the Ponzo illusion. Of particular interest, however, is the fact that the greatest illusion was demonstrated by subjects of medium hypnotizability, while subjects of high and low hypnotizability produced smaller illusions. This curvilinear relationship could explain the difficulty encountered by previous experimenters who have tried to demonstrate correlations between hypnotizability and measures of perception. In effect, the curvilinear relationship masked the correlation. The relationship between hypnotic susceptibility and the magnitude of illusion is of interest to students of hypnosis because it may provide the stable quantitative measure required to establish correlations between hypnotizability and perception.

I should add that the Ponzo illusion appears to be a highly stable measure. In a recent study, we attempted to change the magnitude of the illusion by hypnotically 'ablating' the background lines of the figure (Miller, Hennessy and Leibowitz 1973). This procedure involves suggesting to highly hypnotizable subjects that the background lines of the Ponzo figure will not be visible. Hypnotic ablation can be accomplished with only a very small number of the most hypnotizable subjects. In spite of the fact that some of the subjects indicated that the background lines were not visible, their illusion magnitudes were the same as for normal observation. These results suggest that hypnotic ablation, as is true for many other 'perceptual' effects, should be explained in terms of response rather than perceptual variables. At the same time these data provide reassurance of the stability of the Ponzo illusion which, in the present study, cannot be altered even by what are probably among the most demanding instructions that can be given to experimental subjects. Such data are reassuring in view of the extensive use of the Ponzo illusion in developmental and cross-cultural studies.

Whatever the nature of the final data on this topic, and its relationship to hypnosis theory, this research is important in identifying a major source of variability for the Ponzo and perhaps other illusions as well. This is not an unreasonable conclusion, since an illusion stimulus bears some similarity to hypnotic suggestion – both tend to alter perception in a manner deviating from objectivity. It is obvious that research in this field has barely begun, and I would predict that the future will produce additional interesting data regarding these relationships.

SECTION III

Cross-cultural differences in human development

The individual in developmental theory: Cross-cultural perspectives

A. A CONCEPTUAL MODEL FOR STUDY OF INDIVIDUAL DEVELOPMENT IN DIFFERENT CULTURES

by S. Schludermann and Eduard H. Schludermann, *University of Manitoba, Winnipeg, Canada*

This symposium attempts to deal with the development of individual uniqueness and the related problem of causes of individual differences studied in cross-cultural perspective. One immediately becomes aware that in North America very little systematic theorizing on the issue and few studies of the individual in different cultures have been done. This paper offers some suggestions as to (a) why developmental psychologists may have neglected cross-cultural studies of individuality; (b) how one may conceptualize the development of individual differences as an interaction between the characteristics of the individual and of his society; and (c) suggests steps to apply the suggested conceptual model to the scientific study of individual development in different cultures.

A conceptual model. Within developmental psychology in North America, the study of individual development and causes of individual differences are a neglected topic. There is no doubt that individual variations in cognitive processes have been subjected to much more systematic study (e.g., Kagan and Kogan 1970) than the development of individual differences in personality and social behavior. Perhaps one reason for this lack of research is that many psychologists doubt that 'individuality' is amenable to scientific study, as distinct from biographical and historical study. 'Individual uniqueness' by its very nature may not be compatible with scientific generalizations, since science attempts to establish general principles which abstract that which many individual cases have in common.

The main obstacle to cross-cultural research in the development of individual differences seems to be conceptual. Part of the problem may be attributed to the lack of integration among various areas of theorizing and research. Workers interested in developmental theory were usually not interested in cultural differences. Researchers in cross-cultural psychology were frequently neither interested nor knowledgeable about developmental theory. But there is another very basic problem: The theoretical formulations, the research strategies, and the methods of data analysis of researchers in developmental psychology as well as in cross-cultural psychology tended to discourage concern with the developing individual.

Basic developmental theories (e.g., Baldwin 1967; Langer 1969; Goulet and Baltes 1970) define the concept of development in such a way as to make irrelevant the concern with individuality. Development is usually defined in terms of regular sequences of psychological changes which are characteristic of the species. The research design and the methods of data analysis are conducted in such a way that common features are brought out into sharp forms and individual peculiarities in psychological development are ignored, e.g., comparison of groups, establishment of age norms or developmental stages, etc.

In various research areas of 'cross-cultural psychology' the emphasis was on qualitative or quantitative group differences in psychological characteristics. The study of individual differences within a cultural group was deliberately deemphasized. Studies of national character (e.g., Inkeles and Levinson 1969) compare the psychological characteristics (modal personality) of people in one culture with those of people in another culture. Even though research on this topic now emphasizes the study of many individuals (rather than the study of cultural group-products), the emphasis is on the statistical distribution of psychological characteristics within a culture. Another prominent area of cross-cultural research involves the comparison of people from several societies on a single psychological variable. Here the explicitly comparative group research design precludes the consideration of individuality. The relatively few cross-cultural studies which focus on psychological development (e g., LeVine 1970) tend to emphasize differences between cultures (rather than individual differences within a culture) in patterns of motor, perceptual, and cognitive development, as well as in factors related to the psychological environment of the developing child. There is a lack of theoretical integration and of focused research which deals with the development of individuality in different cultures. In order to study individuality in various cultures, it is helpful to supplement insights and data from the above two approaches by insights from other areas usually not considered part of cross-cultural developmental psychology. There are several areas of theorizing and research which are relevant here.

Theories and models in differential psychology and psychogenetics dealing with the sources of individual differences are especially relevant even though they are restricted in scope. Human psychogenetics emphasizes the complex interaction patterns that are possible between different genotypes and different environments and thereby produce large individual variations in psychological traits (e.g., Anastasi 1958a, 1958b; McClearn 1970). Concepts derived from such research, such as range of reaction (variation), expressive vs. restrictive environment, and phenocopies, etc., suggest analogies. If one wants to develop a conceptual model describing how individual differences might be brought about by the interaction of individual characteristics and specific cultural experiences, such analogies may be useful.

Many theories and research projects in abnormal psychology are concerned with the etiology of behavior disorders – i.e., the problem as to why some individuals develop behavior disorders. Such a concern encourages an interest in the study of individual differences in patterns of psychological development (e.g., Anthony 1970). Insights which result from such research involve concepts like constitutional, environmental, situational, and developmental risks; vulnerability and resilience; predisposing and precipitating causes, etc.

Concepts and models derived from cross-cultural mental health research are especially relevant here (Kiev 1972). Individual differences cannot be ignored because only a few individuals in a given culture develop mental illnesses. On the other hand, the effect of specific cultural influences is emphasized in bringing about behavior problems which are peculiar to that culture. A few of the major emphases resulting from this approach can be cited here. Within a given culture mental problems develop most frequently in certain age groups or in individuals exercising certain occupational and family roles. The same behavior symptoms may have different meanings in different societies. There is a relationship between the epidemiology of mental illness and cultural practices and expectations. Thus different cultures make different demands on members of their society and expose them to different types of stress.

Insights from sociological and psychological studies of family life in different societies can also make important contributions to the under-standing of individuals (e.g., Ross 1961). Most developmental psy-chologists regard data from family studies to be especially relevant because they subscribe – almost as an article of faith – to the hypothesis that early experience within the family is unusually important for later psychological development. Individuals who occupy different roles within the family (e.g., oldest son, youngest daughter, daughter-in-law, etc.) have to face different expectations and are exposed to different kinds of psychological stress (e.g., Rin 1969). Studies relating parental attitudes, family roles, and socialization techniques to psychological development should greatly increase our understanding of the influences which shape the developing individual.

Integration of some of the insights obtained from these diverse sources can provide a tentative framework which would make the study of individual development in different cultures a meaningful and feasible research problem. Even though at this stage it is only a preliminary attempt, it is hoped that it will encourage further thinking about research on the individual in different cultures. Further theorizing and especially the collection of new relevant data should lead to progressive modifications resulting in a more adequate conceptual framework than at present. Such a model might also stimulate more meaningful research on mental health problems in different societies.

Key concepts. At the present state of knowledge a finalized model is quite premature. The suggested frame of reference does not summarize an established body of factual knowledge. It merely tries to integrate concepts and insights from various sources and tries to relate them to the cross-cultural study of the developing individual. It contains suggestions as to the complex interaction patterns whereby different causal factors might account for the great range of individual differences found in every culture. It also suggests how systematic research on psychological development in different cultures might also enrich our understanding of the developing individual.

The suggested model is basically an interaction model: At every stage of the life cycle individual differences result from the interaction of individual peculiarities present at that stage and the cultural influences to which he is exposed at that stage. The same cultural influences have different consequences depending on the characteristics of the individual who is exposed to them. For instance, heavy social pressure on academic achievement during late adolescence may have different effects on a person with low tolerance for stress than it has on a person with high tolerance. The model also suggests that there is a sequential series of interactions between individual characteristics and cultural influences. At birth there are already some individual characteristics resulting from genotype – prenatal environment interactions. Babies with different temperaments respond differently to different child rearing practices. The result is an increase in individual differences. The individual characteristics resulting from this interaction interact anew with cultural influences to which the individual is exposed at the next stage – resulting in a further increase in individual differences. One would, therefore, expect an increasing amount of individual uniqueness as the individual proceeds through the life cycle.

A second feature of the model emphasizes the individual as an active agent (rather than a passive product) playing an important role in his own development. Zigler and Child (1969) give a concise overview of the new trends of thinking about psychological development. This view goes beyond the view that the individual influences in addition to being influenced. The individual is conceived of as an open system having important inherent characteristics and transacting with the environment, rather than being merely a reactor or integrator. The individual is an active processer of the norms of his society. The view is related to the recognition that biological factors and individual differences in cognition are important in producing individual differences in socialization. In the subsequent section some of the factors which should be considered if one studies how the developing individual 'transacts' with cultural influences are outlined.

In every society individuals show great differences in constitutional make-up – differences in physique, the reactivity of the autonomic system, timing of hormonal changes and physical growth patterns, as well as differences in original temperamental tendencies. Recent research (e.g., Thomas *et al.* 1963) on constitutionally based temperamental differences suggests that a child's 'activity type' may influence the quality of parent-child relationships; e.g., a quiet reaction may predispose toward a dependent relationship. Males and females whose reactivity type is in line with the culturally defined sex roles (i.e., active boy, quiet girl) may face fewer adjustment difficulties than those who deviate. Children tend to cope with difficulties in accordance with their temperamental make-up. Thus, different temperamental tendencies may predispose an individual to use certain escape and defence mechanisms, as well as certain kinds of symptom formation in case the individual becomes mentally ill.

There are many levels where constitutionally based individual differences may interact with cultural norms. Different cultures may attach different levels of social desirability to different physiques and temperaments. The degree of congruence between a person's basic temperament and cultural expectations is an important variable affecting psychological development and individual adjustment. The individual's basic temperament may determine the degree of success he will have in coping successfully with the stresses to which he is exposed in his society. In our studies (Schludermann and Schludermann 1971a, 1971b, 1971c, 1971d) on psychological development in the society, we found that Hutterites strongly prefer individuals who are passive, conforming, and non-assertive. Since great pressure is exerted on individuals to develop this desired type of personality, adolescents of an active and assertive temperament find it difficult to meet these expectations.

Because of differences in constitutional make-up which interact with differences in earlier experiences, individuals within a given culture differ with respect to the specific vulnerability to specific stresses. Specific vulnerability may be defined as the individual's capacity to cope with the problems posed by specific stresses, especially the emotional arousal induced by these stresses (e.g., Anthony 1970, pp. 692-693). The concept of specific vulnerability implies that a given individual may have a greater capacity to cope with some stresses (e.g., demand for academic achievement) than to cope with some others (e.g., facing the hostility of others). Individuals differ in resilience, i.e., the ability to overcome malfunctioning after the termination of stress.

May's illustration (quoted by Anthony 1970) of the relationship between stress and differences in vulnerability suggests the possibility that certain individuals may respond to heavy stress with highly superior modes of behavior, e.g., creativity, whereas others may break down.[1] May's

---

1. 'It is as though I had on a table three dolls, one of glass, another of celluloid and third of steel, and I chose to hit the three dolls with a hammer using equal strength. The first doll would break, the second would scar, and the third would emit a pleasant sound.'

analogy is basically a 'challenge and response' formulation – individual differences are more likely to show up under stress than in non-demanding situations.

When studying individuality cross-culturally it is important to note that different societies subject individuals living in the societies to different types of specific stress, such as economic insecurity, achievement in a competitive society, handling interpersonal conflict in the crowded household of an extended family, occupying a family role with little power and prestige, meeting conflicting social role expectations, etc. There are many examples in the cross-cultural mental health literature which emphasize such differences in specific stresses (e.g., Sechrest 1969; Doi 1969; Levy 1969). Different types of personal resources are required to cope successfully with these different types of specific stresses. A given individual may find it easier to meet the demands of one society than the demands of the other society.

Cultures differ considerably in their socialization practices whereby they encourage conformity to cultural demands. There are also cultural differences in the methods, intensity, and timing of socialization practices. Individuals of different temperamental make-up may respond differently to the socialization practices to which they are exposed in their culture. Complex interaction patterns between socialization practices and peculiarities of the individuals exposed to socialization increase greatly the range of individual differences found in a given society.

Some of the concepts derived from national character research are also relevant to cross-cultural studies of individual development. In contrast to earlier thinking about 'culture and personality' the modal personality need not be congruent to the socially required personality. There are different degrees and types of congruence between the modal personality structures and the psychological requirements of a given society. For the study of individual development it is not only necessary to compare the individual's characteristics with the social requirements of that society but also to the modal personality pattern in that society. An incongruity between an individual's personality and the psychological requirements of his society may be less stressful if he shares this incongruity with most other members of his society.

Cultures differ greatly in the extent to which individual identity versus group identity is encouraged. They also differ in the means whereby an individual achieves status and self-esteem. In some societies, status may be ascribed to the individual because of age, sex, family, background, etc., while in other societies the status has to be achieved by the individual. Of special interest are societies where rapid social change alters the means whereby an individual's status is determined. Zaide (1969) points out that urbanization frequently involves moving from a village where status is ascribed to a city where it has to be achieved. This transition may threaten an individual's self-esteem and may require a drastic readjustment of his self-concept. Individuals differ in their capacity to deal with this transition.

For the developmental psychologist it is important to note that different cultures expose the individual to different kinds of stresses and different developmental tasks at different stages of the life cycle. Cultures also differ with respect to continuity versus discontinuity of social expectations and abruptness versus gradual transition in social roles from one developmental level to the next. The interaction between culturally specific developmental tasks and individual peculiarities may best be conceptualized in terms of a 'challenge and response' model of individual differences. As the individual proceeds from birth to senescence his culture presents him with a series of challenges with which the individual has to cope. The individual's unique personality is determined to a considerable degree by the outcome of such coping.

Steps in the use of the model for scientific study. The first prerequisite to the study of individual development within a given society is a thorough acquaintance with that society's social history, culture, and language (e.g., Ho 1972). LeVine (1969, pp. 567-570) emphasizes the importance of obtaining extensive and valid ethnographic information before planning the research design. One should search sociological and anthropological studies in addition to psychological surveys for information such as cultural expectations for different age groups, variations in family structures and family roles, differences between subcultures, socialization methods, and mental problems, etc.

It is necessary to supplement the existing literature with field studies designed to provide the necessary background information. Several methodological discussions of cross-cultural research emphasize the desirability that both insiders and outsiders be involved in the research design, data collection, and interpretation of the results. It is also desirable that research involves the collaboration of behavioral and social scientists from different disciplines. The emphasis should be on actual individual behavior rather than on cultural ideals or norms. In several cross-cultural mental health surveys Leithton (1969) notes that insiders and outsiders can show a high level of agreement about overt behavioral symptoms even though they may differ sharply about explaining their etiology and interpreting the social significance of these symptoms.

After the necessary background information is available, one can then design studies focused on the development of individual characteristics and the maintenance of individuality. Such research involves of necessity obtaining information on how the individual is changing or has changed over time, e.g., longitudinal studies, studies of antecedent consequent relationships, studies of the appearance, persistence, and disappearance of behavior symptoms, etc.

Especially closer examination should be made of an individual's coping behavior at those points of the life cycle where there is a drastic transition (e.g., onset of adolescence, retirement, etc.) or which are especially stressful in that society. Larger individual differences are more likely to be produced and observed when the individuals are under stress than when stress is absent or very mild.

B. ERIKSON'S THEORY IN CROSS-CULTURAL PERSPECTIVE: SOCIAL CLASS AND ETHNICITY IN 'THIRD WORLD' COMMUNITIES

by N.V. Ciaccio, *American University in Cairo, Egypt*

In the first of a series of validational studies of Erikson's theory of ego epigenesis, Ciaccio (1971) reported an investigation of the two basic postulates of this theory – *ego stage progression with increasing age* through *psychosocial crisis* – using a specially designed projective technique and coding system with a sample of 120 white American middle-class males (5-, 8-, and 11-year olds). The present paper represents an attempt at cross-cultural validation of the theory with samples drawn from 'Third World' communities. The designation 'Third World' refers here to either one or a combination of the following variables: poverty level subsistence which engenders significantly different life styles from those of the dominant middle classes in Western societies (such as poor whites or Blacks living in North American ghetto areas); or groups of individuals from 'non-Western' cultures or ideologies (i.e., Egyptian Arabs residing in urban Cairo or Blacks living in North America who identify more readily with African cultural patterns).

Emphasis will be given to data drawn from the North American samples (Black and white poverty groups as compared to the white middle-class) but other data, gathered from middle-class children in London and Paris and from Egyptian children of the middle- and poverty-level classes will also be considered in the discussion section. The research reported here was prompted by the fact that although many investigators have studied single ego variables such as language and perception among many various ethnic and poverty groups, none had specifically addressed himself to the issue of a constellation of ego variables changing over time.

Method. The first investigation (Ciaccio 1971) involved the testing of 120 white middle-class males (5-, 8-, and 11-year olds). For the second study, 60 Black males – twenty for each of the age levels represented – and 60 white males were selected for testing. These children were students from five schools in Chicago's inner-city, and the major criterion for their participation was poverty-level subsistence as defined by welfare receipt or Hollingshead's Occupational Category VII. For the European samples,

60 British and 60 French males were randomly selected from schools which served the middle- and upper-middle classes. In Egypt, where children from both the middle-class and poverty groups were tested, Ss were identified on the basis of place of residence (the former from the Cairene suburb of Maadi, the latter from the area of Bulaq, one of Cairo's most densely populated slum areas).

The projective technique (Boyd 1964; Ciaccio 1969) which was utilized for all Ss consists of a series of five pictures, each designed to depict a basic component of one of the first five Eriksonian stages. Ss were asked to tell a story for each of these pictures, and these stories were broken down into discrete units dealing with one theme. Each such unit was then examined to determine the appropriate stage code (1-5) by referring to the coding system manual (Ciaccio 1969) which was based on a content analysis of these stages as presented by Erikson in his published writings (1953, 1968). All codable units also received a 'valence rating' of either *plus* (indicating the positive aspects of the stage or the 'psychosocial strengths') or *minus* (reflecting conflict or perceived inability to resolve conflict).

This method provided a frequency count yielding a graphic quantitative profile – 'ego development profile' – of each child in terms of the number of coded units in each of the ego stage categories. For group comparisons, individual profiles were converted into grand percentage profiles depicting the ego stage development of each age, ethnic, and socioeconomic group. It was hypothesized, according to theoretical expectations, that the 5-year-old groups would be most concerned in their stories with the Stage II issues of autonomy versus shame and doubt, that the 8-year-olds would concentrate on the initiative versus guilt themes of Stage III, and that the 11-year-olds would show peak interest in the industry versus inferiority issues characteristic of Stage IV.

Results: Five-year-olds. Table 1 presents a general summary of the data for white middle-class Ss, Black poverty Ss, and white poverty Ss. (a) Poverty Ss (both Black and white) clearly gave the majority of their responses to Stage II, in contradistinction to white middle class Ss who showed almost equal peak distributions for both Stages II and III. (b) Poverty Ss gave more negatively scored responses; however, all 5-year-olds concentrated these valences in the Stage II category. Specific autonomy issues tended to vary: White middle class Ss most frequently related incidents of parental domination and interruption of the child's activity, accompanied by oral rages, tantrums or withdrawal, episodes of sibling rivalry, and punishments for 'going too far'. Poverty Ss almost never mentioned sibling rivalry or parental intrusiveness as such; they seemed to prefer 'acting out' their perceived lack of autonomy more directly by describing instances of destructive behavior (what Erikson terms 'willfull destruction'), and active resistance to and defiance of authority. Poverty Blacks most frequently described punishment as coming from the mother, physical in nature but rarely 'brutal'. Poverty whites, on the other hand, reported physical punishment from the father, often underscoring the severity of the punishment. (c) Both poverty groups gave more Stage I responses (usually with a negative valence, indicating a sense of mistrust) than did their middle-class peers. These responses rarely involved instances of perceived lack of proper 'mothering' or protection (as was typical for white middle class Ss when they gave Stage I responses), but rather mistrust of oneself.

Results: Eight-year-olds. (1) The Black poverty Ss again peaked at Stage II but also showed a strong interest in Stage III. (b) Although white poverty Ss peaked at Stage III in terms of the percentage of units, the distribution for both Stages II and III are almost equal. They are, in fact, strikingly similar to those of the five-year-old white middle class. (c) When compared to their middle-class peers, the two poverty groups

Table 1. Ego stages for white middle-class, Black poverty, and white poverty children

Group	Stages					Valence	
	I	II	III	IV	V	+	—
White middle class							
5-year-olds	5.0	46.0	41.9	6.4	0.7	43	57
8-year-olds	3.1	20.3	55.7	19.0	1.9	80	20
11-year-olds	5.3	16.1	26.1	44.3	8.2	82	18
Black poverty							
5-year-olds	11.6	61.9	21.0	5.5	0.0	28	72
8-year-olds	13.2	44.3	35.4	4.2	2.9	48	52
11-year-olds	8.3	26.8	29.6	13.8	21.5	69	31
White poverty							
5-year-olds	8.9	56.3	29.8	4.3	0.7	36	64
8-year-olds	9.0	38.5	42.6	8.7	1.2	61	39
11-year-olds	5.1	24.7	37.6	28.3	4.3	74	26

showed only minimal interest in Stage IV. (d) All three 8-year-old groups showed a marked decrease in the percentage of negatively scored responses, with the white middle class decline being most dramatic. Again, all three groups clustered the majority of their negative responses around Stage II issues, but poverty children continued to give consistently more mistrust responses than the middle class. It is interesting to note that a dichotomy emerges in the poverty data here: White poverty children continued to mistrust themselves, whereas Black children indicated mistrust of others, especially school officials and other persons in authority.

Results: Eleven-year-olds. (a) The 'relative homogeneity' of the poverty group data ends with an analysis of the material collected from the eleven-year-olds. White poverty Ss peaked at Stage III, with sub-peaks for Stages II and IV. Thus, the configuration of their distribution of responses resembled that of the white middle-class 8-year-olds. Only 4.3% of the total number of coded responses fell into the Stage V category. Black poverty Ss showed a much different picture, however. Although they also peaked at Stage III (29.6%) this was closely followed by Stages II (26.8%) and V (21.5%). Compared to either of the white groups, they showed considerably less interest in Stage IV (13.8%). Indeed, the data seems to suggest that these children almost bypassed Stage IV in their definitive move to Stage V issues. (b) Furthermore, the majority of the Black poverty Ss' Stage V responses were scored within the positive range (80%), while some 60% of their Stage II responses remained negative.

Discussion. The American middle-class data tend to support Erikson's first postulate, namely, that of orderly ego stage progression with increasing age. It is interesting and perhaps important to note that European (English and French) and Egyptian middle-class children showed highly similar developmental configurations, showing orderly progression from earlier to later stages, corresponding to the age parameters and hierarchy patterns according to theoretical expectations. Although differences in ego development were noted, especially with regard to the manner in which conflict was expressed, the general configuration is strikingly similar across cultures.

Erikson's second postulate, that the ego develops as it meets with *different* crises at each developmental stage, did not receive the degree of confirmation expected. The only exceptions to this were the Stage II or autonomy crisis, and to a much lesser extent the inferiority crisis of Stage

IV where much of the projective material involved situations in which the child felt that he did not measure up to the autonomy expressions of others. Also, since Erikson's treatment of the identity crisis at Stage V is largely in terms of the re-enactment of autonomy struggles, it might be argued that the first five crises are merely different expressions of autonomy strivings, each reflecting different levels and dimensions of the same underlying crisis.

As seen in the previous section of this paper, poverty group data presented some important differences when contrasted with those of the middle class. While both Black and white poverty 5-year-olds peaked at Stage II; they did not move as readily into Stage III issues as did their middle-class peers. Thus, they appeared to be somewhat 'behind' in the ego developmental time-table. A possible explanation for this could lie in the finding that both poverty 5-year-old groups showed a much higher percentage of negatively scored Stage II responses (as well as negatively scored Stage I responses), indicating more conflict centering around the establishment of autonomy patterns, thereby having comparatively less 'ego energy' available for Stage III concerns.

The discrepancy between the classes becomes even more apparent when the data for the next age level is examined. Black poverty 8-year-olds peaked at Stage II while white poverty 8-year-olds showed almost simultaneous peaks for Stages II (38.5%) and III (42.6%), yielding distributions that strikingly resembled those of the white middle-class 5-year-olds. In very gross categorical terms, it could be stated that both poverty 8-year-old groups were fully one stage behind their white middle-class peers.

The white poverty 11-year-olds peaked at Stage III, with sub-peaks for Stages II and IV, yielding distributions that resembled those of the white middle-class 8-year-olds. Again, in gross categorical terms, white poverty 11-year-olds appear to be one stage behind white middle-class 11-year-olds, continuing the slower developmental pace trend found for the other poverty Ss.

Black poverty 11-year-olds seemed to be working on a number of different ego-stage issues almost simultaneously: Their peak at Stage III (19.6%) was closely followed by Stages II (26.8%) and V (21.5%). The most striking finding is, of course, the precocious interest in Stage V. Black 11-year-olds often gave stories which clearly illustrated perceptions of 'belongingness' in which Ss related instances of group membership, clear role patterns within those groups, and feelings of security and accomplishment within those roles. They were also quite clear about image-ideals which were rarely related to family members but rather to models of leadership within the peer group, their own communities, and the 'Black Community' at large. Their descriptions of specific role behaviors often included what might be termed 'nurturing activities' in which younger or incapacitated members of the community were cared for or given some specific service connected with group programs. Negatively scored Stage V units were often found to be examples of what Erikson calls the 'negative identity' – attempts to be exactly what significant others feel the individual should not be by experimentation with roles not condoned by the reference group.

These results tend to support the conclusions of Proshansky and Newton (1968) in their interpretation of an extensive literature review of Black identity: '...negative self-identity is frequently rooted in negative group identification ... positive self-identity is dependent on positive group identification ... considerable evidence supports the idea that personal or self-pride is essentially the expression of group pride.'

Another significant finding is the continued conflict over autonomy, especially in the face of so many positive identity scorings. Protocol analysis revealed that the 5- or 8-year old Black *S*s' 'struggle for autonomy' was most often focused on specific individuals such as mother, teacher, or some specific school official. The 11-year-old Black was more likely to see the battleground in more general terms, referring to the 'school system', the 'pigs', or elements of the racist socio-political establishment. The emphasis thus changed from the younger *S*s' perceptions of individuals who could grant autonomy to older *S*s' perceiving that institutions would never do so. By way of contrast, it is interesting to note that middle-class 11-year-olds rarely spoke in institutional terms but continued to see autonomy in essentially personal or individual terms. Furthermore, identity scorings were most often given to their responses on the basis of their indicating career and future role possibilities within traditional societal contexts.

These findings are congruent with the interpretations of Proshansky and Newton (1968). 'The minority group member – child or adult – needs to understand the source of his group dilemma. If he is Negro, he needs to view the social system and the white man, not himself, as the source of his difficulties. For some Negroes, the blame has finally been shifted from themselves to the social arrangements of the white society.'

We have already noted these *S*s' lack of 'age appropriate' interest in

Stage IV – a finding which can almost be categorized as 'skipping' a developmental stage. 'School' in the sense of a formal academic enterprise seems to have been excluded as irrelevant and without reward. Response scorings in the Stage IV category only infrequently showed a 'sense of inferiority', however; rather, they included descriptions of non-academic work situations, perceptions of self and others as workers (rather than as students), development of special work skills, and an occasional reference to academically oriented tutoring projects.

The data suggest that a radical shift in ego development occurs for the Black males between the ages of 8 and 11 years – a shift that is not in keeping with either Erikson's re-statement of the epigenetic principle in psychosocial terms or his outline of the 'developmental time-table'. The 8-year-old Black poverty male presents an ego development profile which indicates that he is concerned with developmental issues more characteristic of the 5-year-old from a middle-class background; indeed, the finding that both in Black and white poverty group 8-year-olds are 'in gross categorical terms' one stage behind their middle-class peers seems to support much of the research on 'disadvantaged' populations which catalogs so-called 'developmental lags', deficiencies, etc. One might suspect, therefore, that this trend (the 'slower developmental pace') would continue in full force for the 11-year-old poverty Ss. The fact is that it does appear to continue for the white but not for the Black 11-year-old.

Between the ages of 8 and 11, the Black male begins to dramatically shift his 'radius of significant relations' to peer groups, outgroups, and models of leadership, reflecting ideological perspectives more characteristic of the adolescent. Furthermore, the strong autonomy conflict component appears to facilitate this shift by re-defining the battleground in more institutional terms which reinforces identifications with peer and other reference groups and their leaders and programs, and identifications against outgroups.

Some very interesting perspectives are added to these when one considers the data collected from poor Egyptian children. In this developing country, 5-year-olds are still actively struggling with basic trust issues: Their world is potentially overwhelming, and, although the family offers a possible sense of security, it is often seen as too restrictive and binding. Projective material indicates the early development of strong peer-group identifications (rarely seen in 5-year-olds from other groups) and selective experimentation with trust through prosocial behavior. For the 8-year-old, autonomy – defined quite literally within this context as 'the ability to fend for oneself' – is often forced upon the child by life circumstances rather than by developing, according to Erikson, within a framework of mutually reciprocal encounters between parents and child. Some 60 percent of these children were already engaged in work experiences which contributed in some way to the economic maintenance of themselves and their families. Projective responses did not show the 8-year-olds' characteristic preoccupation with Stage III (initiative versus guilt) but rather the poor Egyptian child's growing sense of autonomy (as well as his conflicts over this issue) through his experiences in the world of work.'

Profiles from the 11-year-olds often reflected conflict over continued acceptance of roles which had been selected for them and fantasies of a 'better life' for themselves and families. Such material is usually not considered as 'typical' for 11-year-olds and presented a highly devergent picture from that of the Egyptian middle-class who tended to be highly similar to the American and European middle-class in terms of their developmental patterns.

It is this author's contention that the 'world views' and socialization patterns of the middle classes in the societies in which he has done research are more similar than many previous cross-cultural studies would have us believe. The data suggest that Erikson's theory has been tailored to describe the Western and middle-class experience of reality. This is perhaps inevitable, but Blacks and members of other Third World communities have contributed 'generation styles' which add unique historical and cultural perspectives to the 'established' social environment. These styles will undoubtedly force a revision of current developmental and social theory which could effect important changes in the social action programs upon which they are supposedly based.

C. THEMATIC STRUCTURATION IN ADOLESCENCE: FINDINGS FROM DIFFERENT EUROPEAN COUNTRIES*

by Franz J. Mönks and Henk G. Heusinkveld, *University of Nijmegen, the Netherlands*

Human behavior is mediated by cognitive and evaluative representation. This is made quite clear in research data related to functions of conscience (Aronfreed 1968; Hoffman 1970). Representation plays an important role in research on personality variables. Research concerning an adolescent's identification and modelling by means of self-report must be seen as an approach to a cognitive and evaluative representation of future plans. We will present here some data on adolescent identification derived from a research project conducted by Lutte (1971) and discuss them within the theoretical framework proposed by Thomae (1969).

Methodologically there are still problems in this area (Mönks 1967). Nevertheless it is suggested that self-report is as valid a method as a rating scale (in which one measures the cognitive representation of the rater) and as an objective test (in which one measures culturally manipulated factors).

Theory formation. A theory about the development of adolescents can be considered as a special case of thematic structuring (Thomae 1969). By thematic structuring we mean an internalization of experience, meaningful for the person himself. According to Thomae, creative and regulative themes are meaningful points of departure for a theory of adolescent development (Thomae 1969).

The homeostatic principle postulates a regulation of all changes in so far as these are consciously experienced; it involves a pragmatic reduction of disturbing stimuli. The individual adjusts himself to reality. This regulative principle appears especially in the significant constriction or expansion of subjective life space. The regulation may have an anticipatory character in the form of behavior adjustment to promote continuity.

The creative principle is especially directed toward the future; it is a tendency to search for new responses, independent of current, generally

* We wish to thank Nan Stevens and Lynn Hewitt for editing the English version of this article.

accepted modes of behavior. Individual possibilities are involved here especially. This theme stresses an individual's own efforts. The creative principle expands and intensifies possibilities for experiencing. At the same time it promotes self-realization. These themes are not classifications but are dynamic principles. We consider the process of identification during adolescence as a form of cognitive and evaluative representation. Our purpose is to examine data obtained in earlier research (Lutte, Mönks, Kempen and Sarti 1969; Lutte, Mönks, Sarti and Preun 1970; Lutte 1971) to determine, *post hoc*, whether empirical support exists for Thomae's proposals.

Method. The research referred to here was carried out in 1965 under the direction of G. Lutte in seven European countries: Belgium, France, Italy, Netherlands, West Germany, Portugal and Spain. The question posed in this research was adopted from Havighurst and McDonald who asked their subjects to write a self-report under the title: 'The person I would like to be like ...'. In each country, one or more random samples were taken. Responses from 19,250 male and female persons, aged 10-17 years, were available for analysis. The repeated measures of inter- and intra-rater reliability were very high (.87 and .86). Table 1 gives the choice of ideal persons in different European countries. Detailed information about age-related changes in ideal persons can be found in Lutte *et al.* (1970), Lutte, Mönks, Kempen and Sarti (1969) and Lutte (1971).

Although there is a strong interplay between homeostasis and self-realization in each change of the subjective lifespace, we shall nevertheless treat the appearance of the principles separately for convenience. We limit ourselves to a qualitative analysis of the development of the ideal self, passing over social-economic, cultural, and other such factors. (a) We consider growth toward independence and self-realization as indications of a *creative tendency*. (b) The *regulating tendency* is expressed by concepts of safety, self-defense, need for approval. We shall deal with these themes side by side. We shall divide the period into three parts for convenience although there is no indication of an age-specific development. Male development will be considered first.

Creativity-boys. Age group 10/11 to 13 years: Sharp decline in choice of parents and family as ideal figure in favor of a remote ideal. The average age of the ideal person still lies between 31 and 40 years but begins to decline. We see an increase in self-realization in the age decline of the

Table 1. *Choice of ideal persons in different European countries reported in percentages.**

	Germany	Netherlands	Belgium	France	Italy	Spain	Portugal
Number of subjects	2400	2400	3050	1800	4800	2400	2400
Near ideals							
parents	10.6	3.7	5.7	3.1	5.6	3.4	9.0
other members of family	5.5	5.9	4.6	4.7	5.7	3.0	6.5
teachers	6.5	2.1	6.0	3.1	4.8	7.4	3.2
sympathetic adults	13.0	11.7	18.0	16.3	9.9	14.5	14.1
girlfriends and boyfriends	9.9	23.6	12.5	9.8	18.6	17.6	18.1
Remote ideals							
religious personalities	4.5	0.2	4.4	4.0	5.2	10.8	10.8
heroic figures	13.7	5.3	5.6	6.6	5.3	4.6	2.4
famous people	13.0	29.4	13.9	25.8	14.2	13.4	9.2
Tarzan figures	0.5	3.4	0.9	1.4	3.0	1.4	1.0
composite or abstract ideal	19.6	11.4	26.9	24.0	24.5	20.6	22.7
unclassifiable	3.2	3.3	1.5	1.2	2.8	3.3	2.9

* Regarding the significance of the differences between the countries, we can say the following: For such a large number of subjects ($N = 19{,}250$) the differences above 2 or 3% are significant at the 1% level (see McNemar; t-test for difference between proportions).

model; increase in choice of science and technical work as profession; intelligence is more frequently chosen as a character trait; professions in the social area decline; a clear, increasing choice of sociability occurs (not in relation to a profession). There is an increasing need to realize creative thinking in the choice of profession; the creative element in social skills remains present, but not in relation to a profession.

Age group 13/14 to 15 years: Decline in age of ideal person (26-30 years); sharp decline in identification with model from one's environment. The activity 'studying' reaches its maximal value. Except for attractiveness, the importance of external things declines. An increase in cultural relaxation begins; choice of playing games declines. Sociability as a personality trait continues to rise rapidly. The direct environment begins to work oppressively. A new orientation can occur via the ideal, 'to be a student', who is perceived as having more freedom. The breaking

Figure 1. *Age-related choices of concrete and abstract models in girls and boys (N = 19250).*

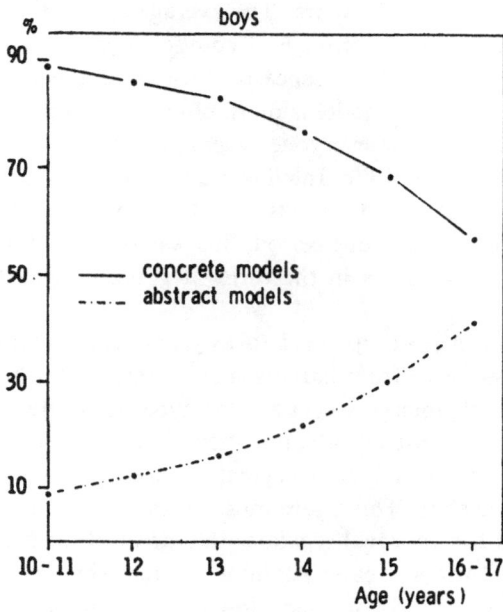

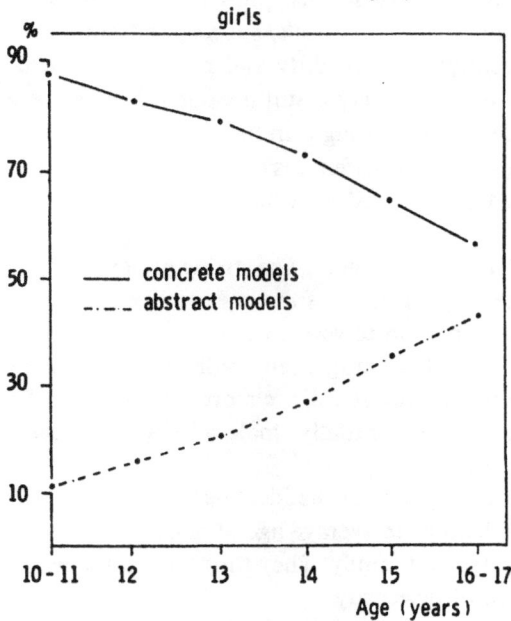

through of the home sphere occurs here (playing games). To spend free time, to go out with others reflects creativity.

Age group 14/15 to 16/17 years: The average age of the ideal person falls to 21-25 years; the percentage of composite ideal figures increases to 45%. The choice of independence is 10 times as great as in the first period. The identification model is more often described as tolerant. No rigid rules govern life for everyone; every individual has the right to create his/her own style of life. Intelligence is chosen twice as often as at age 11 years. The ideal person has sociability as the most frequently chosen quality; in the previous period, this was sense of duty. There is a sharp increase in recreation in the form of going out, parties, theater.

Regulation – boys. Age group 10/11 to 13 years: The threat posed by an increasing independence from parents is compensated for by an increase in the choice of a religious person as an ideal type. There are more frequent choices for courage, sense of duty, devotion, and later, strength of will as character traits. The ideal figure has great stature, is attractive, e.g., sport heroes, pop-music stars. This figure must mean something in the eyes of adults. The need for approval regulates the threat of independence.

Age group 13/14 to 15 years: Along with increasing individualization and self-realization is a diminished preference for heroes; the choice of sympathetic adults reaches its peak; success and fame come forth more and more frequently; sense of duty and responsibility are chosen more often. The club begins to play a still greater role as a social context for passing free time. Safety is sought in being accepted in the closed society of peers of both sexes. Self-defence is apparent in the portrait of a success- ful, appealing adult, admired as a hero, i.e., the person who makes an impression.

Age group 14/15 to 16/17 years: The strong preference for independence also has threatening facets. Despite the decline in the concrete ideal there is a slight regression toward increasing preference for parents and family. Strength of will, courage, self-confidence, and success represent a pragmatic reduction of unrest and are more often chosen. The importance of great stature increases initially; male adolescents choose again more often for attractiveness.

For girls, the average age of the ideal person remains constant at 19 to 20 years, that is, below the average age of marriage. Only 10% of the girls mentioned marriage and family. They thus limited themselves to the near future (regulation of insecurity).

Creativity – girls. Age group 10/11 to 13 years: The sharp decrease in choice of parents and other family members is compensated for by an increase in the choice of sympathetic adults, and sometime later, of boyfriends. There is a sharp increase for sociability. We also see here breaking away from one's own family with the limit extended to the trusted sphere outside one's own home.

Age group 13/14 to 15 years: A sharp decline occurs in choice of teacher or sympathetic adult as ideal. Singing stars are especially chosen; the nearly ideal declines sharply. The seemingly free lives of top musicians attract. Studying reaches its peak as chosen work. Study expands the individual's view of the world. Self-realization is stronger; the ideal adult disappears as a model.

Age group 14/15 to 16/17 years: The concrete ideal declines to 55%. The composite figure is chosen in 45% of the cases, with sociability and altruism as the major qualities. A sharp increase in the choice of parties and cultural recreation and an increasing preference for mixed clubs, and organization occurs in the professional area; the service professions are most frequently chosen; preference for the status of student reaches its minimum (even lower than at 10 years). The identification model corresponds more to the adolescent's own identity. An adult role of service to others affords the possibility for a culturally defined form of self-realization. The independence of students and stars gives way to a self-chosen balance of freedom and constraints.

Regulation – girls. Age group 10/11 to 13 years: Almost 60% choose an ideal close by, compared to 30% who choose a distant figure. The preference for friends and the decrease in choice of family members is accompanied by insecurity. There is a clear increase in choice of sense of duty, courage and strength of will due to the regulating principle. Reality must be seen with one's own eyes without anxiety.

Age group 13/14 to 15 years: Self-confidence (chosen four times as often as at age 1) must regulate this transition. Along with the choice of beauty (50%), great stature is the most frquently chosen (25%) external aspect. A girl apparently needs to identify with the young woman full of confidence in order to be able to make the step toward abstract figures.

Age group 14/15 to 16/17 years: Self-confidence is often sought. A girl chooses an independent position. With her eyes on reality, she already thinks of an ideal self with qualities which fit the cultural pattern for women who have the greatest possibilities for a good marriage. It is striking that 20% of the girls choose an ideal figure from the male sex. They are apparently not secure about their female status. They experience subordination and seek greater security through identification with a male ideal. Thus the threat is lessened.

Discussion. Our reported data and qualitive analysis demonstrate that both themes are present. With increasing age the creativity theme emerges more clearly with regard to the central personality factors (independence, self-confidence, identity); at the same time, the regulating theme emerges clearly as responsibility, is more consciously seen and strived for, that is, as one takes environmental factors more into consideration. The composite ideal self becomes more differentiated and more realistic, with maintenance of many possibilities for creative self-realization.

Both themes have structuring functions. The environment can determine to a great degree whether there is a healthy balance between both or if one of the two will dominate. We notice that the development of modern youth in the industrialized countries (e.g., the Netherlands vs. Spain and Portugal) is determined to a greater degree by the creative theme. We find indications in the material from Spain and Portugal that choice of the ideal person is determined by culturally defined values (religion).

This is not apparent in other countries. We see this latter phenomenon as related to the structure of modern society; the adolescent continually finds himself confronted with divergent values; he must make an independent choice. Thus there are high demands made on both creative and regulative principles. It is clear that the contents of the dynamic principles of homeostasis and creativity are determined by the functional relation between the individual and the environment.

In a theoretical study on 'egocentrism in adolescents', Elkind (1971, p. 136) suggests that the final stage of egocentrism during early adolescence is characterized by the belief that the thoughts of others are directed toward the self. This phenomenon has been termed 'imaginary audience' by Elkind. This form of egocentrism is finally abandoned when the adolescent perceives the disparity between the reactions that he expects from others (creative principle) and the reactions that he actually receives (homeostasis). Elkind further discusses the 'personal fable', referring to the adolescent's belief in the uniqueness of his feelings. Both 'imaginary audience' and 'personal fable' can be seen as creative themes in our theoretical framework. If adolescents do not learn to adapt these forms of behavior to the reality of the environment, then they do not proceed further in their development. We see here, in the cognitive approach, development which is determined by creative and homeostatic principles.

Similar views are expressed by Hornstein (1970), who defines adolescence as a 'sensitive stage for change', that is, a very fruitful stage for developmental possibilities (creativity). In this didactic model, however, Hornstein stresses that such development is channelled by the adolescents' learning possibilities (homeostasis). Again adolescent development is seen to be determined by both principles.

Thomae's proposal for a theory of adolescence has some empirical evidence. The reported data and the data of Elkind and Hornstein support an adolescence theory which is based on the creative and homeostatic principle. We need more research, especially more direct observation. Self-reports cannot give a real picture of the dynamic mechanisms of adolescents' development. Self-reports are meaans to add information to data derived from observation.

D. THEMATIC STRUCTURATION IN ADOLESCENCE: FINDINGS FROM PEDI ADOLESCENTS

by Johan G. Garbers, *Rand Afrikaans University, Johannesburg, Republic of South Africa*

This paper is based on an investigation by the author, published under the title 'Pedi Adolescence: The educational situation and image of adolescence of the Pedi school child'. The present aim is to use the findings of this research in an effort to test a proposed theory of adolescence put forward by Thomae (1969, pp. 234–236). Thomae suggests that adolescence can be described and interpreted as a special case of 'thematic structuration' which implies a principle of creative self-realization of the adolescent on the one hand, and on the other the principle of the striving to arrive at a balanced adaptation to the realities of life. The creative principle does not necessarily imply clever behavior of a high scientific or artistic quality, but behavior which is properly integrated in the adolescent's life, which is directed towards a fairly distant future, and which crystalizes as an own plan of life amongst a score of available possibilities. This creative aspect is, however, always influenced, balanced or nuanced by the homeostatic principle which is represented in society and which regulates change. The basic idea implied by Thomae's theory also exists in the ideas of many specialists in the field of adolescence.

My study of Pedi adolescents was undertaken against the background of Ausubel's outline of theme and cultural variations put forward in his study of Maori youth (1965). Although this frame of reference has much in common with Thomae's theory, the empirical findings will have to be reinterpreted.| The operationalizing of Thomae's frame of reference poses obvious problems, the most difficult of which is to relate the findings to the cultural set-up of the Pedi at the present time. The relationship that will be outlined is bound to be vague and explorative of nature. For this reason I will merely try to arrive at a formulation of feasible hypotheses of probable relationships.

The problem of the individual in developmental theory had been in a very direct sense the impetus to my investigation into Pedi adolescence. While setting up and trying to run a child guidance clinic for Pedi people, it was very soon realized that the image of adolescence depicted in the literature simply was not appropriate or specific enough for purposes of individual guidance. (For this reason too the emphasis was not so much on the cognitive but rather on the affective domain.) We know that the placing of the individual within developmental theory is methodologically a most debatable point. A wide spectrum of views is held – from the view that individual uniqueness is of no scientific significance to the belief that the essence of human life and behavior can only be revealed in the unique sample of human behavior (Van Strien 1966). We also know from experience that an individual very seldom completely fits into a developmental theory. I shall try to arrive at possible functional relationships between cultural milieu and adolescent behavior.

Context and method. The Pedi, about 1,097,080 in number, live in the Northern Transvaal, Republic of South Africa. Socialization within the traditional Pedi culture (Mönnig 1968; Shapera 1953; Duminy 1967) starts with an extremely close, prolonged, and rather exclusive contact of the very young child with its mother. After a fairly late weaning the child becomes a member of a peer group in which it spends most of its time. These peer groups are strictly dichotomized on the basis of sex, are relatively isolated from the adult generation, and carry collective responsibilities. Fear of the irrational is the main means of disciplining children, and punishment is mostly collective and can be given by any adult in the village. To secure conformity, compliance, and subordination to tribal custom are very important aims in education. The fashioning or shaping of the sentiments and attitudes rather than the mind or intellect is the main concern in Pedi education. Vocational education takes place by way of spontaneous imitation of adult activities. Throughout, its development stages are demarcated by various developmental rites, the most important being initiation and ritual preparatory to marriage.

A marked remolding and reorganisation of Pedi society was necessitated by the compulsory adaptation to an advanced and different economic structure. Manifold intermediate strata at present exist between the almost untouched traditional situation on the one hand and the far-reaching adaptation to a Western way of life on the other. Families became, to a varying extent, isolated individual units, and scholastic education became an established and highly desired part of Pedi culture. The traditional tribal education was shaken to its foundations by the contact with technological society, Christian teachings, and a Western type of school education. It is impossible to describe what may be termed the representative educational pattern of the Pedi of today.

The sample drawn for this investigation included 1,718 pupils 11 to 19 years old in the 5th to 12th grade at school. For a score of practical reasons this sample was not representative of all 11 to 19 year old Pedi, but mainly because youth in this age group who were not at school or who have just started school were not represented in the sample. The data was gathered by means of (a) a simple partially pre-coded questionnaire, and (b) the F.S. Go Bana – meaning 'Frustration Study for Youth'. The F.S. Go Bana is a translation and adaptation of Coetsier's (1961) 'F.S. voor de Jeugd' to the Pedi language and life situation. For our purposes this test – devised according to the picture frustration studies of Saul Rosenzweig (1944, 1948) – was most appropriate because it could give an impression of the Pedi adolescent's approach to and behavior in typical life situations. Moreover, from Coetsier's data on 5,000 Flemish adolescents an impression was gained of how adolescents from a typical technological society react to the same typical life situations.

The reactions of the adolescents to each one of the 30 situations were codified according to the following scheme: The direction of the reaction to frustration can be either extrapunitive (an outward orientation), in which case aggression is turned upon the environment (E); intra-punitive (a self-orientation) in which case aggression is turned by the subject upon himself (I); or impunitive (a passive orientation), in which case aggression is evaded in an attempt to gloss over the frustration (M). The types of reaction include obstacle dominance – in which the barrier occasioning the frustration is pronounced in the responses (O-D) (also called obstacle orientation); ego-defensive – in which the ego of the subject predominates (E-D) (also called blame orientation); and need-persistence – in which the solution of the frustrating problem is emphasized (N-P) (also called goal orientation). From a combination of these six categories, nine possible scoring factors result for each item. To the above, two extra scoring categories were added, namely, two typical super-ego reactions in which the person either aggressively denies that he is responsible for an offence with which he is charged or admits guilt but denies any fault by referring to unavoidable circumstances. Separately and in combination 21 coding categories representing specific symptom values were elaborated. T-scores were computed for every subject for each of these 21 coding categories.

In the analysis, the mode of reaction to frustration was compared (a) between various categories of adolescents (chronological age groups, school grade groups, urban-rural residents, those having conflicts with their parents for various reasons, etc.); and (b) within specific categories of life situations (confrontation with adults, peer-group relationships, denial of independence, thwarting of ambition, etc.) – the latter also in comparison with the mode of reaction of Flemish adolescents.

Thematic structuration in the case of Pedi adolescents. The following trends were observed, which probably reflect the creative self-realization of the Pedi adolescent: (a) Ample proof of a development towards greater independence with increasing age is reflected by the decreasing incidence of conflicts between adolescent and parents; the growing concern with the future occupation; the overt and increasing questioning of the educational authority of the adults; the increasingly persistent efforts to pacify frustrated needs; the increasing ability and inclination to pass individual judgments, to hold his own, and to arrive at solutions to frustrating situations. (b) Increasing realism and foresight is reflected in the Pedi adolescent's preoccupation with concrete, practical, and material-istic problems which decreases with increasing age, while the care for the family and parents, the future vocation and education become increasingly important to the older adolescent. With increasing age they are also progressively more able to get an over-all view of situations, to look beyond frustrating situations which face them, and to face and solve such situations; they are increasingly directing blame and aggression upon themselves and increasingly persistent in their efforts to pacify frustrated needs and to solve frustrating situations facing them; and they are progressively more inclined towards forgiveness. (c) Finally, in the assimilation of values and norms of conduct the Pedi adolescent demon-strated an increasing expediency, equity, and reciprocity of obligations with increasing age.

The above-mentioned trends presuppose an urge towards self-realiz-ation. In this the cognitive growth during adolescence is probably a most important precondition. These trends already represent a response to a unique socialization context. Let us now try to relate the creative self-realization to specific regulative contexts within society. It is very difficult to define these contexts in a systematic way. An attack on the problem via the developmental tasks of Ausubel (1954) or Chickering (1969), or the aspects of adulthood of Langeveld (1969), or the dimensions of identity formation of Erikson (1963), or Bühler's four basic trends (1962) places the emphasis predominantly upon the aspect of self-realization of the individual himself and not so much on the regulative social context. Our data, however, implied the following domains:

(a) The very clear trend regarding adaptation to adult generations coming to the fore in our findings is that the Pedi adolescent does not find it difficult to free himself from parental authority. The Pedi adolescent, having undergone initiation (still a fairly general practice also amongst urban dwellers), is readily accepted within adult life with all its privileges. Should there then be an infringement upon their independence by adults, the Pedi adolescent reacts to such an inflicted frustration in an uncompromising, aggressive, extra-punitive way. It appears as if conflicts between adolescent and parent are not typical occurrences in traditional Pedi culture.

Comparison of the reactions of Pedi and Flemish adolescents to frustration inflicted in a confrontation of the adolescent with an adult revealed significant differences: The Pedi adolescent overtly questions the educational authority of the parents with greater ease; is less able to cope with or solve such frustration; is more susceptible to self-defensive reactions; is not touched in his conscience faculty by such encounters; and is less persistent in his attempts to pacify frustrated needs.

An analysis was also made of the matters causing conflicts between adolescent and parent. It was evident that those adolescents who had conflicts with their parents were strikingly in the minority. Those matters which caused conflicts (such as the spending of money, boy-girl relationships, veto of decisions, excessive restriction of freedom) showed marked differences in incidence in the lives of individual adolescents. A comparison of those adolescents who have had conflicts with their parents about specific matters and those who did not revealed that a specific type of conflict an adolescent has with his parents is supported by a corresponding typical mode of reaction to frustration which makes the specific conflict logical. So, for instance, the boys experiencing conflicts with their parents about the latter's veto of their decisions are significantly more inclined than those not having such conflicts to point out persistently the presence of frustrating obstacles, less inclined to expect solutions from other people, more inclined to direct aggression towards the environment, less patient and conforming, less inclined to evade aggression, more inclined to merely stress and point out the barriers occasioning the frustration, and less directed towards the frustrated needs.

The teacher, however, is almost blindly accepted as a person of authority by the Pedi adolescent – in contrast to the Flemish one. Pedi adolescents accept the authority of their teachers (Pedi teachers) even to the point of lacking self-defence in such confrontations. This phenomenon obviously should be related to their strong desire for education and the persistence with which they go to work to achieve this.

The above-mentioned trends are logical if interpreted against the background of the tribal education of Pedi youth. The uninitiated youth form a society of their own. Even legally their parents are not held liable for the deeds of their uninitiated children. The group members are controlled strictly and often harshly by their own leaders. Any adult may, however, give an erring youth a thorough hiding. The uninitiated youth have a form of life and a code of their own. The boys are expected to be insubordinate and cheeky (Mönnig 1969). A very real distance, therefore, exists between successive generations, but it cannot be considered an alienation of generations, as is claimed to exist in the modern technological society. An educational intention by the adult generations does exist, but it is a collective one.

It appears, therefore, that the Pedi adolescent – and for that matter probably many adolescents in developing countries – lives in two worlds: Firstly in the traditional context in which after initiation full adult status is granted and accepted. Because of the introduction of the new social institution, the school, the hierarchical peer group structure is overthrown and new representatives of authority (the teacher or instructor) are introduced. Thus the Pedi adolescent, also being a pupil, partially subjects himself to the extended period of sub-adulthood posed by the longer period of formal education. Therefore he is at the same time being accepted as an adult in Pedi society but as a child within the school situation.

(b) An analysis was made of the mode of reaction of the Pedi adolescent to frustration inflicted in situations of peer-group life (the denial of dignity by peers, confrontation in the company of peers with a negative accusation, and the confrontation with a positive realization of values in a social context of peer accomplishment). The Pedi adolescent, if compared with his Flemish counterpart, is significantly more inclined to accept group relations and this derived status in a matter of fact way; to evade such alienation and to accept the verdict of the group; not to be forcefully motivated by accomplishments of members of the peer group but nevertheless experiencing it as a source of uneasiness and displeasure; and to meet the denial of group participation with overt aggressive reactions.

The Pedi adolescents who indicated that they were members of a group who spend as much time as possible in each other's company differed significantly in their mode of reaction to frustration from those who, according to themselves, were not members of such a group. The group participants (it was accepted that they interpreted group membership here not in the sense of the normal membership of the generation group, but rather as that of a gang type of group) proved to be of a more happy-go-lucky personality type; to be unwilling to accept responsibility; to be less inclined to that type of reflection touching upon the conscience faculty; to be less persistent in their motivation; and to be less forgiving.

In the traditional Pedi society the peer group fulfils a very definite function. The socialization of the individual adolescent is regulated by his peers, so that this status is a derived one. This derived status continues to be a significant source of self-esteem during adult life, and the ego-aggrandizing type of primary status is rare. Hierarchical positions, according to Mönning (1968), are sorted out only within the leseboro (uninitiated boy) and lethumasa (uninitiated girl) groups, when a leader is selected on a basis of excellence in fighting and an ability to sing and dance (pp. 108–109). During initiation, however, leaders are chosen on grounds of social hierarchy: 'The boys are thus forcefully shown that, whereas previously, with the same switches, their leader was chosen on the grounds of strength and ability, rank and status will henceforth be decided by birth and social superiority' (p.115).

Because of the effects of acculturation, many avenues of primary status can be attained. From our data it seems that peer accomplishment has not (yet?) become a forceful motivator for the Pedi adolescent, but it seems to be merely a source of displeasure. Thwarting of scholastic ambition within the context of peer accomplishment, however, is met with an exceptionally strong (much stronger than was the case with the Flemish adolescent) but more nuanced (more evasive and less extra-punitive) aggression – probably a sign of the emerging of the typical image of cultural adolescence. The excessive group activity, which reflects negatively on these group participants, probably represents a symptom of an unsuccessful adaptation to a situation of acculturation.

(c) The predominant impression gained as far as the Pedi adolescent's future perspective is concerned is his vague and inaccurate image of the future. This is noticed in a gross overestimation of his own abilities; a more realistic future perspective by the girls than by the boys; a lack of comprehension of the real content of and insight into the preconditions for intended vocations; and an ignorance regarding the preconditions for entering into vocations. Interest and money are the two most important reasons for choosing a vocation, with aptitude only the third consideration, though considered as of much less relative importance.

In the untouched Pedi society the 'distance' of anticipation, as well as the nature and complexity of the anticipated future, is known. The transition to adulthood does not pose serious problems as it is formalized in the various initiation rites. Contact with technological culture has complicated their future. Consequently the anticipation of the future and the transition towards it have become tremendously complicated. The vague future perspective of the Pedi adolescent is, as we all know, not a unique phenomenon. In their situation of acculturation very optimistic but unrealistic aspirations prevail. Because a situation of cultural contact usually has the greatest impact on the vocational situation of the male, the consequences of a vague future perspective are more grave for the boys than for the girls. This situation poses big challenges to the education and guidance of the Pedi adolescent.

(d) An effort was made to get some impression of the impact of the contact with the urban environment and formal education on Pedi adolescence. The mode of reaction to frustration of the urban dwellers was compared with those of the rural ones. The urban group was significantly more inclined than the rural one to overcome obstacles frustrating them; to turn aggression and direct blame and censure upon themselves; to have more patience and to conform; to be more able to circumvent the barriers facing them; to put more effort into attaining their aims and pacifying their needs; to admit guilt; and to forgive blame or fault. The image of the urban adolescent, therefore, on many points approaches the typical image of adolescence in our modern technological society. The following factors peculiar to the urban environment might be significant here: Its greater appeal to the individual person; the absence or reduced effect of a general ruling tradition which more or less offers directions for behavior; the individual's responsibility for holding his own, and the presence and confrontation with conflicting norms.

In the case of the Pedi no compulsory school education existed at the time of the research (1965). Consequently a very marked age span existed in each school grade. Developmental trends with respect to the various variables were analyzed in terms of chronological age as well as school level. In both cases the same trends in the mode of reaction to frustration were observed. Even though no effort was made to isolate the effect of formal schooling, the impression was that it exerts a very powerful effect on development. This impression appears logical against the background of Perquin's (1967) outline of the influences of schooling on a pupil's personality development. These influences are conducive to the creation of a personality development like that of the cultural adolescent.

It appears, therefore, that the urban environment and formal school teaching effect a development in Pedi adolescence much like that of the adolescent in our technological society.

(e) Most striking differences regarding individual and social control were noticed between the Pedi and Flemish adolescents. In the mode of reaction to frustration the former's less prominent self-critical faculty was striking. The Pedi group is strikingly more inclined to direct aggression against the environment or to evade the frustration altogether. As they grow older, and/or come into contact with the urban environment and with formal schooling, etc., this inclination lessens.

In traditional Pedi society the individual is attuned to the voice of traditional opinion. Numerous pressures towards the creation of conformist personality operate, namely through taboos, rituals, initiation, school, and the inculcation of group values, rather than through personal moral precepts of parents or other individual authorities. Because of social and economic changes, the breakdown of the family tribal group, urbanization, general technological progress, Christian teachings, etc., radical structural changes took place. In the latter set-up progressively more emphasis is placed upon the individual and individual conscience as such. In this development personal confusion and disablement will most probably occur. Our findings seem to reflect in the image of adolescence the changes taking place in Pedi society.

(f) Sex differences in adolescent behavior were also explored. The male Pedi adolescent is more inclined than the female to direct blame or censure upon himself, but to deny any essential fault on his part by referring to unavoidable circumstances; to offer amends to solve a problem; to evade frustration; and to hope that time or circumstances will bring about a solution to his problems. The image of the females appears to be more positive than that of the males. Whether this difference crystalizes as a response to the respective roles of the male and female in the traditional Pedi society, in which the female carries the major burden in various spheres of life and/or whether it refers to the general phenomenon that boys experience more developmental problems than girls at this stage remains a matter of speculation.

Conclusion. The empirical explication of Thomae's theory of thematic structuration for adolescence seems to be a very worthwhile but no easy task. It necessitates, however, a team approach in which the psychologist needs the help of the educationist, sociologist, social anthropologist, politician, criminologist, and others. Comparable cross-cultural data is indispensable, and this presupposes rigorous empirical investigations and the solving of many problems of cross-cultural methodology. Apart from the scientific interest of such work, there is hardly a better way of making a long-term evaluation of the effects of the socialization context which we create and manipulate in society.

Problems of cross-cultural research

A. THE PROBLEM OF THE PACKAGED VARIABLE

by Beatrice Whiting, *Harvard University, Cambridge*

Social scientists studying the nature and developmental history of cognitive processes and individual and social behavior have concentrated their attention on the problem of identifying and measuring the dependent variables and have devoted less attention to the study of factors associated with differences in these processes and behaviors. Frequently after exhaustive pretesting of instruments for measuring the individual's performance on a battery of tests they satisfy themselves with the easily measured independent variables – sex and age, and throw in other packaged variables such as culture, social class, or socioeconomic status – variables which have proved good predictors of differences. Having progressed in solving some of the problems of identification and measurement of the dependent variables, it is time to put effort into unwrapping these packaged independent variables. What are the components of sex, age, culture, social class and socio-economic status which account for their consistent association with differences in test performance? What are the processes associated with these variables?

In discussing the problems faced by the researcher who endeavors to unwrap the packaged variables I will use examples from studies conducted in countries in the non-Western world. Some of these studies contrast the behavior of groups from geographically diverse culture areas, some contrast cultural groups living in contiguous areas and still others, contrast individuals or groups within a culture. Some studies combine all three types of samples (for a review of studies see LeVine 1970). In general the size of the packaged variables decreases as one moves from studies using culturally diverse samples to those making within-culture comparisons based on individual scores.

Independent variables used in cross-cultural studies. Studies of the first kind using geographically and culturally diverse samples and group means have macro antecedent variables. Thus in the cross-cultural studies of visual illusions conducted by Segall, Campbell and Herskovits (1966) the predictor variable included gross features of the physical environment – open terrain with full vision of the horizon as contrasted with forested terrain, a carpentered world of right angles, rectangular houses, and geometric art forms contrasted to houses, tools, and art forms using predominately circular or elliptical shapes, variables which were not difficult to identify and which were judged to be shared by discrete groups of people. Similarly in the early work of Berry (1966), the variable of 'low and high accumulation' was adopted from Barry, Child and Bacon's (1959) cross-cultural study and 'restrictive' socialization isolated and considered the process variable. Barry, Child and Bacon, on evidence from published ethnographies, rated societies on the degree to which they accumulated property. 'Low accumulation' societies were predominantly nomadic hunters and gatherers and rudimentary horticulturalists who did not live in settled nucleated villages with superordinate political and judicial control system. 'High accumulation' societies were predominantly a combination of herders and agriculturalists. Barry, Child and Bacon reported that 'high accumulation' societies pressured children toward obedience and responsibility but not toward self-reliance and achievement, traits associated with 'low accumulation' societies. Berry labeled the type of training which encouraged obedience and responsibility 'restrictive socialization'. In his studies he measured this variable by a combination of ratings based on ethnographic accounts and retrospective interviews with individuals who were tested on Kohs Blocks, Ravens Matrices, Morrisby Shapes, and Witkin's Embedded Figures Test. He found that individuals judged to have had 'restrictive socialization' performed less well on these tests purported to measure spatial ability. His initial study was a comparison of the Temne, settled agriculturalists in West Africa, and an Eskimo group. Since that time he has increased his sample of societies and has done within-culture comparisons so that he can no longer be accused of the type of comparison Donald Campbell has characterized as uninterpretable – the comparison of two naturally occurring cases (1961).

It should be noted, however, that even in his most recent studies Berry does not dedicate as much time to exploring the independent variable, 'restrictive socialization', as one would wish. The differences in life style of 'low' and 'high accumulation' societies are many. As Barry, Child and Bacon point out, the members of 'high accumulation' societies live more frequently in settled communities with more social stratification. The women participate more in the economy, assign more tasks to the children, are more frequently polygynously married. There is less work to be done in the 'low accumulation' societies (see Lee 1969). The children are assigned fewer chores and have more time to play, often engage in competitive games of skill associated with hunting techniques (activities which Barry, Child and Bacon scored high on achievement pressure). How shall we know if we compare the cognitive, individual, and social behavior of samples of children in populations which vary along these dimensions which of the many experiences associated with these types of societies accounts for the differences in behavior. 'Low and high accumulation' and 'restrictive socialization' are packaged variables.

Robert and Ruth Munroe (1971a, 1971b) have attempted to unwrap the 'restrictive socialization' variable by isolating freedom to wander further from home and consequent exploration of the environment. In their two studies in Kenya of age-matched boys and girls they have found that children who during free time or while herding are found further from home have more highly developed 'spatial' ability as measured by their ability to copy block patterns and geometric figures and their greater success on Porteus Mazes.

Among the most popular independent variables used in within-culture comparison in cross-culture studies in the non-Western world are schooling, social class or socioeconomic status, urbanization, or modernization (Greenfield 1966; Dawson 1967; Berry 1971; Goodnow 1969; LeVine 1970). Thus Greenfield compares means of test scores for four groups – children living in country and city, some attending and some not attending school. All of these variables are packaged. They include clusters of correlated and often ill-defined traits. With a few notable exceptions – the Munroe study cited above, Price-Williams, Gordon and Ramirez's (1969) study of Mexican potters, Cole, Gay, Glick and Sharp's (1971) study of strategies of memory among the Kpelle, Fjellman's (1971) studies of category formation among the Kamba, and Dasen's (1973) recent comparative study of conservation – little attempt is made to understand the individual experiences the packaged variables imply – to understand the processes by which individuals growing up in one or the other group develop different profiles of behavior. Furthermore, since the variables are not separated into their component parts, the identification of groups labeled by dimensions such as social class, urbanity, modernity, etc., is problematic. For this reason when these variables are used in comparative studies it is impossible to define them in transcultural terms.

Review of African studies attempting to identify process variables. The identification of process variables requires, first of all, detailed studies of life styles, learning environments, and techniques used in the socialization of children. Secondly, when some of the process variables have been identified, studies should be done within cultures isolating groups which differ on some but not all of the variables. And thirdly, all promising studies should be replicated among other populations and in other societies.

The first type of study is underway in several parts of the world. I am most familiar with the work completed or in process in three parts of Africa: in the Kalahari Desert project directed by Irven DeVore and Richard Lee, in the Kpelle project in Liberia directed by Michael Cole and John Gay, and in the Child Development Research Unit in Kenya formerly directed by John Whiting and myself. In the Kalahari, Mel Konner has observed the life of infants and Patricia Draper the life of children 2-14 years of age. In the Kpelle project I am most familiar with the observational study conducted by Gerald Erchak. In all three of these projects an attempt has been made to observe and record the details of daily life and learning experiences paying attention to those which have been identified as important predictor variables in studies conducted in the Western world, but being constantly alert for variables which have not been identified because of culturally induced blindness. The contrast between the experience of children in the various cultures often suggests new variables which should be investigated.

I will limit my remarks here to studies made in our research unit in Kenya.[1] Liederman (1973), following the work of Geber (1958) and others,

1. Research in Kenya was funded by a grant from Carnegie Corporation and NIMH Research grant MH1096-18.

reported that Kikuyu infants in Kenya are precocious in their mental and physical development as measured by the Bayley Infant Scales but lose their precocity in later infancy. Super (1973), who is working in a Kipsigis community in Western Kenya, has been investigating the learning environment of infants and scrutinizing their performance on the various items of the Bayley Scales. He has singled out the life style of the mothers and certain aspects of the technology as environmental predictors. Kipsigis mothers who have no cribs, high chairs, baby carriages, or infant proppers and who do have many economic responsibilities want their children to sit and walk early. They believe that these skills must be taught, and they start such training early. These infants score precociously on those items of the Bayley Scales which are related to sitting and walking – one of the reasons sub-Saharan infants have been rated as precocious. On the other hand they have no experience in climbing stairs and when the items on the Bayley Scales tap these skills the precocity disappears. If Super's findings replicate in a Kikuyu sample, as he is row investigating, and in other parts of the world, they demonstrate the importance of looking at the details of learning environments and incidentally the importance of unpackaging in this case the dependent variable and making item analyses of such widely accepted tests as the Bayley Infant Scales.

In our work in Kenya Thomas Weisner and I have been attempting to unwrap the urban-rural package as it affects the social behavior of children. Weisner's research (1972, 1973) indicates the importance of exploring the details of urbanization. The urban dwellers in his Kenya samples maintain two households – one in their native village, the other in a housing estate in Nairobi. We have been fortunate in our observational study in having a sample of mothers and children who spend some time in both environments as well as a sample of families living most of the time in Nairobi and a sample of close friends or relatives of these urban dwellers who have remained in the country. We hope from this observational study to get insights into the details of the contrasting experience which will enable us to design more precise research on the effects of urban vs. rural living on the socialization of these children and the development of their social behavior.

Once the researcher has unwrapped the packaged variables he may find it difficult to identify any social group in which he can isolate the important component parts of the package. Thus in the developing countries and the Third world it is difficultt to separate the degree of education from economic well-being and status. In Kenya these two variables are further associated with monogamous nuclear as contrasted with polygynous and extended families. It is urgent, however, that we try and find situations where we can study the effect of these individual variables.

Sex and age as examples of package variables. In conclusion I would like to comment on two of the independent variables which have been considered the least open to criticism, namely, sex and age. It has been the practice of researchers to report differences in individual scores by sex and age without any detailed analysis of what traits are packaged together. Age implies changes in the size of the body, neurological changes, modifications in life style, changes in activities and spheres of social interaction. The young two- and three-year-olds are closer in space to adults, more frequently interact with children of the opposite sex, perform less chores, percentage-wise behave more individually, i.e., non-socially, than older children (Whiting and Whiting in preparation, Edwards 1972, Erchak 1973). If one could vary these experiences would age in years and months still be the best predictor? Assuming there is a 5–7 shift in cognitive abilities are there any experiences which result in an earlier shift in some children? Landauer and Whiting are attempting to determine the effect of physical growth, age of parents, family size, and certain measures of economic well-being such as house type, number of acres of land owned, occupation, and ownership of radios, automobiles, and other items of material culture on the earliness of the shift. If these prove important, the details of life in homes characterized by these variables may lead to further fruitful hypotheses.

Similarly with sex differences. If mothers interact with female more than male children, assign more chores to girls, interrupt them more frequently, expect them to stay closer to home and do the type of work women do (Nerlove 1969, Whiting and Edwards 1974), can differences in their performance on tests be considered to be biologically determined? When one is able to contrast populations controlling for some of these variables some of the characteristics identified as probably biologically determined appear to have strong environmental components. Thus boys who perform baby tending and cooking chores and hence stay closer to home have behavior profiles which approach the stereotype of girls (Ember 1973, Whiting and Edwards 1974). Girls living a life very similar to boys do not differ significantly on many types of social behavior. Those on which they do differ when training is more similar, and those which are significantly different in all samples of individuals studied in various cultural groups seem to be the best candidates for the biological label.

In sum, as researchers interested in understanding cognitive and individual and social behavior, we should pay more attention to analyzing our independent variables and to identifying the processes which may be associated with different types of behavior. To advance along these fronts we need more detailed analyses of the learning environments of the children we study and the details of their experiences in growing up in these various environments. Anthropologists have developed techniques for gathering relevant descriptive data and should collaborate with psychologists and other social scientists in conducting these studies.

B. SITUATING THE EXPERIMENT IN CROSS-CULTURAL RESEARCH

by Sylvia Scribner,* *Rockefeller University, New York*

Of the many methodological problems in cross-cultural research I have selected the experiment as the point of emphasis because it seems to me that the role of the experiment needs to be clarified if we hope to resolve a central dilemma in the field of culture and cognition.

In a sense, the experiment has created the dilemma. In the last several decades, there has been a substantial increase in the number of cross-cultural psychological studies of cognition in which the principal research tool has been the experiment or a task derived from an experiment. In the same period, there has been an upsurge of interest in cognitive phenomena among anthropologists and the initiation of new lines of research based principally on the methods of field observation and interview.

Ordinarily, this shared interest and intensive research effort by two disciplines should promote a more rapid growth of knowledge and understanding. This seems to have been the case in the field of culture and personality, which also arose as a specialized domain of inquiry sitting astride the two disciplines of psychology and anthropology. But in culture and cognition, the multiplication of psychological and anthropological studies has not yet resulted in an integrated body of data or in a set of unifying constructs. On the contrary, it has brought sharply into focus the discontinuities in the evidence each of these sciences presents of cultural variations in cognition.

Discontinuities between anthropology and psychology. I will illustrate the problem with a few sketchy and admittedly over-simplified examples. Many carefully conducted experiments using Piagetian tasks have found a considerable number of *adults* in nontechnological societies failing to show behavior associated with the possession of logical structures of intelligence assumed to be characteristic of 8 to 12-year-old children in

* The views here expressed have developed in the course of collaborative work with Michael Cole and owe much to his formulations on cross-cultural experimentation. Preparation of this paper was supported by a grant from the Carnegie foundation to Michael Cole and U.S.P.H.S. Grant GM 16735 from the Institute of General Medical Sciences to C. Pfaffman.

anthropologists by means of new analytic techniques are identifying complex logical structures underlying conceptual systems within these cultures (Wallace 1962, for example). Moreover, ethnographic studies reveal that individuals within these cultures engage in elegant processes of technological societies (Dasen 1972 reviews many of these studies). Yet, inferential reasoning as they go about the everyday business of settling disputes (Gibbs 1962) or the more exotic business of bargaining on the terms of their participation in some Western-inspired research project (Kulah 1973).

Evans-Pritchard (1963), Albert (1964), Bellman (1968), and other anthropologists have documented the complex communication skills involved in patterns of verbal exchange among the Zande, Burundi, and Kpelle peoples of Africa. Cole and his associates, on the other hand (1969), found that Kpelle adults performed poorly in an experimental situation that was specifically designed to tap communication skills.

As a final example, antropological reports of feats of memory on the part of nonliterate people in traditional societies date back to as early as the seventeenth century (Evreux 1614). But ever since the 1920s, psychologists using methods and procedures developed in the laboratory to test memory performance have failed to confirm these generalizations about extraordinary mnemonic powers.

These examples indicate that the divergencies in data and generalizations between anthropology and psychology on various topics of cognition generally run in the same direction: contemporary anthropological evidence highlights the commonality in the cognitive skills of populations in technological and nontechnological societies; psychological evidence, for the most part, emphasizes either the absence of certain skills or the lower levels of skill of nontechnological peoples. The problem and dilemma is how to reconcile these two sets of data and interpretations.

One response to this problem has been the denial that there is any need for reconciliation because the two research approaches and two sets of evidence really speak to different questions. Thus, some psychologists feel that ethnographic descriptions of performance in naturally occurring situations are useful for many purposes but have little to contribute to an understanding of the basic psychological processes underlying performance in different cultures. They feel that such knowledge can only be generated by the laboratory experiment which permits the isolation and systematic manipulation of various components of the performance.

Critiques of experimental method. Some anthropologists, on the other hand, question whether the laboratory situation yields findings that have any trans-situational generality at all. One objection is that experimental materials, tasks, and procedures developed in industrial societies are ethnocentric and culturally biased. Others go beyond this in asserting that the experiment itself, as a context for the elicitation of behavior, has no ecological validity in the cultures to which it has been transported. Whatever limitations are imposed by the artificiality of the experiment in the societies in which it originated, they argue, are magnified many times over in traditional societies whose people lack experience with test-like situations. Granted that experimental methods make it possible to analyze processes underlying performance. But if the performance itself is non-representative and distorted, what can be learned from such an analysis that has any relevance for the understanding of cultural deter-minants of behavior?

This position, which is essentially an attempt to draw a line between what anthropology and psychology can tell us about cognition, does not seem to be a very fruitful way of handling the problem. Psychologists would hardly be willing to accept the conclusion that experiments can do little to illuminate the problem of cultural influences on cognition. And anthropologists, I am sure, would be equally resistant to the notion that evidence of cultural skills is not relevant to an understanding of individual cognitive processes. But even if, as psychologists, we were ready to ply our narrow trade, we would still have to take into account the questions that have been raised about the use of the experiment as a tool in cross-cultural research. It certainly seems precarious to pursue ambitious in-vestigations that seek to compare cognitive processes among populations of *different* cultures, if we cannot reconcile the comparative evidence of psychological and anthropological studies of cognitive processes within the *same* culture.

To meet some of these criticisms, cross-cultural psychologists have devoted considerable attention in recent years to reducing sources of cultural bias in the experiment. The idea that an experiment consists of a fixed set of materials and operations that can be taken abroad like a piece of luggage has been replaced by an emphasis on the need to adapt features of the experiment to the culture in which the research is being carried out. The contemporary view, as Glick (in press) puts it, is that 'The logic of comparative study involves the testing of people in a *comparable* (note, not *identical*) manner'. Lloyd (1972) agrees that the investigator's concern is not to duplicate the original experiment but to 'ensure that it will produce data in the new setting which can be compared with that collected in the original Euro-American situation' (p. 21). Frijda and Jahoda (1966), Berry (1969), and others have made important contributions toward solution of problems of comparability in materials, procedures, experimenter-subject communication, motivations, etc.

While these are important, they leave untouched the perhaps more fundamental criticism that the experiment, by its very nature, rather than by this or that feature of it, cannot be considered an equivalent or comparable performance situation in all societies. To handle this criticism, we have to go beyond the consideration of specific features of the experiment and explore what the experiment represents as a context for the manifestation of cognitive skills within the traditional cultures to which we carry it. What are the naturally occurring contexts in the culture in which these same skills are elicited? How does the experimental paradigm compare to these naturally occurring situations? Are there situations similar to the experimental situation (such as test-taking in school, for example) that individuals encounter in some cultures and not in others? (See Scribner and Cole, in press.) These are some of the questions we would want to ask simply to meet the criterion of establishing comparability between experimental investigations in one culture and another.

The experiment as an un natural situation. But this is essentially the same set of questions that arises when we confront the problem of comparing and integrating data from psychological experiments with data for field research within *one* culture. To relate the two sets of data to each other we are led to ask questions about the contexts in which the behavior we are investigating was elicited. When we observe a Kpelle child trying to memorize word lists in a free recall experiment and when we observe him trying to memorize the names of nine leaves in a singing game on the road behind his house, we are in each case studying the act of memorizing as it occurs in a given situation with a given set of features. Looking upon the experiment this way it makes sense to ask about the similarities and differences between these situations and, most particularly, about the similarities and differences in the *cognitive demands* they make upon the child. Can these differences be characterized in any generalized or formal way? If we can identify dimensions along which the experimental situation can be compared to the naturally occurring situation we will have a better possibility of achieving some integrated interpretation of performance in the two situations.

This approach suggests that it might be valuable to make the experiment itself an object of cross-cultural inquiry. Our aim would then be to identify certain distinctive features of the experimental situation as a context for cognitive behavior and to fit it into the range of situations in the culture in which this behavior is manifested.

This is a very general statement and an ambitious manifesto. I have no blueprint to propose and no developed line of investigation to use as a model. But some contemporary lines of research suggest certain techniques that might be useful in helping us understand what is going on in the experiment when we are investigating cognitive phenomena in other cultures. I will pick up on these and draw them out to show that this line of inquiry is a feasible one.

Investigating subject's understanding of the experiment. A number of years ago Webb, Campbell, and their colleagues (Webb, Campbell, Schwartz and Sechrest 1966) analyzed the special problems involved in drawing inferences from experimental data which stem from the fact that the experiment is a reactive situation. By this term, they emphasized that the performance outcome in an experiment is determined not merely by the conditions the investigator establishes but by the subject's awareness that he is an object of study.

Orne (1970) has systematically investigated the contribution this awareness makes to a variety of behavioral responses in experimental situations, ranging from hypnotic phenomena to galvanic skin responses. He identified as significant variables such factors as the subject's construction of the hypothesis under investigation – what he thinks the experimental question really is, what he identifies as the relevant variables, and what he thinks constitutes appropriate behavior in the experimental situation. Orne calls these the 'demand characteristics' of the experiment – the information the experimental situation conveys to the subject over and beyond what the experimenter tells him. One of the most interesting features of Orne's work is that, in spite of the investment of a great deal of effort and ingenuity, he found it impossible to design an experiment *without* demand characteristics – that is, an experiment that was totally meaningless to his subjects!

If, as Orne has demonstrated, it is important for the experimenter to take the subject's definition of the experiment into account, even when he is working with a familiar and relatively homogenous subject population, how much more crucial this is when an experimenter is working in an unfamiliar culture with subjects for whom the experiment is an alien situation. Yet, to my knowledge, there has been no systematic attempt to study demand characteristics in a cross-cultural setting. There is some anecdotal material, however, that suggests how this might be done.

Glick (1969), for example, was investigating what attributes of objects traditional Kpelle rice farmers use in classification tasks. His experimental procedure was the standard one in which the subject is presented with an array of familiar objects and told to put together those that belong together. He found that the great majority of subjects made groupings that were based on functional or perceptual relations between items rather than on their common membership in a taxonomic category. Other investigators have interpreted similar findings as an indication that individuals displaying this behavior are deficient in conceptual thinking. Glick, however, asked his subjects why they grouped the items in the way they did. Many answered that this was the clever way to do it, the way that made 'Kpelle sense'. This reply suggested to him that subjects were construing his request to group the items as a test of their cleverness and were responding according to the culturally accepted view of what cleverness is. Glick followed up his hunch, asking a subject to group the items again, this time as a stupid person might do it. Interestingly, under these instructions, he secured perfect taxonomic grouping!

This can be construed as a role-playing approach and many modifications come to mind: Villagers might be asked to group the objects as students attending school might do it, as Westerners might do it, or as elders might do it. Another manipulation might be to vary the role of the experimenter instead of the subject: Are different task expectations conveyed by an experimenter identified with traditional ways and one identified with foreign ways?

In doing pilot work among Kpelle villagers in West Africa on solution of verbal syllogisms, I tried another technique for eliciting information on subject's perception of the task. I was asking individuals to answer classical syllogisms of the following type: All stores in Kpelleland are in a town. Mr. Ukatu has a store in Kpelleland. Is it in a town? Earlier research by Cole and his colleagues (Cole *et al.* 1971) showed that traditional Kpelle villagers handled these problems on no better than a chance basis while young Kpelle adults attending high school performed in a manner comparable to that of American students. I was interested in finding out what features might account for the poor performance of the villagers.

One hypothesis was that they were failing to grasp the nature of the task as one that involved reasoning to reach a conclusion. It seemed from other evidence that they might be conceiving of the problem as a test of their knowledge of facts. So, working with expert translators, we prepared a set of instructions carefully explaining the hypothetical nature of the problems. We also gave a series of practice problems in which we helped the subject arrive at the right answer and demonstrated the peculiarities of the syllogism – how the answer can be derived simply from the information contained in the premises of the problem without any knowledge of the factual situation to which the premises refer.

After the series of test problems, we asked the subject some questions about the experiment and then requested him to give us a problem just like the ones we had given him. This was our test of how the subject construed the experimental task. Here is a typical problem offered by a village tailor: 'Suppose you see your son climbing up in a palm tree and start cutting nuts. You go and begin cooking for him. You hear a sound. How can you find out whether the palm nut fell down or your son?'

This problem and others like it are very instructive. First it tells us that the tailor had correctly grasped the purpose of the psychological game we were playing – his problem, indeed, is one that involves a reasoning process. But it also tells us that he did not grasp the *distinctive* features of the verbal syllogism. An important characteristic of the tailor's problem is that it has a number of correct answers. Among several possibilities, you can find out what has happened to your son by going to the palm tree and looking for him or by staying home near the cooking fire and listening for another sound. The information given in the problem does not in any way dictate the choice of a particular alternative. We know from previous ethnographic research that this problem is similar to a whole class of Kpelle riddle problems that furnish the material for verbal battles of wit in the villages. These problems do not have a single right answer, nor is there necessarily a social consensus as to which answer is the best one; honors go to the participant who delivers the most persuasive and unshakeable argument for the answer he chooses to give. In this respect, traditional Kpelle reasoning problems stand in sharp contrast to the verbal syllogisms we were using in our experiment. The defining attribute of a syllogism is that the answer or conclusion is a necessary one, whether or not it is reasonable, sensible, or clever.

We also learn from the problems given us about the limitations of verbal instructions and brief practice procedures. Our instructions seemed to meet all formal requirements in the sense that they covered the essential features of the task, and they seemed to meet all linguistic requirements as well – they simply failed to communicate what we thought we were communicating, and that was the special nature of the problem material.

The repertoire of problems we secured from our subjects also helps us in interpreting their performance on our test problems. We have the suggestion that one of the factors leading to poor performance might be the assimilation of the syllogism to the traditional riddle problem. If this were the case, subjects may have considered the choice of a Yes or No answer relatively unimportant in comparison to the clever reason they could construct to support it.

Certain testable hypotheses open up from this line of reasoning. One is that villagers might do better when the content of verbal syllogisms is made as unfamiliar as possible since this might counter their tendency to assimilate syllogisms to the traditional problem form. This would be an interesting hypothesis to test because it implies that achieving equal familiarity of problem content in two cultures or in two population groups within a culture does not ensure comparable task difficulty; the dimension of familiarity may be an irrelevant dimension for one group, a facilitating dimension for a second, and a disruptive dimension for a third.

In addition to suggesting modifications in the experiment, this hypothesis suggests a new line of ethnographic research which might help us link the investigation of reasoning processes in the laboratory with those occurring in everyday life. Is there an analog of the Western logic problem in the language games of the Kpelle – that is, a language game in which the response is determined by the formal or structural features of the material and not by its content? If so, we might have more suitable material for experimental purposes. If not, we might want to identify individuals renowned for their skill at traditional riddle-problems to see how they do on our syllogistic problems. Do we observe negative transfer from one class of problems to another or do we observe a generalized verbal problem-solving skill? Through an interweaving of experimental and ethnographic research, we should make progress toward identifying the characteristics of problems and problem-solving situations that influence how reasoning processes are manifested.

Experimenting with the experiment. A second strategy for studying the cognitive demands of a particular experimental paradigm, proposed by Cole (Cole *et al.* 1971), is to subject it to systematic variation until the investigator achieves equal levels of performance among populations that may have initially differed in performance. This research strategy shifts the principle class of independent variables under investigation from those related to characteristics of populations to those related to characteristics of experiments. Instead of carrying one fixed paradigm to many different cultures, the researcher works with many different variations of a single paradigm within one culture. This approach is exemplified by a series of free recall studies conducted by Cole, Gay, Glick and Sharp (1971). These began with the standard free recall paradigm in which the experimenter read a list of disconnected words naming objects belonging to four Kpelle language semantic categories (food, tools, clothes, utensils). In the United States, when lists of this kind are presented in random order, school children from the upper elementary grades on, and middle-class adults, typically reorder the list and recall words clustered together by category rather than in their original order. The amount of clustering in recall has been found to be positively associated with number of words recalled. In the first studies, Kpelle villagers showed little learning of the list and little evidence of clustering.

Cole and his colleagues, however, did not terminate the experimentation at this point. They raised the question: What does it take in the way of experimental procedure to secure clustering and recall performance among the Kpelle villagers comparable to that of educated populations? After failing with some experimental manipulations, they hit on three tasks that dramatically shifted performance. In one, the objects to be remembered were associated with external cues, such as chairs; in another, to-be-remembered words were embedded in narrative stories of a traditional style; in the third successful manipulation, subjects were asked at recall to give back the items of one category at a time – that is, the experimenter instructed the subject to recall all the *foods*, then all the *clothes*, and so on. In all these situations, there was not only an increase in the amount recalled but an analysis of the order in which the items were recalled showed that villagers were engaging in grouping or categorizing operations.

Under these special conditions, the retrieval processes of nonliterate Kpelle farmers seemed very much like those of American or Kpelle students: Both intracultural and intercultural differences were greatly reduced. Cole (1972) offers the following interpretation of these findings:

'This series of experiments taken as a unit certainly seems to bear out the dictum that people will be able to perform well at tasks they find normal and which they often encounter. As such, it confirms anthropological doctrine. But ... it specifies somewhat more closely than usual what "normal" conditions are. And it turns out that "normal" cannot be simply equated with "encounter often". Some of the experimental situations eliciting fine recall were *abnormal* in the sense of infrequently encountered ... What the successful conditions seem to share with "frequently encountered" situations is a lot of structure. Where life or the experimental procedures do not structure the memory task, the traditional person has great difficulty. "Normal" in this case refers to the presence of certain structural features.'

This work is interesting from our present point of view because it identifies a specific cognitive demand present in the experimental situation that is presumed absent from naturally occurring situations. The argument is that the free recall paradigm, unlike situations in everyday life, fails to provide external cues or structure for recall and requires the subject to produce internal cues or structure to support the mnemonic performance. How well he does this, or whether he adopts this strategy at all, may depend on how often his culture confronts him with a similar cognitive demand. This leads to as specific hypothesis about how cultural circumstances may contribute to differences in memory performance – that is, the hypothesis that a member of a traditional society will rarely encounter situations in everyday life that require him to make his own retrieval plan.

To confirm that this is the case among the Kpelle requires an extensive program of field research to identify the contexts in which Kpelle need to learn, store, and retrieve masses of information. The leader of a cooperative work group must remember the work days, hours, and places put in by every one of the twenty or more individuals who constitute the group. Does he have any specific devices for doing this? What are the memory demands required by other activities, such as ritual ceremonies or instruction of the young in bush schools? Can we identify any devices built into these contexts that may serve as retrieval cues?

I am not suggesting that this kind of research will yield analytic knowledge of component processes of recall. But that is not its purpose. Its purpose is to tell us something about how situations vary in their cognitive demands and how the particular experimental paradigm we are using fits into this spectrum.

Studying naturally occurring and quasi-experimental situations. We have seen in all these examples how questions arising in experimental research lead to questions that can best be explored in field research, and the other way around. In closing, I should like to take this approach one step further and suggest the value of a research strategy that seeks from the outset to investigate some particular cognitive phenomenon in a range of situations, from the naturally occurring to the experimental. This strategy requires that we go beyond the use of ethnographic data to set a performance baseline for experimental findings and beyond their use as a source of hypotheses to be tested in experimental research. It means employing a full range of research techniques – both those of anthropology and those of psychology – to study a *single question* concerning cognitive performance.

Without trying to push the parallel, this strategy has been fruitfully employed in the comparative study of animal behavior, principally by Schneirla and his associates (Schneirla 1972). Schneirla's own studies of ant behavior show the complementary nature of observation in the field and experimentation in the laboratory. Field work gives the investigator access to the complete natural phenomenon; selected aspects of this phenomenon can then be isolated and studied quantitatively in the laboratory. One of Schneirla's contributions that has a special relevance for our topic is his emphasis on the possibility of intervention in the field – that is, introducing some experimental manipulation in the naturally occurring situation to test a specific hypothesis about conditions controlling the behavior in question. I have borrowed the term *quasi-experiment* (Campbell and Stanley 1963) to designate this manipulation of conditions in the field.

Again, to keep the discussion concrete, let me work out a specific example. Dr. Akki Kulah, a Kpelle colleague, has described a game called *kolon* (1973), widely played by young and old, whose function seems to be that of teaching young children proverbs. *Kolon* is a competitive game played by two opposing teams whose members vary in age from six to adulthood. The game begins when the leader of one team calls out a phrase to the youngest member of the opposing team who must respond with the 'answer' which is a particular proverb. If the child fails to respond correctly the turn passes to the next older team member.

Kulah has recorded a number of *kolon* games and is now analyzing this material to stipulate the rules of the game and to develop some hypotheses about the relations between the stimulus material and the proverb responses. This analysis will not in itself tell us much about component learning and memory processes of the individual players. Since we do not know the history of the participants, we cannot tell when a child fails to respond correctly whether he has lost the association between the stimulus and the proverb, whether he has forgotten the proverb, or whether he never knew it. When we fully understand the structure of the game, however, we can intervene in it, turning it into a quasi-experimental situation. We might introduce new material to be learned in a format similar to the customary one so that rounds of the game are equivalent to learning trials. We might then begin to manipulate features of the game to see how learning and memory are effected – what happens when we change the structure of the material, that is, vary the relations between the stimulus and response members? What is the influence of the social structure of the game – are there memory cues in the interrelationships of game participants? What happens when it is converted into an individual learning situation? At this point we might return to the laboratory and set up a formal paired associate learning experiment and then gradually reintroduce features of the *kolon* game.

This strategy will clearly not be equally useful for the study of all cognitive phenomena, and for some it may be inapplicable. But it seems feasible and appropriate for pursuing many controversial issues in memory, problem-solving, classification, learning, communication, and related areas. At the least, the systematic study of a given phenomenon in a range of situations, including the quasi-experimental, should help us use the experiment to greater advantage in cross-cultural research. At the best it will move us along toward identifying the formal features of situations that affect cognitive performance. As we develop a framework which relates cognitive processes to their contexts, we may overcome the old dichotomies that have stood in the way of our fuller understanding of the interrelations between culture and cognition.

C. CROSS-CULTURAL RESEARCH AND PIAGETIAN THEORY: PARADOX AND PROGRESS

by Patricia M. Greenfield, *University of California, Los Angeles*

Approaching the methodology of cross-cultural Piagetian research from the perspective of Piagetian theory, I was struck by a series of paradoxical contradictions between the rich potential of the major theoretical constructs and their realization in empirical methods. The three paradoxes upon which my paper will focus are the paradox of the clinical method, the paradox of a developmental endpoint, and the paradox of adaptation and constructionism. For my examples, I will stick to tasks from the period of concrete operations, for this is where the largest and most varied body of research is to be found.

The paradox of the 'clinical method'. The 'clinical method' is a key theoretical element in Piaget's methodology. Applicable to Piaget's entire range of experimental techniques, it consists at base of individualized in-depth exploration of a given child's performance in such a way as to reveal underlying competence in the conceptual area being studied. Instead of a standardized procedure, later stimuli in an experimental session are based on the child's earlier responses (Flavell 1963). In Piaget's early applications of the method, it was heavily dependent on verbal interchange; in 1929 Piaget compared the clinical method to the psychiatric interview. The paradox is that while the original procedures were poorly suited to cross-cultural research, the theory of the clinical method offered some valuable concepts. The tension of this paradox led in turn to a change of emphasis in the clinical method itself.

The original procedures were poorly adapted to cross-cultural research because they often involved verbal explanation of one's own thought processes as well as hypothetical reasoning about the concrete task at hand. For instance, in a conservation of liquid situation, a child is first asked if the amount of liquid changes when it is poured from a container of one shape into a container of another shape. But 'true' conservation as defined by Piaget was diagnosed in terms of an ability to give reasons for the quantity judgment. Although it is possible to modify procedures to make the request for reasons more understandable in a non-Western culture (e.g., Greenfield 1966), nonetheless, the requisite ability to verbalize about one's own thought processes is extremely variable from culture to culture; this ability appears relatively lacking in traditional cultures, where informal learning is the dominant mode of education. Scribner and Cole (1972) summarize the findings by saying that the observational character of informal learning does not promote verbal formulation on the part of the learner anymore than it does on the part of the teacher. To base a diagnosis of conservation or other concepts on the ability to give reasons for one's judgment is thus to allow a general mental characteristic quite independent of specific concepts to overwhelm one's assessment of particular conceptual domains.

Furthermore, if the conservation subject correctly answers that the amount has not changed as a result of its transformation in appearance, then a 'counter-suggestion' is often given to probe for underlying conceptual structure: 'Last week a little boy told me that it is not still the same amount to drink; it's more because we poured the water into a taller glass. Is he right?' The validity of this hypothetical probe in many cultural settings is affected by the fact that skill in comprehending verbal material in the absence of a concrete referential context varies from culture to culture and, in fact, may be tied to the presence of a written language (Greenfield 1972) or more generally to formal school education. Experimental study in our own culture indicates that supportive nonverbal context is particularly important at the early stages of learning (Greenfield 1971) when concepts are unfamiliar. Thus, it may well be that hypothetical reasoning, in which one must imagine a context, so to speak, is particularly difficult when the material is unfamiliar, as Scribner and Cole (1972) suggest. A conservation experiment would of course constitute an unfamiliar and therefore hard to imagine context in many cultures; hence the difficulty in responding appropriately to the hypothetical probe of the Piagetian 'counter-suggestion', independent of one's understanding of the concept of quantity.

Thus defined, the irony of the clinical method applied cross-culturally is that the 'deeper' the experimenter tries to go in probing the foreign child's mental structures, the more superficial the level he is likely to tap.

Although the procedures are too self-conscious and hypothetical for meaningful cross-cultural translation, the theory of the clinical method is, at a more abstract level, a valid guideline for cross-cultural research. In fact, it shows a surprising congruence with the methodological principles proposed by Michael Cole and his colleagues (Cole, Gay, Glick and Sharp 1972; Cole and Bruner 1973). This group takes the view that because universal human cognitive competencies may be manifest in very different situations from culture to culture, the same underlying competency should be assessed in a wide variety of concrete situations or experimental tasks. Just like Piaget, they recommend variations around a theme in order to extract a picture of competence from a multitude of performances. In a sense this conception actualizes the 'clinical method' as a cross-cultural tool, for it involves designing a different range of testing situations from culture to culture, just as Piaget presents a different range from individual to individual within the same culture.

Dasen (1972) says that the 'clinical method' is attractive to cross-cultural research because it may be adapted to each cultural situation, but he fails to note the problems inherent in certain types of verbal questioning. More recently, however, Berry and Dasen (1974) state a need for nonverbal methods, but the work of Heron and his colleagues with purely nonverbal conservation tests in Zambia and Papua demonstrates (Heron and Simonsson 1969; Heron and Dowell 1973) that this is not the solution either in theory or practice.

In Papua, direct comparison of the nonverbal with the 'clinical method' indicated that maximum elimination of verbal discourse does not increase the chances of correctly solving the problem of weight conservation (Heron and Dowel 1973). In the Zambian study, extensive training in the nonverbal method and use of minimal verbal cues were necessary (Heron and Simonsson 1969). Thus the elimination of verbal instructions and responses seems neither to have made the conservation problems easy to administer nor easy to solve.

The problem of out-of-context communication involved in Piaget's clinical method may however be solved by presenting the necessary nonverbal referential context in the experimental situation itself. The use of demonstrations accompanying verbal instructions, as in Greenfield and Childs' (1973) pattern representation study among the Zinacantecos, is one way of doing this. A redundant perceptual-action context seems to be an important part of the earliest verbal interaction in language acquisition; and this fact ought to make a useful addition to the cross-cultural methodology for designing the most communicative experimental procedures. On the other hand, the complete elimination of language for symbolic-relational tasks, which language is specialized to handle, must add ambiguity rather than clarity.

The paradox of a developmental endpoint. One major criticism of Piaget's theory of development for cross-cultural research is that his notion of development is really the development of a Western scientist.[1] Gardner (1972) in comparing two major structuralists, Piaget and Levi-Strauss, points out that 'Western scientific thought, however crucia it may seem today, does not represent with any fidelity or comprehensiveness, the forms of thought valued in other cultures or during other periods' (p. 202). While Piaget himself (1966) recognized the need for studies to describe the final adult stages of cognitive development in other cultures, his concern was restricted to the operational level of these groups, in other words, to the development of Western scientific thinking. The paradox of the developmental endpoint has been that cross-cultural researchers failed to follow Piaget's own demonstration that, to study development, one must first understand the endstate toward which the developmental process is veering. An implication of Piaget's example for cross-cultural research is to ascertain the characteristics of an ideal type in a non-Western culture. Ideally, development in non-Western societies should be studied by members of the society itself. That way, the ideal type is a living reality rather than merely a theoretical abstraction, just as the model of the Western scientist is a living reality for Piaget, informing all his work. This ideal will become more and more realizable as scientific training becomes increasingly available in Third World countries. A second best approach is for a foreign social scientist to ascertain the ideal type through empirical research – interviews and the like. Wober (1974) has made just such an analysis of the Kiganda concept of intelligence in Uganda. Following such an analysis, the scientist is in a position to find out the developmental steps by which an infant grows up to this culturally defined endstate: what, to take the example of Kiganda intelligence, is the developmental process like by which the child achieves a measured, unhurried approach to affairs, one of the hallmarks of Kiganda intelligence? This principle of defining the developmental endstate, intrinsic to Piaget's own work, would paradoxically, lead away from Piagetian procedures.

Childs and I applied this methodological principle in studying cognitive development among the Zinacantecos, a Mayan group in Southern Mexico. Ethnographic study revealed that one of the hallmarks of the mature Zinacanteco woman is her skill in weaving. What we did was to

---

1. John Gabriel (1972) arrives at this same conclusion, although I have strong doubts about tthe particular line of argument that leads him there.

make videotapes of the weaving process carried out by young adults, acknowledged by other members of the community to be skilled weavers. At the same time we made tapes of girls at various definable stages in the process of learning to weave, starting with girls weaving their very first piece of cloth. We hope to put together this data to get a picture of the cognitive steps by which this highly valued Zinacanteco skill is attained and the nature of the instructional process by which it is accomplished.

Gay and Cole's (1967) work on quantitative concepts among the Kpelle provides another interesting example of the same principle. They looked at Kpelle skills in using quantitative concepts indigenous to the Kpelle culture – rice measures and so forth. Although this work was developed outside the Piagetian developmental tradition, it actually accomplishes for Kpelleland what Piaget accomplished for Switzerland in carrying out conservation experiments: the study of indigenous quantity concepts. In this sense, some non-Piagetian cross-cultural research comes paradoxically closer to the Piagetian spirit than most overtly Piagetian studies.

The paradox of adaptation and constructionism. No concept is more basic in Piagetian theory than adaptation. Adaptation occurs whenever an organism-environment encounter modifies the organism in such a way that further interchanges, favorable to its preservation, are enhanced (Flavell 1963). Adaptation as a psychological concept includes interpreting the outside world in terms of preexisting mental organization (assimilation) as well as making changes in that organization in response to particular properties of the world (accommodation). Piaget believes, furthermore, that cognitive development is not a given but rather a process of construction taking place through continuous interaction of organism with environment and always involving components of both assimilation and accommodation (Piaget 1970). The notions of adaptation and constructionism would seem to make cross-cultural research a natural for Piagetians. The study of environment-organism interactions under different conditions and their effects on the constructive process would seem an obvious method for studying the processes of adaptation so critical to cognitive development in Piaget's own scheme. The paradox is that this approach has been extremely rare in cross-cultural Piagetian research. A landmark study in this regard is that by Price-Williams, Gordon, and Ramirez (1967) in which early conservation of clay substance was shown to be an adaptation to the pottery-making process. These researchers demonstrate that, without the cultural environmental stimulus of learning to pot, conservation of clay occurs at a much later chronological age. So, the interactive process with clay whereby the potter transforms the shape of a constant quantity stimulates the construction of the conservation concept.

Why did this type of study occur so late, if adaptation and organism-environment interaction are such central concepts in Piaget's theory? The paradoxical reason is that although the role of organism-environment interaction is central to his constructionistic theory, Piaget has never specified the nature of these interactive processes nor has he himself made them the object of empirical study (even though all his experiments are in fact dynamic interactive situations, as specified by the clinical method). The study of Price-Williams and his colleagues contributed our first hint of naturally occurring organism-environment interactions through which Piagetian concepts are constructed by the child. For this reason, it makes a large contribution to Piagetian theory, as well as to the general field of cross-cultural psychology.

Recently, Durojaye (1972) has demonstrated a connection between other types of naturally occurring organism-environment interaction and order and rate of acquisition of various concrete operational concepts in six African cultures. For instance Durojaye finds that bead stringing hastens the development of conservation of number. Dasen (1973, 1974) has extended the study of the relation between Piagetian concepts and environmental adaptation to Australian Aborigines and Alaskan Eskimos. These studies integrate Piagetian tasks into the framework of ecological functionalism first conceived by Berry (1966). Although Piaget has a concept of horizontal *décalage* to describe time differences in the acquisition of various manifestations of concrete operational thought, he has dealt not at all with the problem of how time differential or *décalage* varies as a function of environment. Cross-cultural studies like the ones under discussion ought to contribute greatly to the solution of this problem within Piagetian theory.

A final step in actualizing Piaget's concept of constructive development through interaction is to analyze these interactive experiences themselves in addition to assessing their results. An important step has been taken in a thesis by Fitzgerald (1970) at Berkeley. She analyzed teaching-learning interactions between mothers and their children in three Ga subcultures in Ghana and correlated the interactive patterns with performance on several concrete operational tasks. Although subcultural membership was correlated with performance on the Piagetian tasks, a number of features of maternal teaching style showed an even stronger relation to Piagetian task performance. Fitzgerald concludes that the effect of subculture on test performance is mediated through mother-child interactions. The results of this study are an important step toward analyzing gross cultural variables into the interactive components by which they achieve their effects.

The paradox of the clinical method resolved. Cole (1973) points out that my research on the development of conservation of liquid quantity in Senegal is an early example of situational variation involving a Piagetian task. Looking at my study from this point of view modifies the interpretation of my findings in a Piagetian direction. Among the Wolof of Senegal, only about half the unschooled children manifested conservation of liquid quantity between eleven and thirteen years of age in two standard testing situations, (a) where the experimenter poured the liquid from one glass to a longer, thinner glass, and (b) where the experimenter poured the liquid from the same initial glass into six smaller glasses. In my original interpretation I stressed the fact that a large proportion of the oldest (11–13 years of age) unschooled Wolofs failed to attain conservation in both these situations, thus challenging the universality of Piaget's theory. While this remains an interesting and important fact, equally interesting is the fact that many 'nonconserving' children of a certain age did manifest conservation in two situations, (a) the first part of the 'standard' test involving the longer, thinner glass, or (b) both parts of the procedure where they transferred the water themselves. This could be considered an example of Cole's situational variation or Piaget's clinical method. In either case, my interpretation of cultural differences would be moderated to emphasize similar underlying competence[2] of all groups tested. Both aspects of the results – similarity and difference – are equally important to a valid and fair interpretation, just as Goodnow (1969) and Cole and Bruner (1971) have suggested in recent years.

But Piaget's own concept of the clinical method was not a static one. In his review of the book (Bruner, Olver, Greenfield *et al.* 1966) in which my Senegalese results appeared, Piaget (1967) began to stress the importance of testing concepts in a variety of action contexts, implicitly reducing the emphasis on the child's verbal analysis of his own thought processes.

2. A paper by Allean Keniston (1973) was very helpful to me in applying the competence-performance distinction to my conservation results in Senegal.

In the case of conservation of liquid, one of Piaget's suggested action variations was to ask the child to put equal amounts of liquid in two containers differing in shape. Would the child try to equalize levels, indicating a lack of conservation, or would he compensate for the lesser width of a container by pouring the liquid to a greater height, thus manifesting through his action at least one component of the conservation concept? The shift in emphasis exemplified by this procedure made a lot of sense in terms of Piaget's own theory, for action, not language, is seen as the basic mode of knowing in Piaget's system. Thus, the emphasis in the clinical method changed from diagnosis through verbal variation to diagnosis through action variation. Note, though, that Piaget makes no attempt to eliminate language, unlike Heron and Simonsson's (1969) approach. Rather language sticks close to the action context at hand instead of delving beneath it in a verbal explanation of thinking or going beyond it in creating an imaginary transformation of the present situation.

The inclusion of action variation in some cross-cultural research later carried out in Algeria by Bovet (1968), a member of Piaget's own team, confirmed my results and led to the first recognition of a culturally specific stage in a foreign culture by a Genevan researcher. This was the stage of pseudo-conservation. Unschooled five- and six-year-old Algerians were similar to the youngest unschooled Wolof group both in the absence of conservation judgments and in the attention to the experimenter's pouring action reflected in their reasons; seven- and eight-year-olds, in contrast, gave conservation judgments when water was poured from one container to another of a different shape. These same children, however, could not deal with the action variations such as the one just described where the child tries to equalize amounts in glasses of two different shapes. These children were called 'pseudo-conservers'.

Although I did not find such a stage among the Wolofs, this seems due to a procedural difference rather than to an actual difference in results. As mentioned earlier, I used a second Piagetian test of liquid quantity conservation not present in Bovet's study: The water was poured from a single glass into six shorter, narrower glasses. As I mentioned in my original article, this task was more difficult than the transfer to a single narrower glass, probably because it involved inequality in the sphere of action as well as perception. To be called a conserver in my study it was necessary to judge the amounts equal in both parts of the conservation test. In fact, most members of the middle (eight and nine) and oldest

(11 through 13) age groups classified as nonconservers made conservation judgments in the first part of the procedure where there was but a single pouring action; these children would have been classified as pseudo-conservers by Bovet. While this result thus parallels that of Bovet, an important difference remains. With increasing age, the pseudo-conservation pattern in Algeria gives way, first to nonconservation responses and then. by age eleven, to conservation – these latter two stages are a somewhat delayed version of the familiar pattern first observed in Switzerland (Piaget and Inhelder 1941). Among the unschooled Senegalese children in contrast, this 'pseudo-conservation' pattern persists among the eleven through thirteen-year-olds, a group even older than Bovet's Algerian conservers.

If my analysis is correct, then there is greater, although not complete, compatibility between Bovet's results in Algeria and my results in Senegal than she has noted. The exaggeration of the discrepancy points up, however, the necessity of situational variation. One more situational variant in Bovet's study and separate presentation of the data for the two different conservation situations in my own article would have eliminated the confusion and made the interpretation of both studies more accurate. In terms of the evolution of Genevan research and theory, it is interesting that a member of Piaget's own team has acknowledged the need for action variations in the cross-cultural context, thus completing the circle and bringing the clinical method into harmony with Cole's principle of situational variation. The lacunae in each study, my own and Bovet's, point up the need for even more systematic situational variation in cross-cultural Piagetian research (Cole 1973).

In a more recent article Bovet (1974) also recognizes that Piaget's earlier emphasis on verbally describing one's own reasoning is undesirable in comparative research; hence her analysis of the strengths and weaknesses of the clinical method, totally in harmony with my own, indicates that it has become a valuable tool for Genevan researchers, abroad as well as at home.

The paradox of the developmental endpoint resolved. Again, with respect to the developmental endpoint, Piaget shows himself far from static, his own major revisionist as he has said (1970). In a 1972 article on 'Intellectual evolution from adolescence to adulthood' Piaget talks about the diversification of development with age. The import of such diversification is that different individuals have different endpoints of cognitive development according to differences in aptitude and experience, especially occupational training. The Western scientist is in theory no longer the only possibility. Piaget leaves it as an open question whether this developmental diversification means that formal operational thinking, the highest stage in his developmental theory, will appear in different domains for different people, according to occupational role (e.g., law students will reason at the formal level about juridical but not physical concepts) or 'whether there will appear new and special structures that still remain to be discovered and studied' (p. 11). The latter alternative supports, by extension, a position of extreme cultural relativism, something very new in Piagetian theory. Piaget's question concerning the possibility of cognitive structures still to be discovered poses an important challenge for comparative study both within and between cultures.

Bovet's recent article also takes a large step toward resolving the second paradox of the developmental endpoint within the context of a Piagetian framework, for she tests Algerian adults from the same milieu as her younger subjects and relates their performance on various tasks (tests of quantity, weight, length, and time) to the skills required of male and female adults in this particular sociocultural milieu. For instance, adult male subjects showed immediate conservation of length while female subjects gradually reached the correct responses by a process of trial and error. (To give an example of how one tests for conservation of length, one task involved recognizing that changing the position of one of two equal lines does not destroy their equal length.) This sex difference corresponds to a difference in adult roles: Women are very much tied to their homes, while men spend much time away from home and frequently walk considerable distances. In another example, a particular way of comparing weights by weighing quantities in one's two hands, a method used by Algerian women in daily life, appears in response to a conservation of weight test. Thus, definition of cultural differences in the endstate of development and the relation of these differences to cognitive skills has been recognized in Geneva as a principle of cross-cultural research, thus bridging the gap between Piaget's definition of development in terms of the Western scientist and the varied application of Piagetian theory to other cultures (or subcultures) having different ideal types.

The paradox of adaptation and constructionism resolved. Finally, Bovet (1974) explicitly recognizes that Piaget's principles of interaction and construction, as well as his biological leanings (closely related to the notion of adaptation) 'provide a fitting framework for cross-cultural research' (p. 313). She adopts training procedures as a necessary aspect of cross-cultural research. Although she recognizes training procedures as situational variants that help in diagnosing the competence of people in very different cultures, she gives almost no recognition to these procedures as tools to discover what kinds of interactions with the environment are required for the construction of operational Piagetian concepts in the course of development. Perhaps this is why she fails to recognize the contribution of my pouring procedure to the conservation of quantity in unschooled Wolof subjects. As mentioned earlier, when these children did the pouring themselves – both to a single taller, thinner beaker and to six smaller beakers, they typically realized that the quantities were still the same; and their justifications referred back to the initial equalizing operation. Bovet implies that this was probably pseudo-conservation because the equalizing operation, being difficult, has done nothing more than capture their attention. This fact cannot, however, explain our results because the matched group in the standard procedure also equalized the water in the two identical glasses at the beginning of the procedure, although the experimenter carried out the subsequent transfer of liquid from one container to another. Yet that group did not show conservation in both parts of the test.

Bovet also does not account for the fact that older (eight-through thirteen-year-old) unschooled Wolof subjects who had the experience of transferring liquid from container to container also manifest conservation on two subsequent posttests where the experimenter once again did all the pouring. The phenomenon seems in fact very similar to Bovet's own account of conservation of weight in Algerian adults for whom weight concepts are used in daily life:

'For some of the nonconserving subjects, all that was required for them to grasp the notion of conservation, was to weigh the two pieces of clay once on a pair of scales in front of them. They then accompanied their judgments by logical justifications and, what is more, generalized their conservation responses to various changes in shape.

'It has been noted that in the case of children, a single demonstration is not sufficient to elicit a more advanced judgment (Smedslund, 1961). We conclude therefore that in these adult subjects an underlying logical way of apprehending the problem coexists with an intuitive approach' p. 325).

Another interpretation may be more revealing: The weighing experience is the organism-environment interaction which allows the construction of the operational concept out of intuitive knowledge, just as the pouring experience is the crucial environmental interaction for the Wolof children. Amount is important in the daily life of Wolof children, just as weight is for the Algerian adults. Bovet's results suggest that such practical usage is an important factor in the successful effect of a one-time 'training' experience.

My original interpretation of the training effect stressed the change in thinking that seemed to result from the experience. Equally important to a balanced interpretation is another set of facts. The first fact is that the inferred change resulted from a single brief experience, indicating a preexisting competence on the part of the subjects. This competence consisted partly of maturational readiness, for the magnitude of the training effect was proportional to age. It may also have resulted from interactions concerning quantity in everyday life, for Bovet found that short-term experience with concepts irrelevant to everyday Algerian life – such as speed and time – did not have such an effect on operational thinking. Thus, Bovet may have contributed to a specification of the interactive processes by which concepts are constructed by making this distinction between the effects of operational training in adults with and without related practical experience. Bovet's study (1974) thus makes a large contribution to the analysis of environmental interaction required for the construction of an operational concept. Because this interactive process of construction is theoretically central to Piaget, Bovet's Algerian study exemplifies the enormous value of cross-cultural research to Piagetian theory.

In conclusion, if Piaget has, in the past, led the cross-cultural enterprise astray, it is because researchers have followed his procedures rather than his theory. Deviations from the procedures, past and present, have, on the other hand, enhanced the theory, especially contributing to the concept of development as a constructive process occurring through interaction with the environment. While Piaget's writings do not suggest the new techniques necessary for further advance, it is hard to imagine future cross-cultural research that will fail to harmonize with and further actualize Piaget's basic notion of development as a constructive process involving the adaptive interaction of a biological organism with its environment.

D. CROSS-CULTURAL PIAGETIAN STUDIES: WHAT CAN THEY TELL US?

by Jerry S. Carlson,* *University of California, Riverside*

Piaget (1966) suggests four basic factors which affect the progressive hierarchization and differentiation involved in cognitive development. They are: (a) biological factors, which relate to genetic potential and maturation of the nervous system; (b) equilibration factors, which are viewed as autoregulatory and in continuous interaction with the biological potential of the individual and his environmental circumstance and which are assumed to be ubiquitous; (c) general social factors independent from formal schooling which engender social contact, exchange, collaborations, and so forth; and (d) factors of educative and cultural transmissions which include social pressures and language patterns. All of these factors are interactive. For example, for the individual to be affected by any aspect of socialization, he must actively assimilate the data from his milieu. This presupposes some level of cognitive organization or operatory structure and the general process of equilibration. Development, as affected by these four factors, progresses through the integration of successive structures which are manifested through stages and substages, each having criterial attributes, each forming the necessary precursor to a higher level of organization.

What Piaget suggests concerning this progress is (a) that the order is constant through the stages, though differences in environmental milieu may be related to accelerations or retardations in age of acquisition; (b) that each stage is characterized by a general structure; and (c) that as progression is made through the stages, preceding structures are integrated into successive ones.

In a recent article, Piaget (1972) has reemphasized the importance he attaches to sociocultural factors, and professional and work specialization. He maintains and reaffirms, however, the necessity for an invariant sequence of development as well as the hypothesis that formal operational thought is available in general, rather than to specific 'culturally advantaged' groups, albeit that in certain environmental contexts formal

* The author is grateful to Dr. Pierre Dasen for his many helpful comments and criticisms of an earlier extended version of this paper.

operations might not be attained until relatively late (15 to 20 years of age). Assessment of this might be difficult, though, as 'They (individuals whose schooling is limited) would, therefore, be capable of thinking formally in their particular field, whereas faced with our experimental situations, their lack of knowledge or the fact they have forgotten certain ideas that are particularly familiar to children still in school or college, would hinder them from reasoning in a formal way, and they would give the appearance of being at the concrete level' (Piaget 1972, p. 10).

Description of approaches taken to cross-cultural research has been made by several authors (Berry 1969; Berry and Dasen 1973; Cole and Bruner 1971; Cole, Gay, Glick and Sharp 1971; Frijda and Jahoda 1966; Jahoda 1970; Le Vine 1970; Piaget 1966; Vernon 1969). One approach of cross-cultural research in cognitive development is to collect comparative data from different cultural or ethnic groups and compare these data with the results obtained in the milieu in which the tests were designed. This, the etic approach described by Berry (1969) assumes the universality of the criteria involved as well as the functional equivalence of these criteria as phenomena occurring naturally within the target society.

Lack of confirmation of the etic assumption can lead to more refined approximations of the universality of categories and comparison with criteria which are internal (emic in nature) and not dependent on universal assumptions. From the approach of the etic assumption, the *modus operandi* of most Piagetian cross-cultural research, poor performance on a particular test does not necessarily imply psychological deficit. It could be that the materials used, the questions asked, and the procedures employed simply didn't elicit the 'appropriate' responses, strategies, or processes. And, perhaps, under appropriate 'elaboration' conditions, or clever modifications of the test materials – Price-William (1961) for conservation concepts among the Tiv children in Nigeria, and Gay and Cole (1967) for classification for Kpelle children in Liberia – very different patterns of responses might be obtained.

When one considers cross-cultural Piagetian research there are several questions which should be dealt with. (1) What types of questions within Piagetian theory are amenable to cross-cultural research? (2) How well can Piagetian studies help determine the importance of and differentiate between the factors affecting mental development, i.e., those proposed by Piaget, Vernon, and LeVine? (3) Of what practical significance is cross-cultural Piagetian research? (4) What types of research within the Piagetian framework might be helpful in the future? In some ways these questions are interrelated; in some ways they are independent. For sake of clarity they will be discussed independently and in order.

What types of questions within Piagetian theory are amenable to cross-cultural research? (a) For Piaget, logic mirrors thought. It is a natural consequence of the development of intelligence, for at the base of rational thought, logic must exist. The logical analysis Piaget applies to thinking processes allows for formalization of their contents and their commonalities. Hence, an appropriate mode of analysis of structures is through the logical properties they possess. Concerning the universality and relevance of the development of logical processes, Piaget argues that logical formulation is essential; it is a necessity for the development of thought.

Lévi-Strauss (1966) points out that logic is the basis of action and rational inquiry in both technologically advanced and nontechnological societies. He suggests that there are certain universals such as the forming of classes. Although such formations manifest themselves in different ways and at different levels of abstraction between groups of people, they are based on the same types of mental operations.

Smedslund (1969) posits that logic is a necessary precondition for effective mental functioning and that there are indeed some logical universals. He suggests that one such universal is the elementary notion of number. This concept is not based upon specific content but reflects basic operations that cannot be understood or specified in any way other than logical. The central question of exactly what these forms of logic are and how helpful analysis in Piagetian terms is is now an area of research. Such an analysis necessarily depends not only on the study of the development of logical thinking in children but also on an understanding of the logics employed by the adult population. It might turn out that the logical bases for classifactory behavior, number, and other areas requiring concrete operational thought are universal. But would such universality hold for all stages of development, e.g., formal operational thought?

(b) Though considered important at one time by researchers in the field, Piaget has essentially discounted the importance of finding children from various cultures passing through the same stages at the *same ages*. He points out (Piaget 1972, p. 7) that 'the average age at which children go through each stage can vary considerably from one social environment to another, or from one country or even region within a country to another'. This he posits to be due to the quantity and quality of the intellectual stimulation afforded by the environment and suggests that these factors are of increasing significance as one moves up through the stages.

Support for the differential effects environmental stimulation plays in development during the sensorimotor stage has been offered by Paraskevopoulos and Hunt (1971). Using age as a dependent variable, they compared the ages of infants living in Athenian orphanages with different infant-caretaker ratios (10:1 and 3:1) with home-reared infants on a criterion from the ordinal scales developed by Uzgiris and Hunt. The children in the 10:1 ratio could follow an object through hidden displacement without reversibility at 45 months of age; for the children in the 3:1 ratio, the average was 30 months. The results were interpreted as showing the strong effects of environment on age of acquisition of the criterion.

Similar findings of differential ages of acquisition of concrete operational thought due to milieu are numerous (Bovet 1968; Dasen 1973; deLacey 1970; Goldschmid et al. 1973; Goodnow 1962). It is important to note that in each of these investigations it was shown that concrete operational thought was obtained, although often delayed by environmental factors. Conversely, Price-Williams, Gordon and Ramirez (1969) found acceleration for the conservation of substance for pottery-making children in Mexico over a group of non-pottery-making children matched on age, years of schooling, and socioeconomic level. They found no differences between the groups for conservation of number, liquid, weight, and volume, however.

The age of acquisition though of formal thought seems to be much more variable and related to milieu effects than development during the sensorimotor period or the acquisition of concrete operational thought. For example, severe delay and even nonacquisition of formal operational structures for lower SES American samples has been found (Graves 1972). Similar results of nonacquisition of formal thought for non-American samples have been reported by Goodnow (1962).

(c) The question of stage sequence is more critical than age of acquisition. Three interpretations of sequence need to be distinguished: (i) succession of global stage (sensorimotor, concrete operational, and formal), (ii) discrepancies due to horizontal *décalages*, and (iii) the sequence of substages for any particular test.

Concerning the succession of global stage, Flavell (1971) tentatively suggests that such a sequence is neither due to genetic programing nor the way in which the environment affects the individual. The sequence from concrete to formal thought is logically necessary inasmuch as those operations which are required for formal thought are the results of already available concrete operations. This interpretation, though not necessarily implying that formal thought will be acquired, would mean that sequence is unalterable.

The second point concerning horizontal *décalage* raises some very difficult and certainly unresolved issues. Piaget (1971) suggests that time lags are due to the resistances which objects offer. For example, in a classification task some types of materials will present greater difficulty for the child than other types of materials. Hence, a lower level of performance will be obtained. These differences cannot be predicted in advance by his theory, however, and become evident only after the fact.

Though a number of reversals of acquisition have been reported (see Dasen 1972a), they are not based on longitudinal data. Too, since horizontal *décalage* is accepted as a general, though perhaps pesky, phenomenon, it is not crucial to confirmation of Piaget's general theory. It is certainly of lesser significance than the issue of global sequence or sub-stages on a particular test.

The third point is on stage progression on individual tests. The overwhelming majority of research studies has found the same stages as Piaget has described. It is possible that Piagetian tasks are less 'culture-bound' than other assessment devices and that the 'natural' environment of the child is such that etic approximations can be found. A central question remains, however, and it pertains to process rather than product: Although children seem to be giving correct responses to a Piagetian problem, say conservation or classification, are they really employing the same, or at least very similar, conceptual bases for their responses? It seems as though we know very little about the conceptual bases actually employed, and it might be that attention of cross-cultural Piagetian researchers should be directed toward this area.

(d) Generally when one thinks of causation he refers to factors in an individual's or in a group's genetic make-up as well as all the factors from the individual's or the group's environmental milieu which contribute in some way to the acquisition of a particular characteristic, behavior, or developmental pattern. What is meant here by causation is much more circumscribed and refers to specific postulates that certain sets of environmental circumstance are related to a particular acquisition or developmental sequence. An example which might be used to make this clearer comes from the area of moral development.

Piaget (1965) views the development of moral judgment to be strongly related to cultural-environmental factors. For example, in the area of justice two divergent attitudes present themselves: punishment by expiation, which is stern, unbending, arbitrary, and not specifically related to the act of transgression, and punishment by reciprocity, which is imposed in a sense relative to the content and nature of the transgression. The latter has value in terms of the prevention of future transgressions. Piaget considers the movement from expiatory punishment to punishment by reciprocity to be largely due to the relationships which hold between children. He suggests that 'the sense of justice, though naturally capable of being reinforced by precepts and practical example of the adult, is largely independent of the influences, and requires nothing more for its development than the mutual respect and solidarity which holds among children themselves' (Piaget 1965, p. 198). It is clearly hypothesized that the quality of peer group relationships is of great significance and that punishment by reciprocity and mature view of the effect of punishment on later deed are related.

In a recent study (Carlson 1973) it was found that for Laotian children, ages six through fourteen, there were many more mature responses, even for the youngest groups of children, to a protocol separating punishment by expiation from reciprocity than one finds for European children. On the other hand, for an item dealing with the effect of punishment on later deeds, there seemed to be no developmental pattern at all. It was concluded that these two areas, in contrast to conclusions based on data from Western cultures, are quite distinct and that the latter, effect of punishment on later deed, cannot be attributed to the quantity and quality of peer-group interactions, which in Laos are very highly developed. This gives just one example where divergencies in development, studied in a cultural setting different from the one in which the original work was done, can shed light on developmental phenomena which otherwise might be assumed to be structurally related or to stem from certain environmental conditions.

How well can cross-cultural Piagetian studies help differentiate and determine the importance of the factors of mental development? (a) As far as can be determined there is only one investigation which gives support to the notion of a strong hereditary factor to Piagetian cognitive development (deLemos 1969). DeLemos administered conservation of number, substance, length, weight, area, and volume tests to two groups of Australian Aboriginals: one group with mixed blood, one group totally Aboriginal. Her findings were as follows: (1) There was a similar, though much retarded, progression on the Piaget measures as found for European children; (2) there was a reversal in the expected order of conservation, conservation of quantity followed conservation of weight; and (3) there was evidence of better performance by the mixed-blood than the full-blood Aboriginals. The latter finding was interpreted as being due to genetic factors as it was argued that the environments of the two groups were the same. Eysenck (1971) used the deLemos results to support his argument that there is a large genetic component in IQ and that individuals with more negroid blood are more deficient on measures of IQ than those with mixed blood. From the deLemos study such a conclusion is inappropriate for a number of reasons of which only three shall be mentioned here.

First, it cannot be argued, as Eysenck (1971, p. 95) does, that just because a progression of development similar to European children was found, that the tests themselves were relevant to the Aboriginal samples Second, although it has been shown that conservation and mental age are fairly closely related in American samples (Anooshian and Carlson 1973; Goldschmid 1967), it doesn't necessarily follow that such a relationship will obtain for individuals from vastly different environmental circumstances. Third, and perhaps more important, Dasen (1972b) was unable to replicate deLemos' findings and in another study (Dasen, deLacey and Seagrim 1972) found that Aboriginal children raised in European families attained concrete operations at almost the identical rate as middle-class European children.

Based on Piagetian cross-cultural research, it would appear that too little is known about genetic factors to warrant the conclusion of their relative importance or unimportance to development. Furthermore the interactive aspects of genetic potential and environmental stimulation play a central role in Piaget's theory and perhaps cannot be separated in a quantitative manner (Furth 1973; Overton and Reese 1973).

(b) The effects of early stimulation on development during the sensorimotor period have been discussed (Paraskevopoulos and Hunt 1971). In a study of considerable interest Dasen (1973) examined the relationship between divergent ecological demands and the development of (i) conservation of quantity, weight, volume, and length; (ii) seriation; and (iii) spatial tests of orders rotation and horizontality. Three groups of subjects were used: Australian Aboriginals with medium contact with

European culture, Aboriginals with low contact with European culture, and a European group. It was hypothesized that (1) though differential rates of development would be found, the stage sequence of the Aboriginals development would be the same as that found for the Europeans; (2) the rate of development would be faster in the medium as opposed to the low contact Aboriginals; and (3) due to the ecological and cultural background of the Aboriginals, especially the low contact group for whom survival requires the use of detailed 'cognitive maps', spatial concepts would develop more readily than logico-mathematical ones (i.e., conservation and seriation).

All of Dasen's hypotheses were supported. There were some unexpected results, though, as he found greater lag in performance for the Aboriginals than expected. Too, although performance on the spatial relations test was higher than on the logico-mathematical test for the Aboriginals (the opposite was found for the Europeans) and the medium contact Aboriginals out-performed the low contact group on the logico-mathematical relations test, no difference in performance between the medium and low contact Aboriginal groups was found on the spatial relations test. This was surprising as the low contact group is dependent on nomadic hunting and was expected to develop spatial skill at a faster rate than the medium contact group which is less dependent on traditional food-gathering techniques.

The results of research concerning the effects of formal schooling on the on the acquisition of Piagetian concepts are divergent. A number of studies (Goodnow and Bethon 1966; Mermelstein and Shulman 1967; Heron 1971) have shown the relative lack of importance of schooling for the development of concrete operational thought. Other investigators (Greenfield 1966) dispute this, however, and argue for the importance of schooling as an aid in the development of concrete operational thought. Certainly the effects of schooling on development are not clear. One reason for the confused results might be that the *nature* of the schooling involved has not been adequately examined. Perhaps only certain types of school experiences will make significant contribution to the development of children's logical thinking capabilities. Evidence for this has been offered by Allen (1968). He found performance for children exposed to a cognitively based science curriculum (Science Curriculum Improvement Study) was significantly better on Piagetian measures of logical thinking than performance for children whose science instruction followed the traditional pattern. The question is not schooling versus no schooling, rather type of schooling versus no schooling. If this question is to be seriously investigated cross-culturally, it would require an experimental and interventionist approach, an approach which heretofore has been lacking in cross-cultural Piagetian research.

As development progresses it might well be that environmental factors, including schooling, play an ever more important role. This implies that formal thought would be more affected by these variables than concrete operational or sensorimotor development. The few studies (Collis 1971; Graves 1972) done to date on formal operational thought and the schooling variable suggest that this is the case, but again, clarity of *type* versus amount of schooling is necessary.

What this implies is a model that shows not only increasing variability of performance with increasing age, but greater importance of environmental factors with age. The latter is in contrast to the model posited by Bloom (1964) in which environmental circumstance plays a decreasing role in development with age, although individual variation might continue to increase.

Another area of differentiation which should be drawn is between general versus specific effects of environment on Piagetian development. Indeed a number of studies have attempted to do this (Furby 1971) but a more 'anthropologically based' approach might be necessary for the types of distinction desired. As Galperin (1967) has pointed out, one must consider the societal nature and organization of all symbols (including all the forms of work engaged in by individuals) within the society. This requires a thorough knowledge of societal organization and transmission as well as an understanding of how the individual will be affected and will affect such organization. To look at just the 'tools' of the society and infer how they affect individual development is not enough. The nature of these tools and their dialectical relationship to societal organization and individual cognition must be understood. For such an analysis, fusion of the efforts of psychologists and anthropologists is necessary.

Little work has been done in the assessment of personality factors as they relate to acquisition of such Piagetian concepts as conservation. Using American samples, the investigations of Goldschmid (1968) and Peters (1967) are instructive, however. Goldschmid found that such affective variables as objectivity of self-evaluation, peer preference, less domination by mothers, and general social attractiveness and passivity were related to various measures of conservation. Peters found attentiveness, impulse control, resistance to distraction, independence to task-oriented situations, and friendly assertiveness to be correlated with acquisition of conservation of number. The generality of such findings has not been adequately tested through cross-cultural research, however, and work along these lines could be most informative.

In summary, cross-cultural research efforts designed to differentiate between and determine the importance of the many factors related to cognitive development is in its infancy. We are in position of having many more questions than answers.

Of what practical significance is cross-cultural Piagetian research? One area of great practical significance and applicability of Piagetian research is education. It has been clearly demonstrated that level of cognitive function is of critical importance to performance on cognitively based curricula (Freyburg 1966; Field and Cropley 1969) and, in turn, exposure to such a curriculum can affect level of cognitive functioning (Allen 1968). Knowledge of a child's level of development can and should be used to help 'make the match' between capability and expectation.

Hunt (1967) makes this point in respect to general motivation. He suggests that there is an optimum level of incongruity between the incoming information and the level of development which the individual is at. Too little incongruity probably produces boredom; too much incongruity produces emotional stress; just the right amount of incongruity produces the motivation underlying intellectual growth.

The evidence presented on the relationship between school achievement and level of development was for science and the methods of instruction accompanying this curriculum area. Unfortunately, far too little effort is made in both technologically advanced and nontechnological countries to develop curricula which go beyond memory and rote learning. (Or even if the effort is made, as it has been done in the United States, it remains largely unimplemented.) It has been demonstrated that cognitive variables account for only 30% to 50% of the variance for school achievement in the U.S.; non-intellective predictors account for the rest (Fend 1971). One can more than surmise that in nontechnological societies even less variance in school achievement would be in the cognitive domain. Accordingly, schools seem to require a great deal about which Piaget's theory of intellectual development has little to say. This conclusion reflects not on Piagetian theory so much as on the goals and practices which one finds in education today.

What types of research within the Piagetian framework might be helpful in the future? In this section only a summary of avenues of research which would appear to be fruitful for the future will be dealt with. In many instances these have been anticipated in the previous discussion.

A strategy which has only very rarely been employed in cross-cultural research is the longitudinal approach. The longitudinal approach can be used in the study of causal factors involved in growth and can ably describe both childhood experiences and the result, adult behaviors. Too, through the use of longitudinal studies with co-twin controls, a closer approximation of the relative effects of environment and heredity factors can be gained.

Often cross-cultural research compares one age sample in a particular culture with the same or a similar age sample from another milieu. Such studies are of interest but do not provide for analysis of developmental trends. Developmental data are needed in order to make appropriate comparisons so that problems of time displacement *(décalage)* will not lead to the perhaps spurious conclusion that a true deficit exists. Fortunately most of the recent cross-cultural Piagetian studies take this consideration seriously and look for developmental trends rather than single age groups comparisons.

A basic problem remains though: lack of intensive knowledge of the culture under study. The psychologist and anthropologist must combine their efforts so that a genuine understanding of the processes of development might be arrived at. A study of the products of development through comparative studies is informative but necessarily falls short without the necessary analysis of the societal conditions, in all their complexity, in which the individual grows and develops. What this implies is the requirement of combining the emic approach described by Berry (1969) with the etic assumptions which might have motivated the research question in the first place.

Another approach which would be helpful in understanding processes of development would be through the use of experimental studies in conjunction with *ex post facto* designs. Correlational methods can provide baseline data and indications of the probable causal effects of a variable or a number of variables. Extending this approach to the manipulation of variables thought to be causal in an experimental design would lead to extension of external validity and perhaps confirmation of etic processes. There is a wealth of data, for example, from a host of training studies carried out in the U.S. and Europe on acquisition of various Piagetian concepts. The question of how widely these findings are applicable is still open, however.

In summary, this paper has attempted to outline some basic aspects of Piaget's theory and place them in cross-cultural perspective. Several questions concerning approaches and the relevance of cross-cultural research for clarification of Piagetian theory were discussed. It was concluded that although a great deal of information has been gained from cross-cultural investigations, many critical research questions are still outstanding.

Cultural differences in socialization techniques

A. MATERNAL SOCIALIZATION PRACTICES AND SPATIAL-PERCEPTUAL ABILITIES IN NEWFOUNDLAND AND LABRADOR*

by Pauline A. Jones, *Memorial University of Newfoundland, St. John's, Canada*

Prominent among current theories of intelligence is the hierarchical model proposed by Vernon and earlier suggested by Burt. Vernon conceives abilities as if organized in a hierarchy where the g-factor or general intelligence is the most prominent component in that it accounts for the greatest proportion of differences in abilities. Over and above this he sees abilities as falling into two major types – the verbal-educational and the spatial-perceptual-practical. This paper will deal with the relevance of cultural variables, including socialization practices, for performance on tasks which may be viewed as measures of the spatial-perceptual factor.

Goodnow (1969) has cited studies which suggest that one of the sharpest differences among cultural groups may lie in imaging or spatial-type tasks. While explanations of how such differences arise are varied, they seem to fall into two groups, cultural and ecological. On the one hand, Goodnow (1969), for example, has suggested that the availability of such factors of industrialized society as television and quality schooling may be especially

* This research was supported by Canada Council Research Grants S70-1063 and S71-1263.

important for the development of spatial-type skills. Vernon (1966) and MacArthur (1973), however, have both shown that Eskimos are close to English norms on most perceptual-spatial tasks, thus indicating that good spatial performances occur without exposure to such cultural stimulation as is commonly provided by quality schools and other social media. Vernon looks to another environmental variable, namely, the extent to which the boy's background is purposeful, planful, and male-oriented. Berry's (1966) results confirm Vernon's findings, and, like Vernon, he stresses the importance of socialization practices but has detailed (1971) how such factors arise to supplement ecological characteristics in producing certain spatial skills. Berry argues that traditional hunting and fishing ecologies, like that of the Eskimo, necessitate the development of spatial-perceptual skills in order to hunt and fish effectively. Following Barry, Child, and Bacon (1959) he has further suggested that certain cultural variables, such as socialization practices, are functionally related to the physical environment and mediate the predicted relationship between ecology and the development of particular skills. Specifically, hunting, fishing, and food-gathering peoples are thought to stress more resourceful traits. Berry (1966) found that the Eskimo tended to be less severe in disciplining children, but he has indicated that his assessment of socialization practices was weak.

Child-rearing practices have also been related to the development of spatial ability through research by Witkin (1967) concerning the construct, field dependence. Embedded Figures, used as a measure of field dependence, may be considered as a measure of Vernon's spatial-perceptual-practical factor and of Thurstone's original spatial factor. Vernon (1972) has in fact shown that there is no evidence, in the field independence group tests which he used, of a perceptual independence ability distinct from the spatial ability or visualization factor. Witkin has emphasized the importance of mother-child relationships for the development of field independence. The closely interrelated factors, handling of separation, regulation of impulse expression, and personal characteristics of parents affecting their part in these processes constitute a socialization cluster which was found to relate to the child's progress toward the development of field independence (Dyk and Witkin 1965).

In order to clarify the relative importance of both ecological and cultural variables for the development of spatial-perceptual skills, a study was carried out using five subgroups of subjects from communities in the province of Newfoundland and Labrador. The study was initially designed to test two hypotheses, namely, that (1) cultural stimulus, independent of ecological press, is positively related to spatial skill, and that (2) ecological press, independent of cultural stimulus, is positively related to spatial skill. The study was designed also to examine the relationship between socialization practices and spatial ability and to determine whether socialization practices are functionally related to the demands of a fishing ecology.

Method. Initially, four samples of grade VI boys were selected from contrasting areas of Newfoundland. One sample ($N = 25$) whose fathers were fishermen came from the extremely isolated communites of southern Newfoundland. Two samples were selected from towns in northeast Newfoundland. Fathers of one of these groups ($N = 26$) were fishermen; thus this sample was equated with the south coast sample in terms of ecological demands but was higher in cultural stimulus, as a result of the larger size of the communities, and their closer contact with other parts of the Province. A comparison of these two groups provided the primary test of hypothesis 1. The second sample from the same northeast communities consisted of boys whose fathers were not fishermen but who were of a similar occupational level ($N = 25$). Using Blishen's index for occupations in Canada (1967), this sample had a mean occupational level of 31.85. Since the two subgroups from northeastern Newfoundland were exposed to the same cultural stimulus, but to different ecological demands, they served to test hypothesis 2. A fourth group ($N = 26$) was selected from the city of St. John's. Fathers were engaged in work other than fishing but were matched with the other samples for occupational level. This sample had a mean occupational level of 31.45. The St. John's sample was included for comparison purposes and to provide further variation in terms of cultural stimulus. Additionally, a sample ($N = 22$) of grade VI boys from southern Labrador was obtained. These boys, the sons of fishermen, came from communities where the pattern of life revolves more around the traditional fishery than it does in south coast Newfoundland communities. Inclusion of the Labrador sample provided a second test of hypothesis 1 and allowed a further examination of a functional relationship between socialization practices and the demands of a fishing ecology. Each of the five samples was composed of Caucasian subjects.

Three measures were used to assess spatial-perceptual ability. The Embedded Figures Test (Witkin, Oltman, Raskin and Karp 1971) was used as measure of perceptual field independence. This test, individually administered, consisted of 12 figures with a three-minute limit per trial. The Block Design from the WISC was administered as a measure of spatial ability as was the spatial subscale from the Primary Mental Abilities Test. The latter was given on a group basis. Raven's Progressive Matrices was given primarily for control of the general intellectual factor. While there were no differences in mean Progressive Matrices score among the preliminary four samples, the Labrador sample was, however, significantly lower in mean Matrices score.

Socialization practices were assessed by means of a 100-item questionnaire developed by Witkin and colleagues to classify mother-child interactions as fostering or interfering with the development of field independence. The questionnaire, consisting of 11 subscales, was developed on the basis of interview data such as were reported by Dyk and Witkin (1965) and was in an early stage of validation up to the time of use in the present study. In this case the questionnaire was administered during a home visitation of approximately one hour, and each question was discussed with the mother. Additionally, on the basis of observation and discussion with the mother during the course of administering the questionnaire, each mother was rated as fostering or interfering with the development of differentiation. Home interview responses were also supplemented by a brief interview with each boy based on questions used by Berry (1966, p. 221) to assess severity of discipline.

Results and discussion. Hypotheses 1 and 2 were tested through use of the t-ratio for independent samples. A test for the possible relevance of cultural stimulus, independent of ecological press, was made by comparing scores for the northeast fishing sample, first with those for the south coast fishing sample, and second with those for the Labrador fishing sample. Spatial-perceptual ability as indicated by both the time score ($t = 2.49$, $p < .05$) and the number of correct responses ($t = 2.33, p < .05$) on the EFT was significantly different across samples in the first comparison. The respective means were 1345.9 versus 1589.2 for the score in seconds and 6.73 versus 5.08 for number correct on the EFT. The difference in these measures across the Labrador and northeast fishing samples was of borderline significance ($t = 1.65$ and 1.68 respectively). These findings with reference to the Embedded Figures thus supported the hypothesis that cultural stimulus is positively related to spatial skill. Results from the Block Design and the PMA spatial test both tended to support the hypothesis; however, differences did not reach the significance level.

Neither of the spatial-perceptual measures was significantly different across the northeast fishing and non-fishing samples, thus refuting the hypothesis of an independent effect for ecological press. In fact, whatever differences were found were in the direction of the non-fishing sample.

Failure to support the relevance of ecological demands for spatial ability may be explained by one or both of two factors. While it was postulated that socialization practices among families engaged in fishing would differ from those of the other families and would be such as to further enhance the development of spatial-perceptual ability, this assumption was not empirically validated as may be seen from Table 1. It may also be that the fishing communities sampled were not characteristic of the traditional subsistence level societies described by Berry (1971). Findings relating specifically to hypotheses 1 and 2 are more fully discussed in Jones (1973), where spatial-perceptual measures for the five samples are presented. Discussion in the present paper will focus primarily upon the relevance of socialization practices for the development of spatial ability and upon the relationship of such practices to the fishing ecology.

Following the suggestion made by Berry (1971) for subsistence level societies, it was postulated that socialization practices among families engaged in fishing would be such as to enhance the development of spatial-perceptual ability. Whether or not the fishing communities, either from Newfoundland or Labrador, are characteristic of the subsistence level society for which Berry's model may have relevance is, of course, open to question. However, the present three fishing samples may undoubtedly be placed on a continuum anchored by the subsistence level economy. The pattern of life in the Labrador communities revolves more around the traditional fishery than it does in south coast Newfoundland communities and certainly more than in the northeast Newfoundland communities. While occupational alternatives to the fishery are available within the northeast communities, the fishermen of Labrador have no alternative unless they were prepared to abandon their homes and way of life, possessions which on the contrary they appear to be striving to maintain. The shortness of the fishing season on the Labrador, coupled with the greater economic requirements of larger families, also support the closer proximity of the Labrador fishing communities to the subsistence level society. The mean number of siblings for the Labrador sample was 7.32 as compared with 6.44 for the south coast and 4.67 for the northeast Newfoundland fishing samples. A test of the hypothesis regarding a relationship between ecological press and socialization practices was made by examining such practices across the three fishing samples. Differences across the groups were examined by the use of one-way analyses of variance. Table 1 presents the means for the various socialization measures across the three fishing samples and also presents the F ratios obtained.

Table 1. *Summary of means and F ratios for socialization measures across three fishing samples*

| Variables | Samples | | | F ratio[a] |
	Northeast fishing	Southcoast	Labrador	
M-C interaction fostering field independence	409.9	398.4	357.3	8.68
Mother views self as successful mother	71.3	70.0	60.4	8.47
Wife-husband relations in childrearing	18.3	15.8	16.9	1.85
Mother satisfied with motherhood	25.8	25.2	25.6	0.10
Childrearing not a burden	40.4	38.2	36.0	1.47
Child not viewed as delicate	30.3	29.9	24.4	3.78
Child responsible for own care	6.5	7.2	6.4	0.33
Independence training	91.1	86.9	72.1	8.14
Training, discipline, punishment, aggression	77.4	78.5	76.7	0.16
Individuality	28.5	27.8	21.8	8.23
OK for child to be loner	9.9	9.5	8.2	1.32
'Good student' important	10.4	9.3	9.0	1.90
Mother strictness	1.5	1.3	1.5	1.46
Father strictness	1.6	1.7	1.5	0.41
Embedded figures	1345.9	1589.2	1525.1	3.08

[a] F ratio required for significance at .05 level: 3.14.

As may be seen in row 1, mother-child interactions foster the development of field independence to a significantly greater extent in the least traditional of the fishing samples. Validation for the fostering of such interactions is given by also noting that the mean level of spatial ability is also higher in the least traditional of the fishing samples. The following rows of Table 1 indicate that with respect to all socialization measures, either there is no difference across samples increasing in the extent to which they are engaged in the traditional fishery or where there are significant differences they are opposite to prediction. It should be especially noted that independence training, which is the best single predictor of level of spatial ability, is significantly lower in the more traditional fishing samples. While, as already suggested, the fishing communities sampled may not have been characteristic of the traditional subsistence level societies described by Berry (1971) they may be said to represent different levels on a continuum towards traditional subsistence level societies. To the extent, therefore, that characteristics of the fishing communities sampled, do represent ecological pressures, present findings bring into question the relevance of these pressures for socialization practices, as well as for the development of spatial ability.

As indicated earlier, socialization practices assessed were those suggested by Witkin as having relevance for perceptual field independence. A factor analysis of these various practices was performed on data from the present study in order to clarify the nature of the domain of possible relevant variables. The solution resulting from Promax rotation indicated that the main cluster of practices fostering the development of field independence includes five variables. Mothers theoretically fostering such development are concerned with independence training and with a form of discipline which is not overly indulgent but consistent and rational. Such mothers do not view the child as delicate and do not overly suppress aggression. They do not view childrearing as a burden and appear satisfied with motherhood. Each of these five socialization behaviors showed a significant correlation with measures of spatial-perceptual ability, with independence training showing the highest relationship with both the Embedded Figures and Block Design. It is also of interest to note that other childrearing practices, while seeming to form meaningful clusters, were not related to performance on spatial-perceptual tasks.

Considering these five socialization variables as defining the main dimension of mother-child interactions fostering differentiation, what mothers are likely to be high on such variables? Judging from the matrix of interrelationships between mother and father characteristics and these socialization variables, it would seem more appropriate to speak of parent-child interactions rather than mother-child interactions, as there is indirect evidence for the father's role in fostering differentiation. While admitting that the father's contribution to the child's development needs to be considered, Witkin has tended to stress the importance of mother-child interactions. Within each of the five samples presently being described, it would appear that mother's education is predictive of the extent to which she is concerned with independence training. Within the total sample mother's education correlates .46 with independence training.[1]

1. Correlations with parental education within each sample were based on an n of approximately 20, since education levels were not available for all families.

On the other hand, father's education tends within each sample to be more predictive of the quality of discipline exercised within the home. It was noted that the level of mother's and particularly of father's education were in fact the best predictors of spatial-perceptual ability especially as measured by the EFT ($r = .31$ and $.38$ respectively). It would appear that level of parental education operates upon the development of spatial-perceptual ability through its influence upon socialization. The model perhaps most appropriate sees the mother as the one who, being mainly responsible for child care, creates behavioral opportunities for the child's assumption of responsibility and for his development of independence generally. The father, it is suggested, plays a role more specifically in applying punishment and in setting standards for discipline and the display of aggression. This may be contrasted with a conclusion by Corah (1965) to the effect that the opposite-sex parent rather than the mother contributes to the development of autonomy. It is appropriate to stress that the above statement relative to the role of mother and father in the development of spatial-perceptual ability is not one of definite conclusion but merely a suggestion arising from observations of findings from the present samples. These samples were small and rather homogeneous with respect to many of the variables being measured. All subjects were boys whose parents had the lowest levels of occupation and education that are found within the Province of Newfoundland and Labrador. The measures of relationship derived from these samples are understandably not high, but in areas where conclusions have been tentatively stated these measures have been consistent and significant.

By way of conclusion it would appear that measures of spatial-perceptual ability (in particular as obtained from the Witkin Embedded Figures Test) show a systematic decrease as one moves within a lower-class segment of society from families at the urban end to families in small, rather isolated communities. While perhaps quality of schooling and availability of television and other general indices of intellectual stimulation are relevant variables, it would also appear that characteristics of parent-child interactions are important. In general, it seems that as the level of parental education is lowered, which more often is associated with large families where mothers indicate that childrearing is a burden, there is less emphasis on independence training and the development of differentiation. The hypothesis of ecological press exerting a systematic influence upon the childrearing process for the positive development of particular skills would not appear to have explanatory value for the variations observed within the subgroups described.

B. A TEST OF THE UNIVERSALITY OF AN 'ACCULTURATION GRADIENT' IN THREE CULTURE-TRIADS*

by Robert F. Peck, Guy J. Manaster and Gary Borich, *University of Texas, Austin*
Arrigo L. Angelini, *University of Sao Paulo, Brazil*
Rogelio Diaz-Guerrero, *National University of Mexico, Mexico*
Shunichi Kubo, *National Institute for Educational Research, Tokyo, Japan*

According to acculturation theory (and common sense) migrants from one culture embody the values and aspiration patterns of their original culture. When they move into a new culture, it is commonly assumed that they gradually change their values until, usually after several generations, their descendants no longer resemble people in the original, ancestral culture but closely resemble those in the 'new' culture where they are living. The simplest model to represent this trend would be a linear 'acculturation gradient', whereby a migrant population would start out identical with its original culture and move, through intermediate degrees, closer and closer to the 'new' culture.

Anyone who knows migrant populations, whether as a social scientist or through first-hand encounters, probably knows intuitively that such a model is much too simplistic to fit the facts. It makes a useful frame of reference, nonetheless, for examining data on different migrant groups who enter different cultures.

In the course of the Cross-National Study of Coping Styles and Achievement, carried out in eight countries from 1965–73, it became possible to collect a diverse array of data on children who made up three 'culture-triads': (1) Japanese – Brazilian-Japanese – Brazilians, (2) Mexicans – Mexican-Americans – Anglo-Americans, and (3) Southwestern Blacks – Northern Blacks – Northern Anglo-Americans. These data permit a test of hypothetical universality of a straight-line acculturation gradient, regardless of the specific populations or the specific values at issue. Much

* This study was supported in part by U.S. Office of Education Contract No. OE-5-85-063, Coping Styles and Achievement: A Cross-National Study of School Children. The opinions expressed herein do not necessarily reflect the position or policy of the Office of Education and no official endorsement by the Office of Education should be inferred.

more important, they permit examination of some of the complex factors that influence the acculturation process in the real world. Out of the array of data, the present, preliminary report uses only information about the children's occupational aspirations and about the career values they would seek to fulfill in their adult occupations. The data can be used to test the general proposition that immigrant groups are intermediate between the original and the new cultures.

The sample. The 2,640 children in the population were boys and girls who were 10 or 14 years old at the time of testing. All of the subjects were classified as being in the upper lower or skilled working class. The method employed for measuring socioeconomic status utilized the International Scale of Occupations and an Educational Scale adjusted for each country. Briefly, the measurement of socioeconomic status consisted of a combination of the weighted scale scores for father's occupation (weighted by three) and father's education (weighted by two), giving a total range from 5 (high status) to 30 (low status). The working-class group in this sample had total scores from 19 to 25.

There were three culture-triads in this study, each composed of three sub-samples, of either 50 or 100 subjects, depending on the location. The first sample represents the country or area from which the mobile or minority group most recently migrated. The second sample in each triad is the migrant group. The third sample in each triad represents the majority group in the country or area to which the mobile or minority group migrated. The size of each sample is shown in Table 1.

Table 1. *Mean aspiration and value scores of the culture-triad groups*

Item	Mexican-American triad			Black-Anglo triad			Japanese-Brazilian triad		
	M	MA	AA	AB	CB	CA	J	BN	B
Aspirations	2.26	3.07**	2.882	2.72	2.82	2.68	2.81	2.36**	2.17
Expectations	2.52	3.41**	3.168	3.02	3.29*	2.96	3.22	2.45**	2.27
Discrepancy	7.70	7.47**	7.315	7.71	7.79	7.62	7.29	8.75	8.57
Intrinsic values	7.09	7.16*	6.99	7.10	6.84**	7.22	7.18	7.19**	6.77
Extrinsic values	6.89	6.12**	7.01	6.29	6.25**	6.76	6.80	5.97**	7.27

* $p < .05–.001$
** $p < .001$

The first group in the Mexican-American triad is from Mexico City and was tested in public and private schools in that city. The mobile or minority group is a Mexican-American sample drawn from the public schools in Austin, Texas. The majority group, Austin Anglo-Americans, was also drawn from the Austin schools.

The first group in the Black-Anglo triad is a Black sample collected in the Austin public schools. The mobile or minority group is a Black sample (Chicago Blacks) drawn from the public school systems of Gary, Indiana, and suburbs south of Chicago, Illinois. The third, 'majority' group, Chicago Anglos, was drawn from these same cities in the Chicago area.

The country-of-origin group in the Japanese-Brazilian triad is from Tokyo, Japan, where they were tested in the public schools. The mobile or minority group are Japanese-Brazilians, tested in public and private schools in Sao Paulo, Brazil. The third, majority group, Brazilians of European descent, was also tested in Sao Paulo.

The first real-life complication in this study arises from the fact that the 'migrant' groups in the triads did not necessarily come originally from a population that is entirely like the currently available, highly urbanized 'country of origin' sample in that triad. Consequently, it does not do to take these acculturation triads uncritically at face value. Some of the differences in value patterns to be reported, for at least two of the triads, probably stem from important pre-existing differences between subcultures within the country of origin. Many Mexico City inhabitants, for example, do not derive their 'inherited' values from the rural, indigenous folk-culture of Northern Mexico from which many of the 'migrant' sample of Austin Mexican-Americans undoubtedly came. Moreover, these Austinites of Mexican descent could be anything from first- to sixth- or seventh-generation Americans. The original migrant family member may have come from Mexico City but more probably came from Eastern or Northeastern Mexico.

The Chicago Blacks may also be from first to fourth generation in the North. They may originally have come from Texas but probably most of their ancestors came from more easterly portions of the American South.

The Brazilian-Japanese are mostly third to fifth generation in Brazil, the descendants of low-income farmers who came from Japan. Certainly, a good proportion of the Japanese sample in Tokyo are descendants of persons who migrated from rural areas to the big city within the last three generations (as must be the case with the Sao Paulo, Brazil, sample), but it cannot be known with any assurance just how closely similar were the value patterns of the particular ancestors of the Tokyo sample and the Brazilian-Japanese sample.

The problem is not one that could easily be resolved by a different selection of samples, although a study focused exclusively on the acculturation process would ideally try to match more closely the backgrounds of the 'migrant' and 'country of origin' samples in a triad. In fact, what with the rapid rate of social change in recent generations in almost every developing or developed country, it would be extremely difficult to find present populations, even in still-rural areas, whose values and aspirations would really match those of the ancestors of the contemporary 'migrant' samples. Consequently, instead of being able to mount a classically controlled experimental design and derive clean-cut answers about the relative influence of background differences or of acculturation phenomena on the observable values of present-day descendants of migrant groups, the social scientist is perforce constrained by great social changes, which have nowhere been minutely recorded, to trace out probable, *not certain*, patterns of causation. At the very least, some of the observable differences among the samples in the present triads, for instance, must be due to differences in original cultural background, *not* to the process of acculturation to a new society. Much more sophisticated (and expensive) research designs, probably longitudinal in nature, will have to be carried out before the precise degree of influence of different factors can be established, even approximately. Meanwhile, it is at least possible to be more realistic, and perhaps more accurately insightful into the acculturation process, if these other influences on sub-cultural value patterns are explicitly taken into account.

Instruments and procedures. The Occupational Interest Inventory (OII) was developed as part of a complex battery of achievement, attitude, and coping-skill measures in the project, 'Coping Styles and Achievement: A Cross-National Study of School Children'. It was collected in classroom settings by the project staff. The instrument is composed of a number of items; however, only three will be reported here. These consist of three questions, scored according to the status level of the occupation named. The questions are: (1) 'What job would you like to have when you grow up?', the *aspiration* question; (2) 'What job do you think you probably will have when you grow up?', the *expectation* item; and, (3) 'At what job does your father work?', the *father's occupation* item.

Space was provided for the subjects to give the name of a job in response to each of the above questions. After this space, an additional question asked the subject to describe the tasks involved in the job mentioned. The added question served to clarify the specifics of the job title given in the first question for each item. The answers to these two questions allowed each job to be scored according to an occupational prestige scale modified somewhat for each country. The International Scale of Occupations developed by Havighurst was employed (Peck *et al. The conceptual system: The instrumentation and the design of the study,* Volume I of seven volumes of final reports of project, Coping Styles and Achievement: A Cross-National Study of School Children, Project No. HRD-167-65, U.S. Office of Education Contract No. 5-85-063, and Texas Education Agency Contract No. 29390, in preparation). The scale runs from the highest prestige level, scored 1, to lowest prestige level, scored 6. The scoring was highly reliable (above .90) between scorers within each country; and the principal investigators of the Coping Style study, whose scoring provided the criteria within each country, had highly reliable inter-country scoring reliability (above .90).

It is important to note that the highest prestige scores have the lowest absolute numbers. That is, the highest score is always a 1, and the lowest score is always a 6. This needs to be kept in mind in reading Table 1, since groups naming jobs that are higher in prestige have mean scores that are lower than the groups to which they are being compared.

A discrepancy score was developed to indicate mobility aspirations. This is the discrepancy between the objective status level of the subjects' aspiration level and the occupational status level of the subject's father. The discrepancy score was derived by the following formula:

(6 + father's job level) minus subject's aspiration level.

The addition of 6 as a constant excludes the occurrence of zero or a negative number among the discrepancy scores. The possible range of derived discrepancy scores is from 1-11, meaning that scores below 6 indicate aspirations lower than father's job level, while scores above 6 indicate aspirations above the level of the father's job.

The Occupational Values Inventory is composed of 15 work values in a paired comparison format (Peck *et al. Cultural patterns of coping,* Volume II of seven volumes of final reports of project, Coping Styles and Achievement: A cross-National Study of School Children, Project No. HRD-167-65, U.S. Office of Education Contract No. 5-85-063, and Texas Education Agency Contract No. 29390, Personality Research Center, The University of Texas at Austin, 1972, 1092, pp., ERIC # ED 065825). Eight of the items were called Intrinsic items and seven, Extrinsic, after Super's usage.

Results. Three-way analysis of variance was performed on these data at the Computation Center at The University of Texas at Austin, using age, sex, and ethnic group membership as the independent variables. Table 1 shows the mean scores on the aspiration measures and the Intrinsic/ Extrinsic value scores for each of the samples, whether the samples within any one triad differed significantly, and the direction of the difference. One of the striking findings is that the simple 'acculturation gradient' hypothesis is *not* supported by most of the data.

In the Mexican-American triad the 'migrant' group, the Mexican-Americans of Austin, were *not* intermediate between the two 'core culture' samples in their levels of occupational aspiration or expectation. The children of Mexico City expressed the greatest ambition on both of these measures; the Austin Anglos scored much lower; and the Austin Mexican-Americans expressed the least ambition for occupational status, although even they expected to rise to lower-middle class status. This 'migrant' group of Mexican-Americans did score midway between the other two samples in their degree of ambition to exceed their fathers' status levels.

On the two, almost-reciprocal summary scores for Intrinsic and Extrinsic values, the Mexican-Americans scored highest of all three groups in their triad on Intrinsic values and were much the lowest on the Extrinsic values. Taking the fifteen values separately, the Mexican-Americans scored significantly highest on their interest in esthetic careers, self-satisfaction, intellectual stimulation, variety in the work and the chance to achieve managerial status. Except for the last item, this pattern may explain why they scored lower on aspiration level. Their values are oriented more toward intrinsic, personal satisfactions than toward competitive success or prestige.

Of no little interest is the reversal of the traditional stereotypes in the other two groups. Instead of the Yankees, it was the Mexico City youth who hungered for success and prestige, with an interest in the chance to be personally creative. They also were relatively more willing to follow their fathers' occupational footsteps (although this was not really a popular idea in *any* sample). The Austin Anglos, rather than showing the aggressive enterprise of American legend, stressed altruism, job security, pleasant surroundings, and pleasant work associates, although also valuing independence of action and economic rewards.

Thus, each of the three culture samples showed a unique, significantly distinctive pattern on most of these measures, both in aspiration level and in career values. The 'migrant' Mexico-Americans were different from either the Anglo or Mexican 'core-culture' samples, but they were not in between, as the acculturation gradient model would predict. They do hope to advance substantially in their adult careers but their values look like a fusion of some 'passive', traditional values from the Northern Mexican folk culture with the self-oriented, humanistic values that have recently won growing acceptance among American youth, as the Austin Anglo sample vividly demonstrates.

The Black-Northern Anglo triad similarly refuted the 'acculturation gradient' model. The 'migrant' Chicago Blacks were not intermediate on any of the six measures shown in Table 1. On the contrary, they scored lower than either the Austin Blacks or the Chicago Anglos in the occupational status level they expected to achieve, although they showed a greater desire to exceed their fathers' status. Clustering the Occupational Values items differently from Super's Intrinsic/Extrinsic classification, they scored lowest of the three samples in their triad in both their Intrinsic and Extrinsic summary scores.

The 'migrant' Chicago Blacks stressed the importance of income and success (the chance to get ahead) more than either of the other groups and gave as high weight to job security as did the Chicago Anglos. Overall, these Northern Blacks showed the greatest desire to get ahead. The fact that they *expect* somewhat less success in this endeavor than youth in the other two groups may both reflect and explain some of the frustration and cynicism of Northern Blacks about succeeding within the existing social system. Even so, as a group, they expect to rise to lower-middle class status. They do not, by age 10 or 14, feel locked into an economically or socially deprived world.

The Austin Blacks expected as much occupational success as did the Chicago Anglos. They had outstanding value scores only on their desire for variety and for prestige.

The Chicago Anglos did not differ from the other two groups in their aspiration levels. They did show a distinctive pattern in valuing altruism, self-satisfaction, job security and pleasant asssociates. They most closely resembled the Austin Anglos in these respects.

The Japanese-Brazilian triad came closer to an acculturation gradient than the other triads, on the occupational aspiration measures, though not on the career value measures. The Brazilian-Japanese were intermediate in their levels of occupational aspiration and expectation. On the desired-mobility measure they outscored both the Japanese and the Brazilian core-culture samples. Thus, the Brazilian-Japanese may have moved away from the more conservative expectation-pattern of the Japanese, as found in Tokyo, toward the highly confident optimism of the Paulistas of European descent.

In their career values, however, the Brazilian-Japanese were not at all intermediate. On the contrary, they tied the Japanese sample for a high score on the Intrinsic values and scored lowest, by far, of the three samples on the Extrinsic cluster of values. They scored particularly high (relative to the other samples) in their interest in esthetic careers, the desire for self-satisfaction, and the desire to follow their fathers, occupationally. They scored low on concern for job security, unlike either of the other samples. Like the Brazilians, they scored relatively lower on altruism and concern about being creative; but, like the Japanese, they also scored lower on their desire for prestige.

The Japanese of Tokyo had the most modest expectations and ambitions in this triad – indeed, they just about tied for low with the Austin Anglos and Austin Mexican-Americans, in these respects, in the total research population. They stressed the career values of altruism, creativity, security, and pleasant surroundings, not at all the entrepreneurial values one might infer from Japan's recent history of explosive economic growth. They relatively disvalued esthetic careers, pay, success, prestige, and following father, occupationally. In most ways, this pattern was quite different from the Brazilian-Japanese pattern of values.

The Paulistas of European descent were extremely optimistic in both their desires and expectations. They wanted to rise far above their fathers' level of occupation. What is more, they expected to succeed so far as to achieve nearly upper-middle class status – this, starting from the skilled working class. Their optimism was approached only by the youth of Mexico City.

Their career values were highly pragmatic and extrinsic. They wanted success, prestige, high income,and job security. They also thoughta rtistic careers attractive. They relatively disvalued altruism, self-satisfaction, creativity, pleasant surroundings, or following father, occupationally.

Thus, while the Brazilian-Japanese resembled the other Brazilians in their *level* of ambition, the kind of working life and career rewards they seek is very different from what motivates the European Brazilians. They have a unique value pattern that cannot be explained in any simple way as a direct product of Brazilian values supplanting Japanese values.

Summary. Data were collected on three culture triads, each including a group who could be viewed as migrants from one 'core' culture to another 'core' culture. The results indicate that a simple 'acculturation gradient' model is neither sufficient nor accurate as an explanation of the comparative similarity of aspiration and value systems within any of the three acculturation triads. Interpretation is complicated by the fact that the 'migrant' samples probably did not originate in exactly the same culture group within the 'country of origin' as the contemporary sample drawn from the 'country of origin'. This problem is not just an accidental defect arising from the sampling design of the present study; to some degree, it probably is an irreducible discrepancy created by the rapid and widespread social changes of the last fifty years.

The hopes, expectations, and career values of Black Americans in the northern United States, Mexican-Americans in the southwestern United States, and Japanese-Brazilians in southern Brazil can only be explained by considering, not only some culturally inherited values they brought with them, generations back, but by the actual opportunities the 'new' society affords them. Deep, detailed field study will be necessary if one is ever to trace the complex interactions among the traditions, the available rewards, and the values of the two core cultures these 'migrants' are striving to synthesize. In each culture triad in the present study, the 'migrant' group shows a pattern of values and expectations that is considerably unique and is not explainable simply as a direct, linear derivative of either the 'old' culture or the 'new' culture. The 'new' values of the migrants appear to reflect the present realities of career opportunities and the prevailing economic mood of the 'new' society; but these presumed 'shifts' do not appear to happen as a series of increasingly close approximations to the 'new' society's values. The 'melting-pot' does not dissolve the partially unique value patterns of migrants, even after several generations in a new society.

C. A CROSS-CULTURAL VIEW OF ADULT LIFE IN THE EX-TENDED FAMILY

by David Gutman, *University of Michigan, Ann Arbor*

The extended family as hero. The social sciences have become, in Riesman's term, 'Other Directed'. They are less interested in internally based, intra-personal sources of security – conscience, identity – and more interested in those externally based, interpersonal sources of security that are found in the various forms of collective life. Thus, many social scientists now study, generate, and celebrate those collective enterprises in which inter-individual boundaries, distinctions, and rivalries are blurred over or dissipated in favor of some harmonious 'group process'. What is studied is also valued; and we now find that many social scientists assert the superiority of collectivist over individual enterprise: the encounter group is valued over individual psycho-therapy; Maoist collectivism is valued over democracy; the communard is valued over the entreprenuer; and the extended family is valued over the nuclear family. Thus, partially in deference to the ideas of Women's Lib, social scientists have begun to dis-parage the nuclear family as though it were the nuclear bomb. It is stigma-tized as a hot-bed of sex-ism, double-binding, age-ism, capitalist ethics, and generational discontinuities. By contrast, the extended family – largely found in rural settings – is eulogized. The extended family takes on the postorale mystique and is depicted as a panacea against human woe. Thus Germaine Greer (1971) is so taken by the extended family that she even accepts the patriarchal rule that usually accompanies it: 'The head was the oldest male parent, who ruled a number of sons and their wives and chil-dren. The work of the household was divided according to the status of the female in question: The unmarried daughters did the washing and spinning and weaving, the breeding wives bred, the elder wives nursed and disci-plined the children, and managed the cooking, the oldest wife supervised the smooth running of the whole. There was friction but it had no chance to build itself into the intense introverted anguish of the single eye-to-eye confrontation of the isolated spouses. Family problems could be challenged openly in the family forum and the decisions of the elders were honored.'

In this Rousseauan and essentially 'outside' view, the extended family is seen to give, automatically and without stint, the kinds of love and security that the nuclear family either withholds or poisons. If the nuclear family represents an authentic circle of hell, then the extended family is our life in Eden, before the fall from grace.

Inside the extended family. However, this public relations picture of the extended family is not always corroborated by its members. For the past nine years I have done field research into the comparative psychology of aging and have interviewed Navajo, Maya, and Druze subjects – all of them residents of one or another version of the extended family. But my middle-aged and elderly respondents (in the age-range 35–95 years) have reported grave difficulties in family living, as well as bonuses of the sort noted by social scientists. My subjects mention the support provided by relatives; but these admittedly helpful relatives might also be involved in family feuds. Complaints about mother-in-laws, stepmothers, or heavy-handed older brothers come as easily from the members of each form of family, extended or nuclear. Furthermore, across cultures, younger subjects are likely to chafe under the heavy weight of social control: The extended family in the small village is the ideal repository of tradition, and woe to the adventurous spirit who enters into an unsanctioned marriage or some deviant line of work. In the folk society the deviant is not only 'bad' in the moral sense, he is also eerie, not quite human. Accordingly, the tradition breaker who stays in or returns to his native village risks much trouble; he, his wife, and children will be the target of unrelenting gossip, even witchcraft accusations.

Clearly, then, the extended family – which typically gives power to the older generation over the younger – is not receptive to innovation. Thus, while younger men defer publicly to their fathers, they will often complain behind his back, calling him an obstacle to progress. Incidentally, revolutionary regimes typically regard the extended family as the major enemy of the new older that they are trying to build; and they work ruthlessly – as in the case of Red China – to disband it.

Comparing the nuclear and extended families. In sum, judging from the accounts of actual members, the extended family is not a piece of our lost perfection nor a reproach to our urban venality. It is not a philosopher's stone for transmuting human hate into human love. The extended family and the nuclear family do not represent moral polarities, but contrasting human arrangements, each of which has its own optimal social setting, its distinctive evolutionary history, and its distinctive functions. Each form of family life stresses and delivers the benefits that the other tends to neglect. For example, when we assess the nuclear family for its strengths and weaknesses, we do indeed find important deficiencies. The nuclear family is centered on two parents, and this limited personnel cannot provide a deep sense of security, nor help children whose love is tangled with their hate to resolve the terrible problem of ambivalence. But, by the same token, the reduced complement of the nuclear family is the basis of its particular strength. Because it is centered on a few members, individual differences are underlined; the nuclear family is not composed of replaceable social parts, but of unique individuals. Accordingly, the nuclear family sponsors individual differences, the sense of personal uniqueness and individual initiative. In effect, the nuclear family is packaged for physical and social mobility, and it prepares its children for successful adaptation in new and unpredicted environments. The child reared in the nuclear family carries the ultimate sources of his security within himself, but he must leave home in order to discover and lay claim to his strength. By contrast, the resources, prestige, and logistics of the cumbersome extended family are inevitably tied to and identified with a particular place, a home range, and the individual member who might want to explore new horizons is in for trouble: He cannot introduce innovations within the tradition-hallowed rigidities of the family; yet if he leaves, he must risk complete up-rooting from his accustomed psychosocial supports. Thus, while the nuclear family erodes the sense of collective resource lodged in the group, in the land, and in the household gods, it does replace it with a sense of individual resource lodged within the self – the kind of resource that is vital to mobility and discovery.

Clearly, these contrasting arrangements, the nuclear and the extended families, fluctuate in value according to historical circumstance, cultural values, and the life cycle position of the component members. The nuclear family tends to be valued over the extended family by emerging societies, by societies which value individual initiative and by those individuals – particularly the young – who are interested in exploring new life ways. The extended family is valued in rural settings, in cultures which resist change, and which value stability over innovation. Furthermore, the extended family tends to be valued by those who give priority to conformity over expressiveness; and within the life cycle, it is valued either by the very young or by the old.

The comparative psychology of adult life. I am not against the extended family *per se;* I am only against those who would take it out of its socio-historical framework and turn it into some object of cult worship. A determinedly relativistic approach informs the rest of this paper, which outlines some ideas, based on field work, concerning the coordination of the extended family system with the stages of the male life cycle in the middle and later years. We will consider the ways in which the various themes of the adult life stages mesh, or fail to mesh, with the extended family system in which these themes emerge and are expressed. By way of preface, some general findings concerning the normative psychological developments of later life that have been identified in the course of my comparative studies will be briefly summarized. Details of data collection and analysis have been reported elsewhere (Gutmann 1969). Here, I will only present those still tentative findings which are pertinent to this discussion.

Generally speaking, it appears that younger middle-aged men – those in the age range 35 through 54 – are characterized by psychological stances or postures which differentiate them from older men as well as from younger women across the range of study sites. In general, we find that younger men are characterized by an active mastery or active-productive orientation: It is very important for them to control the resources on which the physical well-being of themselves and their families depend. This generative posture of younger men goes very deep, mobilizes a great deal of energy, and is supported by a great deal of self-discipline: In the service of husbandry, younger men repress their own need to be taken care of by others, as well as most needs for comfort and sensual pleasure. In younger men this capacity for delay of gratification is sponsored by early training against laziness, by puberty rituals which test their capacity to endure deprivation, and by the experience of marriage and fatherhood. It is particularly this latter event which seems to mobilize a disciplined 'emergency response': Paternity as well as maternity has its imperatives. Though younger men still need, at least unconsciously, to be indulged, they tend to live out these needs vicariously – by identifying with the wife and/or the children that they themselves nurture and indulge. Younger men make difficult inner adjustments – away from dependency, away from comfort seeking, and away from a combative to a productive use of their energies. Having accomplished this internal engineering, young men can be trusted to do what has to be done – regardless of the hardships involved – by way of providing physical security to their dependents. By the same token, younger wives tend to give up the aggressive potentials that would interfere with their ability to provide emotional security to the infants in their charge. They too live out lethal aspects of their nature vicariously: They surrender their own claims to aggression and instead identify with the prowess of the husband. They literally send their dangerous aggression out of the house with him and identify with the husband's struggle against natural and human enemies.[1]

At any rate, once the period of chronic emergency that we know as parenthood has passed, and children can demonstrate their own capacity for active mastery, the massive repression of passive-dependency in the male and aggression in the case of the female is no longer either required or justified. As a result there takes place in both sexes a transcultural 'return of the repressed'. By contrast to younger men – and to their younger selves – the older male subjects (those in the age range 55–95 years) reverse the usual 'masculine' priorities; they become more dependent, more diffusely sensual, more sensitive to the incidental pleasures and pains of the world. They become particularly interested in food, in pleasant sights, in harmonious sounds, and in supportive human 'relationships'. Clearly, older men become less aggressive than younger men; older men are more affiliative, more interested in love than in conquest or power, more interested in community than in agency. By the same token, older women reclaim the aggression that can no longer hurt their young. Even in the patriarchal Druze culture older women become more intrusive, more domineering, and less sentimental. In effect, with the phasing out of the gender-specific emergency reactions that we call sex role behavior, each sex becomes to some degree what the other used to be, and there is ushered in the normal unisex of later life.

The stages of adult life in the extended family. However we characterize these transformations, it is clear that they involve important age-shifts in relational styles; we are describing sex and age related changes in the mode

---

1. Thus, the usual rigid sex-role distinctions of young and middle adulthood serve to convert dangerous inter-community male and female aggression to useful extra-communal, outwardly directed aggression. That is, *via* his role as husband and father the younger man deflects the wife's aggression away from their children, and his own aggression away from the community as a whole. He 'removes' it from within the domestic precincts to the outer defense line of the community.

Clearly, the sex role distinctions that routinely occur in small communities living under conditions of hardship and necessity were not invented to swell the egos of chauvinist males; they are evolutionary outcomes, designed to provide maximum physical and emotional security to the vulnerable young.

of relating to others, in the satisfactions derived from social relationships, in the expectations and demands that are brought to relationships, and in the relative importance of human relationships as against other sources of security and satisfaction. Clearly, given the magnitude of the age change in the inner orientations that individuals bring to their social investments, there should be corresponding shifts in the subjective involvement with that pivotal system of intimate relationships, the extended family, as its members age. Again, my field observations were mainly confined to men, and I will only try to delineate the age changes in masculine priorities within the extended family. Turning first to the younger men, we find that their favored ego style – that of Active Mastery – has important consequences for their relations to and within the extended family. In general, younger men seem to be at best ambivalent towards the ready-made forms of security that are provided for them by their parents and relatives. True enough, younger men love their kin, and they appreciate the various forms of support that the family provides, but they are at the same time very conscious of the price – in autonomy, in authority, and in privacy – that they have to pay for the gratuitous security provided by their family. They are quite often aware that the family's support is bought at the price of free marital, residential, occupational, and religious choice. Furthermore, within the confines of the extended family the future is already predicted. Within its daily rounds, the family presents the picture of the way life has been, will be, and should be. Though the future is depicted as secure, it may contain little room for a younger man's fantasies of challenge, innovation, and high achievement. Accordingly, while many younger men do remain in the ancestral village, accept their place within the family, work their portion of the father's land, and wait to inherit, there is always a minority of restless ones – both married and unmarried – who hive off, who leave the secure but confining life. Some of these outmigrants are clearly motivated by economic necessity: There is not enough land for all the brothers. But others are driven by some inchoate ferment within the blood: They are urged away from the safe harbor precisely because it is too secure. In Shakespeare's words, they are driven 'by the winds that blow young men through the world, to seek their fortunes far from home, where small experience grows'.

The extended family may look good to us, the rootless children of rootless pioneers. But we must remember that cities are founded and settled by the young refugees from the extended family. We are constantly reminded, as part of the new sentimentality, that the city is a harsh and alienating environment; but the critics of the urban experience forget that while the city alienates the individual it also frees him. The usual charge against the city is that one can drop dead in public without being noticed; but the corollary is that one can enjoy any legal or even para-legal life in the city without being restrained, or gossiped over. In the city the refugee from the extended family can experiment with vocational, religious, political, and sexual possibilities without suffering the usual social consequences of his explorations, and without making final choices. He is not surrounded by a review panel of concerned and keenly observant relatives who will not forget his past sins, and who treat his tentative experiments as though they were final life choices. Thus, if the extended family offers community at the price of freedom, the city offers freedom at the price of community. In effect, the priorities of the city match the priorities of young men. Accordingly, it is not strange that younger men often leave their parental village and their extended family for some strange city halfway around the world.

However, just as young men leave the village and the family for the rootless city, many older men leave the now lonely and frightening city, and cycle back to their native village and kinsmen. In the apt Indian term, they 'return to the blanket'. Increasingly, the village becomes the retirement community for the older man who has had a moderate success in the city, and who has come back to buy the house, the land, and herds that he could not afford in his youth. Clearly, the prospect of being a big shot, of being a big frog in a small puddle, will draw many men back to the village of their birth and to their family of orientation.

The recycling of the future. Thus, by providing a haven, the extended family meets the personal needs of those older men who cycle back to their origins at the end of life. But there are many men who have lived out their lives, and reached middle age, without ever leaving the confines of village and family. In their case, as they reach middle life, the extended family and the village ambiance serve to convert some of the personal, intrinsic developments of later life into transactions that have important social utility. This mediation of the life-cycle is very evident in regard to a characteristic phenomenon of the middle years that might be termed 'the re-cycling of the future'. By this I refer to the readiness of older traditionals to concede their own future hopes and plans to their maturing sons. This development is facilitated by the patterning of interpersonal experience in the small traditional community, and by the blurring of interpersonal boundaries that takes place there. The redundant lifestyle, the high degree of consensus and the pooling of individuals into larger social categories of village, clan, and tribe, reduces self-boundaries and sponsors a fractionation or distribution of the elements of self into their outer exemplars or representations. As regards inter-generational relations, this phenomenon of the 'distributed self' makes for a strong sense of identification and relatedness between fathers and sons, across the generations. The father can re-experience his younger self in his son; the son can see his future self represented in the father. This trans-generational homogeneity becomes particularly useful at that point – usually in his early fifties – when the father concedes that he has 'peaked', and that he cannot expect his remaining fantasies of wealth or power to be realized in the future. Typically, the middle-aged peasant looks to a future in which his strength for meeting the continuing demands of the agricultural life will decline. However, while his own future closes off it is possible for the peasant father, within the extended family, to transfer his personal hopes and fantasies from himself to that son with whom his own ego is blended. The father joins the future through his younger self, his son, and therefore finds it easy to concede the future to him. On the filial side, while sons may grumble about the father's authority, or his old fashioned methods, they do tend to share his overall values and goals. Accordingly, there is little evidence in extended family relationships of the so-called 'Generation Gap'.[2]

The old man as hero. But cross-generational identification is not the only feature of life in the traditional community that facilitates the recycling of the future. The older traditional can concede the future to his son because doors to particular forms of prestige and power have opened to him that are largely closed to his son. That is, in the traditional community, as the man ages, he may disengage from the technical-productive order, which

2. Perhaps the generation gap is a product of urban society and the nuclear family, both of which sponsor a higher degree of individuation in all its members, including fathers and sons. The self-aware person is likely to cling – well into middle life – to the idea that his future goals will be realized, *by himself,* at some later date. Accordingly, urban fathers are not as likely as traditional fathers to concede the future to their sons. They often continue to work on their own career long into middle and even later life. By the same token, the individualized son, product of nuclear family and urban experience, will not easily accept his father's idea of what the future ought to be. He will not accept or strive towards some vision of the future that was promulgated for him by the past. Acoordingly, in the nuclear family and in the urban society, fathers and sons tend to fight each other for the ownership of the future. We call this struggle 'the generation gap'.

he concedes to his son, but he tightens his linkage to the traditional order, the moral core of the society, and he thereby gains a privileged status largely closed off to the younger individuals who have not yet lived a full life under the discipline of the tradition, and who have not yet proved their moral worth.

In effect, the older man in the traditional society gives up the idea that he is the center of executive action in exchange for a refreshed sense of junction with the executive powers of the Gods (Gutmann 1972). The traditional order of society provides the institutional structures and practices through which this sense of connection to the vital powers of the Gods can be enacted. The older man is humble; therefore his prayer is particularly acceptable to the deity and serves to bring his sustaining powers into the life-forms of community and its ecology. In effect, the social structure of the traditional society acts so as to translate the normal male passivity of later life into the very pivot of the older man's renewed prestige in the community at large.

The recovery of the past. The older man's enhanced moral prestige allows his son to inherit the future; and it also allows the old father to regain the past. Having dispensed with the future, he can begin to again enjoy the pleasures of the past that were ruled out in the service of productive parenthood. Within the larger community, in his public aspect, the old man is a sort of hero; but within the extended family he can live out some of his wishes to be the recipient of that which he used to provide to others. As these yearnings emerge or re-emerge, the older man quite naturally turns back to that setting wherein he received his first provisions of affection and support. He turns to the family. His parents have long since passed on; but the family which included the subject and his parents still persists relatively unchanged. The extended family relates the past to the present; therefore the old man in the bosom of the extended family can relive the past through his participation in the present life of the family; he can recapture the sense of being again included in a 'parenting' milieu.

By helping him to relive his beginnings the extended family also aids the old man towards his central goal – the denial of the end. The parental or 'species' function of the old man has ended; weakness, disease, and the death of peers remind him of the end. His natural impulse, since he cannot project himself into the future, is to deny the end by returning to his own beginnings. His wish is to deny the end by creating some of the weather, some of the ambiance of his own inception as a protected and relatively indulged child. The extended family supports his denial by providing the human raw materials out of which the old man can reconstruct the early world of attentive and reliable kin. Furthermore, the members of the extended family offer automatic, unquestioned respect to the older man; and by so doing they help to revive childhood memories of total and unconditional acceptance. The extended family gives to the older man a panel of caretakers – daughters-in-law, daughters, nieces, sons, and sons-in-law – around whom he can live out some of the fantasies and expectations that he once held towards the older paternal and maternal figures of his childhood. Thus, the extended family allows some of the regressive developments of later life to take place in benign circumstances, in a setting which accepts the 'childish' needs of the old man as these emerge.

In effect then, the major 'social ecologies' of the folk society – the formal, traditional institutions and the extended family – between them provide settings in which the older man can live out discrepant aspects of his nature, without these coming into conflict. Within the prayer house he can be the autocrat with special entrée to the deity, and he can look down on the younger men who do not share his special knowledge; but within the family he can live out and enjoy his need to be indulged and taken care of. Having access to both these settings, he does not have to make some final choice between being either the patriarch or the child.

Finally then, when we view the ways in which the structures and usages of the extended family interface with the changing themes of the adult male life cycle, we do not find unrelieved integration and harmony between social pressures and personal needs. Quite the contrary, it appears that the extended family as an institution is quite discordant with the periods of young adulthood and early middle age – those in which the sense of individual agency and responsibility are being developed, tested, and enacted. These are the age-grades which are most likely to generate refugees and drop-outs from the extended family. On the other hand, the extended family is well fitted to, even homologous with, the later stages of the life cycle during which individual agency, individual responsibility and orientation to the future are being abandoned and turned over to others. The extended family is particularly useful to men who are preparing to relive the past rather than shape the future. Perhaps those social scientists who romanticize the rural and communal past find the extended family attractive for the same reasons.

Subcultural differences in language aquisition

A. SOME THEORETICAL CONSIDERATIONS OF SUBCULTURAL DIFFERENCES IN LANGUAGE DEVELOPMENT

by Klaus F. Riegel, *University of Michigan, Ann Arbor*

Black English can be considered to be a structural system distinctly different from Standard English. Undoubtedly, this proposition will be considered controversial by some, especially since detailed inquiries into the distinctive properties of Black English have begun only recently. But even if scholars could never agree that Black English is sufficiently different from Standard English and, thus, would not consider it to be an independent language or a main dialect, for the sake of the language learning children, they ought to segregate both systems as forcefully as possible. Only through such constructive efforts can we sufficiently aid the deprived child in his formidable task.

At the present time, culturally deprived groups represent the largest contingent of bilinguals in the United States. There exists, however, a small group of bilingual children from homes with high educational and economic levels. These are the children of professionals who have emigrated to this country and found it advisable to raise their children under bilingual and often bicultural conditions. Needless to say, both groups of bilinguals are psychologically and sociologically far apart.

In the past, notably during the 1930s, a considerable number of psychological investigations have been conducted with bilingual children from both groups. The reports on the well-educated children have provided important insights into the compatibility of two linguistic systems and about some psychological problems in processing such information (Leopold 1939–49). The bulk of research was conducted, however, on children from the ghetto areas. Not surprisingly, most of the results revealed serious short-comings and deficiencies not only in the use of language but in other psychological skills as well. In the interpretations, the socio-linguistic bases of psychological performances were rarely emphasized with sufficient strength. The research was, all too often, restricted to sets of purely psychological variables, and subsequently conclusions were drawn about the lack of effort and motivation, ability, and intelligence of these children.

As argued elsewhere (Riegel and Riegel 1972), the consideration of psychological factors in a socio-historical vacuum leads to fictitious constructions which are, by and large, of little value both for gaining knowledge in science as well as for helping these children in gaining knowledge in their world. In the following presentation, we will retain the same viewpoint and, therefore, shift the emphasis from psychological constructions to linguistic contingencies of the physical-social environment.

Before such an attempt can be made a few comments are necessary about the structural properties of the linguistic system to which the growing child is being exposed. Structures are based upon relations. Elements alone do not provide structure but mere conglomerates; stronger yet, relations are prior to the elements which they connect. To use but one simple example, we always transmit information about relations, never about elements alone. We will tell the child that 'A rose is a flower', thereby implying the relationship of class inclusion, or we point at a rose in a book and pronounce its name, thereby implying an extralingual relation between an object and a label. We never – except for Gertrude Stein – tell a child that 'a rose is a rose, is a rose, is a rose...' Only after a sufficient amount of relational information has been provided, will a child be able to identify words, explicate their meanings, and abstract semantic classes.

In terms of a simple schema presented in Figure 1, the child acquires information represented by the cells of the matrix. Only after he has received a certain amount of such relational information is he able to move conceptually toward the margins of the matrix, i.e., to extrapolate words. Of course, the child will originally produce single word utterances in his own speech, but this merely indicates limitations in his performance by which part of the intended relations remain suppressed. Recently, Lois Bloom has called attention to this issue (1973).

Types of bilingualism. In extending the relational matrix shown in Figure 1, we can distinguish two types of bilingualism with a third intermediate type between these extremes. Such a distinction is not new. In contrast to earlier discussions, we emphasize exclusively the external contingencies rather than intervening psychological conditions.

First, we find a situation in which at time t_1 a second language, such as standard English, is introduced to a child who, up to this point, was exclusively exposed to another language, e.g., Spanish. In the extreme case, e.g., of a child who has lost his parents and is being brought up by another family who does not speak his native language, no provision for the transfer of his first language knowledge is made. Subsequently, this knowledge will be slowly lost. We will call the case in which both languages are introduced and used in complete separation the condition of *independent bilingualism*.

Second, a child might be exposed to conditions in which two languages are almost randomly mixed. In this case he not only acquires two sets of intralingual relations (as the independent bilingual child does also) but two additional sets of interlingual relations as well. Intuitively we feel that such a condition, which we shall call *confounded bilingualism*, can not lead to an efficient acquisition of either the first or of the second language. If a child during a given time period can be exposed to and, subsequently, can acquire only a fixed amount of relational information, represented by a small subsection or frame within the matrix of Figure 1, the confounded bilingual child is exposed to four times and the independent bilingual

Figure 1. *Three types of bilingualism*

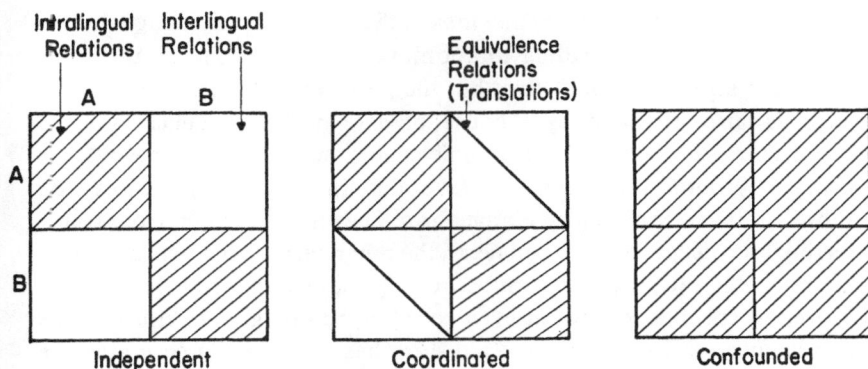

child to twice as much relational information as a monolingual child. Thus these children, especially the confounded bilinguals, receive less information in either of the two languages, and it becomes very unlikely that they will ever be able to compete successfully with their monolingual age mates.

Both conditions described so far are unrealistic extremes which are not desirable for second-language training. The confounded condition overburdens the child and fails to assist him in separating the two languages. The independent condition prevents the child from transferring his first language knowledge to his second language and, thereby, to facilitate its acquisition. No wonder that parents and teachers are applying a modified combination of second-language training schedules which lead to what we will call *coordinated bilingualism*.

Under the simplest but by no means most efficient form of coordinated condition, the second language is introduced with the aid of equivalence relations or translations. Such a procedure allows for a limited transfer of first-language knowledge to the second language but neither for sufficient explorations of the conceptual similarities between the two languages nor for complex translations which rely on more than one-to-one equivalence between items. While such a condition represents a minimal degree of coordination, a maximum is attained under confouded contingencies where theoretically every item can be connected with every other item across the two languages. Optimal bilingual contingencies are provided through an extended set of equivalence relations which captures the conceptual and semantic properties in a contrastive manner. More will be said about these issues in our section on interlingual relations further below.

Children raised under favorable educational and economic conditions are commonly exposed to the most efficient form of bilingual contingencies, i.e., those leading to coordinated bilingualism. In this case, both languages are kept distinct but the possibility for transfer of knowledge is also provided by the use of extended equivalence systems. Children raised under poor economic conditions, on the other hand, are commonly raised under the least favorable linguistic contingenices, i.e., those leading to confounded bilingualism. They are prevented from transferring knowledge in one language to the other because the two languages are not sufficiently separated. Subsequently they can not possibly succeed as well as the independent or even coordinated bilingual in either of the two languages. The first step to aid them has to consist in accepting the two languages, e.g., standard and non-standard English, as separate and equal. Such a segregation is the prerequisite for an intelligent transfer of knowledge, thus making an increased success in second-language learning possible.

Stages in bilingual development. The different bilingual types can be regarded as levels in developmental progression with the independent and coordinated types as early transitions and the confounded type as the terminal stage. In particular, we have proposed the following sequence (Riegel 1968):

Stage I characterizes the very early steps in the acquisition of the first language during which parts of the vocabulary A are provided through the use of extralingual relations. Thus, the interconnections are of a special type, namely, between words and the objects, events, or qualities which they denote. The number of these extralingual relations, appropriately placed into the cells of the main diagonal of the $A \times A$ matrix, is equal to or less than A. At Stage I no second language is acquired, thus $B = 0$.

At Stage II various interconnections in A will be presented. Theoretically, every item could be connected with every other item and (as at Stage I) with the object, event, or quality which it denotes. Thus, the maximum number of relations will be A^2. At this stage, too, $B = 0$.

At Stage III parts of a vocabulary B are provided through the use of equivalence relations. Equivalence relations appear on the main diagonals of the two interlingual quadrants of Figure 1 and connect items in B to their translations in A and vice versa. Thus, the total vocabulary equals $A + B$, but it is likely that at first $B < A$. The total number of possible relations equals $A^2 + 2B$, whereby the second term refers to the equivalence relations $A \Rightarrow B$ and $B \Rightarrow A$. The number of equivalence relations going in either direction may be unequal if the two languages differ in the size of their vocabularies.

Stage III resembles Stage I and is important for the initiation of second-language learning, often presented by instructions such as 'In German, table is called Tisch.' This type of information will be quickly supplemented by more complex messages. Under independent bilingual conditions and as a function of the teaching technique applied, Stage III may be substituted (or supplemented) by a modified form of Stage I relating the vocabulary items of the second language to the objects, events, or qualities which they denote, rather than to their translated labels. In this case, the set of relations equals $A^2 + B$ rather than $A^2 + 2B$.

At Stage IV items in B are also interconnected. The relations with A remain of the equivalent type. Thus, the total vocabulary equals A + B, whereby B may approach A, and the total number of relations consists of those in A, those in B, and the equivalence relations A $\Rightarrow$ B, and B $\Rightarrow$ A, that is, $A^2 + B^2 + 2B$. The extralingual relations might be placed along the main diagonal of the second language matrix, represented by the term B^2. If they do not appear, the above expression should be reduced by B. In any case, the learner may derive the extralingual relations in B without further instructions on the basis of the extralingual relations in A and the equivalence relations A $\Rightarrow$ B and B $\Rightarrow$ A.

At Stage V all items are interconnected. The vocabulary remains A + B. The number of relations equals $A^2 + B^2 + 2AB = (A + B)^2$. The proficiency of most bilinguals will remain at Stage IV, but under exceptional circumstances Stage V may be attained. Paradoxically, it is again the disadvantaged ghetto child who is exposed to these circumstances, and, worse yet, he is not exposed to them at the very end of long language acquisition history, but at the beginning when he cannot possibly cope with this information.

The major differences between the five stages have been summarized in Table 1. The stages must be regarded as transitional conditions in a continuous process of change. They overlap greatly. Thus, while an individual continues to be exposed to extralingual relations, he may already face intralingual relations between the different items of the first language. Also, while still being taught equivalence relations, he will be exposed, at the same time, to intralingual relations within his second language or to other interlingual relations between the two languages.

Taking all these variations into account we can, nevertheless, agree that Stage II follows I and Stage IV follows III. (However, Stage III may be

Table 1. *Qualitative stages of bilingual development*

(A = Size of repertoire in first, B in second, language)

Stage	No. of relations	No. of elements
I	A	A
II	A^2	A
III	$A^2 + 2B$	A + B
IV	$A^2 + B^2 + 2B$	A + B
V	$A^2 + B^2 + 2AB$	A + B

substituted by a special condition, whenever the second language is introduced by extralingual rather than equivalence relations.) Stage V either follows II or IV or co-occurs with them, whenever both languages are simultaneously introduced under confounded conditions. Thus, the five stages, much like current theories of cognitive development, meet the requirement of partially ordered scales of developmental progression (see Reese 1973; Riegel 1972; Van den Daele 1969, 1973).

The five stages described represent an idealized sequence of bilingual development, i.e., development as it 'ought to be'. The few children who may ever follow such a progression most likely belong to the culturally favored group of well-educated bilingual parents. In contrast, the disadvantaged child of the ghetto is likely to be subjected to a pathological reversal of this sequence. He enters the linguistic community at the most advanced stage, i.e., at the stage of confounded bilingualism, and has to proceed backwards, most often left all on his own, in order to separate the two linguistic systems from one another as well as to apprehend the complex transformation matrices of interlingual relations. Is it any wonder that few of these children will succeed?

Interlingual relations. Undoubtedly, one-to-one equivalence relations are the exception rather than the rule and occur among the most common terms only, such as Table ⟺ Tisch, Horse ⟺ Pferd, etc. In most instances equivalence has either to be established at higher ranks, such as at the level of sentence parts, phrases, or whole utterances, or equivalence has to be sought between semantic classes rather than between its elements, i.e., words.

The issue of equivalence at higher ranks touches upon differences between languages in syntactic organization. To give but one example, languages differ in their degrees of inflection which are marking differentially the various sentence parts. Subsequently, in highly inflected languages such as Latin, Russian, or German, the word order can be varied more widely. Since inflected languages use specific word orders for different types of sentences but non-inflected languages do not, words will have to be shifted around in translation. Such operations tax the capacity of the translator and, in particular, rely on interlingual relations between various, non-equivalent items.

Lack of strict equivalence is also characteristic for members of semantic classes upon which not only second- but also first-language acquisition relies to an extent still not fully recognized in the literature. Membership in semantic classes is generally determined by asymmetric relations which group items together that, for instance, *do* similar things (predication), have similar *parts* (attribution), are found at similar *places* (location), or are *logically* included in the same class (superordination). If classes are formed on this basis in two languages, a higher-order equivalence can be established between them although their composition may vary. Instead of a simple one-to-one equivalence we are, thereby, considering a many-to-many equivalence.

We have proposed earlier (Riegel 1957, 1970; Riegel and Riegel 1963) that the apprehension of semantic classes and their constituting relations form the most important basis of language acquisition. We have extended this argument for the discussion of second-language acquisition (Riegel 1968) and have drawn particular attention to the interlingual connections between the semantic classes of two languages. Although considerable evidence now exists in support of such an interpretation of first-language acquisition (Riegel 1970; Bloom 1970; Brown 1973; Schlesinger 1972; for general operations of learning and memory, Kintsch 1972; Rummelhart, Lindsay, and Norman 1972), no supportive records are available for bilingual comparisons. In particular, we are not able to pinpoint the differences and similarities in semantic organization and, subsequently, in semantic equivalence structure between standard and non-standard English.

Environmental utility. Let us return to our example of a child skimming over the matrices of intra- and interlingual relations, his intake being limited during a given time period to a constant amount of relational information which might be visualized as a small subsection bounded by a frame of a given size. The longer the child has been scanning the matrix, i.e., the longer he has lived, the more likely it becomes that he will encounter information which he has already received once or several times before. With advancing age the individual depletes more and more the information provided; it becomes less likely that he discovers something new.

On the basis of such reasoning it is possible to generate a growth function in which the depletion of the outer linguistic contingencies is plotted against age. As academic as such enterprise might seem, it opens important possibilities for evaluating the utility or efficiency of various bilingual contingencies. Although the details of such models can not be presented at this occasion (see Riegel 1968), some inferences concerning the conditions of the ghetto child will be discussed.

Figure 2 shows some growth curves, on the left for independent and on the right for confounded bilingual development. In both instances the shift into bilingual contingencies occurs at the relative late age of about 17 years; also in both cases the distribution between languages A and B is even, i.e., half of the time is devoted to the first language, the other half to the second language. In general, the main purpose of models like ours is, of course, to vary both the time of shift and/or the proportions of exposures in order to study the efficiency of the bilingual contingencies.

The two diagrams, in comparison to one another, reveal once more the problems of confounded bilingualism. Here, most of the efforts are devoted to the set of interlingual relations. More detailed information on the utility of these bilingual conditions can be obtained by using the monolingual curve as upper boundary and comparing the areas below it with those of the different bilingual curves. The closer the approximation of the monolingual curve, the greater the utility of the condition.

On the basis of such calculations utility curves have been derived (see Riegel 1968, Figure 2). Keeping again the proportional distribution constant at 50%, the utility is a function of the time of the switch into the bilingual condition. If this switch occurs early in life, the first language will suffer greatly over an extended period of time; second language acquisition, will make relatively quick advances, however. If the switch occurs late, the first language is less effected but the progress in the second language is retarded. Special inferences about shifts in dominance between the two languages can be made if the proportional distribution is varied in conjunction with the time of the switch. Although these comparisons are purely theoretical, they allow for detailed predictions of bilingual development and subsequently for planned arrangements of optimal environmental conditions. In this regard it is again most obvious that the confounded contingencies under which most of the efforts are directed to the interlingual matrices are by far the least desirable conditions for both first- and second-language acquisition.

Conclusions. (a) An answer to the question whether one should or should not aim toward bilingual education lies outside the conceptual framework presented here, but by implication we have maintained that monolingualism is a true form of cultural deprivation. After all, the majority of the world's population are bilingual. From this point of view, Black children are advantaged. Since monolingualism provides restricted information in an effective manner, however, we have to search for the

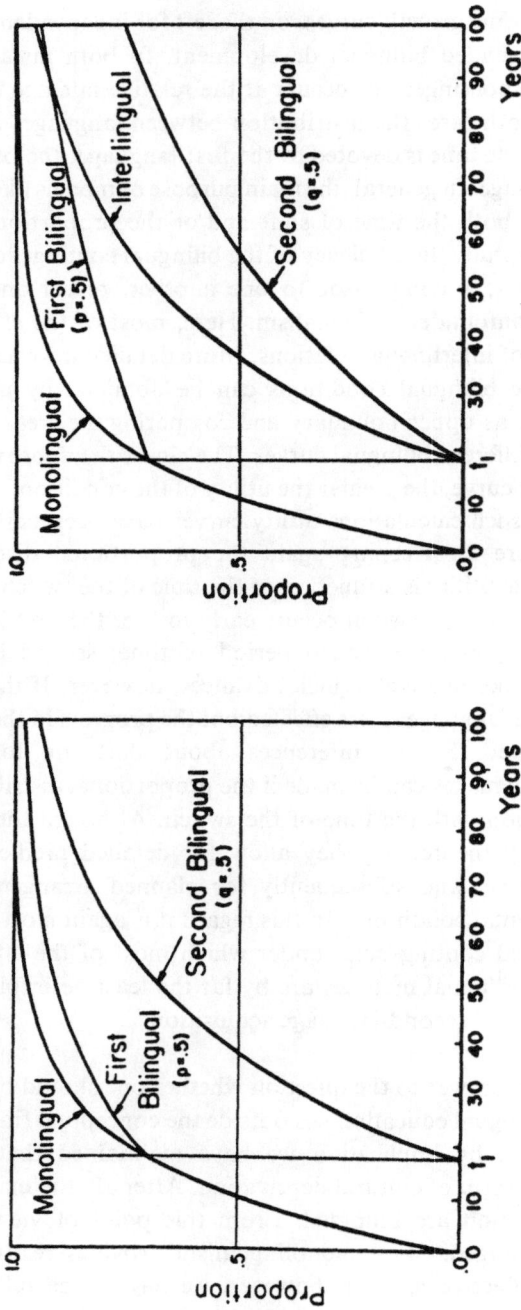

Figure 2. *Comparisons of growth curves for independent (left figure) and confounded bilingual (right figure) conditions. Age for introducing second language is 17.5 years.*

optimal progression of bilingual development. (b) Neither independent nor confounded bilingualism in their extreme constitute reasonable and efficient conditions of progression. A coordinated form is ideal which maximizes transfer of knowledge across languages and minimizes interferences. Such a form can only be established through explorations of semantic interlingual structures or what might be called semantic-syntactic transformation matrices. At the present time, such explorations are lacking. (c) If raised under such conditions, the independent bilingual will, then, be able to transfer a much greater share of his first language knowledge to his second language. The confounded bilingual is still not much assisted because he has, first, to differentiate the two language systems from one another before, second, such transfer can take place. (d) In returning to our introductory statements, we request that, regardless of whether Black and white English dialects are linguistically sufficiently distinct, for the benefit and well-being of the confounded child, they ought to be treated as such. Only when conceptually a clearer separation is created can we expect the child to progress efficiently in either of the two languages.

B. AN INFORMATION PROCESSING APPROACH TO SOME PROBLEMS IN DEVELOPMENTAL SOCIOLINGUISTICS

by Roy O. Freedle, *Educational Testing Service, Princeton,* and William S. Hall, *Vassar College, Poughkeepsie*

It seems useful to address ourselves to the cultural context of language use in attempting to place an information-processing approach to developmental sociolinguistics in proper perspective. To accomplish this, we shall rely in part on some recent work in ethnopsychology – especially that of Cole, Gay, Glick, and Sharp (1971).

A portion of Cole *et al.*'s empirical work suggests to us the possibility that there are at least some experimental tasks which different races and different language users respond to in basically the same manner. By this we mean that the information-processing steps by which some problem is solved can be isomorphic across the various subject populations tested. One example in the Cole *et al.* book which leads us to this conclusion is their revision of what is called the Kendler Inference Experiment (see Kendler, Kendler and Carrick 1966). The abstract characterization of the experiment is what concerns us at the moment and not the specifics of the task.

The Kendler task has two major considerations for cross-cultural comparisons: (a) the familiarity of the objects which comprise the inference task; and (b) the degree to which a prelearned associative link has been established across the task objects. Cole *et al.* tested seven variants of these task features and concluded that Kpelle and American children of several ages respond in very similar fashion for many variants of this task. This result can be interpreted to mean that if a full information processing analysis of the inference task were constructed, then the same underlying cognitive steps (decisions) would be required to explain the data of each population of subjects; the only differences, if there are any, presumably would be reflected in the magnitude of the model parameters which characterize each step of the decision process. If the task happens to emphasize aspects of the culture which are unique to that culture then it may be necessary to postulate cognitive decisions which differ across the populations tested. If, however, the task has been carefully constructed so as to tap cognitive decisions which are universal to all cultures then the decision parameters may well be statistically identical across populations. Finally, there may be tasks which favor a mixture of these two basic types, that is, wherein some of its steps favor unique cultural knowledge while the remaining steps in the task cut across the universal features of all cultures. In terms of guideline principles, a critical feature of the above comparisons may involve some function of the similarity of one culture to another. Subcultures of the same basic culture such as one finds in America may be so similar that every such task on which the subgroups are compared may be assumed *a priori* to be isomorphic in their basic underlying information-processing steps.

This latter assumption is precisely the one that we shall make now in fitting an information processing model for a sentence imitation task in two dialects. The task was presented to 240 eight- and ten-year-olds consisting of an equal number of Blacks and whites, males and females, and lower and middle socioeconomic levels. The members of each of the populations can be considered to be members of highly similar subcultures in contemporary urban America. Each group responded to sentences presented in either standard or so-called nonstandard English.

Let's consider what a subject must do in responding to this task. On any one trial he is read a sentence that either matches or mismatches his preferred dialect. If it matches his preferred dialect we assume that this may influence his ability to code the semantic and syntactic information in his short-term memory; also it may affect the accuracy with which he can retrieve the information when he starts his overt recall of the sentence. Each one of these three aspects (preference, coding in memory, and retrieval) can be considered to be steps in an information-processing model. A full elaboration of this model would help to account for errors and deletions that are made in this task by introducing steps in the process that reflect, for example, failure to store information in short-term memory and/or failure to retrieve the information stored in memory.

Notice that some of the factors which affect the covert information processing decisions may in this present task be identified as cognitive ability parameters such as memory; other factors will be more appropriately characterized as ones which are identified with those qualities which are unique to the subcultures tested, namely, their preference for using one dialect over another. Thus, this latter factor of the decision model which measures degree of preference for one dialect system over another should be a function of what race and social class the experimental subject belongs to.

The sentence imitation task that we have examined at this point seems to represent a mixed system inasmuch as we can identify memory coding steps which should yield the same parameter values for the populations tested, and it also involves a dialect preference 'step' for which the various subcultures are likely to differ significantly. Clearly, finding significant differences on the dialect preference part of the task cannot be construed as implicating the superiority or inferiority of any subcultural group over another. Finding significant differences, if there are any, on the memory parameter would require a more careful examination of the sources of these differences. For example, if it is found that the memory parameter interacts with the type of dialect sentence with which the subject is presented, then one is not justified in pretending that the steps in the information processing model are independent. Also, if interaction occurs one would not be justified in concluding that one subgroup is superior to the others if they have a significantly higher memory parameter value. Instead, one should attempt to track down the source of the interaction in terms of the task requirements as a function of the subcultural differences.

In the title to this paper we have promised to deal with developmental changes that occur across various social groups of basically the same culture. Recall that we are testing 8- as well as 10-year-olds in this sentence recall task. The same information processing model is assumed to be appropriate at both these age groups inasmuch as both these age groups share basically the same culture. Had the two age groups been widely different (say, a group of 3-year-olds were contrasted with a group of 70-year-olds) then we may well question whether the same information-processing model is appropriate to these several age groups. Again, the underlying conception of the similarity of one subpopulation to another is the source of this intuition just as the similarity of the subcultures of the same basic culture was the source of intuition that the same information-processing model should apply to each population tested. We can anticipate that age differences will show up as primarily differences in magnitude of the memory parameter. Furthermore we can expect that each subpopulation will show an increase in the memory parameter as a function of increasing age (here, from age 8 to 10). We shall not make similar regularizing assumptions about how the magnitude of the dialect preference parameter will change with age for each of the subpopulations inasmuch as we can anticipate that a much more complex network of social pressures is operating so that some social groups might show a decrease in preference for a given dialect while other social groups might show an increase in preference. The nature of the information-processing model that we are fitting is such that we still shall be able to make intelligible statements regarding changes in the magnitude of the dialect preference parameter after each set of data has been fitted.

An information-processing model. We shall now construct the specifics of an information processing model for a sentence recall task using standard and nonstandard English sentences as stimuli. Eight groups of subjects will be examined separately: 8-year-old white lower class, 10-year-old white lower class, 8-year-old Black lower class, 10-year-old Black lower class, 8-year-old white middle class, 10-year-old white middle class, 8-year-old Black middle class, and 10-year-old Black middle class. In each group there are an equal number of male and female subjects. Every subject received 30 sentences to imitate; half of these were presented in standard English and the remaining half in nonstandard English. Using a scoring scheme given in greater detail by Hall and Freedle (1973) we obtained the proportion correct imitations, the proportion deletions and/or substitutions, as well as the proportion translation responses for each of the following fourteen grammatical structures: standard third person singular, standard copula, standard negation, standard use of the conditional 'if' clause, standard past marker, standard possessive, and standard use of plural nouns, nonstandard third person singular, nonstandard copula, nonstandard negation, nonstandard use of the 'if' conditional, nonstandard past marker, nonstandard possessive, and nonstandard use of the 'be' construction. Examples of these are found in Table 1.

Table 1. *Some examples of syntactic differences between standard and nonstandard English*[a]

Variable	Standard English	Black nonstandard English
Linking verb (copula)	He *is* going.	He __ goin'.
Possessive marker	John'*s* cousin.	John cousin.
Plural marker	I have five cent*s*.	I got five cent__.
Third person singular (verb agreement)	He live*s* in New York.	He live__ in New York.
Past marker	Yesterday he walk*ed* home.	Yesterday he walk__ home.
'If' construction	I asked *if he did it.*	I ask *did he do it.*
Negation	I *don't* have *any.*	I *don't* got *none.*
Use of 'be'	Statement: he is here *all the time.*	Statement: He *be* here.

[a] This table is adapted from one presented by Joan Baratz 1969, pp. 99–100.

As already alluded to, several things can occur in responding to a particular structure. The subject may correctly repeat it, or he may translate it into a form appropriate to the other dialect, or he may fail to respond and/or he may use some novel response in place of the correct one. Deletions and novel reponses were scored together. The information-processing model that we shall now describe is intended to account for all the patterns of correct repetitions, deletions, and translations that occur for each grammatical structure within and across dialects for each of the eight groups of subjects.

By following Figure 1 the information-processing model should become clear to the reader. Each branch of the model is labelled by a Roman numeral to facilitate reference to each branch of the tree structure.

Figure 1. *Information-processing assumptions for a sentence imitation task in two dialects*

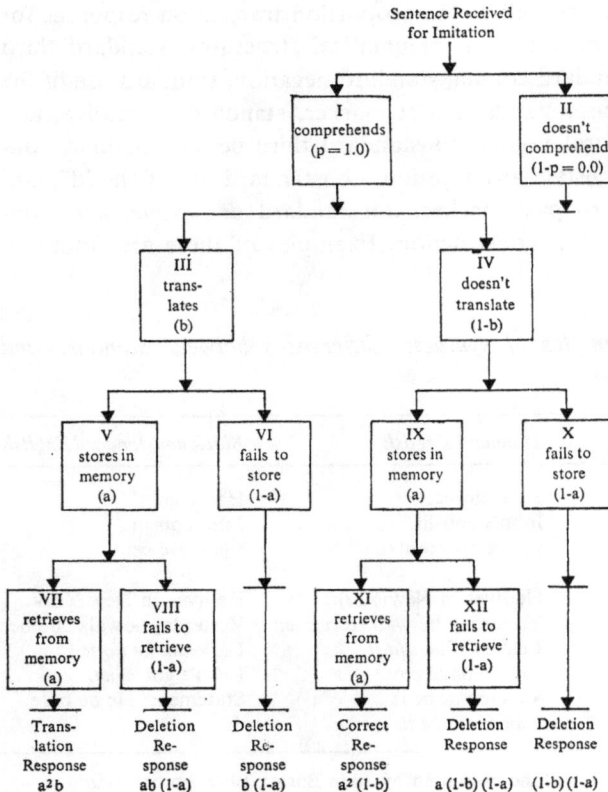

At the top we see indicated the presentation of a particular stimulus sentence. We need not distinguish at this point whether the sentence is given in standard or nonstandard English because the same abstract model is used for both types of structures. Once the stimulus sentence is received the subject either comprehends it (I) or fails to comprehend it (II). Since all of the subjects with whom we are dealing in this experiment are older subjects, it will greatly simplify our model if we assume here that for all intents and purposes all subjects comprehend the import of each sentence that is presented them even though we admit that the white middle-class subjects may find some of the sentences which are presented in nonstandard English strange.

Following comprehension, the subject will either translate (III) the sentence or sentence phrase or sentence fragment into the dialect opposite the one in which the stimulus sentence was presented (the degree to which this is done will be a function of his preference for coding in one dialect over the other), or he will fail to translate it (IV). The probability that he will translate is given by the parameter b. Thus b can be interpreted as a dialect preference parameter.

Below Roman numerals III and IV we see that the model is quite similar. For example, we see that in each case the subject either successfully stores the results of the prior decision (III) in memory (V) or he fails to store it (VI); similarly, below decision IV, the subject will either store the outcome of decision IV in memory (IX) or he will fail to store it (X). Also, if he stores the information successfully at (V) he will either successfully retrieve this information when it comes time to overtly recall it (VII) or he will fail to retrieve it (VIII). When he fails to retrieve the information it is assumed that this results in a Deletion Response. Also if the subject fails to store the information at VI this too will contribute to the observed magnitude of the Deletion Response. Below branch IX we see the same kind of structure: Either the subject retrieves the information in the form that he stored it in (XI) or be fails to do so (XII). Failure to do so again contributes to the magnitude of the Deletion Response as does failure to store the information at step X. Thus there are four pathways of the decision tree which contribute to a Deletion Response; each of the four pathways has a different probability of occurring as we see indicated in Figure 1 below branches VIII, VI, XII, and X. The probability $ab(1-a)$ is obtained by multiplying the parameter estimates encountered from the top of the figure down to branch VIII. Thus at branch I one has the value 1.0, this is multiplied by the parameter *b* that occurs at branch III, which in turn is multiplied by the parameter *a* which occurs at branch V, and finally parameter (1–a) which occurs at branch VIII is multiplied by all the above. The net result is ab (1–a).

A correct response has probability $a^2(1-b)$ of occurring as Figure 1 illustrates. A translation response has probability a^2b of occurring; finally, a deletion response has an overall probability of $1-a^2$ of occurring. All three of these probabilities sum to 1.0.

Results for the unrestricted model. The unrestricted model refers to the *a* and *b* parameters which were estimated for each age group. (Later we shall present a restricted model which makes a linearity assumption about how the magnitude of the memory parameter *a* changes from age 8 to age 10 – the reason for this restricted model is to gain degrees of freedom so as to fit the model to the data in a nontrivial way; the unrestricted model exhausts all the degrees of freedom, and in so doing, achieves a perfect fit to the data.) We shall now use the parameter values from the unrestricted model to compare the several subcultural groups to determine possible significant differences in some or all of the parameters.

Memory: Parameter a comparisons. Ignoring age, Black middle class equals white middle class in memory for standard sentences ($p = .395$, 1-tailed, n.s.). Also middle class Blacks are not different from middle class whites in memory for nonstandard sentences ($p = .212$, 1-tailed, n.s.). Again, ignoring age effects, Black lower class equals white lower class in memory for standard sentences ($p = .092$, 2-tailed, n.s.). However, Black lower class is significantly higher in memory parameters than white lower class when nonstandard sentences are examined ($p = .002$, 2-tailed).

Still ignoring age effects and comparing SES effects within each racial group, we find that Black middle-class subjects do better, but not significantly so, than Black lower class on standard sentences ($p = .090$, 1-tailed). Black lower class does significantly better than middle-class Blacks on nonstandard sentences ($p = .046$, 1-tailed). This latter effect is easy to understand if we remember that lower-class Blacks probably speak Black dialect on more occasions than do middle-class Blacks. This fact also presumably could be used to explain why middle-class Blacks do somewhat better (but not significantly so) on standard sentences. White middle class does significantly better than white lower class in memory for standard sentences ($p = .001$, 1-tailed). However, less easy to understand is the fact that white middle class also does significantly better than lower class on the nonstandard structures ($p = .001$, 1-tailed).

Every group improved significantly in its memory parameter when 8-year-olds were contrasted with the same parameter at age 10. This was true for nonstandard as well as standard structures.

For each of the eight subject groups there was significantly better performance on standard structures than nonstandard. This particular result is important inasmuch as it means that the ability to store and retrieve information is not independent of the dialect code in which it is presented by the experimenter. The surprise in this is that our Black subjects found it easier to store and retrieve standard stimulus sentences (the reader is cautioned here that we are not talking about proportion correct repetitions, but rather the magnitude of the under-lying memory ability parameter a). This perhaps makes some sense if we recall from the Hall and Freedle (1973) study that in a communication task these same Blacks spontaneously produced more standard forms than nonstandard forms. Since our 8- and 10-year-old black subjects in the imitation study appear to use predominantly standard dialect (at least in the setting in which we tested them – a school setting), this helps us explain why these same subjects found it easier to store and retrieve standard grammatical forms better than nonstandard – it is because they use these forms to a greater extent in their spontaneous speech. We see that what appears at first to be a counterintuitive result with the memory parameter for these Black subjects can be partially interpreted with the aid of data obtained from other experimental settings – in particular, a communication study. This points up the need for data on the same subjects in a variety of different settings and tasks when attempting to inter-pret dialect usage from a psychological modelling point of view.

Dialect preference: Translation parameter b comparisons. Eight- and 10-year-old middle-class Blacks show a significantly greater tendency to translate *from standard to nonstandard* than do 8- and 10-year-old middle-class whites ($p < .001$, 2-tailed). This is somewhat interesting inasmuch as we have already noted that with respect to the memory parameter, these same subjects are equal to the whites. This suggests that in some cases a dialect preference difference need not alter or interact with memory ability. On the other hand, 8- and 10-year-old middle-class whites show a significantly greater tendency to translate *nonstandard into standard* forms ($p < .001$, 2-tailed) than middle-class Blacks. This is hardly surprising inasmuch as these whites are probably quite unfamiliar with the syntax of nonstandard grammatical forms.

Eight- and 10-year-old Black lower-class children showed a significantly stronger preference (parameter *b*) for coding in nonstandard dialect when nonstandard stimuli were presented in comparison with 8- and 10-year old white-lower class children ($p < .001$, 1-tailed). When standard sentences were presented black lower class children again showed a significantly greater tendency to code in Black English than do the white lower-class children ($p < .001$, 1-tailed). Both of these findings are consistent with common sense inasmuch as the Black children first learn so-called nonstandard English and speak this dialect more frequently than do white children. Because of this, one would expect this dialect to be stronger for them (in a preferential sense) than it is for whites of the same social class.

A restricted information processing model. The unrestricted model presented above exhausted all the degrees of freedom in the data. In so doing it resulted in a perfect fit to the data. Our purpose in presenting the parameters for the overly restrictive model was to examine the relative magnitudes of the values across different subject populations so as to determine wherein the various subgroups differ and wherein they are similar. Thus, the unrestricted model served a limited but useful purpose: group comparisons in parameter magnitudes. To be scientifically interesting, though, a model should not exhaust all the degrees of freedom. One way of gaining degrees of freedom in such a model is to introduce restrictive or regularizing assumptions across the different subject populations in one or more of the underlying parameter values. Since the age effects for each population appear to be quite regular in its memory parameter results, we decided to introduce our simplifying assumption at this point in the model. The degree to which a linear relationship assumption holds across the memory parameter *a* as a function of age (the restrictive information processing model) is very high. A figure which presents the observed and predicted proportion of correct repetitions, deletions, and translations for standard as well as nonstandard grammatical forms can be scanned for four groups: lower-class Blacks, lower-class whites, middle-class Blacks, and middle-class whites. Visual inspection indicates that the observed and predicted values cluster close to the line of perfect fit thereby suggesting that our assumption, about how the memory parameter *a* increases linearly from age 8 to 10, may be a fairly accurate one.

At this point in fitting the model to the data and observing, visually, how well the data and model appear to agree, one is caught midstream in the scientific enterprise of deciding whether to leave the model stand in its current form or modify it. The possibility of further modification is mentioned here for the following reason. It is possible to detect a very slight deviation of observed from predicted values when tables of parameter values for standard and nonstandard structures are examined (these tables are available upon request). The discrepancy, though small, has the following source: In fitting a memory parameter across the two age samples it was assumed that the same linear increase would hold regardless of whether standard or nonstandard forms were being considered. This latter assumption turns out to be erroneous inasmuch as the memory parameter a is slightly underestimated for standard forms and slightly overestimated for nonstandard forms. This deviation can of course be quickly removed by fitting a different linear increase for standard and nonstandard forms. The reason this has not been pursued here is that the degree of improvement is quite negligible. It is possible, of course, that in future elaborations of this information-processing model in new experimental settings, a more dramatic departure of observed and predicted values might be traceable to this interaction of memory parameter magnitude with dialect. If this is found, then of course it would become advisable to separately estimate the linear increase in the memory parameter a for each set of sentences presented in a given dialect.

Conclusions. Sociolinguistic theory has not been directed at asking basic psychological questions concerning the source, cognitive processes, and perceptual mechanisms that lead to observable differences in speech behavior as a function of social-class variables. With the awareness that such an enterprise is not only feasible, but that it lies well within the current capabilities of psychological theory, we see that a part of sociolinguistic theory and its findings can be recast as psychological in its underpinnings. One seeks therefore those perceptual, preferential, and process mechanisms that will help explain not only the short-range effects of psychosocial phenomena on speech, but also long-range effects. Regarding long-range effects, at the group level, one would wish to uncover psychological mechanisms that lead to historical changes in semantic, syntactic, and stylistic forms. At the individual level one would like to describe how the uses of language alter the manner in which the prelinguistic infant and child (see Lewis and Freedle 1972) comes to learn his language from his parents and peers (see Hall and Freedle 1973). Thus one is led to postulate models for developmental sociolinguistics that interrelate such variables as basic abilities (memory), social preferences (dialect preferences), social pressures to conform to the primary speech community (standard dialect), and so on. In addition, postulates are needed to specify how these abilities, preferences, and pressures change over an individual's lifetime as a function of who he is, how he is viewed by others, etc.

In the modest information-processing model that we have presented above, we can find many of these sociolinguistics factors operating. For many of these factors, we have postulated psychological mechanisms such as comprehension routines, memory storage, dialect preferences, and retrieval capabilities which not only help account for the detailed patterns of the data but also serve as numeric indices which can be contrasted across subcultural populations. Further we have used the same structural approach to account for developmental changes over time in our subcultural groups. Needless to say, such cross-group comparisons are only valid providing that the same underlying information-processing mechanisms are at work in each subgroup. In spite of this caveat, we are encouraged that viable psychological mechanisms can be uncovered and used to explain data which previously was the province of linguists. We do not thereby usurp their territory or call into question the regularities they have uncovered; rather, we seek alternative explanations for these regularities.

Additional studies that tap other language levels such as semantic comprehension which are studied as a function of social variables would presumably also lend themselves to an information-processing approach. In addition, conditions which affect sentence production, stylistic shifts, and so on, as a function of the sociolinguistic setting, may eventually lend themselves to a similar approach, although models of language production are harder to construct than are language comprehension (see Trabasso 1972) and language repetition tasks (see Freedle and Hall 1972a, 1972b).

To sum up, our generally good fits of model to data for eight sociolinguistic groups of subjects and the rather compelling identification of the information-processing steps with basic psychological mechanisms have persuaded us of the viability of studying similar subcultures via the same basic model. The results of having applied this model suggests to us that Blacks and whites do not differ in the abstract structures of their underlying decisions. In particular, the same branching structure lent itself to good fits for every group. When one examines the magnitudes of the resulting parameters for each stage of the decision tree, one finds evidence for the equality of the races in terms of memory storage and retrieval operations. Differences were primarily due to nonability factors such as the degree of preference one had for one dialect over another. Additional psychological theory is required however to untangle why there is occasionally an interaction between the magnitude of the memory parameter and the particular dialect that the linguistic stimuli are presented in; since this occurred not only for true bi-dialectal speakers (the Blacks) as well as for middle-class whites (who are largely single dialect speakers) it suggests that cognitive mechanisms are used differently in some as yet unspecified way to account for this interaction effect.

C. SOME PSYCHOLINGUISTIC AND SOCIAL PREDICTORS OF DIALECT USAGE AMONG SUBJECTS AND THEIR MOST PREFERRED PEERS*

by William S. Hall, *Vassar College, Poughkeepsie*, and Roy O. Freedle, *Educational Testing Service, Princeton*

Who are those who most influence language acquisition in children and later in adolescence? For the earliest phase, is it the members of the immediate family, in particular the mother and older sibs, rather than people outside the household who most influence the acquisition of language forms? As the child gets older, do the same people continue to influence his language, or do other sources, especially peers, begin to exert a more powerful effect on both his grammatical forms and the frequency with which these forms are used? These questions take on another level of complexity when we address issues of the acquisition of one or more dialects. Carroll (1968) has pointed out that aspects of language learning with respect to syntax and vocabulary, as well as reading and writing skills, continue to grow well beyond the early years. This is partly in contrast to a widely held viewpoint that virtually all language syntax is acquired by the age of four for monolingual children. Because of Carroll's (1968) work one sees the legitimacy of inquiring about the relative effects of peer vs. family influence on language after the age of four.

While Carroll's (1968) review has covered language development of the monolingual child, we know of no review which covers the degree to which language skills continue to grow for American populations in which two or more dialects are spoken. An educated guess would lead us to suspect that similar growth in syntactic competence occurs for diglossic language users. While our primary focus in this paper is an examination of the degree to which peers influence aspects of language usage of their friends, we shall first review the general literature on peer influence for those variables which will be implicated in the research reported here. Those wishing a more comprehensive review in this regard are referred to Hartup's excellent review (1970).

* The research on which this paper is based was supported by a grant from the Carnegie Corporation of New York to Princeton University for William S. Hall. The preparation of this manuscript was supported in part by Educational Testing Service and Princeton University.

Peer-influence research. The research on age differences suggests that there is a curvilinear relation between age and peer conformity (Berenda 1950; Hunt and Synnerdale 1959; Starkweather 1964; Marple 1933; Patel and Gordon 1960; McConnell 1963; Iscoe, Williams and Harvey 1963; Costanzo and Shaw 1966; and Harvey and Rutherford 1960). While the age at which peer influence is greatest is not agreed upon by all researchers, middle childhood appears to be the peak period for responsiveness to such influence. The inexactness regarding age implicates other factors such as cultural experience. Iscoe, Williams and Harvey (1964), for example, found that peer conformity among white children increased between 9 and 12 years and then decreased, and that conformity among Black children increased between 7 and 9 years and decreased steadily thereafter. The white children, as a whole, were found to be more conforming than the Black children. The research on age supports Piaget's (1932) theoretical statement about social development which posits a curvilinear relation between chronological age and conformity in children.

Under most conditions, girls are more likely to yield to peer pressure than are boys. However, situational factors can either enhance or reverse this difference. Iscoe *et al.* (1964), for example, found a significant race-by-sex interaction in conformity. Specifically, white females conformed more than white males. On the other hand, Black males were more conforming than Black females. Further, Maccoby (1961) notes that acceptance of role enforcement from peers is significantly related to boy's own enforcement of rules over others. This was not the case, however, for girls. The data on sex cannot be interpreted to mean that females conform more than males. The fact of the matter is that situational factors, if they elicit sex-typed behavior, can serve either to enhance sex differences or reverse them.

Family and sib influence on language. Lewis and Freedle (1972) have argued that the primary caretaker can be shown to have a powerful influence on prelinguistic vocalization behavior. Across situations and socioeconomic level, they found differences in the patterned aspects of mother-infant vocalization interactions. In addition, they present evidence that these early vocalization behaviors are correlated with language behaviors at age two. Gelman and Shatz (1972) have touched upon issues indicating that both mother and slightly older sibs alter the complexity of their speech patterns presumably to increase the likelihood of young children's comprehension of them. This interesting fact points up the possibility that older sibs, as well as the mother, can have an impact on language development at the earliest ages. These researchers were also able to determine that a child with whom the subject was not familiar showed simplification of speech when directing his communication to the younger child. This fact merely illustrates the possibility that children outside the main household can contribute to language development in the child. These studies suggest that while the mother and sibs are probably the main influence on early language development, the possible influence of members outside the main household cannot be totally ruled out. Indeed Freedle and Hall (1973) have developed a rationale for why peers become more important influences on language while the nuclear family decreases in importance as the child grows older. In particular they implicate the increasingly complex locales to which the growing child is exposed. They indicate typically that the home is the primary locale for the infant. Later the home plus the immediate neighborhood become the major locales which can influence the semantic knowledge acquired by the child. This gets reflected in his speech. These increasingly complex locales also make available the language patterns of people external to the household and immediate neighborhood, but in addition the local town and still later the cities and more distant locales. If we accept such premises, each of these new locales opens up potential sources of language influence and semantic growth. Obviously, too, with each new locale the opportunity to engage in conversation with speakers of varying speech patterns also increases. Thus, it is possible that others can become a predominant influence on one's language usage as one gets older.

Method. One hundred and twenty children, randomly chosen from a population of 5-, 8-, and 10-year-olds, provided the subject sample for this research. At each age level an equal number of subjects were male and female, lower and middle class, Black and white. Subjects were asked to name their best friend in two instances, namely, in school and out of school. In 98% of the cases this proved to be the same person. These persons constituted the peers in this research. The total N here including subjects and peers was 248.

Subjects and peers were administered a Sentence Imitation Test containing 14 grammatical forms, 7 of them in standard English and 7 in Black dialect. Some examples which illustrate these different forms are as follows:

The copula in standard English in contrast to Black nonstandard

English is illustrated by the following pair of sentences: 'He is going' versus 'He goin'. Possessive marker differences are illustrated by 'John's cousin' versus 'John cousin'. Plural marker by 'I have five cents' versus 'I got five cent'. Third person singular by 'He lives in New York' versus 'He live in New York'. Past tense marker by 'Yesterday he walked home' versus 'Yesterday he walk home'. The 'If' construction by 'I asked if he did it' versus 'I ask did he do it'. Negation difference is illustrated by 'I don't have any' versus 'I don't got none'. And finally, use of 'be' is illustrated by the contrast between 'He is here all the time' as opposed to 'He be here'. These examples have all been adapted from Baratz (1969, pp. 99–100).

Prior to presenting our main results relating language similarities across subjects and their peers, we shall first present some results indicating the degree to which social background indicators influence peer choice. These social indicators will later be merged with the language ones in discussing subject-peer similarities. Blacks choose progressively fewer Blacks as friends as they get older. On the other hand, whites choose the same proportion of white friends irrespective of their age. Our data suggest that 5-year-olds invariably choose 5-year-olds, 8-year-olds tend to choose friends from a wider age range, and 10-year-olds tend to choose other 10-year-olds. Thus, a curvilinear trend is evident. With regard to sex group membership of peer choice, 5e- and 10-year-olds choose friends from the same sex group as their own, while 8-year-olds show a minor inconsistency in this regard. There appears to be curvilinear effect over age for friendship choice with respect to SES.

The data reveal perhaps two surprises. The first of these has to do with the race of the peers chosen by Black subjects. In a society that is only marginally pluralistic one might predict otherwise. The fact of the matter is that the children studied here live in a community where there is widespread bussing of children to achieve racial balance in the schools. This situation undoubtedly accounts in large measure for the cross-race choices of peers. Attending school outside of one's immediate neighborhood provides the opportunity to meet persons from an SES level different from one's own. The choice of peers outside of one's own SES level represents the second surprise here.

Results. We wish to present two kinds of results in support of our interpretation of predictors of dialect usage among subjects and their most preferred peers. First, we will present tables showing correlational data for subjects and peers. In this regard we only use overall scores received by subjects and peers on the sentence imitation task. Second, we present some regression results for language and social indicators.

Language correlations. We note in Table 1 that there is an age effect regarding total standard structures such that peers are most similar at age 10 and least so at age 5. This suggests that there is enough variability in either the grammatical forms that are being learned across dialects or in the frequency of usage of these once learned to permit these significant correlations to occur. Thus, this initial result can be considered an indirect support for Carroll's (1968) viewpoint that aspects of language usage continue to change for many years after the age of 4.

The data reported in Table 1 also indicate that peer similarity is best reflected in standard English performance on the sentence imitation task, while little peer similarity can be inferred from performance on the non-standard sentences. This partially dovetails with results obtained by Hall and Freedle (1973), who found that there was a higher intra-person correlation across language tasks when standard dialect scores were correlated and zero intra-person correlations for nonstandard scores.

Table 1. *Correlations for total standard and total nonstandard structures across subjects and peers*

	Standard		Nonstandard	
Age	Black	White	Black	White
5 years	.07	.08	.05	.00
8 years	.27	.44	.16	.08
10 years	.77*	.90*	.16	.06

* Significant beyond the .05 level

This was true for Black and white subjects considered separately. The above results suggest that a similar pattern holds for inter-person correlations.

The correlations listed in Table 1 might be interpreted as an indication that peers have an increasingly strong influence on each other as they approach adolescence. This interpretation takes on greater plausibility when we consider the fact that the correlations at age 5 are not significant. It raises the possibility that significant correlations at this age occur not with peers but with family members (see, for example, Hess and Shipman

1965). Moreover, we have some evidence that language measures on our 5-year olds do correlate significantly with measures of their mother's free production. We only allude to these results here because the measures are not strictly comparable to those used with peers. This finding, however, is quite plausible in light of our introductory comments which suggested that early in life immediate family members are by virtue of their proximity and frequent encounters in a position to exert a maximum influence on the language forms used by young children. As the child gets older he spends increasingly more time with others outside the household, and this provides a necessary, if not a sufficient, condition for his peers to exert influence on his language usage. This observation appears to hold regardless of race. The interpretation of peer influence seems plausible in the light of two findings: (a) the significant correlations at age 10 and at none of the other age periods studied; and (b) the significant relationship between child's language and mother's language at age 5 and at none of the other age periods studied.

Regression results for language and social indicators. In Table 2 a number of regression results are presented using all subjects ($N = 120$). The following format was followed. Each subject's scores on the standard grammatical forms, nonstandard grammatical forms, total standard grammatical forms, and total nonstandard grammatical forms, were used as dependent variables. The social indicators (age, race, class, and sex) were also used as dependent variables where appropriate. Each peer's scores on the standard grammatical forms, nonstandard grammatical forms, total standard grammatical forms, and total nonstandard grammatical forms were used as independent variables. Again, the social indicators (age, race, class, and sex) were used where appropriate. The analyses mentioned above represent the influence of peers on subject's scores. There is a reciprocal relationship of the subject's influence on the peer's scores. To study this second problem a similar set of regression analyses was run. Each peer's scores on the standard grammatical forms, nonstandard grammatical forms, total standard grammatical forms, and total nonstandard grammatical forms were used as dependent variables. The social indicators (age, race, class, and sex) were also used as dependent variables where appropriate. Each subject's scores on the aforementioned were used as independent variables.

Tabel 2. *Regression analysis for all subjects**

Column	A	B	C	D		E	
	Percent of variance without with social social indicators indicators		*F*	*t* of predictors largest		next largest	
Standard:							
3rd person	51	61	8.89	Totstan	3.47	S, 3rd	−2.90
copula	32	40	3.76	Age	2.69	S, 3rd	−1.39
negation	14	25	1.87	Age	2.25	NS, Poss	2.12
if	33	38	3.50	NS, 3rd	−2.14	NS, 'be'	2.12
possessive	30	42	4.03	Totstan	2.87	S, If	−2.71
plural	37	51	5.75	Age	2.47	Totstan	2.19
Nonstandard:							
3rd person	14	27	2.04	Race	−2.83	NS, 3rd	−1.92
copula	11	15	0.96	Totstan	−1.97	S, Neg	1.74
negation	18	26	2.02	NS, Poss	−2.79	Race	−2.27
if	34	45	4.60	S, 3rd	−2.38	Age	2.24
possessive	09	24	1.75	NS, Poss	−3.22	S, Neg	3.17
'be'	12	24	1.73	Age	2.89	Totstan	−2.09
Total standard	54	68	12.19	Age	3.51	Totstan	3.06
Total nonstandard	18	40	3.70	NS, Poss	−3.64	Age	2.70
Social indicators:							
Age	—	93	69.41	Age	11.57	Class	−8.06
Race	—	36	3.17	Race	3.07	NS, Poss	1.21
Class	—	26	1.93	Class	2.87	Sex	1.94
Sex	—	97	96.00	Sex	51.37	Race	4.76

* The regression analyses are based on $N = 120$ subjects. The F values are significant at the .05 level when $F = 2.14$ or larger. The regression results showing the reciprocal effect of peer back upon the subject are not shown.

Table 2 is organized to reflect only one kind of regression analyses: the effect of peer on subject. While the relationship among these variables can be viewed in several ways, we shall focus on the following three: (a) the degree to which each language indicator is predicted by all of the other language indicators; (b) the degree to which the same language indicators are predicted by the social indicators plus the language scores of the peer; and (c) the degree to which the social indicators of the subject are predicted by the language plus social indicators of the peer. The same three foci are addressed for peer to subject comparisons. Analyses were done by total sample, racial groups, social class groups, and sex groups. Space limitations allow us to present only the total sample results in great detail.

Attending first to the total sample in Table 2 we note several regularities. In Column A we find the percent of variance accounted for by language scores on both standard and nonstandard grammatical forms. The significance levels indicate that five of the six standard scores are significantly predicted by the peer's language scores, while for the nonstandard, only one of the six is significant. Further, total standard score is significantly predicted by peer's language scores. Clearly, standard English scores are more closely related across subjects and peers – perhaps this is to be expected, given the generally high salience of Standard English in the culture. That is to say, most of the subjects and their peers speak in standard English (see Hall and Freedle 1973). If this is so, it is precisely these forms that should extend the strongest influence.

In Column B we find the degree to which the various dependent variables are predicted by language and social indicators. Standard forms are better predicted than nonstandard ones. As before, total standard scores are still significantly predicted by the peer's scores. When social indicators are added, we find that nonstandard scores are significantly predicted by the peer's scores.

In addition, Table 2 lists the two best predictor variables that account for each dependent variable. It contains considerable surprises. To understand this consider the following argument: If one is attempting to predict a language score, it would seem likely that the best possible predictor would be another language score. Table 2 indicates that this is in general a false assumption. When both language and social indicator variables are present, the social indicators turn out to carry greater weight in predicting the language scores. This can be seen by scanning Columns D and E. For example, standard negation is best predicted by the age variable as indicated in Column D. Moreover, the column also indicates that when a social indicator is itself the dependent variable it is best predicted by the identical social indicator of the peer. For example, the age variable is best predicted by the peer's age variable.

Despite the fact that there was a preponderance of language over social indicators, the latter still emerged as powerful predictors of the language forms, particularly the standard ones. Before interpreting the import of these powerful social predictors, let us enumerate some additional findings for some of the special groups studied.

The results of separate regression analyses for Blacks and whites will now be briefly described. The method of analysis was identical to those for the total sample as presented in Table 2. Some interesting contrasts across racial groups can be noted. The peer choices for Black subjects exert only one significant effect for standard English (3rd person singular) and only one significant effect for nonstandard English (the 'if' construction). The peers chosen by whites, on the other hand, exert a consistent significant effect for four of the six standard forms (3rd person singular, copula, if, and possessive). They exert no significant effect for nonstandard forms. When social indicators are added along with language variables the pattern of significance shifts somewhat for Standard English irrespective of the subject's race.

For Black subjects, as far as language indicators go, total standard grammatical forms are significantly predicted by both language and social indicators. (The same does not hold for non-standard.) Furthermore, when social indicators are added they figure among the most significant predictors. When social indicators are themselves the dependent variables we find that they usually are best predicted by other social indicators; however, the results are not as uniform as those for the total sample.

For whites, on the other hand, total standard grammatical forms are significantly predicted by both language and social indicators. (Again, the same does not hold for non-standard English.) When social indicators are the dependent variables they usually are best predicted by other social indicators. The results here resemble in many respects those for the total sample as reported in Table 2. It is important to note here that there is a uniformity in the results for Blacks that does not occur for whites. For Blacks the peer's linguistic scores best predicted nonstandard English, whereas the peer's social 'scores' best predicted standard English. The data for whites do not show this uniformity.

Social class was also separately analyzed. For middle-class subjects we obtained the following: (a) For standard English, the peer choices exert a significant effect for third person singular, copula, and plural; (b) for nonstandard English a single structure is implicated – the if construction. The peers chosen by lower-class subjects exert a consistently significant effect on only two standard grammatical forms, the 3rd person singular and the if construction. However, when social indicators are added only the 3rd person singular is significant. Again, for non-standard English the if construction is the only form that is significantly predicted. For total standard structures, both language and social indicators exert influence on lower- and middle-class subjects. But, when we consider total nonstandard structures only social predictors are significant for lower-class subjects. For middle-class subjects, none of the *F*s are significant for total nonstandard grammatical forms. When social indicators are the dependent variables, they are usually best predicted by other social indicators, irrespective of social class.

Male and female samples were also separately analyzed. Looking first at the males, three linguistic variables exert a powerful influence when standard English is the point of departure – 3rd person singular, copula, and plural. The if construction again is implicated when nonstandard English is the point of departure. When social indicators are added as predictors, the same dependent variables are significant. Regarding total standard structures, both language and social indicators are significant predictors for males. For nonstandard English the pattern is less clear. When social indicators are the dependent variables they are usually best predicted by other social indicators. Few new surprises occur when we shift our focus to females. The copula drops out for standard English, but 3rd person singular and plural remain, while if and possessive are added. The if construction continues to remain central when we attend to nonstandard English. For total standard structures both linguistic and social indicators exert an influence, but this is not the case for nonstandard structures. Again, when social indicators are employed as dependent variables, other social indicators are by and large the best predictors of them.

Summary of results. Overall, we see that only 3rd person singular in standard English is significant across all analyses. It is interesting that this particular form is the most consistently significant variable since Hall and Freedle (1973) found this form to be of importance. This form is almost invariably best predicted by the social indicators. While the prior analyses done by Hall and Freedle (1973) were for intra-individual consistencies, the current findings show the 3rd person to be of special importance in relating inter-individual differences in peer choices. Again, scanning all results for the nonstandard forms we see that the if construction is invariably significant, with the exception occurring for whites. We further note that the best predictors of this are the other language forms. This again suggests some similarity to the findings previously reported by Hall and Freedle (1973) for nonstandard English. Another consistent finding is that total standard scores are consistently significant with social indicators almost invariably being the most important predictors of them. In addition, total nonstandard scores typically fail to yield significant F values. Generally speaking, in every analysis, when social indicators were dependent variables they almost always were best predicted by the same social indicator of peer choice.

As a final observation one can see evidence that there usually are more standard forms which are significant as compared to nonstandard forms. This may account for the consistent significance of the total standard score noted above. The fact that only one of the six nonstandard scores was usually significant probably helps to account for the fact that the total nonstandard score was typically not significant. We interpreted the large number of significant standard scores across peer choices to be traceable to the presumed fact that most of our subjects speak predominantly standard English – with 5-year-old Blacks being a possible exception (see Hall and Freedle 1973).

Conclusions. Our results clearly suggest that there are significant influences on language use after the age of 4. This supports Carroll's conclusion that a person's language skills continue to evolve through a longer period than early childhood. Further, we have already noted that there is a developmental trend to peer's influence on language usage. This appears to be true irrespective of racial group membership.

A central question that comes to mind in contrasting social milieu influences versus those of particular friends and immediate family members on a person's language is of interest here. We have noted that for 5-year-olds the peer has no detectable influence on either standard or nonstandard English. Moreover, we have alluded to the fact that the mother of the 5-year-old does have a significant effect on his language. If the social milieu were the primary determinant on dialect usage, it would seem to us that mother and peer would have been of equal importance. By this view we mean to say that a person's use of language is predictable from knowledge of his particular social milieu. Since we have found a differential influence of mother vs. peer at age 5 (and another pattern at age 10), we are led to conclude that knowledge of the social milieu does not exhaust all of the important information concerning language usage. We raise these issues because many of our regression analyses have indicated that the social milieu indicators (age, race, sex, and SES) were often the most potent predictors of language usage. Because of this, one might have maintained that knowledge of the milieu was the single most important element in interpreting our results. Our several analyses by age, however, indicate that this cannot be the full explanation. The particular individuals that one knows and interacts with presumably have a differential effect over age which goes beyond the effect of the milieu. In particular, the mother (or immediate family) has a strong early influence, while peers have a strong late influence.

Bibliography

Abelson, R.P., Aronson, E., McGuire, W.J., Newcomb, T.M., Rosenberg, M.J., & Tannenbaum, P.H. (Eds.), *Theories of cognitive consistency: A sourcebook.* Chicago, Rand McNally, 1968.

Adam, J. The relationship between visual illusions and figural aftereffects. *Australian Journal of Psychology*, 1966, *18*, 130–136.

Adams, M. The single woman in today's society. *American Journal of Orthopsychiatry*, 1971, *41*, 776–786.

Aebli, H. *Piaget and beyond.* Toronto, Ontario Institute for Studies in Education, 1973.

Ajuriaguerra, J. de, Boehme, M., Richard, J., Sinclair, H., & Tissot, R. Désintégration des notions de temps dans les démences dégénératives du grand âge. *Encephale*, 1967, *5*, 385–438.

Ajuriaguerra, J. de, Kluser, J., Velghe, J., & Tissot, R. Praxies ideatoires et permanence de l'objet. Quelques aspects de leur désintégration conjointe dans les syndromes démentiels du grand âge. *Psychiatry et Neurology*, Bâle, 1965, *150*, 306–319.

Ajuriaguerra, J. de, Richard, J., Rodriguez, R., & Tissot, R. Quelques aspects de la désintégration des praxies ideomatrices dans les démences du grand âge. *Cortex cérébral*, 1966, *2*, 438–462.

Albert, E.M. 'Rhetoric', 'logic', and 'poetics'. In Burundi, Culture patterning of speech behavior. *American Anthropologist*, 1964, *66*, 35–54.

Allen, L. An examination of the visual classificatory ability of children who have been exposed to one of the 'new' elementary science programs. *Science Education*, 1968, *52*, 532–539.

Allport, D.A. Studies in the psychological unit of duration. Unpublished doctoral dissertation, University of Cambridge, 1966.

Allport, G.W. European and American theories of personality. In H.P. David & H. v. Bracken (Eds.), *Perspectives in personality theory.* New York, Basic Books, 1957. Pp. 3–24.

Allport, G.W. The open system in personality theory. *Journal of Abnormal and Social Psychology*, 1960, *61*, 301–310.

Allport, G.W. *Personality: A psychological interpretation.* New York, Holt, 1937.

Allport, G.W. The personalistic psychology of William Stern. In B.B. Wolman, *Historical roots of contemporary psychology.* New York, Harper & Row, 1965. Pp. 321–337.

Allport, G.W. William Stern 1871–1933. *American Journal of Psychology*, 1938, *51*, 770–773.

Allport, G. W., & Vernon, P. E. *A study of values*. Boston, Houghton Mifflin, 1931 (new ed. with G. Lindzey, 1952).

Ananev. B. G., Dvorashina, M. D., & Kudryavtseva, N. A. *Human individual development and constancy of perception*. Moscow, Izd. Prosveshchenie, 1968.

Anastasi, A. *Differential psychology: Individual and group differences in behavior* (3rd ed.). New York, Macmillan, 1958.(a)

Anastasi, A. Heredity, environment and the question 'How?'. *Psychological Review*, 1958, *65*, 197–208.(b)

Anderson, G. C. Self regulatory mother-newborn interaction deprivation: A theoretical framework. Unpublished masters thesis, University of Wisconsin, Madison, 1972.

Anosohian, L., & Carlson, J. A study of mental imagery and conservation within the Piagetian framework. *Human Development*, 1973, *16*, 382–394.

Ansbacher, H. Adler, Alfred, & Hall, G. Stanley. Correspondence and general relationship. *Journal of the History of Behavioral Science*, 1971, *7*, 337–352.

Anthony, E. J. Behavior disorders of childhood. In P. H. Mussen (Ed.), *Carmichael's manual of child psychology*, vol. 2. New York, 1970, pp. 692–705.

Antsyferova, L. I. Psikhologiya lichnosti kak 'otkrytoy sistemy'. O kontseptsii G. V. Olporta [The psychology of personality as a 'open system'. On the conception of G. W. Allport]. *Voprosy psikhologii*, 1970, *16*, 168–177.

Aristotle, *The works of Aristotle*, vol. 2. Chicago, Encyclopaedia Britannica, 1952.

Aronfreed, J. *Conduct and conscience*. New York, Academic Press, 1968.

Arrington, Z. Future implications of increased labor force participation of older women. Paper presented at the 25th Annual Gerontological Society Meeting, San Juan, P. R., December, 1972.

Ausubel, D. P. *Theory and problems of adolescent development*. New York, Grune & Stratton, 1954.

Ausubel, D. P. *Theory and problems of adolescent development* (5th ed.). New York, Random House, 1962.

Ausubel, D. P. *Maori youth: A psychological study of cultural deprivation*. New York, Grune & Stratton, 1965.

Baer, D. M. An age-irrelevant concept of development. *Merrill-Palmer Quarterly*, 1970, *16*, 238–246.

Bähr, H. W. Nachwort. In H. W. Bähr (Ed.), *Eduard Spranger: Gedanken zur Daseingestaltung*. München, Piper, 1954.

Bakan, D. *Sigmund Freud and the Jewish mystical tradition*. Princeton, New Jersey, Van Nostrand, 1958.

Baldwin, A. D. *Theories of child development*. New York, Wiley, 1967.

Baldwin, A. L. A cognitive theory of socialization. In D. A. Goslin (Ed.), *Handbook of socialization theory and research*. Chicago, Rand McNally, 1969. Pp. 325–345.

Baley, S. *Zarys psychologii w związku z rozwojem psychiki dziecka* [Outline of psychology in connection to the psychic development of the child]. Wrocław-Warszawa, Książnica-Atlas, 1946.

Baltes, P. B. Longitudinal and cross-sectional sequences in the study of age and generational effects. *Human Development*, 1968, *11*, 145–171.

Baltes, P. B. Prototypical paradigms and questions in life-span research on development and aging. *Gerontologist*, 1973, *13*, 458–467.

Baltes, P. B., & Goulet, L. R. Status and issues of a life-span developmental psychology. In L. R. Goulet & P. B. Baltes (Eds.), *Life span developmental psychology: Theory and research*. New York, Academic Press, 1970. Pp. 3–21.

Baltes, P. B., & Nesselroade, J. R. The developmental analysis of individual differences on multiple measures. In J. R. Nesselroade & H. W. Reese (Eds.), *Life-span developmental psychology: Methodological issues.* New York, Academic, 1973. Pp. 219–251.

Bandura, A., & Walters, R.H. *Social learning and personality development.* New York, Holt, 1963.

Baratz, J.C. A bi-dialectal task for determining language proficiency in economically disadvantaged Negro children. *Child Development,* 1969, *40,* 889–902.

Barber, T.Z. *LSD, marijuana, yoga and hypnosis.* New York, Van Nostrand, 1969.

Barry, H., Child, I., & Bacon, M. Relation of child training to subsistence economy. *American Anthropologist,* 1959, *61,* 51–63.

Bart, P. Depression in middle age. In J. Bardwick (Ed.), *Readings on the psychology of women.* New York, Harper & Row, 1972. Pp. 134–142.

Bart, P. Mother Portnoy's complaint. *Trans-Action,* 1970, *8,* 69–74.

Bayley, N. The life-span as frame of reference on psychological research. *Vita Humana,* 1963, *6,* 125–139.

Baylor, G.W., Gascon, J., Lemoyne, G., & Pothier, N. An information processing model of some seriation tasks. *Canadian Psychologist,* 1973, *14,* 167–196.

Beilin, H. On the development of physical concepts. In T. Mischel (Ed.), *Cognitive development and epistemology.* New York, Academic, 1971. Pp. 85–119.(a)

Beilin, H. The training and acquisition of logical operations. In M. Rosskopf, L. Steffe & S. Taback (Eds.), *Piagetian cognitive development research and mathematical education.* Washington, D.C., National Council of Teachers of Mathematics, 1971. Pp. 81–124. (b).

Bekesy, G. von. *Sensory inhibition.* Princeton, New Jersey, Princeton University Press, 1967.

Bekhterev, V.M. *La Réflexologie collective,* 1953. Traduit du Russe, adapté et complété, par N. Kostileff. Neuchatel, Delachaux & Niestlé, 1957.

Bell, E.T. *The development of mathematics.* New York, McGraw-Hill, 1970.

Bell, I. The double standard of aging. *Trans-Action,* 1970, *8,* 75–80.

Bell, S.G. (Ed.) *Women: From the Greeks to the French revolution.* Belmont, Calif., Wadsworth, 1973.

Bell, S.M. The development of the concept of object as related to infant-mother attachment. *Child Development,* 1970, *41,* 291–312.

Bellman, B.L. Unpublished field notes. 1968.

Bem, S.L. The role of task comprehension in children's problem-solving (Report No. 62, Center for Human Growth and Development). Ann Arbor, Michigan, University of Michigan, 1968.

Benussi, V. Zur Psychologie des Gestalterfassens (die Müller-Lyersche Figur). In A. Meinong (Ed.), *Untersuchungen zur Gegenstandstheorie und Psychologie.* Leipzig, Johann Ambrosius Barth, 1904.

Berenda, R.W. *The influence of the group on the judgments of children.* New York, King's Crown Press, 1950.

Berg, E.E. L.S. Vygotsky's theory of social and historical origins of consciousness. Unpublished doctoral dissertation, University of Wisconsin, 1970.

Bernshteyn, N.A. Methods for developing physiology as related to the problems of cybernetics. In M. Cole & I. Maltzman (Eds.), *A handbook of contemporary Soviet psychology.* New York-London, Basic Books, 1969. Pp. 441–451.

Bernstein, N. *The co-ordination and regulation of movements.* New York, Pergamon Press, 1967.

Berry, J. Independence and conformity in subsistence level societies. *Journal of Personality and Social Psychology,* 1967, *7,* 415–18.

Berry, J. On cross-cultural comparability. *International Journal of Psychology,* 1969, *4,* 119–128.

Berry, J. & Dasen, P. *Culture and cognition: Reading in cross–cultural psychology.* London, Methuen, 1973.

Berry, J., W. Ecological and cultural factors in spatial-perceptual development. *Canadian Journal of Behavioral Science*, 1971, *3*, 324–336. (a)

Berry, J. W. Mueller-Lyer susceptibility: Culture, ecology, or race? *International Journal of Psychology*, 1971, *6*, 193–197. (b)

Berry, J. W. Temne and Eskimo perceptual skills. *International Journal of Psychology*, 1966, *1*, 207–229.

Bertalanffy, L. v. *Modern theories of development.* London, Oxford University Press, 1933.

Berthoff, W. *The ferment of realism: American literature 1884–1919.* New York, Free Press, 1965.

Bertlein, H. *Das Selbstverständnis der Jugend.* Berlin-Hannover, Schroedel, 1961.

Beth, E. W., & Piaget, J. *Epistémologie mathématique et psychologie.* Paris, P.U.F., 1961. (*Mathematical epistemology and psychology.* Dordrecht, Holland, D. Reidel, 1966.)

Bever, T. G. The cognitive basis for linguistic structures. In J. R. Hayes (Ed.), *Cognition and the development of language.* New York, Wiley, 1970. Pp. 279–362.

Binet, A. De la fusion des sensations semblables. *Revue Philosophique*, 1890, *10*, 284–294.

Binet, A. La measure des illusions visuelles chez les enfants. *Revue Philosophique*, 1895, *40*, 11–25.

Binet, A. La peur chez les enfants. *Année Psychologique*, 1895, *2*, 223–254.

Binet, A. Le Dantec's work on biological determinism and conscious personality. *Psychological Review*, 1897, *4*, 516–522.

Binet, A. *L'Etude expérimentale de l'intelligence.* Paris, Schleicher Frères, 1922.

Binet, A. Notes on the experimental study of memory. *American Naturalist*, 1897, *31*, 912–916.

Binet, A. Perceptions d'enfants. *Revue Philosophique*, 1890, *30*, 582–611.

Binet, A. Plural states of being. *Popular Science Monthly*, 1897, *50*, 539–543.

Binet, A. Recherches sur les mouvements chez quelques jeunes enfants. *Revue Philosophique*, 1890, *29*, 297–309.

Binet, A. Review of recent French works on psychology. *Psychological Review*, 1896, *3*, 551–556.

Binet, A. The mechanisms of thought. *Fortnightly Review*, 1895, *55*, 785–799.

Binet, A., & Charcot, J. M. Un calculateur de type visuel. *Revue Philosophique*, 1893, *35*, 590–594.

Binet, A., & Henri, V. Recherches sur le développement de la memoire visuelle des enfants. *Revue Philosophique*, 1894, *37*, 348–350.

Binet, A., & Vashide N., The influence of intellectual work upon the blood-pressure in man. *Psychological Review*, 1897, *4*, 54–66.

Birren, J. E. Principles of research on aging. In J. E. Birren (Ed.), *Handbook of aging and the individual: Psychological and biological aspects.* Chicago, University of Chicago Press, 1959. Pp. 3–42.

Birren, J. E. Toward an experimental psychology of aging. *American Psychologist*, 1971, *25*, 124–135.

Blakeley, Th. J. *Soviet theory of knowledge.* Dordrecht, Holland, Reidel, 1964.

Blishen, B. R. A socio-economic index for occupations in Canada. *Canadian Review Sociology and Anthropology*, 1967, *4*, 41–53.

Blonskii, P. P. *Memory and thinking*, 1935. In *Selected psychological works.* Moscow, Izd. Prosveshchenie, 1964.

Blood, R., & Wolfe, D. *Husbands and wives.* New York, Free Press, 1960.

Bloom, B. *Stability and change in human characteristics.* New York, Wiley, 1964.

Bloom, L. *Language development: Form and function in emerging grammars.* Cambridge, M.I.T. Press, 1970.

Bloom, L., *One word at a time: The use of single word utterances before syntax.* The Hague, Mouton, 1973.

Boat, B. M., & Clifton, C. Verbal mediation in four year old children. *Child Development,* 1968, *39,* 505–514.

Boring, E. G. *A history of experimental psychology.* New York, Appleton-Century-Crofts, 1929. (2nd rev. ed., 1950.)

Boston, L. M. *The children of Green Knowe.* New York, Harcourt-Brace, 1955.

Boston, L. M. *Yew Hall.* London, Faber & Faber, 1954.

Botwinick, J., Robbin, J. S., & Brinley, J. F. Reorganization of perceptions with age. *Journal of Gerontology,* 1959, *14,* 85–88.

Boulding, K. E. Dare we take the social sciences seriously? *American Psychologist,* 1967, *22,* 879–887.

Bovet, M. C. Cognitive processes among illiterate children and adults. In J. W. Berry & P. R. Dasen (Eds.), *Culture and cognition: Readings in cross-cultural psychology.* London, Methuen, 1974.

Bovet, M. Etudes interculturelles du développement intellectuel et processus d'apprentissage. *Schweizerische Zeitschrift für Psychologie und ihre Anwendung,* 1968, *27,* 189–199.

Bower, T. G. R. Conflict and development in infancy. Paper presented at the Merrill-Palmer Conference on Research and Teaching in Infant Development, Detroit, Michigan, February, 1973.

Bower, T. G. R., Broughton, J. M., & Moore, M. K. Development of the object concept as manifested in changes in the tracking behavior of infants between 7 and 20 weeks of age. *Journal of Experimental Child Psychology,* 1971, *11,* 182–193.

Bower, T. G. R., Broughton, J. M., & Moore, M. I. Infant responses to approaching objects: An indicator of response to distal variables. *Perception and Psychophysics,* 1970, *9,* 193–196.

Boyd, R. Analysis of the ego-stage development of school-age children. *Journal of Experimental Education,* 1964, *32,* 249–257.

Bracken, H. v. Anglo-amerikanische Persönlichkeitstheorien. In A. Wellek (Ed.), *Bericht 19. Kongreß Deutsche Gesellschaft Psychologie* (Köln 1953). Göttingen, Hogrefe, 1954. Pp. 89–111.

Brainerd, C. J. Continuity and discontinuity hypotheses in studies of conservation. *Developmental Psychology,* 1970, *3,* 225–228.

Brainerd, C. J. Order of transitivity, conservation, and class-inclusion of length and weight. *Developmental Psychology,* 1973, *8,* 105–116.(a)

Brainerd, C. J. The stage problem in behavioral development. Unpublished manuscript, University of Alberta, 1973. (b)

Brainerd, C. J., & Allen, T. W. Experimental inductions of the conservation of 'first-order' quantitative invariants. *Psychological Bulletin,* 1971, *75,* 128–144.

Brainerd, C. J., & Kaszor, P. An analysis of performance explanations of children's failures on the class-inclusion problem. Unpublished manuscript, University of Alberta, 1973.

Bransford, J. D., & Johnson, M. K. Considerations of some problems of comprehension. In W. G. Chase (Ed.), *Visual information processing.* New York, Academic Press, 1973. Pp. 383–438.

Brazelton, T. B. Effect of maternal medication on the neonate and his behavior. *Journal of Pediatrics,* 1961, *58,* 513–518.

Bridges, K. M. B. Emotional development in early infancy. *Child Development,* 1932, *3,* 324–341.

Brinley, J., & Fichter, J. Performance deficits in the elderly in relation to memory load and set. *Journal of Gerontology*, 1970, *25*, 30–35.

Bronckart, J.-P. Le role regulateur du langage chez l'enfant: Critique experimentale des travaux d'A. R. Luria. *Neuropsychologia*, 1970, *8*, 451–463.

Brown, R. *A first language*. Cambridge, Mass., Harvard University Press, 1973.

Brown, R. Grammatic morphemes and the modulation of meaning. Unpublished manuscript, Harvard University, 1972.

Brožek, J. &, Slobin, D.I. (Ed.) *Psychology in the USSR: An historical perspective*. New York, International Arts and Science Press, 1972.

Bruner, J.S. Competence of infants. Paper presented at the meeting of the Society for Research in Child Development, Minneapolis, April 1971.

Bruner, J.S., & May, A.A. Cup to lip. New York, John Wiley & Sons, 1972. (Film)

Bruner, J.S., May, A.A., & Koslowski, B. Intention to take. New York, John Wiley & Sons, 1972. (Film)

Bruner, J.S., Olver, R.R., Greenfield, P.M., *et. al. Studies in cognitive growth*. New York, Wiley, 1966.

Brunswik, E. *Perception and the representative design of psychological experiments* (2nd ed.). Berkeley, California, University of California Press, 1956.

Bühler, C. *Values in psychotherapy*. New York, Free Press, 1962.

Bühler, K. *Die Krise der Psychologie*. Jena, Fischer, 1927.

Bunge, M. *Method, model and matter*. Boston, D. Reidel Publishing, 1973.

Bunge, M. *Teoria y realidad*. Barcelona, Ariel, 1972.

Burnham, C.A. Decrement in the Mueller-Leyer illusion with saccadic and tracking eye movements. *Perception and Psychophysics*, 1968, *3*, 424–426.

Calhoun, A.W. *A social history of the American family*. New York, Barnes and Noble, 1966.

Campbell, D.T. The mutual methodological relevance of anthropology and psychology. In F. Hsu (Ed.), *Psychological anthropology*. Homewood, Ill., Dorsey Press, Inc., 1961.

Campbell, D.T., & Stanley, J.C. *Experimental and quasi-experimental designs for research*. Chicago, Rand McNally, 1966.

Campbell, J. *The masks of God: Occidental mythology*. New York, The Viking Press, 1964.

Carlson, E., & Carslon, R. Male and female subjects in personality research. *Journal of Abnormal and Social Psychology*, 1960, *61*, 482–483.

Carlson, J. Moral development in Lao children. *International Journal of Psychology*, 1973, *8*, 25–35.

Carnap, R. *Meaning and necessity*. Chicago, University of Chicago Press, 1958.

Carnap, R. *The logical structure of the world and pseudoproblems in philosophy*. Berkeley, California, University of California Press, 1967.

Carroll, J.B. Development of native language skills beyond the early years (Research Bulletin, RB-68-23). Princeton, N.J., Educational Testing Service. 1968.

Carter, D.J. Response to the successively presented Mueller-Lyer illusion as a function of interstimulus interval. Paper presented at 78th Annual Convention of the American Psychological Association, 1970.

Carter-Seeman, D.J. Temporal integration. Paper presented at the 79th Annual Meeting of the American Psychological Association, 1971.

Carter-Seeman, D.J. Temporal integration and development. Unpublished dissertation, University of Georgia, 1972.

Cassirer, E. *Language and myth*. New York, Dover, 1946.

Castaneda, A., Fahel, L. S., & Odom, R. Associative characteristics of sixty-three adjectives and their relation to verbal paired-associate learning in children. *Child Development*, 1961, *32*, 297–304.

Cavan, R. S., Burgess, E., Havighurst, R., & Godhamer, H. *Personal adjustment in old age*. Chicago, Science Research Associates, 1949.

Cellérier, G. Information processing tendencies in recent experiments in cognitive learning – theoretical implications. In S. Farnham-Diggory (Ed.), *Information processing in children*. New York, Academic Press, 1972. Pp. 115–123.

Chaing, C. A. A new theory to explain geometrical illusions produced by crossing lines. *Perception and Psychophysics*, 1968, *3*, 174–176.

Charlesworth, W. R. The role of surprise in cognitive development. In D. Elkind & J. H. Flavell (Eds.), *Studies in cognitive development*. New York, Oxford, 1969. Pp. 257–314.

Chaucer, G. *Canterbury tales*. Baltimore, Penguin Books, 1952.

Chickering, A. W. *Education and identity*. San Francisco, Jossey-Bass, 1969.

Chomsky, N. *Language and mind*. New York, Harcourt, Brace & World, 1968.

Ciaccio, N. V. Erikson's theory of ego epigenesis: Empirical and theoretical perspectives for human development. Unpublished doctoral dissertation, Pennsylvania State University, 1969.

Ciaccio, N. V. A test of Erikson's theory of ego epigenesis. *Developmental Psychology*, 1971, *4*, 306–311.

Coates, B., & Hartup, W. W. Age and verbalization in observational learning. *Developmental Psychology*, 1969, *1*, 556–562.

Coetsier, L., & Lagae, C. *Frustratie-studie; een experimentele bijdrage tot de Jeugdpsychologie*. Deinze, Caecilia Boekhandel, 1961.

Cole, M. An ethnographic psychology of cognition. Paper presented at the Conference on the interface between culture and learning, Honolulu, February 1973.

Cole, M. Toward an experimental anthropology of thinking. Paper presented at the joint meeting of the American Ethnological Society Council on Anthropology and Education, Montreal, April 1972.

Cole, M., & Bruner, J. Cultural differences and inferences about psychological processes. *American Psychologist*, 1971, *26*, 867–876.

Cole, M., Gay, J., & Glick, J. Communication skills among the Kpelle of Liberia. Paper presented at the Society for Research in Child Development Meeting, Santa Monica, Calif., March 1969.

Cole, M., Gay, J., Glick, J., & Sharp, D. W. *The cultural context of learning and thinking*. New York, Basic Books, 1971.

Cole, M., & Maltzman, I. *Handbook of contemporary Soviet psychology*. New York, Basic Books, 1969.

Cole, M., & Scribner, S. *Culture and thought: A psychological introduction*. New York, Wiley, 1974.

Collis, K. A study of concrete and formal reasoning in school mathematics. *Australian Journal of Psychology*, 1971, *23*, 289–291.

Coombs, C. H., Dawes, R. M., & Tversky, A. *Mathematical psychology*. Englewood Cliffs, N. J., Prentice-Hall, 1970.

Corah, N. L. Differentiation in children and their parents. *Journal of Personality*, 1965, *33*, 300–308.

Coren, S. The influence of optical aberrations on the magnitude of the Poggendorff illusion. *Perception and Psychophysics*, 1969, *6*, 185–186.

Coren, S. Lateral inhibition and geometric illusions. *Quarterly Journal of Experimental Psychology*, 1970, *22*, 274–278.

Coren, S. A size contrast illusion without physical size difference. *American Journal of*

Psychology, 1971, *84*, 565–566.

Coren, S., & Girgus, J.S. Differentiation and decrement in the Mueller-Lyer illusion. *Perception and Psychophysics*, 1972, *12*, 466–470.(a)

Coren, S., & Girgus, J.S. Illusion decrement in intersecting line figures. *Psychonomic Science*, 1972, *26*, 108–110.(b)

Coren, S., & Girgus, J.S. Density of human lens pigmentation: *In vivo* measures over an extended age range. *Vision Research*, 1972, *12*, 343–346.(c)

Coren, S., & Hoenig, P. Eye movements and decrement in the Oppel-Kundt illusion. *Perception and Psychophysics*, 1972, *12*, 224–225.

Corman, H.H., & Escalona, S.K. Stages of sensorimotor development: A replication study. *The Merrill-Palmer Quarterly*, 1969, *15*, 351–361.

Costanzo, P.R., & Shaw, M.E. Conformity as a function of age level. *Child Development*, 1966, *37*, 967–975.

Cronbach, L.J. Two disciplines of scientific psychology. *American Psychologist*, 1957, *12*, 671–684.

Crovitz, E. Reversing a learning deficit in the aged. *Journal of Gerontology*, 1966, *21*, 236–238.

Cunningham, M. *Intelligence: Its organization and development*. New York, Academic Press, 1972.

Curry, K.B. *Foundations of mathematical logic*. New York, McGraw-Hill, 1963.

Darwin, C. *The expression of the emotions in men and animals*. London, Methuen, 1872.

Dasen, P.R. Concrete operational development in three cultures. Paper presented to the First Regional Conference in Africa, International Association for Cross Cultural Psychology, Ibadan, Nigeria, 1973.

Dasen, P. Cross-cultural Piagetian research: A summary. *Journal of Cross-Cultural Psychology*, 1972, *3*, 23–39.(a)

Dasen, P. The development of conservation in Aboriginal children: A replication study. *International Journal of Psychology*, 1972, *7*, 75–85.(b)

Dasen, P. The influence of ecology, culture and European contact on cognitive development in Australian Aborigines. In J. Berry & P. Dasen (Eds.), *Culture and cognition: Readings in cross-cultural psychology*. London, Methuen, 1973.

Dasen, P., deLacey, P., & Seagrim, G. An investigation of reasoning ability in adopted and fostered Aboriginal children. In G. Kearney, P. deLacey & G. Davidson (Eds.) *The psychology of Aboriginal Australians*. New York, Wiley, 1973.

Davidson, R.E. Mediation and ability in paired-associate learning. *Journal of Educational Psychology*, 1964, *55*, 352–356.

Davis, E.G. *The first sex*. Baltimore, Penguin Books, 1971.

Davis, J.K. Mediated generalization and interference across five grade levels. *Psychonomic Science*, 1966, *6*, 273–274.

Dawson, J. Cultural and physiological influences upon spatial processes in West Africa, Part 1. *International Journal of Psychology*, 1967, *2*, 115–128.

Day, R.H. On the stereoscopic observation of geometric illusions. *Perceptual and Motor Skills*, 1961, *13*, 247–258.

Day, R.H., Pollack, R.H., & Seagrim, G.N. Figural after-effects: A critical review. *Australian Journal of Psychology*, 1959, *11*, 15–45.

de Beauvoir, S. *The coming of age*. New York, Putman, 1972.

De Goncourt, E., & De Goncourt, J. *The woman of the eighteenth century*. London, Allen & Unwin, 1928.

deLacey, P. A cross-cultural study of classificatory ability in Australia. *Journal of Cross-Cultural Psychology*, 1970, *1*, 293–304.

deLemos, M. The development of conservation in Aboriginal children. *International*

Journal of Psychology, 1969, *4*, 255–269.

de Lorde, A. & Binet, A., *L'horrible expérience: drama en deux actes*. *Repertoire du Grand Guignol Librairie Théâtrale du 'Nouveau Siecle'*. Paris, 1910.

Dewar, R. E. Distribution of practice and the Mueller-Leyer illusion. *Perception and Psychophysics*, 1968, *3*, 246–248.

Dickinson, E. *Final harvest: Emily Dickinson's poems*. Boston, Little-Brown, 1961.

Doi, L. T. Japanese psychology, dependency need, and mental health. In W. Caudill & T. Y. Lin (Eds.), *Mental health research in Asia and the Pacific*. Honolulu, East-West Center Press, 1969. Pp. 335–242.

Draper, P. Social ecology of 'Kung childhood. In R. B. Lee & I. DeVore (Eds.), *Kalahari hunter-gatherers*. Cambridge, Harvard University Press, in press.

Duminy, P. A. (Ed.), *Irends and challenges in the education of the South African Bantu*. Pretoria, Van Schaïck, 1967.

Durojaye, H. Conservation in six cultures. Paper presented at the Twentieth International Congress of Psychology, Tokyo, August, 1972.

Dyk, R. B., & Witkin, H. A. Family experiences related to the development of differentiation in children. *Child Development*, 1965, *36*, 21–55.

Ebert, P. C., & Pollack, R. H. Magnitude of the Mueller-Lyer illusion as a function of hue, saturation and fundus pigmentation. *Psychonomic Science*, 1972, *26*, 225–226.(a)

Ebert, P. C., & Pollack, R. H. Magnitude of the Mueller-Lyer illusion as a function of lightness contrast, viewing time and fundus pigmentation. *Psychonomic Science*, 1972, *26*, 347–348.(b)

Eckensberger, L. H. Methodological issues of cross-cultural research in developmental psychology. In J. R. Nesselroade & H. W. Reese (Eds.), *Life-span developmental psychology: Methodological issues*. New York, Academic, 1973. Pp. 43–64.

Editorial. On the subject matter and tasks of psychology. *Sovetskaya Pedagogika*, 1955. *9*, 73–84.

Edwards, C. Dependency as a system of behavior in children. Qualifying paper submitted to Harvard Graduate School of Education, 1972.

Elder, G. H. jr. Adolescent socialization and development. In E. F. Borgatta & W. W. Lambert (Eds.), *Handbook of personality, theory and research*. Chicago, Rand McNally, 1968. Pp. 239–364.

Eliade, M. *Myths, dreams and mysteries*. London and Glasgow, Harvill Press, 1960.

Elkind, D. Egocentrism in adolescence. In. J. P. Hill & J. Shelton (Eds.), *Readings in adolescent development and behavior*. Englewood Cliffs, New Jersey, Prentice-Hall, 1971.

Elkind, D. Quantity concepts in college students. *Journal of Social Psychology*, 1962, *57*, 459–465.

Elkind, D. Editor's introduction. In J. Piaget, *Six psychological studies*. New York, Random House, 1967, Pp. i-xx.

Elkonin, D. E. *Child psychology: The child's development from birth to seven years*. Moscow, Uchpedgiz. 1960.

El'konin, D. B. K probleme periodizatsii psikhicheskogo razvitija v detskom vozraste [On the problem of periodization of psychic development in childhood]. *Voprosy psichologii*, 1971, *17*, 6–20.

Ember, C. R. The effect of feminine task assignment on the social behavior of boys. *Ethos*, in press.

Eppink, H. An experiment to determine a basis for nursing decisions in regard to time of initiation of breastfeeding. *Nursing Research*, 1969, *18*, 292–299.

Erchak, G. The asocial behavior of young Liberian Kpelle children and its social context. Paper presented to the Department of Social Anthropology, Harvard University, 1973.

Erikson, E. H. *Childhood and society.* New York, Norton, 1950 (rev. eds., 1963, 1966). (a)

Erikson, E.H. Growth and crises of the healthy personality. In M.J.E. Senn (Ed.), *Symposium on the healthy personality.* New York, Macy Foundation, 1950. Pp. 91–146.(b)

Erikson, E. H. *Identity, youth and crisis.* New York, Norton, 1968.

Erikson, E. H. Youth: Fidelity and diversity. In E. H. Erikson (Ed.), *Youth: Change and challenge.* New York, Basic Books, 1963.

Erlebacher, A., & Sekuler, R. Explanation of the Mueller-Lyer illusion: Confusion theory examined. *Journal of Experimental Psychology,* 1969, *80,* 462–467.

Ertl, J. Evoked potentials, neural efficiency and IQ. In L. D. Proctor (Ed.), *Biocybernetics of the central nervous system.* Boston, Little & Brown, 1969.

Evans-Pritchard, E. E. Sanza, a characteristic feature of Zande language and thought. In Evans-Pritchard (Ed.), *Essays in social anthropology.* New York, Free Press, 1963.

Evreux, Y. *Voyage dans le nord du Bresil fait durant les annees 1613 et 1614.* Paris and Leipzig, Franck, 1864.(New Haven, Human Relations Area Files.)

Eysenck, H. J. Genetics and personality. In J. M. Thoday & A. S. Parkes (Eds.), *Genetic and environmental influences on behavior.* Edinburgh, Oliver & Boyd, 1968.

Eysenck, H. *The IQ argument: Race, intelligence and education.* New York, Library Press, 1971.

Eysenck, H.J., & Levey A. Conditioning, introversion-extraversion and the strength of the nervous system. In V.D. Nebylitsyn & J.A. Gray (Eds.), *Biological bases of individual behavior.* New York, Academic Press, 1972.

Farquar, M., & Leibowitz, H. The magnitude of the Ponzo illusion as a function of age for large and for small stimulus configurations. *Psychonomic Science,* 1971, *25,* 97–99.

Fedorov, V. K. *Genetika povedeniya* [Behavior genetics]. Leningrad, Nauka, 1969.

Fend, H. *Konformität und Selbstbestimmung.* Hemsbach über Weinheim, Julius Beltz, 1971.

Fern, F. *Ruth Hall: A domestic tale of the present time.* New York, Mason, 1855.

Festinger, L. Eye movements and perception. In P. Bach-y-Rita (Ed.), *The control of eye movements.* New York, Academic Press, 1971. Pp. 259–273.

Festinger, L., White, C.W., & Allyn, M.R. Eye movements and decrement in the Mueller-Lyer illusion. *Perception and Psychophysics,* 1968, *3,* 376–382.

Feyerabend, P.K. Against method: Outline of an anarchistic theory of knowledge. In W. Radner & S. Winokur (Eds.), *Analyses of theories and methods of physics and psychology.* (Minnesota Studies in the Philosophy of Science, Vol. IV). Minneapolis, University of Minnesota Press, 1970. Pp. 17–130.

Field, T., & Cropley, A. Cognitive style and science achievement. *Journal of Research in Science Teaching,* 1969, *6,* 2–10.

Filehne, W. Die geometrisch-optischen Täuschungen als Nachwirkungen der im körperlichen Sehen erworbenen Erfahrung. *Zeitschrift für Psychologie und Physiologie der Sinnesorgane,* 1898, *17,* 15–61.

Fisher, G.H. Illusions and size-constancy. *American Journal of Psychology,* 1968, *81,* 2–20.

Fitzgerald, L.K. Cognitive development among Ga children: Environmental correlates of cognitive growth within the Ga tribe. Unpublished doctoral thesis, University of California, Berkeley, 1970.

Fjellman, J. The myth of primitive mentality: A study of semantic categorization in Kenyan children. Unpublished doctoral thesis, Department of Social Anthropology, Harvard University, 1971.

Flavell, J.H. *The developmental psychology of Jean Piaget*. Princeton, N.J., Van Nostrand, 1963.

Flavell, J.H. Cognitive changes in adulthood. In L.R. Goulet & P.B. Baltes (Eds.), *Life span developmental psychology: Theory and research*. New York, Academic Press, 1970. Pp. 248–257.

Flavell, J. Comments on Beilin's 'The development of physical concepts'. In T. Mischel (Ed.), *Cognitive development and epistemology*. New York, Academic Press, 1971.

Flavell, J.H. Stage-related properties of cognitive development. *Cognitive Psychology*, 1971, *2*, 421–453.

Flavell, J.H. An analysis of cognitive-developmental sequences. *Genetic Psychology Monographs*, 1972, *86*, 297–350.

Flavell, J.H., Beach, D.R., & Chinsky, J.M. Spontaneous verbal rehearsal in a memory task as a function of age. *Child Development*, 1966, *37*, 283–299.

Flavell, J.H., & Wohlwill, J.F. Formal and functional aspects of cognitive development. In D. Elkind & J.H. Flavell (Eds.), *Studies in cognitive development: Essays in honor of Jean Piaget*. New York, Oxford University Press, 1969. Pp. 67–120.

Flexner, E. *Centuries of struggle*. New York, Atheneum, 1968.

Flitner, A. *Soziologische Jugendforschung: Darstellung und Kritik aus pädagogischer Sicht*. Heidelberg, Quelle & Meyer, 1963.

Fodor, J. Some reflections on L.S. Vygotsky's *Thought and Language*. *Cognition*, 1973, *1*, 83–95.

Fraisse, P., & Piaget, J. *Iraité de psychologie expérimentale* (I. Histoire et Méthode; Chap. I. Les Origines). Paris, Presses Universitaires de France, 1963.

Fraisse, R. *The psychology of time*. London, Eyre and Spottiswodde, 1964.

Frazer, J. *The golden bough*. New York, Macmillan Company, 1955.

Freedle, R. A stimulus similarity scale for temporal measures of attention in infants and children. *Developmental Psychology*, 1971, *4*, 240–247.

Freedle, R., & Hall, W.S. A black and a white dialect: Some quantitative differences. Paper presented at the Annual Meeting of the American Psychological Association, Montreal, 1973.

Freedle, R., & Hall, W.S. A latency analysis of strategies underlying children's recall of sentences (Research Bulletin RB-73-9). Princeton, N.J., Education Testing Service, 1973.

Freedle, R., & Hall, W.S. Effects of prenominal adjective ordering on children's latencies and errors in an immediate sentence recall task (Research Bulletin RB-73-19). Princeton, N.J., Educational Testing Service, 1973.

Freedle, R., Keeney, T.J., & Smith N.D. Effects of phrase structure, mean depth, and grammaticality on children's imitation of sentences (Research Bulletin RB-69-79). Princeton, N.J., Educational Testing Services, 1969.

Freedle, R., & Lewis, M. Application of Markov processes to the concept of state (Research Bulletin 71-34). Princeton, N.J., Educational Testing Service, 1971.

Freeman, M.W. *A New England nun and other stories*. New York, Harper's, 1891.

Freud, S. Psychology of women. In S. Freud, *New introductory lectures on psychoanalysis*. London, Hogarth Press, Ltd., 1962.

Freud, S. *Moses and monotheism*. New York, Alfred A. Knopf, 1939.

Freud, S. *Totem and taboo*, New York, Norton, 1950.

Freyburg, P. Concept development in Piagetian terms in relation to school attainment. *Journal of Educational Psychology*, 1966, *57*, 164–168.

Friedlander, J.W., & Sarbin, T.R. The depth of hypnosis. *Journal of Abnormal and Social Psychology*, 1938, *33*, 453–475.

Frijda, N., & Jahoda, G. On the scope and methods of cross-cultural research. *International Journal of Psychology*, 1966, *1*, 110–127.

Furby, L. A theoretical analysis of cross-cultural research in cognitive development: Piaget's conservation task. *Journal of Cross-Cultural Psychology*, 1971, *3*, 241–255.

Furth, H.G. *Piaget for teachers.* Englewood-Cliffs, N.J., Prentice-Hall, 1970.

Furth, H. Piaget, I.Q., and the nature-nurture controversy. *Human Development*, 1973, *16*, 61–73.

Gabriel, J. Conservation, cognition and culture. Paper presented to the Australian Association for Research in Education, 1972.

Galperin, P.Y. The psychology of thinking and the theory of stages in the development of intellectual actions. In E. V. Shorokhova (Ed.), *Researches on thinking in Soviet psychology.* Moscow, Izd. Nauka, 1966. Pp. 236–277.

Galperin, P. Die Entwicklung der Untersuchungen über die Bildung geistiger Operationen. In H. Hiebsch, F. Klix & M. Vorwerg (Eds.), *Ergebnisse der sowjetischen Psychologie.* Berlin, Akademie Verlag, 1967.

Gal'perin, P.Y. Stages in the development of mental acts. In M. Cole & I. Maltzman (Eds.), *A handbook of contemporary Soviet psychology.* New York, Basic Books, 1969. Pp. 249–273.

Ganz, L. Mechanism of the figural after-effects. *Psychological Review*, 1966, *73*, 128–150.

Garbers, J.G. The image of puberty and adolescence and its educational implications. In P.A. Duminy (Ed.), *Trends and challenges in the education of the South African Bantu.* Pretoria, Van Schaik, 1967.

Garbers, J.G. Die puberteit en adolessensie as opvoedingsopgave. *South African Journal of Pedagogy*, 1968, *2*, 17–38.

Garbers, J.G. *Pedi adolescence: The educational situation and image of adolescence of the Pedi school child.* Port Elizabeth, University of Port Elizabeth Publication Series C1, 1971.

Gardner, H. *The quest for mind.* New York, Knopf 1973.

Garrison, E.C. *Psychology of adolescence.* New York, Englewood Cliffs, 1965.

Gay, J., & Cole, M. *The new mathematics and an old culture.* New York, Holt, 1967.

Geach, P., & Black, M. (Eds.), *Translations from the philosophical writings of Gottlob Frege.* Oxford, Basil Blackwell, 1966.

Geber, M. L'Enfant Africain occidentalisé et de niveau social superieur. *Ouganda Courier*, 1958, *8*, 517–23.

Gelman, R., & Shatz, M. Listener-dependent adjustments in the speech of four-year-olds. Paper presented at the meeting of the Psychonomic Society, 1972.

Gerstmann, S. *Osobowość: Wybrane zagadnienia psychologiczne.* Warszawa, PZWS, 1970.

Gesell, A.L. *The mental growth of the pre-school child: A psychological outline of normal development from birth to the sixth year, including a system of developmental diagnosis.* New York, Macmillan, 1925.

Gibbs, J. Poro values and courtroom procedures in a Kpelle chiefdom. *Southwestern Journal of Anthropology*, 1962, *18*, 341–350.

Gillam, B. A depth processing theory of the Poggendorff illusion. *Perception and Psychophysics*, 1971, *10*, 211–216.

Gilles, B. Rhythmical activity in 6- to 10-year-olds. *Zeitschrift für Entwicklungspsychologie und Pädagogische Psychologie*, 1971, *3*, 89–105.

Gillespie, J.M., & G.W. Allport. *Youth's outlook on the future.* New York, Random

House, 1955.

Ginsburg, H., & Opper, S. *Piaget's theory of intellectual development: An introduction.* Englewood Cliffs, N.J., Prentice-Hall, 1969.

Girgus, J.S., Coren, S., & Agdern, M. The interrelationship between the Ebbinghaus and Delboeuf illusions. *Journal of Experimental Psychology,* 1972, *95,* 453–455.

Girgus, J.S., Coren, S., & Horowitz, L. Peripheral and central components in variants of the Mueller-Lyer illusion. *Perception and Psychophysics,* 1973, *13,* 157–160.

Glick, J. Culture and cognition: Some theoretical and methodological concerns. Paper presented at the American Anthropological Association meetings, New Orleans, November 1969.

Glick, J. Cognitive development in cross-cultural perspective. In J. Horowitz (Ed.), *Review of child development research,* vol. 4, in press.

Glöckel, H. Eine Vergleichsuntersuchung zur Frage des jugendlichen Idealerlebens. *Psychologische Rundschau,* 1960, *9,* 1–20.

Goldschmid, M. Different types of conservation and nonconservation and their relation to age, sex, IQ, MA, and vocabulary. *Child Development,* 1967, *38,* 1229–1246.

Goldschmid, M. The relation of conservation to emotional and environmental aspects of development. *Child Development,* 1968, *39,* 579–589.

Goldschmid, M., *et. al.* A cross-cultural investigation of conservation. *Journal of Cross-Cultural Psychology,* 1973, *4,* 76–88.

Goode, W.J. *The family.* Englewood Cliffs, N.J., Prentice-Hall, 1964.

Goodman, F. Glossolalia: Speaking in tongues in four cultural settings. *Confinia Psychiatrica,* 1969, *12,* 113–129.

Goodnow, J.J. A test for milieu effects with some of Piaget's tasks. *Psychological Monographs,* 1962, *76,* 1–22 (Whole No. 555).

Goodnow, J.J. Cultural variations in cognitive skills. In D.R. Price-Williams (Ed.), *Cross cultural studies.* Baltimore, Penguin, 1969. Pp. 246–264.

Goodnow, J.J. Problems in research on culture and thought. In D. Elkind & J.H. Flavell (Eds.), *Studies in cognitive development: Essays in honor of Jean Piaget.* New York, Oxford University Press, 1969. Pp. 439–462.

Goodnow, J.J., & Bethon, G. Piaget's tasks: The effect of schooling and intelligence. *Child Development,* 1966, *37,* 573–582.

Gough, H.G. *Manual for the California psychological inventory.* Palo Alto, Consulting Psychologists Press, 1969.

Goulet, L.R. The interfaces of acquisition: Models and methods for studying the active, developing organism. In J.R. Nesselroade & H.W. Reese (Eds.), *Life-span developmental psychology: Methodological issues.* New York, Academic Press, 1973. Pp. 281–298.

Goulet, L.R., & Baltes, P.B. (Eds.), *Life-span developmental psychology: Research and theory.* New York, Academic Press, 1970.

Graham, E. Figural after-effects as functions of contrast, area, and luminance of the inspection-figure. *Psychologia,* 1961, *4,* 201–208.

Graves, J. Attainment of conservation of mass, weight, and volume in minimally educated adults. *Developmental Psychology,* 1972, *7,* 223.

Graves, R. *The white goddess.* New York, Farrar, Straus, and Giroux, 1966.

Graves, R., & Patai, R. *Hebrew myths: The book of genesis.* New York, McGraw-Hill Book Company, 1966.

Gray, J.A. (Ed.) *Pavlov's typology: Recent theoretical and experimental developments from the laboratory of B.M. Teplov.* Oxford, Pergamon Press, 1964.

Gray, J.A. Strength of the nervous system, introversion-extraversion, conditionability and arousal. *Behaviour Research and Therapy,* 1967, *5,* 151–169.

Gray, J.A. The psychophysiological basis of introversion-extraversion. *Behaviour Research and Therapy*, 1970, *8*, 249–266.

Greenfield, P.M. On culture and conservation. In J.S. Bruner, R.R. Olver, P.M. Greenfield, et al., *Studies in cognitive growth*. New York, Wiley, 1966.

Greenfield, P.M. Oral or written language: The consequences for cognitive development in Africa, the United States and England. *Language and Speech* 1972, *15*, 169–178.

Greenfield, P.M. Representing mathematical concepts to two- and three-year-olds through action, image, and word: An experimental comparison of teaching methods. Unpublished paper, University of California, Los Angeles, 1971.

Greenfield, P.M., & Childs, C.P. Weaving, color terms, and pattern representation: Cultural influences and cognitive development among the Zinacantecos of Southern Mexico. Paper presented at the First International Conference of the International Association for Cross-Cultural Psychology. Hong Kong, 1973.

Greer, G. *The female eunuch*. New York, McGraw-Hill, 1971.

Gregory, R.L. Distortion of visual space as inappropriate constancy scaling. *Nature*, 1963, *199*, 678–680.

Grushin, B. Razvitiye [Development]. In F.V. Konstantinov (Ed.), *Filosofskaya entsiklopediya* Tom 4. [*Encyclopedia of philosophy* Part 4.] Moscow; Izd-vo Sovetskaya Entsiklopediya, 1967. Pp. 453–454.

Gutmann, D. *The country of old men: Cultural studies on the psychology of later life*. In W. Donahue (Ed.), *Occasional papers in gerontology*, no. 5, Ann Arbor, Institute of Gerontology, The University of Michigan-Wayne State University 1969.

Gutmann, D. Alternatives to disengagement: The old men of the highland Druze. Paper presented at the meetings of the Gerontological Society, San Juan, Puerto Rico, December 1972.

Hagen, J.W., & Kingsley, P.R. Labeling effects in short-term memory. *Child Development*, 1968, *39*, 113–121.

Hall, G.S. *Senescence*. New York, Appleton, 1922.

Hall, St. *Adolescence*. New York, Appleton, 1904.

Hall, W.S., & Freedle, R.O. A developmental investigation of standard and nonstandard English among Black and white children. *Human Development*, 1973, *16*, 440–464.

Halle, M., & Keyser, S.J. *English stress, its form, its growth and its role in verse*. New York, Harper and Row, 1971.

Hamlyn, D.W. Epistemology and conceptual development. In T. Mischel (Ed.), *Cognitive development and epistemology*. New York, Academic, 1971. Pp. 3–24.

Hanley, C., & Zerbolio, D.C. Developmental changes in five illusions measured by the up-and-down method. *Child Development*, 1965, *36*, 437–452.

Hanson, N.R. A picture theory of meaning. In W. Radner & S. Winokur (Eds.), *Analyses of theories and methods of physics and psychology* (Minnesota Studies in the Philosophy of Science, vol. 4). Minneapolis,' University of Minnesota Press, 1970. Pp. 131–141.

Harrelson, W. *From fertility cult to worship*. New York, Doubleday, 1970.

Harris, A., & Meacham, J. Verbal activity in the planning and execution of motor acts. Paper presented at the Ninth International Congress of Gerontology, Kiev, U.S.S.R., July, 1972.

Hart, J.D. *The popular book*. New York, Oxford University Press, 1950.

Hartup, W.W. Peer interaction and social organization. In P. Mussen (Ed.), *Carmichael's manual of child psychology*, vol. 2 (3rd ed.). New York, Wiley, 1970.

Harvey, O.J., & Rutherford, J. Status in the informal group: Influence and influencibility at differing age levels. *Child Development*, 1960, *31*, 377–385.

Hass, W.A. Pragmatic structures of language: Historical, formal and developmental issues. In K.F. Riegel & G.C. Rosenwald (Eds.), *Structure and transformation: Developmental and historical aspects*. New York, Wiley, 1975.

Havighurst, R.J., Dubois, M.E., Csikszentmihalyi, M., & Doll, R. A cross-national study of Buenos Aires and Chicago adolescents. *Bibliotheca Vita humana*, Fasc. 3, Basel, Karger, 1965.

Havighurst, R.J. *Developmental tasks and education*. New York, Mckay, 1948. (3rd ed., 1972).

Hayes, J.R. The child's conception of the experimenter. In S. Farnham-Diggory (Ed.), *Information processing in children*. New York, Academic, 1972. Pp. 176–182.

Hearnshaw, L.S. Temporal integration and behavior. *Bulletin of the British Psychological Society*, 1956, *9*, 1–20.

Heglin, H.J. Problem solving set in different age groups. *Journal of Gerontology*, 1956, *11*, 310–317.

Helmholtz, H. von. *Helmoltz's treatise on physiological optics*. New York, Dover, 1962.

Helson, H. *Adaptation-level theory: An experimental and systematic approach to behavior*. New York, Harper, 1964.

Helson, R. Heroic and tender modes in women authors of fantasy. *Journal of Personality*, 1973, *4*, 493–512.

Hempel, C.G. *Aspects of scientific explanation*. New York, Free Press, 1965.

Hempel, C.G. *Introduction to philosophy of natural science*. Englewood Cliffs, New Jersey, Prentice-Hall, 1966.

Hempel, C.G., & Oppenheim, P. Studies in the logic of explanation. *Philosophy of Science*, 1948, *15*, 135–175.

Heron, A. Concrete operations, 'g' and achievement in Zambian children. *Journal of Cross-Cultural Psychology*, 1971, *2*, 325–336.

Heron, A., & Dowel, W. Weight conservation and matrix-solving ability in Papuan children. *Journal of Cross-Cultural Psychology*, 1973, *4*, 207–219.

Heron, A., & Simonsson, M. Weight conservation in Zambian children: A nonverbal approach. *International Journal of Psychology*, 1969, *4*, 281–292.

Hess, R.D., & Shipman, V.G. Early experience and the socialization of cognitive modes in children. *Child Development*, 1965, *34*, 869–886.

Heymans, G. Quantitative Untersuchungen über die 'optischen Paradoxe'. *Zeitschrift für Psychologie*, 1896, *9*, 221–255.

Hilgard, E. *Hypnotic susceptibility*. New York, Harcourt, Brace and World, 1965.

Ho, D.Y.F. Field studies in foreign cultures: A cautionary note on methodological difficulties. *Psychologia, An International Journal of Psychology in the Orient*, 1972, *15*, 15–21.

Hoffman, M.L. Moral development. In P.H. Mussen (Ed.), *Carmichael's manual of child psychology*. New York, Wiley, 1970.

Holst, E. Von. Aktive Leistungen der menschlichen Gesichtswahrnehmung. *Studium Generale*, 1957, *10*, 231–243.

Holtby, W. *Women and a changing civilization*. London, John Lane the Bodley Head, 1934.

Hooper, F.H. An evaluation of logical operations instruction in the preschool. In R.K. Parker (Ed.), *The preschool in action: Exploring early childhood programs*. Boston, Allyn and Bacon, 1972. Pp. 134–186.

Hooper, F.H. Cognitive assessment across the life span: Methodological implications of the organismic approach. In J.R. Nesselroade & H.W. Reese (Eds.), *Life-span developmental psychology: Methodological issues*. New York, Academic Press, 1973. Pp. 299–316.

Hooper, F.H., Fitzgerald, J., & Papalia, D. Piagetian theory and the aging process: Extensions and speculations. *Aging and Human Development*, 1971, *2*, 3–20.

Hooper, F.H., Goldman, J.A., Storck, P.A., & Burke, A.M. Stage sequence and correspondence in Piagetian theory: A review of the middle-childhood period. *Research Relating to Children*, Bulletin 28, Urbana, Ill., Educational Resources Information Center, 1971.

Hooper, F.H., Sipple, T., & Goldman, J.A. A cross-sectional investigation of children's classificatory abilities. University of Wisconsin, Research and Development Center for Cognitive Learning, Technical Report, 1973.

Hornstein, W. Aspekte und Dimensionen erziehungswissenschaftlicher Theorien zum Jugendalter. In F. Neidhart, R. Bergius, T. Brocher, D. Eckensberger, W. Hornstein, L. Rosenmayr & W. Loch (Eds.), *Jugend im Spektrum der Wissenschaften*. Munich, Juventa, 1970.

Hudson, W. The study of the problem of pictorial perception among unacculturated groups. *International Journal of Psychology*, 1967, *2*, 89–107.

Hulicka, I.M., & Grossman, J.L. Age-group comparisons for the use of mediators in paired-associate learning. *Journal of Gerontology*, 1967, *22*, 46–51.

Hunt, J.McV. Intrinsic motivation and its role in psychological development. In D. Levine (Ed.), *Nebraska symposium on motivation*. Lincoln, University of Nebraska Press, 1965. Pp. 189–282.

Hunt, J.McV. How children develop intellectually. In H. Bernard & W. Huckins (Eds.), *Readings in human development*. Boston, Allyn and Bacon, 1967.

Hunt, R.G., & Synnerdale, V. Social influences among kindergarten children. *Sociological Social Research*, 1959, *43*, 171–174.

Huntington, D. Designs for infant mothering programs to develop a sense of self and competence in infancy. Paper presented at the meeting of the Society for Research in Child Development, Minneapolis, April 1971.

Ikeda, H., & Obonai, T. Studies in figural after-effects: IV. The contrast-confluence illusion of concentric circles and the figural after-effect. *Japanese Psychological Research*, 1955, *2*, 17–23.

Inhelder, B. Foreword. In I.E. Sigel & F.H. Hooper (Eds.), *Logical thinking in children: Research based on Piaget's theory*. New York, Holt, Rinehart and Winston, 1968. Pp. v–vii.

Inhelder, B. Information processing tendencies in recent cognitive learning – empirical studies. In S. Farnham-Diggory (Ed.), *Information processing in children*. New York, Academic Press, 1972. Pp. 103–123.

Inhelder, B., & Piaget, J. *The growth of logical thinking from childhood to adolescence*. New York, Basic Books, 1958.

Inhelder, B., & Piaget, J. *The early growth of logic in the child: Classification and seriation*. New York, Harper & Row, 1964.

Inkeles, A., & Levinson, D.J. National character: The study of modal personality and socio-cultural systems. In G. Lindzey & E. Aronson (Eds.), *Handbook of social psychology*, vol. 4. Readiny, Mass., Addison Wesley, 1969. Pp. 418–506.

Iscoe, I., Williams, M., & Harvey, J. Age, intelligence, and sex as variables in the conformity behavior of Negro and white children. *Child Development*, 1964, *35*, 451–460.

Ivanov-Smolenskiy, A.G. *Ocherki patofiziologii vysshey nervnoy deyatelnosti*. Moskva, Medgiz, 1952. (*Essays on the pathophysiology of the higher nervous activity*. Moscow, Foreign Languages Publishing House, 1954.)

Jahoda, G. Geometric illusions and environment: A study in Ghana. *British Journal of*

Psychology, 1966, *57,* 193–199.

Jahoda, G. Retinal pigmentation, illusion susceptibility and space perception. *International Journal of Psychology,* 1971, *6,* 199–208.

Jaide, W. Über die Einstellung zu Werten auf Seite heutiger Jugendlicher. In *Bericht 22. Kongreß der Deutschen Gesellschaft für Psychologie.* Göttingen, Hogrefe, 1959. Pp. 215–218.

Jaide, W. *Eine neue Generation? Eine Untersuchung über Werthaltung und Leitbilder der Jugendlichen.* München, Juventa, 1961.

Jakobson, R. *Kindersprache, Aphasie, und allgemeine Lautgesetze.* Uppsala, Almquist and Wiksell, 1941. (*Child language, aphasia, and general sound laws.* The Hague, Mouton, 1968.)

James, W. *The principles of psychology.* New York, Holt, 1890.

Jarvis, P. E. Verbal control of sensory-motor performance: A test of Luria's hypothesis. *Human Development,* 1968, *11,* 172–183.

Jenkin, N., & Feallock, S. M. Developmental and intellectual processes in size-distance judgment. *American Journal of Psychology,* 1960, *73,* 268.

Jensen, A. R., & Rohwer, W. D., jr. Syntactical mediation of serial and paired-associate learning as a function of age. *Child Development,* 1965, *36,* 601–608.

Jewett, S. O. *The country of the pointed firs.* London, Jonathan Cape, 1927.

Johnson, N. F. The psychological reality of phrase-structure rules. *Journal of Verbal Learning and Verbal Behavior,* 1965, *4,* 469–475.

Jones, P. A. Intra-cultural differences in spatial-perceptual ability. Paper presented at the Annual Meeting of the Canadian Psychological Association, Victoria, British Columbia, June 1973.

Judd, C. H. Practice and its effects on the perception of illusions. *Psychological Review,* 1902, *9,* 27–39.

Jung, C. G. *Psychological types* (Collected works, vol. 6). Princeton, Princeton University Press, 1971.

Kagan, J., & Kogan, N. Individual variations in cognitive processes. In P. H. Mussen (Ed.), *Carmichael's manual of child psychology,* vol. 1. New York, Wiley, 1970. Pp. 1273–1365.

Kaiser, J., & Niemczynski, A. Tozwój psychiczny jako proces samoorganizacji [Psychic development as a process of self-organisation]. *Przegląd Psychologiczny,* 1970, *20.*

Kaplan, B. Meditations on genesis. *Human Development,* 1967, *10,* 65–87.

Kaplan, B. Genetic psychology, genetic epistemology, and theory of knowledge. In T. Mischel (Ed.), *Cognitive development and epistemology.* New York, Academic, 1971. Pp. 61–81.

Katz, P. A. Effects of labels on children's perception and discrimination learning. *Journal of Experimental Psychology,* 1963, *66,* 423–428.

Keele, S. W. Movement control in skilled motor performance. *Psychological Bulletin,* 1968, *70,* 387–403.

Keeney, T. J., Cannizzo, S. R., & Flavell, J. H. Spontaneous and induced verbal rehearsal in a recall task. *Child Development,* 1967, *38,* 953–966.

Kelchner, M. *Schuld und Sühne im Urteil jugendlicher Arbeiter.* Leipzig, Barth, 1929.

Kelly, E. L. Consistency of the adult personality. *American Psychologist,* 1955, *2,* 659–681.

Kendler, H. H., & Kendler, T. S. Effect of verbalization on discrimination reversal shifts in children. *Science,* 1961, *134,* 1619–1620.

Kendler, H. H., & Kendler, T. S. Vertical and horizontal processes in human concept learning. *Psychological Review,* 1962, *69,* 1–16.

Kendler, T.S., Kendler, H.H., & Carrick, M. The effect of verbal labels on inferential problem solution. *Child Development*, 1966, *37*, 749–763.

Keniston, A.H. Cross-cultural studies of milieu effects on cognitive growth: Some considerations. Unpublished paper, Stanford University, 1973.

Kerckhoff, A. Family patterns and morale in retirement. In A.H. Simpson & J. McKinney (Eds.), *Social aspects of aging*. Durham, N.C., Duke University Press, 1966.(a)

Kerckhoff, A. Husband-wife expectations and reactions to retirement. In A. H. Simpson & J. McKinney (Eds.), *Social aspects of aging*. Durham, N.C., Duke University Press, 1966.(b)

Kessen, W. Research design in the study of developmental problems. In P.H. Mussen (Ed.), *Handbook of research methods in child development*. New York, Wiley, 1960. Pp. 36–70.

Kessen, W. Sucking and looking: Two organized congenital patterns of behavior in the human infant. In H.W. Stevenson, E.H. Hess & H.L. Rheingold (Eds.), *Early behavior: Comparative and developmental approaches*. New York, Wiley, 1967.

Kiev, A. *Transcultural psychiatry*. Harmondworth, Middlesex, England, Penguin Books, 1972.

Kintsch, W. Notes on the structure of semantic memory. In E. Tulving & W. Donaldson (Eds.), *Organization of memory*. New York, Academic Press, 1972. Pp. 247–308.

Klahr, D. A production system for counting, subitizing, and adding. In W.G. Ghase (Ed.), *Visual information processing*. New York, Academic Press, 1972. Pp. 527–546.

Klahr, D., & Wallace, J.G. An information processing analysis of some Piagetian experimental tasks. *Cognitive Psychology*, 1970, *1*, 358–387.

Klahr, D., & Wallace, J.G. The development of serial completion strategies: An information processing analysis. *British Journal of Psychology*, 1970, *61*, 243–257.

Klahr, D., & Wallace, J.G. Class inclusion processes. In S. Farnham-Diggory (Ed.), *Information processing in children*. New York, Academic Press, 1972. Pp. 144–170.

Klahr, D., & Wallace, J.G. The role of quantification operators in the development of quantity. *Cognitive Psychology*, 1973, *4*, 301–327.

Klausmeier, H.J., & Hooper, F.H. Conceptual development and instruction. In F. Kerlinger (Ed.), *Review of research in education*. Washington, D.C., American Educational Research Assoc., 1974.

Koehler, W., & Wallach, H. Figural aftereffects: An investigation of visual processes. *Proceedings of the American Philosophical Society*, 1944, *88*, 296–357.

Kohlberg, L.A. A cognitive theory of socialization. In D.A. Goslin (Ed.), *Handbook of socialization theory and research*. Chicago, Rand, 1969. Pp. 347–480.

Kohlberg, L. Moral development. Paper presented at the Biennial Meetings of the International Society for the Study of Behavioral Development, University of Nijmegen, the Netherlands, 1971.

Kominski, C., & Coppinger, N. The Müller-Lyer illusion and Piaget's test for the conservation of space in a group of older institutionalized veterans. Unpublished Manuscript, College of William and Mary, 1968,

Konner, M.J. 'Kung infant care, behavior and development. In R.B. Lee & I. DeVore (Eds.), *Kalahari hunter-gatherers*. Cambridge, Mass., Harvard University Press, in press.

Konorski, J. On two types of conditional reflex: General laws of association. *Conditional Reflex*, 1973, *8*, 2–9.

Kornilov, K.N. Psychology in light of dialectical materialism. In C. Murchison (Ed.), *Psychologies of 1930*. Worcester, Mass., Clark University Press, 1930. Pp. 243–278.

Kostyuk, G.S. Printsip razvitya v psikhologii [The principle of development in psychology]. In E.V. Shorokhova (Ed.), *Metodologicheskie i teoreticheskie problemy psikhologii [Methodological and theoretical problems of psychology].* Moscow, Nauka, 1969. Pp. 118–152.

Krantz, D.H., Luce, R.D., Suppes, P., & Tversky, A. *Foundations of measurement.* New York, Academic Press, 1971.

Krantz, D.H., & Tversky, A. Conjoint-measurement analysis of composition in psychology. *Psychological Review,* 1971, *78,* 151–170.

Krasusky, V.K., & Fedorov, V.K. (Eds.), *Methodiki otsenki svoystv vysshey nervnoy deyatelnosti [Methods of determination of the properties of the higher nervous activity].* Leningrad, Nauka, 1971.

Kravitz, H., & Boehm, J.J. Rhythmic habit patterns in infancy: Their sequence, age of onset, and frequency. *Child Development,* 1971, *42,* 399–413.

Kroh, O. Psychologie der Oberstufe. Langensalza, Beltz, 1929. (6th ed., 1940).

Kuenne, M.R. Experimental investigation of the relation of language to transposition behavior in young children. *Journal of Experimental Psychology,* 1946, *36,* 471–490.

Kuhn, T.S. *The structure of scientific revolutions.* Chicago, University of Chicago Press, 1962.

Kulah, A.A. The organization and learning of proverbs among the Kpelle of Liberia. Unpublished doctoral dissertation, Harvard University, 1973.

Kussman, T. *Sowjetische Psychologie: Auf der Suche nach der Methode. Pavlovs Lehren und das Menschenbild der Marxistischen Psychologie.* Bern, Huber, 1974.

Kussmaul, A. *Untersuchungen über das Seelenleben des neugeborenen Menschen.* Leipzig, Winter, 1859.

Lacey, W.K. *The family in classical Greece.* Ithaca, N.Y., Cornell University Press, 1968.

Ladefoged, P. *Three areas of experimental phonetics.* New York, Oxford University Press, 1967.

Landy, A., Kwiatowska, M. & Topińska, Z. *Rozwój if wychowanie dziecka w wieku przedszkolnym [Development and education of the child in preschool age].* Warszawa, Nasza Księgarnia, 1970.

Langdon-Davies, J. *A short history of women.* New York, The Literary Guild of America, 1927.

Langer, J. *Theories of development.* New York, Holt, Rinehart & Winston, 1969.

Langer, J. Werner's comparative organismic theory. In P.H. Mussen (Ed.), *Carmichael's manual of child psychology.* New York, Wiley, 1970. Pp. 733–771.

Langer, S.K. *Philosophy in a new key.* Cambridge, Mass., Harvard University Press, 1951.

Langeveld, M.J. *The Columbus – Picture analysis of growth towards maturity.* Basel, Karger, 1969.

Lashley, K. The problem of serial order in behavior. In L.A. Jeffress (Ed.), *Cerebral mechanisms in behavior.* New York, Wiley, 1951.

Laurence, M.W. Memory loss with age: A test of two strategies for its retardation. *Psychonomic Science,* 1967, *9,* 209–210.

LeCompte, G.K., & Gratch, G. Violation of a rule as a method of diagnosing infants' levels of object concept. *Child Development,* 1972, *43,* 385–396.

Lee, R. 'Kung Bushman subsistence: An input-output analysis. In A. Vayda (Ed.), *Environment and cultural behavior.* New York, Natural History Press, 1969. Pp. 47–79.

Leibowitz, H. Apparent size as a function of distance for mentally defective subjects.

American Journal of Psychology, 1961, *74*, 98–100.

Leibowitz, H.W., Brislin, R., Perlmutter, L., & Hennessy, R. Ponzo perspective illusion as manifestation of space perception. *Science*, 1969, *166*, 1174–1176.

Leibowitz, H. & Heisel, L'evolution de l'illusion de Ponzo en function de l'age. *Archives de psychologie*, Geneva, 1958, *36*, 328–331.

Leibowitz, H. & Heisel, M. L'evolution de l'illusion de Ponzo en function de l'age. Ponzo illusion. *American Journal of Psychology*, 1967, *80*, 105–109.(a)

Leibowitz, H.W., & Judisch, J.M. Size-constancy in older persons: A function of distance. *American Journal of Psychology*, 1967, *80*, 294–296.(b)

Leibowitz, H., & Pick, H.A., Jr. Cross-cultural and educationa, aspects of the Ponzo perspective illusion. *Perception and Psychophysics*, 1972, *12*, 430–432.

Leibowitz, H.W., Pollard, S.W., & Dickson, D. Monocular and binocular size-matching as a function of distance at various age-levels. *American Journal of Psychology*, 1967, *80*, 263–268.

Leiderman, H., Babu, B., Kagia, J., Kraemer, H.C., & Leiderman, G.I. African infant precocity: Some social influences during the first year. *Nature*, 1973, 242, 247–249.

Leighton, A.H. Cultural relativity and the identification of psychiatric disorders. In W. Caudill & T.Y. Lin (Eds.), *Mental health research in Asia and the Pacific*. Honolulu, East-Wester Center Press, 1969. Pp. 448–462.

Lenneberg, E. *Biological foundations of language*. New York, Wiley, 1967.

Leontiev, A.N. *Problems of psychical development*, (znd ed.). Moscow, Izd. Mysl, 1965.

Leontiev, A.N. Les besoins, les motifs et la conscience. Paper presented at the eighteenth International Congress of Psychology, Moscow, 1966.

Leontiev, A.N. Problema deyatel'nosti v psikhologii. [The problem of activity in psychology]. *Voprosy psikhologii*, 1972, *18*, 95–108(a)

Leontiev, A.N. Deyatel'nost' i soznanie [Activity and consciousness]. *Voprosy psikhologii*, 1972, *18*, 129–140.(b)

Leopold, W.F. *Speech development of a bilingual child*, 4 vols. Evanston, Ill. Northwestern University Press, 1939–1949.

Levine, R. Cross-cultural study in child psychology. In P.H Mussen (Ed.), *Carmichael's manual of child psychology*, vol. 2. New York, Wiley, 1970. Pp. 559–612.

Lévi-Strauss, C. *The savage mind*. Chicago, University of Chicago Press, 1966.

Levy, R.T. On getting angry in the Society Islands. In W. Caudill & T.Y. Lin (Eds.), *Mental health research in Asia and the Pacific*. Honolulu, East-West Center Press, 1969. Pp. 358–380.

Lewin, K. *Field theory and social science*. New York, Harper Torchbook, 1951.

Lewis, M., & Baumel, M.H. A study in the ordering of attention. *Perceptual and Motor Skills*, 1970, *31*, 979–990

Lewis, M., & Butler, R. Neglected by women's lib: Why elderly females need help against discrimination. *The National Observer*, July 29, 1972, *11*.

Lewis, M., & Freedle, R. Mother-infant dyad: The cradle of meaning. In P. Pliner, L. Krames & T. Alloway (Eds.), *Communication and affect: Language and thought*. New York, Academic Press, 1973.

Lewis, M., & Goldberg, S. Perceptual-cognitive development in infancy: A generalized expectancy model as a function of the mother-infant interaction. *Merrill-Palmer Quarterly*, 1969, *15*, 81–100.

Liberman, A.M., Cooper, F.S., Shankweiler, D.P., & Studdert-Kennedy, M. Perception of the speech code. *Psychological Review*, 1967, *74*, 431–461.

Lieberman, P. *Intonation, perception and language*. Cambridge, Mass., M.I.T. Press, 1967.

Lindsay, P.H., & Norman, D.A. *Human information processing*. New York, Academic

Press, 1972.

Lipsitt, L.P. The experiential origins of human behavior. In L.R. Goulet & P.B. Baltes (Eds.), *Life-span developmental psychology: Research and theory.* New York, Academic Press, 1970. Pp. 285–303.

Lloyd, B.B. *Perception and cognition: A cross-cultural perspective.* Middlesex, England, Penguin Books, 1972.

Locke, J.L., & Fehr, F.S. Young children's use of the speech code in a recall task. *Journal of Experimental Child Psychology,* 1970, *10,* 367–373.

Loevinger, J. The meaning and measurement of ego development. *American Psychologist,* 1966, *21,* 191–217.

Looft, W.R. Egocentrism and social interaction across the life-span. *Psychological Bulletin,* 1972, *78,* 73–92.

Looft, W.R. Socialization and personality throughout the life-span: An examination of contemporary psychological approaches. In P.B. Baltes & K.W. Schaie (Eds.), *Life-span developmental psychology: Personality and socialization.* New York, Academic, 1973. Pp. 25–52.

Looft, W.R., & Svoboda, C.P. Structuralism in cognitive developmental psychology: Past, contemporary, and futuristic perspectives. In K.F. Riegel & G.C. Rosenwald (Eds.), *Structure and transformation: Developmental and historical aspects.* New York, Wiley, 1975.

Lopata, H. Social relations of Black and white widowed women in a northern metropolis. *American Journal of Sociology,* 1972, *78,* 1003–1010.

Luria, A.R. Experimental analysis of the development of voluntary action in children. *Central nervous system and behavior,* 1958, *1,* 529–535.

Luria, A.R. The directive function of speech in development and dissolution. *Word,* 1959, *16,* 341–352.

Luria, A.R. Verbal regulation of behavior. In A.B. Brazier (Ed.), *The central nervous system and behavior.* New York, Josiah Macy Foundation, 1960.

Luria, A.R. *The role of speech in the regulation of normal and abnormal behavior.* New York, Liveright, 1961.

Luria, A.R., & Yudovich, F.Ya. *Speech and the development of mental processes in the child.* London, Staples Press, 1959.

Lütkens, D. *Die deutsche Jugendbewegung.* Frankfurt a. M., Frankfurter Societaets-Druckerei, 1925.

Lutte, G. *Le moi idéal de l'adolescent.* Bruxelles, Dessart, 1971.

Lutte, G., Mönks, F.J., Kempen, G., & Sarti, S. *Ideaalbeelden van de Europese jeugd.* 's-Hertogenbosch, Malmberg, 1969.

Lutte, G., Mönks, F.J., Sarti, S. & Preun, H. *Leitbilder und Ideale der europäischen Jugend.* Wuppertal-Elberfeld, A. Henn, 1970.

Lyublinskaya, A.A. *Detskaya psikhologiya [Child psychology].* Moscow, Izd.-vo 'Prosveshchenie', 1971.

MacArthur, R.S. Cognitive strengths of central Canadian and north-west Greenland Eskimo children. Paper presented at the Annual Meeting of the Canadian Psychological Association, Victoria, British Columbia, June 1973.

MacDonald, E. *Mrs. Pigglewiggle.* New York, Lippincott, 1947.

MacKinnon, D.W. Personality and the realization of creative potential. *American Psychologist,* 1965, *20,* 273–281.

MacNeilage, P.F. Motor control of serial ordering of speech. *Psychological Review,* 1970, *77,* 182–196.

Malmo, R.B. Activation: A neuropsychological dimension. *Psychological Review,* 1959, *66,* 367–386.

Mandelbrot, B. Quelques problèmes de la théorie de l'observation, dans le contexte des théories modernes de l'induction des statisticiens. In A. Jonckheere, B. Mandelbrot, & J. Piaget (Eds.), *La lecture de l'expérience*. Paris, P.U.F., 1958. Pp. 30–47.

Marple, C.H. The comparative susceptibility of three age levels to the suggestion of group versus expert opinion. *Journal of Social Psychology*, 1933, *10*, 3–40.

Marsh, C., & Sherman, M. Verbal mediation of transposition as a function of age level. *Journal of Experimental Child Psychology*, 1966, 4, 90–98.

Martin, J. *Harvest of change: American literature, 1865–1914*. Englewood Cliffs, New Jersey, Prentice-Hall, 1967.

Martin, J.G. Rhytmic (hierarchical) versus serial structure in speech and other behavior. *Psychological Review*, 1972, *79*, 487–509.

Maslina, M.N. The Leontiev critique: For Bolshevik partisanship in questions of psychology. In J. Wortis (Ed.), *Soviet psychiatry*. Baltimore, Williams & Wilkins, 1950. Pp. 295–304.

Massaro, D.W., & Anderson, N.H. Judgmental model of the Ebbinghaus illusion. *Journal of Experimental Psychology*, 1971, *89*, 147–151.

Masters, W.H., & Johnson, V. Sexual response: The aging female and the aging male. In B. Neugarten (Ed.), *Middle age and aging*. Chicago, University of Chicago Press, 1968.

McClearn, C.E. Genetic influences on behavior. In P.H. Mussen (Ed.), *Carmichael's manual of child psychology*, vol. 1. New York, Wiley, 1970. Pp. 39–76.

McConnell, T.R. Suggestibility in children as a function of chronological age. *Journal of Abnormal and Social Psychology*, 1963, *67*, 286–289.

McNeill, D. Developmental psycholinguistics. In K. Smith & C.A. Miller (Eds.), *The genesis of language*. Cambridge, Mass., M.I.T. Press. 1966. Pp. 15–84.

McNeill, D. *The acquisition of language*. New York, Harper & Row, 1970.

Meacham, J.A. The development of memory abilities in the individual and society. *Human Development*, 1972, *15*, 205–228.

Meacham, J., Harris, A., & Blaschko, T. Integration of verbal and motor activities. Paper presented at the biennial meeting of the Society for Research in Child Development, Philadelphia, March 1973.

Mead, M. *Continuities in cultural evolution*. New Haven, Yale University Press. 1964.

Meerloo, J.A.M. Rhythm in babies and adults. *Archives of General Psychiatry*, 1961, *5*, 169–175.

Meichenbaum, D.H. Training of the aged in the verbal control of behavior. *Human Development*, 1974, *17*, 273–280.

Meichenbaum, D., & Goodman, J. The developmental control of operant motor responding by verbal operants. *Journal of Experimental Child Psychology*, 1969, *7*, 553–565.

Meichenbaum, D.H., & Goodman, J. Training impulsive children to talk to themselves: A means of developing self-control. *Journal of Abnormal Psychology*, 1971, *77*, 115–126.

Mermelstein, E., & Shulman, L. Lack of formal schooling and the acquisition of conservation. *Child Development*, 1967, *38*, 39–51.

Michaelis-Stern, E. William Stern 1871–1938: The man and his achievements. *Year Book XVII of the Leo Baeck Institute*. London, 1972.

Michon, J.A. *Timing in temporal tracking*. Assen, The Netherlands, Van Gorcum and Co., 1967.

Miller, R.J. Cross-cultural research in the perception of pictorial materials. *Psychological Bulletin*, 1973, *80*, 135–150.

Miller, R.J. Response to the Ponzo illusion as a reflection of hypnotic susceptibility. *International Journal of Clinical and Experimental Hypnosis*, 1975, *23*, in press.

Miller, R.J., Hennessy, R.T., & Leibowitz, H. The effect of hypnotic ablation of the background on the magnitude of the Ponzo perspective illusion. *International Journal of Clinical and Experimental Hypnosis*, 1973, *21*, 180–191.

Miller, S., Shelton, J., & Flavell, J.H. A test of Luria's hypotheses concerning the development of verbal self-regulation. *Child Development*, 1970, *41*, 651–665.

Minsky, M.L. Matter, mind, and models. In M.L. Minski (Ed.), *Semantic information processing*. Cambridge, Mass., M.I.T. Press, 1968. Pp. 425–433.

Minsky, M.L. Frame systems. Draft manuscript. Carnegie-Mellon University, 1973.

Minsky, M., & Papert, S. Research at the laboratory in vision, language, and other problems of intelligence. Artificial intelligence, Memo No. 252, M.I.T. Artifical Intelligence Laboratory, January, 1972.

Mitchell, N.B., & Pollack, R.H. Block-design performance as a function of hue and race. *Journal of Experimental Child Psychology*, 1974, *17*, 377–382.

Mönks, F.J. *Jugend und Zunkuft*. München, J.A. Barth, 1967.

Mönks, F.J. Hedendaagse Jeugd: Theoretische en empirische kanttekeningen. *Nijmeegs Tijdschrift voor Psychologie*, 1970, *18*, 339–352.

Mönnig, H.O. *The Pedi*. Pretoria, Van Schaick, 1968.

Moss, Z. It hurts to be alive and obsolete: The aging women. In R. Morgan (Ed.), *Sisterhood is powerful*. New York, Vintage Books, 1970. Pp. 170–175.

Mountjoy, P.T. Effects of exposure time and intertrial interval upon decrement to the Mueller-Lyer illusion. *Journal of Experimental Psychology*, 1958, *56*, 97–102.

Munroe, R.L., & Monroe, R.H. Effect of environmental experience on spatial ability in East African society. *Journal of Social Psychology*, 1971, *83*, 15–22.

Mussen, P.H. (Ed.), *Carmichael's manual of child psychology*. New York, Wiley, 1970.

Nagel, E. Determinism and development. In D.B. Harris (Ed.), *The concept of development*. Minneapolis, University of Minnesota Press, 1957.

Nagel, E. *The structure of science*. New York, Harcourt, Brace, & World, 1961.

Nebylitsyn, V.D. *Osnovye svoystva nervnoy sistemy cheloveka*. Moskva, Prosveschenie, 1966. *(Fundamental properties of the human nervous system*. New York & London, Plenum Press, 1972.)

Nebylitsyn, V.D. (Ed.), *Problemy differentsialnoy psichofiziologii [Problems of differential psychophysiology]*. Moskva, Prosveshchenie, 1969.

Nebylitsyn, V.D. Current problems in differential psychophysiology. In L. Mecacci & J. Brožek (Eds.), Soviet psychophysiology. *Soviet Psychology*, 1973, *11*, 47–70.

Nebylitsyn, V.D., & Gray, J.A. (Eds.), *Biological bases of individual behavior*. New York & London, Academic Press, 1972.

Neimark, E.D. Model for a thinking machine: An information-processing framework for the study of cognitive development. *Merrill-Palmer Quarterly*, 1970, *16*, 345–368.

Neimark, E.D., Slotnick, N.S., & Ulrich, T. Development of memorization strategies. *Developmental Psychology*, 1971, *5*, 427–432.

Neisser, U. *Cognitive psychology*. New York, Appleton-Century-Crofts, 1967.

Nerlov, S. Trait disposition and situation determinants of behavior among the Gusu of South West Kenya. Unpublished doctoral thesis, Stanford University, 1969.

Nerlov, S.B., Munroe, R.M., & Munroe, R.L. Effect of environmental experience on spatial ability: A replication. *Journal of Social Psychology*, 1971, *84*, 3–10.

Nesselroade, J.R., & Reese, H.W. (Eds.), *Life-span developmental psychology: Methodological issues*. New York, Academic Press, 1973.

Neugarten B. *et al. Personality in middle and late life*. New York, Atherton Press, 1964.

Newell, A. A note on the process structure distinction in developmental psychology. In S. Farnham-Diggory (Ed.), *Information processing in children*. New York,

Academic Press, 1972. Pp. 126–133.

Newell, A. Production systems: Models of control structures. In W.G. Chase (Ed.), *Visual information processing*. New York, Academic Press, 1973.

Newell, A. & Simon, H.A. *Human problem solving*. New York, Prentice-Hall, 1972.

Nikkel, N., & Palermo, D.S. Effects of mediated associations in paired-associate learning of children. *Journal of Experimental Child Psychology*, 1965, *2*, 92–101.

Nochlin, L. Why are there no great woman artists? In V. Gornick, & B. Moran (Eds.), *Women in sexist society*. New York, Basic Books, 1972.

Norcross, K.J. Effects on discrimination performance of similarity of previously acquired stimulus names. *Journal of Experimental Psychology*, 1958, *56*, 305–309.

Norcross, K.J., & Spiker, C.C. The effects of type of stimulus pretraining on discrimination performance in preschool children. *Child Development*, 1957, *28*, 79–84.

Norcross, K.J., & Spiker, C.C. Effects of mediated association on transfer in paired associate learning. *Journal of Experimental Psychology*, 1958, *55*, 129–134.

Ogasawara, J. Displacement after-effect of concentric circles. *Japanese Journal of Psychology*, 1952, *22*, 224–234.

Ohwaki, S. On the destruction of geometrical illusions in stereoscopic observation. *Tohuku Psychol. Folin*, 1960, *29*, 24–36.

Orne, M.T. Hypnosis: Art or artifact. *Journal of Abnormal Psychology*, 1959, *58*, 173–190.

Orne, M.T. Hypnosis, motivation, and the ecological validity of the psychological experiment. In W.J. Arnold, & M.M. Page (Eds.), *Nebraska symposium on motivation*. Lincoln, Univ. of Nebraska Press, 1970. Pp. 187–265.

Ourth, L., & Brown, K.B. Inadequate mothering and disturbance in the neonatal period. *Child Development*, 1961, *32*, 287–295.

Overton, W.F. Research and application: A philosophical perspective. Paper presented at the meeting of the Society for Research in Child Development, Philadelphia, April, 1973.

Overton, W.F., & Reese, H.W. Models of development: Methodological implications. In J.R. Nesselroade & H.W. Reese (Eds.), *Life-span developmental psychology: Methodological issues*. New York, Academic Press, 1973. Pp. 65–86.

Palermo, D.S., Mediated association in a paired-associate transfer task. *Journal of Experimental Psychology*, 1962, *64*, 234–238.

Papalia, D.E. The status of several conservation abilities across the lifespan. *Human Development*, 1972, *15*, 229–243.

Papashvily, H. *All the happy endings*. New York, Harper, 1956.

Papert, S. Theory of knowledge and complexity. In G.J. Dalenoort (Ed.), *Process models for psychology*. Rotterdam, Rotterdam University Press, 1973. Pp. 1–49.

Paraskevopoulos, J., & Hunt, J.McV. Object construction and imitation under differing conditions of rearing. *Journal of Genetic Psychology*, 1971, *119*, 301–321.

Pareck, U.N. *Developmental patterns in reaction to frustration*. London, Asia Publishing House, 1965.

Pascual-Leone, J. A mathematical model for the transition rule in Piaget's developmental stages. *Acta Psychologica*, 1970, *32*, 301–345.

Pascual-Leone, J., & Bovet, M.C. L'apprentissage de la quantification de l'inclusion et la théorie opératiore. *Acta Psychologica*, 1966, *25*, 334–356.

Pascual-Leone, J., & Smith, J. The encoding and decoding of symbols by children: A new experimental paradigm and a neo-Piagetian model. *Journal of Experimental Child Psychology*, 1969, *8*, 328–355.

Passingham, R. E. The neurological basis of introversion-extraversion: Gray's theory. *Behaviour Research and Therapy*, 1970, 8, 353–366.

Pastore, N. *A history of visual perception*. Oxford, Oxford University Press, 1971.

Patel, H. S., & Gordon, J. E. Some personal and situational determinants of yielding to influence. *Journal of Abnormal and Social Psychology*, 1960, 61, 411–418.

Pavlov, I. P. The physiology of higher nervous activity. In I. P. Pavlov (Ed.), *Conditioned reflex and psychiatry*. New York, International Publishers, 1941.

Pavlov, I. P. *Experimental psychology and other essays*. New York, Philosophical Library, 1957.

Payne, T. R. *S. L. Rubinstein and the philosophical foundations of Soviet psychology*. New York, Humanities Press, 1968.

Perquin, N. *Pedagogische psychologie van de Middelbare scholier*. Roermond, Romen & Zonen, 1967.

Peters, D. Task variations and individual differences in Piaget's conservation of number. *Merrill-Palmer Quarterly*, 1967, 13, 295–308.

Peters, R.S. (Eds.), *Brett's history of psychology*. London, George Allen & Unwin, 1953.

Piaget, J. *The child's conception of the world*. New York, Harcourt, Brace, 1929.

Piaget, J. *Introduction à l'épistémologie génétique*, 3 vols. Paris, Presses Univ. de France, 1950.

Piaget, J. Autobiography. In C. Murchison, & E. G. Boring (Eds.), *A history of psychology in autobiography*, vol. 4. Worcester, Mass., Clark University Press, 1952. Pp. 237–256.(a)

Piaget, J. *The origins of intelligence in children*. New York, International Universities Press, 1952. (b)

Piaget, J. *Logic and psychology*. Manchester, Manchester University Press, 1953.

Piaget, J. *The construction of reality in the child*. New York, Basic Books, 1954.

Piaget, J. Programme et méthodes de l'epistémologie génétique. In W. E. Beth, W. Mays, & J. Piaget, *Epistémologie génétique et recherche psychologique. Etudes d'épistémologie génétique*, vol. 1. Paris, Presses Univer. France, 1957. Pp. 13–84.

Piaget, J. The general problems of the psychobiological development of the child. In J.M. Tanner & B. Inhelder (Eds.), *Discussions on child development: Proceedings of the World Health Organization study group on the psychobiological development of the child*, vol. 4. New York, International Universities Press, 1960. Pp. 3–27.

Piaget, J. *Les mécanismes perceptifs*. Paris, Presses Universitaires de France, 1961.

Piaget, J. Comments on Vygotsky's critical remarks concerning 'The language and the thought of the child' and 'Judgement and reasoning in the child'. Cambridge, Mass., M.I.T. Press, 1962.(a)

Piaget, J. *Play, dreams, and imitation in childhood*. New York, Norton, 1962.(b)

Piaget, J. The relation of affectivity to intelligence in the mental devolopment of the child. *Bulletin of the Menninger Clinic* (Topeka, Kansas), 1962, 26, 167–175.(c)

Piaget, J. Cognitive development in children: Development and learning. In R. Ripple & V. Rockcastle (Eds.), *Piaget rediscovered: Report of the conference on cognitive studies and curriculum development*. Ithaca, N.Y., Cornell University, 1964. Pp. 6–15.

Piaget, J. *The moral judgment of the child*. New York, The Free Press, 1965.

Piaget, J. Nécessité et signification des recherches comparatives en psychologie génétique. *International Journal of Psychology*, 1966, 1, 3–13.(a)

Piaget, J. *The psychology of intelligence*. Totowa, N.J., Littlefield Adams, 1966.(b)

Piaget, J. Review of *Studies in cognitive growth* by J.S. Bruner, R.P. Olver, P. M. Greenfield, *et. al.*, *Contemporary Psychology*, 1967, 12, 532–535.(a)

Piaget, J. *Six psychological studies*. New York, Random House, 1967.(b)

Piaget, J. Explanations in psychology and psychophysiological parallelism. In P. Fraisse & J. Piaget (Eds.), *Experimental psychology: Its scope and method. I. History and method*. London, Routledge and Kegan Paul, 1968. Pp. 153–192.

Piaget, J. *On the development of memory and identity*. Worchester, Clark University Press, 1968.

Piaget, J. *The mechanisms of perception*. New York, Basic Books, 1969.

Piaget, J. *Genetic epistemology*. New York, Columbia University Press, 1970.(a)

Piaget, J. Piaget's theory. In P.H. Mussen (Ed.), *Carmichael's manual of child psychology*. New York, Wiley, 1970. Pp. 703–732.(b)

Piaget, J. *Science of education and the psychology of the child*. New York, Grossman, 1970.(c)

Piaget, J. *Structuralism*. New York, Basic Books, 1970.(d)

Piaget, J. *Biology and knowledge*. Chicago, Illinois, University of Chicago Press, 1971. (a)

Piaget, J. The theory of stages in cognitive development. In D. Green, M. Ford & G. Flamer (Eds.), *Measurement and Piaget: Proceedings of the CTB/McGraw-Hill Conference on ordinal scales of cognitive development*. New York, McGraw-Hill, 1971.(b)

Piaget, J. *Essai de logique opératoire*. Paris, Dunod, 1972.(a)

Piaget, J. Intellectual evolution from adolescence to adulthood. *Human Development*, 1972, *15*, 1–12.(b)

Piaget, J., *et. al.* Recherches sur le développement des perceptions: I. Introduction à l'étude des perceptions chez l'enfant et analyse d'une illusion relative à la perception visuelle de cercles concentriques (Delboeuf). *Archives de Psychology*, Genève, 1942, *28*, 1–107.

Piaget, J., & Inhelder, B. *Le Dévelopment des quantités chez l'enjant*. Neuchatel, Delachaux et Niestlé, 1941.

Piaget, J., & Inhelder, B. *The psychology of the child*. New York, Basic Books, 1969.

Piaget, J., & Lambercier, M. Recherches sur le dévelopment des perceptions: V. Essai sur un effet d' 'Einstellung' survenant au cours de perceptions visuelles successives (effet Usnadze). *Archives de Psychologie*, Genève, 1944, *30*, 139–196.

Piaget, J., Maire, F., & Privat, F. Recherches sur le développement des perceptions: XVIII. La résistance des bonnes formes à l'illusion de Müller-Lyer. *Archives de Psychologie*, Genève, 1954, *34*, 155–202.

Pinard, A., & Laurendeau, M. 'Stage' in Piaget's cognitive-developmental theory: Exegesis of a concept. In D. Elkind & J.H. Flavell (Eds.), *Studies in cognitive development: Essays in honor of Jean Piaget*. New York, Oxford, 1969. Pp. 121–170.

Pineo, P. Disenchantment in the later years of marriage. In B. Neugarten (Ed.), *Middle age and aging*. Chicago, University of Chicago Press, 1968.

Plato. *The dialogues of Plato*. Chicago, Encyclopaedia Brittannica, 1952.

Plutarch. *The lives of the noble Grecians and Romans*. Chicago, Encyclopaedia Brittanica, 1952.

Polanyi, M. *Personal knowledge*. New York, Harper & Row, 1958.

Pollack, R.H. Figural after-effects: Quantitative studies in displacement. *Australian Journal of Psychology*, 1958, *10*, 269–277.

Pollack, R.H. Figural after-effects as a function of age. *Acta Psychologica*, 1960, *17*, 417–423.

Pollack, R.H. Apparent median plane shifts with asymetrical stimulation and fixation. *Australian Journal of Psychology*, 1961, *13*, 195–205.

Pollack, R.H. Application of the sensoritonic theory of perception to figural after-effects. *Acta Psychologica*, 1963, *21*, 1–16.(a)

Pollack, R.H. The after-effects of passive kineasthetic-tactual stimulation of the thumb and forefinger. *Acta Psychologica*, 1963, *21*, 17–23.(b)

Pollack, R.H. Viewing distance and the after-effects of fixation. *Perceptual and Motor Skills*, 1963, *17*, 863–866.(c)

Pollack, R.H. Effects of temporal order of stimulus presentation on the direction of figural after-effects. *Perceptual and Motor Skills*, 1963, *17*, 875–880.(d)

Pollack, R.H. Contour detectability thresholds as a function of chronological age. *Perceptual and Motor Skills*, 1963, *17*, 411–417.(e)

Pollack, R.H. Simultaneous and successive presentation of elements of the Mueller-Lyer figure and chronological age. *Perceptual and Motor Skills*, 1964, *19*, 303–310.

Pollack, R.H. Hue detectability thresholds as a function of chronological age. *Psychonomic Science*, 1965, *3*, 351–352.(a)

Pollack, R.H. Effects of figure-ground contrast and contour orientation on figural masking. *Psychonomic Science*, 1965, *2*, 369–370.(b)

Pollack, R.H. Backward figural masking as a function of chronological age and intelligence. *Psychonomic Science*, 1965, *3*, 65–66.(c)

Pollack, R.H. Effect of figure-ground contrast and contour orientation of the temporal range of apparent movement. *Psychonomic Science*, 1966, *4*, 401–402.(a)

Pollack, R.H. Initial stimulus duration and the temporal range on apparent movement. *Psychonomic Science*, 1966, *5*, 165–166.(b)

Pollack, R.H. Temporal range of apparent movement as a function of age and intelligence. *Psychonomic Science*, 1966, *5*, 243–244.(c)

Pollack, R.H. Changes in the effects of fixation upon apparent distance in the third dimension. *Psychonomic Science*, 1967, *8*, 141–142.

Pollack, R.H. Some implications of ontogenetic changes in perception. In J. Flavell & D. Elkind (Eds.), *Studies in cognitive development: Essays in honor of Jean Piaget*. Oxford University Press, New York, 1969.

Pollack, R.H. Mueller-Lyer Illusion: Effect of age, lightness contrast and hue. *Science* 1970, *170*, 93–95.

Pollack, R.H., & Brenner, M.W. (Eds.), *The experimental psychology of Alfred Binet: Selected papers*. New York, Springer Publishing Co., 1969.

Pollack, R.H., & Carter, D.J. Subjective median plane as a function of age and source of stimulation. *Perceptual and Motor Skills*, 1967, *25*, 691–692.

Pollack, R.H., & Carter, D.J. Effects of age and asymetrical stimulation on the subjective median plane. *Perception and Psychophysics*, 1968, *4*, 264–266.

Pollack, R.H., Carter, D.J., & Ptashne, R. The dark-interval threshold as a function of age. *Psychonomic Science*, 1968, *12*, 237–238.

Pollack, R.H., & Chaplin, M.R. The after-effects of prolonged arm extension. *Acta Psychologica*, 1962, *20*, 24–28.

Pollack, R.H., Ptashne, R., & Carter, D.J. The effects of age and intelligence on the dark interval threshold. *Perception and Psychophysics*, 1969, *6*, 50–52.

Pollack, R.H., & Silvar, S. Magnitude of the Mueller-Lyer illusion in children as a function of pigmentation of the Fundus oculi. *Psychonomic Science*, 1967, *8*, 83–84.

Polya, G. *How to solve it*. New York, Doubleday, 1957.

Pongratz, L.G. *Problemgeschichte der Psychologie*. Bern, Franke, 1967.

Ponser, M.I., & Mitchell, R. A chronometric analysis of classification. *Psychological Review*, 1967, *74*, 392–409.

Power, E. The position of women. In G.C. Crump & E.F. Jacob (Eds.), *The legacy of the middle ages*. New York, Oxford University Press, 1926. Pp. 403–433.

Powers, E.A. The effects of the wife's employment on household tasks among post-parental couples: A research note. *Aging and Human Development*, 1971, *12*, 284–287.

President's Commission on the Status of Women. American Women: Report. Washington, D.C., U.S. Government Printing Office, 1963.

Preyer, W. *Die Seele des Kindes. Beobachtungen über die geistige Entwicklung des Menschen in den ersten Lebensjahren.* Leipzig, Grieben, 1882.

Price-Williams, D. A study concerning concepts of conservation of quantities among primitive children. *Acta Psychologica*, 1961, *18*, 293–305.

Price-Williams, D., Gordon, W., & Ramirez, M. Manipulation and conservation: A study of children from pottery-making families in Mexico. *Memorias del XI Congresso Inter-Americano de Psicologia*. Mexico City, 1967. Pp. 106–126.

Price-Williams, D., Gordon, W.F., & Ramirez, M. Skill and conservation: A study of pottery-making children. *Developmental Psychology*, 1969, *1*, 769.

Proshansky, H., & Newton, P. The nature and meaning of Negro self-identity. In M. Deutsch, I. Katz, & A.R. Jensen (Eds.), *Social class, race, and psychological development*. Holt, Rinehart & Winston, New York, 1968.

Przetacznikowa, M. *Rozwój i wychowanie dzieci i młodzieży w średnim wieku szkolnym [Development and education of children and adolescents in the middle school age].* Warszawa, Nasza Księgarnia, 1971.

Przetacznikowa, M. Rozwój struktury i mechanizmów regulacyjnych czynności ludzkich. [Development of the structure and regulative mechanisms of human actions]. *Psychologia Wychowawcza*, 1971, *2*.

Przetacznikowa, M. *Podstawy rozwoju psychicznego dzieci i młodzieży [Principles of children's and adolescents' development]*. Warszawa, PZWS, 1973.

Quina, M.K., & Pollack, R.H. A parametric investigation of the Ponzo illusion under conditions of tachistoscopic exposure. Paper presented at the Annual Meeting of the American Psychological Association, 1971.

Quina, M.K., & Pollack, R.H. Effects of test line position and age on the magnitude of the Ponzo illusion. *Perception and Psychophysics*, 1972, *12*, 253–256.

Quina, M.K., & Pollack, R.H. Attraction of parallels as a function of intercontour distance. *Perceptual and Motor Skills*, 1973, *36*, 394.

Quine, W.V. *Word and object*. Cambridge, Mass., MIT Press, 1960.

Quine, W.V. Epistemology naturalized. In J.R. Royce & W.W. Rozeboom (Eds.), *The psychology of knowing*. New York, Gordon & Breach, 1972. Pp. 9-24.

Rabbit, P. Age and the use of structure in transmitted information. In G.A. Talland (Ed.), *Human aging and behavior: Recent advances in research and theory*. New York, Academic Press, 1968.

Rabbitt, P.M.A., & Birren, J.E. Age and responses to sequences of repetitive and interruptive signals. *Journal of Gerontology*, 1967, *22*, 143–150.

Rahmani, L. *Soviet psychology: Philosophical, theoretical and experimental issues*. New York, International Universities Press, 1973.

Ramey, C.T., & Ourth, L.L. Delayed reinforcement and vocalization rates of infants. *Child Development*, 1971, *42*, 291–297.

Rank, O. *Truth therapy and truth and reality*. New York, Knopf, 1945.

Rapaport, D. The structure of psychoanalytic theory: A systematizing attempt. In S. Koch (Ed.), *Psychology: A study of a science*, vol. 3. New York, McGraw-Hill, 1959. Pp. 55–183.

Raum, D.F. An evaluation of indigenous education. In P.H. Duminy (Ed.), *Trends and challenges in the education of the South African Bantu*. Pretoria, Van Schaick, 1967.

Reese, H.W. Verbal mediation as a function of age level. *Psychological Bulletin*, 1962, *59*, 502–509.

Reese, H.W. Imagery in paired-associate learning. *Journal of Experimental Child Psychology*, 1965, *2*, 290–296.

Reese, H.W. Verbal effects in the intermediate-size transposition problem. *Journal of Experimental Child Psychology*, 1966, *3*, 123–130.

Reese, H.W. Models of memory and models of development. *Human Development*, 1973, *16*, 397–416.

Reese, H.W., & Overton, W.F. Models of development and theories of development. In L.R. Goulet & P.B. Baltes (Eds.), *Life-span developmental psychology: Research and theory*. New York, Academic Press, 1970. Pp. 115–145.

Restle, F., & Greeno, J.G. *Introduction to mathematical psychology*. Reading, Mass., Addison-Wesley, 1970.

Restle, F., & Merryman, C.T. An adaptation-level theory account of a relative-size illusion. *Psychonomic Science*, 1968, *12*, 229–230.

Riegel, K.F. Untersuchungen der intellektuellen Fähigkeiten älterer Menschen. Unpublished doctoral dissertation, University of Hamburg, 1957.

Riegel, K.F. Some theoretical considerations of bilingual development. *Psychological Bulletin*, 1968, *70*, 647–670.

Riegel, K.F. The language acquisition process: A reinterpretation of selected research findings. In L.R. Goulet & P.B. Baltes (Eds.), *Life-span developmental psychology: Theory and research*. New York, Academic Press, 1970. Pp. 357–399.

Riegel, K.F. Influence of economic and political ideologies on the development of developmental psychology. *Psychological Bulletin*, 1972, *78*, 129–141.(a)

Riegel, K.F. Time and change in the development of the individual and society. In H. Reese (Ed.), *Advances in child development and behavior*, vol. 7. New York, Academic Press, 1972. Pp. 81–113.(b)

Riegel, K.F. Developmental psychology and society: Some historical and ethical considerations. In J.R. Nesselroade & H.W. Reese (Eds.), *Life-span developmental psychology: Methodological issues*. New York, Academic Press, 1973. Pp. 1–24.(a)

Riegel, K.F. Dialectic operations: The final period of cognitive development. *Human Development*, 1973, *16*, 346–370.(b)

Riegel, K.F. Structure and transformation in modern intellectual history. In K.F. Riegel & G.C. Rosenwald (Eds.), *Structure and transformation: Developmental and historical aspects*. New York, Wiley, 1975.

Riegel, K.F., & Riegel, R.M. An investigation into denotative aspects of word meaning. *Language and Speech*, 1963, *6*, 5–21.

Riegel, K.F., & Riegel, R.M. Development, drop and death. *Developmental Psychology*, 1972, *6*, 306–319.

Rin, H. Sibling rank, culture and mental disorders. In W. Caudill & T.Y. Lin (Eds.), *Mental health research in Asia and the Pacific*. Honolulu, East-West Center Press, 1969. Pp. 105–113.

Roberton, M.A. Unidirectionality in life-span development: A necessary or unnecessary corollary of organismic theory? Unpublished manuscript, University of Wisconsin, 1972.

Rodd, W.G. Cross-cultural use of the study of values. *Psychologia* (Kyoto), 1959, *2*, 157–164.

Rohwer, W.D., jr., Lynch, S., Suzuki, N., & Levin, J.R. Verbal and pictorial facilitation of paired-associate learning. *Journal of Experimental Child Psychology*, 1967, *5*, 294–302.

Roodin, M.L., & Gruen, G.E. The role of memory in making transitive judgments. *Journal of Experimental Child Psychology*, 1970, *10*, 264–275.

Rosen, G. The revolt of youth: Some historical comparisons. In J. Zubin & A.M. Freedman (Eds.), *The psychopathology of adolescence*. New York, Grune and

Stratton, 1970. Pp. 1–14.

Rosen, R. Sexism in history or, writing women's history is a tricky business. *Journal of Marriage and the Family*, 1971, *33*, 541–544.

Rosenzweig, S. The Rosenzweig picture frustration study: Form for children. Distributed by author, 1944.

Rosenzweig, S., Flemming, E., & Rosenzweig, L. The children's form of the Rosenzweig Picture-Frustration Study. *Journal of Psychology*, 1948, *26*, 141–191.

Ross, A.D. *The Hindu family in its urban setting*. Toronto, University of Toronto Press, 1961.

Rossi, A. Equality between the sexes: An immodest proposal. *Daedalus*, 1964, *93*, 607–652.

Roth, E. *Der Werteinstellungstest: Eine Skala zur Messung dominanter Interessen der Persönlichkeit*. Bern, Huber, 1972.

Rozeboom, W.W. Problems in the psycho-philosophy of knowledge. In J.R. Royce & W.W. Rozeboom (Eds.), *The psychology of knowing*. New York, Gordon & Breach, 1973. Pp. 25–109.

Rubinshtein, S.L. *Principles and paths of the development of psychology*. Moscow, Izd. Akad. Nauk SSSR, 1959.

Rumelhart, D.E., Lindsay, P.H., & Norman, D.A. A process model for longterm memory. In E. Tulving & W. Donaldson (Eds.), *Organization of memory*. New York, Academic Press, 1972. Pp. 197–246.

Russel, B. *Human knowledge: Its scope and limits*. New York, Simon & Schuster, 1948.

Saint-Anne Dargassies, S. Neurological maturation of the premature infant of 28 to 41 weeks' gestational age. In F. Falkner (Ed.), *Human development*. Philadelphia, Saunders, 1966. Pp. 306–325.

Samarin, W. *Tongues of men and angels*. New York, Macmillan, 1972.

Sander, F. Experimentelle Ergebnisse der Gestaltspychology. *Bericht über den 10. Kongreß der Deutschen Gesellschaft für Psychologie*. Bonn, Jena, S. Fischer, 1928. Pp. 23–88.

Sanders, S., Laurendeau, M., & Bergeron, J. Aging and the concept of space: The conservation of surfaces. *Journal of Gerontology*, 1966, *21*, 281–286.

Schelsky, H. *Die skeptische Generation: Eine Soziologie der deutschen Jugend*. Düsseldorf-Köln, Diederich, 1957.

Schiller, P., & Wiener, M. Binocular and stereoscopic viewing of geometric illusions. *Perceptual and Motor Skills*, 1962, *15*, 739–747.

Schlesinger, I.M. Grammatical development. In E. Lenneberg & H. Lenneberg (Eds.), *Foundations of language development*. 1973, in press.

Schlosberg, H. Stereoscopic depth from single pictures. *American Journal of Psychology*, 1941, *54*, 601–605.

Schludermann, S., & Schludermann, E. Adolescents' perception of themselves and adults in Hutterite communal society. *Journal of Psychology*, 1971, *78*, 39–48.(a)

Schludermann, S., & Schludermann, E. Adolescent perception of parent behavior (CRPBI) in Hutterite communal society. *Journal of Psychology*, 1971, *79*, 29–39.(b)

Schludermann, S., & Schludermann, E. Paternal attitudes in Hutterite communal society. *Journal of Psychology*, 1971, *79*, 41–48.(c)

Schludermann, S., & Schludermann, E. Maternal child rearing attitudes in Hutterite communal society. *Journal of Psychology*, 1971, *79*, 169–177. (d)

Schmeing, K. *Ideal und Gegenideal*. Leipzig, J.A. Barth, 1935.

Schmid, R.C. German youth movements: A typological study. Unpublished dissertation, University of Wisconsin, 1946.

Schmidt, H.D. *Allgemeine Entwicklungspsychologie*. Berlin, VEB Deutscher Verlag der

Wissenschaften, 1970.

Schmidt, R. A. Anticipation and timing in human motor performance. *Psychological Bulletin*, 1968, *70*, 631–645.

Scott, D. S. Background to formalization. In H. Leblanc (Ed.), *Truth, syntax, and modality*. Amsterdam, North-Holland, 1973. Pp. 244–273.

Scribner, S., & Cole, M. The cognitive consequences of formal and informal education. *Science*, 1973, *182*, 553–559.

Sechrest, L. Phillipine culture, stress and psychopathology. In W. Caudill & T. Y. Lin (Eds.), *Mental health research in Asia and the Pacific*. Honolulu, East-West Center Press, 1969. Pp. 306–334.

Segall, M. H., Campbell, D. T., & Herskovitz, M. J. *The influence of culture on visual perception*. Indianapolis, Bobbs-Merrill, 1966.

Serafica, F. C., & Uzgiris, I. C. Infant-mother relationship and object concept. Paper presented at the 79th Annual Convention of the American Psychological Association, 1971.

Shapera, I. (Ed.) *The Bantu-speaking tribes of South Africa*. Cape Town, Longmans, 1953.

Shapiro, A. H. Verbalization during the preparatory interval of a reaction-time task and development of motor control. *Child Development*, 1973, *44*, 137–142.

Shirk, G. B. An examination of conceptual frameworks of beginning mathematics teachers. Unpublished dissertation, College of Education, University of Illinois, 1973.

Sigismund, B. *Kind und Welt*. Braunschweig, Vieweg, 1856.

Silvar, S., & Pollack, R. H. Racial differences in pigmentation of the Fundus oculi. *Psychonomic Science*, 1967, *7*, 159.

Simon, H. A. An information processing theory of intellectual development. In W. Kessen & C. Kuhlman (Eds.), *Thought in the young child. Monographs of the Society for Research in Child Development*, 1962, *27* 150–155.

Simon, H. A. In H. H. Pattee (Ed.), *Hierarchy theory*. New York, Braziller, 1973.

Simon, W. E. Self-concept and the validity of the Allport-Vernon-Lindzey study of values. *Perceptual and Motor Skills*, 1970, *31*, 263–266.

Sinclair de Zwart, H. Sensorimotor action schemes as a condition of the acquisition of syntax. Unpublished paper, University of Geneva, 1970.

Singleton, W. T. The change of movement timing with age. *British Journal of Psychology*, 1954, *45*, 166–172.

Sjostrom, K. P., & Pollack, R. H. The effect of simulated receptor aging on two types of visual illusions. *Psychonomic Science*, 1971, *23*, 147–148. (a)

Sjostrom, K. P., & Pollack, R. H. Simulated receptor aging in the study of ontogenetic trends of visual illusions. Paper presented at the Annual Convention of the American Psychological Association, 1971. (b)

Sjostrom, K. P., & Pollack, R. H. Effect of short-term fixation on perceived size of a circle. *Perceptual and Motor Skills*, 1973, *36*, 1217–1218.

Skinner, B. F. *The behavior of organisms*. New York, Appleton-Century-Crofts, 1938.

Skoff, E., & Pollack, R. H. Visual acuity in children as a function of hue. *Perception and Psychophysics*, 1969, *6*, 244–246.

Slamecka, H. J. A methodological analysis of shift paradigms in human discrimination learning. *Psychological Bulletin*, 1968, *69*, 423–438.

Slavskaya, K. A. *Thinking in action: Psychology of thinking*. Moscow, Izd. Politicheskoi Literatury, 1968.

Smedslund, J. The acquisition of conservation of substance and weight in children: II. External reinforcement of conservation of weight and of the operations of additions and subtractions. *Scandinavian Journal of Psychology*, 1961, *2*, 71–84.

Smedslund, J. The concept of correlation in adults. *Scandinavian Journal of Psychology*, 1963, *4*, 165–173.

Smedslund, J. Meanings, implications and universals: Towards a psychology of man. *Scandinavian Journal of Psychology*, 1969, *10*, 1–15.

Smillie, D. Piaget's constructionist theory. *Human Development*, 1972, *15*, 171–186.

Smith, K. U. Physiological and sensory feedback of the motor system: Neural metabolic integration for the energy regulation in behavior. In J.D. Mazer (Ed.), *Efferent organization and the integration of behavior*. New York, Academic Press, 1973.

Sokolov, A. N. *Inner speech and thought*. New York, Plenum, 1972.

Sontag, S. The double standard of aging. *Saturday Review of Society*, 1972, September 23, 29–38.

Spionek, H. *Rozwój i wychowanie małego dziecka. [Development and education of the little child]*. Warszawa, Nasza Księgarnia, 1967.

Spranger, E. *Wilhelm von Humboldt und die Humanitätsidee*. Berlin, Reuther & Reichard, 1909.

Spranger, E. *Lebensformen: Geisteswissenschaftliche Psychologie und Ethik der Persönlichkeit*. Halle, Niemeyer, 1921.

Spranger, E. *Psychologie des Jugendalters*. Leipzig, Quelle & Meyer, 1924. (27th ed., Heidelberg, 1968.)

Spranger, E. *Die Frage nach der Einheit der Psychologie*. Berlin, Akademie der Wissenschaften, 1926.

Spranger, E. *Pädagogische Perspektiven: Beiträge zu Erziehungsfragen der Gegenwart*. Heidelberg, Quelle & Meyer, 1950. (7th ed., 1962.)

Springbett, B. M. Some stereoscopic phenomena and their implications. *British Journal of Psychology*, 1961, *52*, 105–109.

Starkweather, E. K. Conformity and nonconformity as indicators of creativity in preschool children. Cooperative Research Project No. 1967, United States Office of Education, 1964.

Stern, C., & Stern, W. *Die Kindersprache*. Leipzig, J. A. Barth, 1907.

Stern, C., & Stern, W. *Erinnerung, Aussage und Lüge in der ersten Kindheit*. Leipzig, J. A. Barth, 1920.

Stern, F. The historical setting of student unrest. In *The background of student unrest*. New York, Assoc. Alumni Columbia College, 1966. Pp. 4–18.

Stern, J. A. Toward a definition of psychophysiology. *Psychophysiology*, 1964, *1*, 90–91.

Stern, J. A. Toward a developmental psychophysiology: My look into the crystal ball. *Psychophysiology*, 1968, *4*, 403–420.

Stern, W. *Ueber Psychologie der individuellen Differenzen*. Leipzig, J. A. Barth, 1900.

Stern, W. *Person und Sache: System der philosophischen Weltanschauung*. Leipzig, J. A. Barth, 1906.

Stern, W. *Die differentielle Psychologie in ihren methodischen Grundlagen*. Leipzig, J. A. Barth, 1911.

Stern, W. *Psychological methods of testing intelligence*. Baltimore, Warwick & York, 1914.(a)

Stern, W. *Psychologie der frühen Kindheit bis zum sechsten Lebensjahre*. Leipzig, Quelle und Meyer, 1914.(b)

Stern, W. Psychologists' song. *Journal of Educational Psychology*, 1914, *5*, 413–416.(c)

Stern, W. *Die Intelligenz der Kinder und Jugendlichen*. Leipzig, J. A. Barth, 1920.

Stern, W. *Psychology of early childhood up to the sixth year of age*. London, George Allen and Unwin, 1924.

Stern, W. *Die Anfänge der Reifezeit: Ein Knabentagebuch in psychologischer Bearbeitung*. Leipzig, Quelle & Meyer, 1925.

Stern, W. *Jugendlichen Zeugen in Sittlichkeitsprozessen*. Leipzig, Quelle & Meyer, 1926.

Stern, W. Die Stellung der Psychologie an den deutschen Universitäten. *Die Deutsche Schule*, 1931, *2*, 3–12.

Stern, W. *Allgemeine Psychologie auf personalistischer Grundlage*. The Hague, M. Nijhoff, 1935.

Stern, W. *General psychology from the personalistic standpoint*. New York, Macmillan, 1938.

Stevens, S. S. (Ed.), *Handbook of experimental psychology*. New York, Wiley, 1964.

Stevenson, H. *Children's learning*. New York, Appleton, Century, Crofts, 1972.

Stinnett, N., Carter, R., & Montgomery, J. Older persons' perceptions of their marriages. *Journal of Marriage and the Family*, 1972, *34*, 665–670.

Streicher, H. W. Backward figural masking as a function of inter-contour distance. *Psychonomic Science*, 1967, *7*, 69–70.

Subbotskii, Y. V. On the question of children's behavior in conflict situations. Unpublished dissertation, Moscow State University, 1972. (a) (Unpublished translation by E. E. Berg, 1973.)

Subbotskii, Y. V. The development of an objective attitude toward people in very young children and preschool children. Unpublished dissertation, Moscow State University, 1972.(b) (Unpublished translation by E. E. Berg, 1973.)

Sukhanova, N. V. Formation of the motor component of a verbal reaction in children. *Pavlovian Journal of Higher Nervous Activity*, 1961, *11*, 893–898.

Sumler, D. *A history of Europe in the twentieth century*. Homewood, Ill., Dorsey Press 1973.

Super, C. Infant care and motor development in rural Kenya: Some preliminary data on precocity and deficit. Paper presented at the Regional Meeting of the International Association for Cross-Cultural Psychology, Ibadan, Nigeria, April 1973.

Szafran, J. Experiments on the greater use of vision by older adults. In *Old age in the modern world*. Edinburgh, Livingstone, 1955.

Szuman, S. *Rola działania w rozwoju umysłowym małego dziecka, [Role of activity in the mental development of the little child]*. Wrocław, Ossolineum, 1955.

Tausch, R. Optische Täuschungen als artifizielle Effekte der Gestaltungsprozesse von Grössen- und Formenkonstanz in der naturlichen Raumwahrnehmung. *Psychologische Forschung*, 1954, *24–25*, 299–348.

Teplov, B. M. Nekotorye voprosy izucheniya obschich tipov vysshey nervnoy deyatelnosti cheloveka i zhivotnych. *Tipologischeskie osobennosti vysshey nervnoy deyatelnosti cheloveka*. Moskva: Akad. Pedag. Nauk RSFSR, 1956. (Problems in the study of general types of higher nervous activity in man and animals. In J. A. Gray (Ed.), *Pavlov's typology*. Oxford, Pergamon Press, 1964.)

Teplov, B. M. (Ed.), *Tipologischeskie osobennosti vysshey nervnoy deyatelnosti cheloveka [Typological features of higher nervous activity in man]*, 5vols. Moskva, Akad. Pedag. Nauk RSFSR, 1956–1967.

Thomae, H. Der physiognomische Test. In C. Coerper, W. Hagen & H. Thomae (Eds.), *Deutsche Nachkriegskinder*. Stuttgart, Thieme, 1954.

Thomae, H. Entwicklungsbegriff und Entwicklungstheorie. In H. Thomae (Ed.), *Entwicklungspsychologie*. Handbuch der Psychologie, Band 3. Göttingen, Verlag für Psychologie, 1958. Pp. 3–20.

Thomae, H. *Vorbilder und Leitbilder der Jugend*. München, Juventa, 1965.

Thomae, H. *Das Individuum und seine Welt: Eine Persönlichkeitstheorie*. Göttingen, Verlag für Psychologie, 1968.

Thomae, H. *Beiträge zu einer genetischen Anthropologie*. Frankfurt a.M., Athenäum, 1969. Pp. 213–237.

Thomae, H. *Vita humana: Ansätze zu einer genetischen Anthropologie*. Frankfurt,

Athenaeum, 1969.

Thomae, H. Vorstellungsmodelle in der Entwicklungspsychologie. *Zeitschrift für Psychologie* (Leipzig), 1961, *165*, 41–58.

Thomas, A., Birch, H.G., Chess, S., Hertzig, M.E., & Korn, S. *Behavioral individuality in early childhood.* New York, New York University Press, 1963.

Tiedemann, D. *Beobachtungen über die Entwicklung der Seelenfähigkeit bei Kindern,* 1787. (Reprinted, Altenburg, O. Bonde, 1897.)

Tikhomirova, O.K. The formation of voluntary movements in children of preschool age. In A.R. Luria (Ed.), *Problems of the higher nervous activity of normal and abnormal children,* vol. 2. Moscow, Academy of Pedagogical Sciences of the R.S.F.S.R., 1958.

Tolman, E.C. *Purposive behavior in animals and men.* New York, Century, 1932.

Tolman, E.C. *Behavior and psychological man.* Berkeley, University of California Press, 1961.

Tomaszewski, T. *Wstęp do psychologii.* Warszawa, PWN, 1963. [Introduction to psychology.]

Trabasso, T. Mental operations in language comprehension. In R. Freedle & J.B. Carroll (Eds.), *Language comprehension and the acquisition of knowledge.* Washington, D.C., Winston, 1972.

Trabasso, T. Discussion of the papers by Bransford & Johnson and Clark, Carpenter & Just: Language and cognition. In W.G. Chase (Ed.), *Visual information processing.* New York, Academic Press, 1973. Pp. 439–459.

Travis, L.E. The relation of voluntary movement to tremors. *Journal of Experimental Psychology,* 1929. *12*, 515–524.

Troll, L. The family of later life: A decade review. *Journal of Marriage and the Family,* 1971, *33*, 263–290.

Troshikin, V.A., Kozlova, L.N., Kruchenko, Zh.A., & Sirotskiy, V.V. *Formirovannie i razvitie snovych svoystv tipa vysshey deyatelnosti v ontogeneze. [Ontogenetic formation and development of general properties of types of higher nervous activity].* Kiev, Naukova Dumka, 1971.

Tuchman, B. *The proud tower: A portrait of the world before the war: 1890–1914.* New York, Macmillan, 1966.

Turiel, E. Developmental process in the child's moral thinking. In P.H. Mussen, D. Langer, & M. Covington (Eds.), *Trends and issues in developmental psychology.* New York, Holt, Rinehart, & Winston, 1969. Pp. 92–133.

Uhr, R., Thomae, H., & Becker, J. Verlaufsformen der Entwicklung im Kindes- und Jugendalter. *Zeitschrift Entwicklungs- und Pädagogische Psychologie,* 1969, *1.*

Ullmo, J. *La pensée scientifique moderne.* Paris, Flammarion, 1958.

Undeutsch, U. *Die psychologische Entwicklung der Jugend.* München, Juventa, 1965.

Uzgiris, I.C. Ordinality in the development of schemas for relating to objects. In J. Hellmuth (Ed.), *Exceptional infant,* vol. 1. Seattle, Special Child Publications, 1967. Pp. 317–334.

Uzgiris, I.C. Patterns of cognitive development in infancy. Paper presented at Merrill-Palmer Institute Conference on Research and Teaching of Infant Development, February, 1972.

Uzgiris, I.C., & Hunt, J. McV. Toward ordinal scales of psychological development in infancy. Unpublished manuscript, Clark University and University of Illinois, 1972.

Van den Daele, L.D. Qualitative models in development analysis. *Developmental Psychology,* 1969, *1*, 303–310.

Van den Daele, L. D. Infrastructure and transition in developmental analysis. *Human Development*, 1974, *17*, 1–23.

Van Strien, P. J. *Kennis en communicatie in de psychologische praktijk.* Utrecht, Bijleveld, 1966.

Velikovsky, I. *Oedipus and Akhnaton.* New York, Doubleday, 1960.

Vernon, P. E. Educational and intellectual development among Canadian Indians and Eskimos. *Educational Review*, 1966, *18*, 79–91, 186–195.

Vernon, P. E. *Intelligence and cultural environment.* London, Methuen, 1969.

Vernon, P. E. Intelligence. In W. B. Dockrell (Ed.), *On intelligence.* London, Methuen, 1970.

Vernon, P. E. The distinctiveness of field independence. *Journal of Personality*, 1972, *40*, 366–391.

Vurpillot, E. L'influence de la signification du matériel sur l'illusion de Poggendorff. *Année Psychologie*, 1957, *57*, 339–357.

Vygotsky, L. S. *Collected psychological investigations.* Moscow, Izd. Akad. Pedag. Nauk RSFSR, 1956.

Vygotsky, L. S. *Myshleniye i rech.* Moscow, Izd-vo Sotsekgiz, 1934. (Thought and language. Cambridge, Mass., M.I.T. Press, 1962.)

Wachs, T. D., Uzgiris, I. C., & Hunt, J. McV. Cognitive development in infants of different age levels and from different environmental backgrounds: An explanatory investigation. *Merrill-Palmer Quarterly*, 1971, *17*, 283–317.

Walker, J. B. B. *A study of Frege.* Ithaca, Cornell University Press, 1965.

Wallace, A. F. C. Culture and cognition. *Science*, 1962, *135*, 351–357.

Wapner, S. Organismic-developmental theory: Some applications to cognition. In P. H. Mussen, J. Langer & M. Covington (Eds.), *Trends and issues in developmental psychology.* New York, Holt, Rinehart, & Winston, 1969. Pp. 38–65.

Wapner, S., & Werner, H. *Perceptual development.* Worcester, Mass., Clark University Press, 1957.

Warren, N. African infant precocity. *Psychological Bulletin*, 1972, *78*, 353–367.

Watanabe, M. S. *Knowing and guessing.* New York, Wiley, 1969.

Watanabe, M. S. Pattern recognition and inductive reasoning. In G. I. Dalenoort (Ed.), *Process models for psychology.* Rotterdam, Rotterdam University Press, 1973.

Watson, J. S., & Ramey, C. T. Reactions to response-contingent stimulation in early infancy. *Merrill-Palmer Quarterly*, 1972, *18*, 219–227.

Watson, R. *The great psychologists from Aristotle to Freud.* Philadelphia, Lippincott, 1968.

Webb, E. J., Campbell, D. T., Schwartz, R. D., & Sechrest, L. *Unobtrusive measures: Non-reactive research in the social sciences.* Chicago, Rand McNally, 1966.

Weisner, T. One family, two households. Unpublished doctoral thesis, Harvard University, 1972.

Welford, A. T. *Skill and age.* New York, Oxford University Press. 1951.

Wenke, F. Die Jugend in der Welt. *Studium Generale*, 1951, *4*, 587–609.

Werner, H. Process and achievement: A basic problem of education and developmental psychology. *Harvard Educational Review*, 1937, *7*, 353–368.

Werner, H. *The comparative psychology of mental development.* New York, International Universities Press, 1948.

Werner, H. The concept of development from a comparative and organismic point of view. In D. Harris (Ed.), *The concept of development.* Minneapolis, Minnesota, University of Minnesota Press, 1957.

Werner, H., & Kaplan, E. *Symbol formation.* New York, Wiley, 1963.

Westbrook, P. D. *Mary Wilkins Freeman.* New York, Twayne, 1967.

White, K.D., & Mangan, G.L. Strength of the nervous system as a function of personality type and level of arousal. *Behaviour Research and Therapy*, 1972, *10*, 139–146.

White, S. The learning theory approach. In P.H. Mussen (Ed.), *Carmichael's manual of child psychology*. New York, Wiley, 1970. Pp. 657–702.

White, S.H. Evidence for a hierarchical arrangement of learning processes. In L.P. Lipsitt & C.C. Spiker (Eds.), *Advances in child development and behavior*, vol. 2. New York, Academic Press, 1965.

Whiting, B.B., & Whiting, J.W.M. Task assignment and personality: A consideration of the effect of herding on boys. In W.W. Lambert & R. Weisbrod (Eds.), *Comparative perspectives on social psychology*. Boston, Little Brown, 1971.

Whiting, B.B., & Whiting, J.W.M. *Children of six cultures: A psycho-cultural analysis*. Cambridge, Harvard University Press, 1974.

Whiting, B.B., & Edwards, C.P. A cross-cultural analysis of sex differences in the behavior of children aged three through eleven. In R.A. Levine (Ed)., *Culture and personality: Contemporary readings*. Chicago, Aldine, 1974.

Wicklund, D.A., Palermo, D.S., & Jenkins, J.J. The effects of associative strength and response hierarchy on paired-associate learning. *Journal of Verbal Learning and Verbal Behavior*, 1964, *3*, 413–420.

Wilder, L. The role of speech and other extra-signal feedback in the regulation of the child's sensorimotor behavior. *Speech Monographs*, 1969, *36*, 426–434.

Wilder, L. Relationships between overt and covert verbal responses in the aging process. Paper presented at Ninth International Congress of Gerontology, Kiev, U.S.S.R., July 1972.

Witkin, H.A. A cognitive-style approach to cross-cultural research. *International Journal of Psychology*, 1967, *2*, 233–250.

Witkin, H.A., Oltman, P., Raskin, E., & Karp, S. *Manual for the embedded figures test*. Palo Alto, Consulting Psychologists Press, 1971.

Wittkower, R., & Wittkower, M. *Born under Saturn*. London, Weidenfeld & Nicolson, 1963.

Witz, K. Representations of cognitive processes and cognitive structure in children I. *Achives de psychologie*, 1971, *16*, 61–95.

Witz, K. Structural changes in four- to five-year-olds. Paper presented at the Second Annual Interdisciplinary Meeting in Structural Learning, University of Pennsylvania, Philadelphia, April 1971.

Witz, K. Models of systems of sensory motor schemes in infants. *Journal of Mathematical Psychology*, in press.

Witz, K. Dynamical systems underlying language production in a $1\frac{1}{2}$ year old. Paper presented at the Fourth Annual Meeting on Structural Learning, Philadelphia, April, 1973.

Witz, K., & Duchan, J. Language production in a $1\frac{1}{2}$ year old. Unpublished manuscript, University of Illinois, 1973.

Witz, K., & Easley, J. Analysis of cognitive behavior in children. Final Report, U.S.O.E. Project No. 0-0216, Grant No. OEC-0-70-2142 (508), July 1972.

Wober, J.M. Towards an understanding of the Kiganda concept of intelligence. In J.W. Berry & P. Dasen (Eds.), *Culture and cognition: Readings in cross-cultural psychology*. London, Methuen, 1974.

Wohlwill, J.F. Developmental studies of perception. *Psychological Bulletin*, 1960, *47*, 249–288.

Wohlwill, J.F. Piaget's system as a source of empirical research. *Merrill-Palmer Quarterly*, 1963, *4*, 253–262.

Wohlwill, J.F. Vers une réformulation du rôle de l'expérience dans le développement cogitif. In F. Bresson (Ed.), *Psychologie et épistémologie génétiques: Thèmes*

Index

Piagetiens. Paris, Dunod, 1966.

Wohlwill, J.F. The age variable in psychological research. *Psychological Review*, 1970, *77*, 49–64.

Wohlwill, J.H. The place of structured experience in early cognitive development. *Interchange*, 1970, *1*, 13–27.

Wolanski, N. (Ed.), *Czynniki rozwoju człowieka: Wstep do ekologii człowieka. [Factors of human development: Introduction to human ecology]*. Warszawa, PWN, 1972.

Wołoszynowa, L. *Rozwój i wychowanie dzieci w młodszym wieku szkolnym [Development and education of children in early school age]*. Warszawa, Nasza, Księgarnia, 1967.

Wood, A.D. The 'Scribbling Women' and Fanny Fern: Why women wrote. *American Quarterly*, 1971, *23*, 3–24.

Wood, A.D. The literature of impoverishment: The women local colorists in America 1865–1914. *Womens' Studies*, 1972, *1*, 3–46.

Wozniak, R.H. Verbal regulation of motor behavior: Soviet research and non-Soviet replications. *Human Development*, 1972, *15*, 13–57.

Wozniak, R.H. Speech-for-self as a multiply reafferent source of non-speech motor control. Paper presented at the biennial meeting of the Society for Research in Child Development, Philadelphia, March, 1973.

Wozniak, R.H. Dialecticism and structuralism: The philosophical foundations of Soviet psychology and Piagetian cognitive developmental theory. In K.F. Riegel & G.C. Rosenwald (Eds.), *Structure and transformation: Developmental and historical aspects*. New York, Wiley, 1975.

Wozniak, R.H., Acredolo, C., & Peterson, R. Effects of overt vocalization and silent articulation on elicitation of the orienting reponse. Unpublished manuscript, University of Minnesota, 1973.

Wozniak, R.H., & Eisner, H. Human performance and verbal control in the aging process. Paper presented at the IX International Congress of Gerontology, Kiev, July, 1972.

Wozniak, R.H. & Nuechterlein, P. Reading improvement through verbally self-guided looking and listening. Summary Report, University of Minnesota Research, Development and Demonstration Center in Education of Handicapped Children, 1973.

Yakovleva, S.V. Conditions for the formation of simplest voluntary actions in children of preschool age. In A.R. Luria (Ed.), *Problems of the higher nervous activity of normal and abnormal children*, vol. 2. Moscow, Academy of Pedagogical Sciences of the R.S.F.S.R., 1958. Pp. 47–71.

Yarrow, L., Rubenstein, J., & Pedersen, F. Dimensions of early stimulation: Differential effects on infant development. Paper presented at the biennial meeting of the Society for Research in Child Development, Minneapolis, April 1971.

Zaidi, S.M. Social-cultural change and value conflict in developing countries: A case study in Pakistan. In W. Caudill & T.Y. Lin (Eds.), *Mental health research in Asia and the Pacific*. Honolulu East-West Center Press, 1969. Pp. 415–430.

Zaporozhets, A.V. The origin and development of the conscious control of movements in man. In N. O'Connor (Ed.), *Recent Soviet psychology*. New York, Liveright, 1961.

Zaporozhets, A.V. *et. al. Perception and action*. Moscow, Izd. Prosveshchenie, 1967.

Zazzo, R. *Psychologie differentielle de adolescence*. Paris, Presses Universitaires, 1966.

Zebrowska, M. (Ed.), *Psychologia rozwojowa dzieci i młodzieży [Developmental psychology of children and adolescents]*. Warszawa, PWN, 1966.

Zeigler, H.P., & Leibowitz, H.W. Apparent visual size as a function of distance for children and adults. *American Journal of Psychology*, 1957, *70*, 106–109.

Zhorof, P.A., & Yermolaeva-Tomina, L.B. Concerning the relation between extraversion and strength of the nervous system. In V.D. Nebylitsyn & J.A. Gray (Eds.), *Biological bases of individual behavior*. New York, Academic Press, 1972.

Zigler, E. Metatheoretical issues in developmental psychology. In M. Marx (Ed.), *Theories in contemporary psychology*. New York, Macmillan, 1963.

Zigler, E., & Child, I.L. Socialization. In G. Lindzey & E. Aronsen (Eds.), *Handbook of social psychology*, vol. 3. Reading, Mass., Addison Wesley, 1969. Pp. 468–470.

Zinchenko, V.P. [Perception as action.] *Voprosy Psikhologii*, 1967, *1*, 17–24.

Zivin, G. Speech-for-self as a function of individual styles of central organization. Paper presented at the biennial meeting of the Society for Research in Child Development, Philadelphia, March, 1973.

Zivin, G. How to make some boring thing more boring. *Child Development*, 1974, *45*, 232–236.

For Product Safety Concerns and Information please contact our EU
representative GPSR@taylorandfrancis.com
Taylor & Francis Verlag GmbH, Kaufingerstraße 24, 80331 München, Germany

www.ingramcontent.com/pod-product-compliance
Lightning Source LLC
Chambersburg PA
CBHW021806270326
41932CB00007B/71

9 780202 361291